MW01017140

China's Economic Development

Palgrave Readers in Economics

Titles include:

Hercules Haralambides (*editor*)
PORT MANAGEMENT

Josef C. Brada, Paul Wachtel and Dennis Tao Yang (*editors*)
CHINA'S ECONOMIC DEVELOPMENT

Palgrave Readers in Economics
Series Standing Order ISBN 978–1–137–47589–3 (Hardback)
(*outside North America only*)

You can receive future titles in this series as they are published by placing a standing order. Please contact your bookseller or, in case of difficulty, write to us at the address below with your name and address, the title of the series and the ISBN quoted above.

Customer Services Department, Macmillan Distribution Ltd, Houndmills, Basingstoke, Hampshire RG21 6XS, England

China's Economic Development

Edited by

Josef C. Brada
Professor of Economics, Arizona State University, USA

Paul Wachtel
*Professor of Economics, Leonard N. Stern School of Business,
New York University, USA*

and

Dennis Tao Yang
*Professor of Business Administration, Darden School of Business,
University of Virginia, USA*

Selection, introduction, and editorial matter © Josef C. Brada, Paul Wachtel, and Dennis Tao Yang 2014
Individual chapters © Association for Comparative Economic Studies 2014
Index compiled by Palgrave Macmillan.

All rights reserved. No reproduction, copy or transmission of this publication may be made without written permission.

No portion of this publication may be reproduced, copied or transmitted save with written permission or in accordance with the provisions of the Copyright, Designs and Patents Act 1988, or under the terms of any licence permitting limited copying issued by the Copyright Licensing Agency, Saffron House, 6–10 Kirby Street, London EC1N 8TS.

Any person who does any unauthorized act in relation to this publication may be liable to criminal prosecution and civil claims for damages.

The authors have asserted their rights to be identified as the authors of this work in accordance with the Copyright, Designs and Patents Act 1988.

First published 2014 by
PALGRAVE MACMILLAN

Palgrave Macmillan in the UK is an imprint of Macmillan Publishers Limited, registered in England, company number 785998, of Houndmills, Basingstoke, Hampshire RG21 6XS.

Palgrave Macmillan in the US is a division of St Martin's Press LLC, 175 Fifth Avenue, New York, NY 10010.

Palgrave Macmillan is the global academic imprint of the above companies and has companies and representatives throughout the world.

Palgrave® and Macmillan® are registered trademarks in the United States, the United Kingdom, Europe and other countries.

ISBN 978–1–137–46995–3

This book is printed on paper suitable for recycling and made from fully managed and sustained forest sources. Logging, pulping and manufacturing processes are expected to conform to the environmental regulations of the country of origin.

A catalogue record for this book is available from the British Library.

A catalog record for this book is available from the Library of Congress.

Typeset by MPS Limited, Chennai, India.

Contents

List of Figures and Tables

Figures

Tables

Notes on Editors

Josef C. Brada is Professor of Economics *emeritus* at Arizona State University, USA, Foreign Member of the Macedonian Academy of Sciences and Arts, and President of the Society for the Study of Emerging Markets. His research focuses on international economics, comparative economic systems, and economics of transition. He has served as a consultant to the OECD, the World Bank, and the United Nations Economic Commission for Europe as well as to governments in Europe and Latin America. Born in Czechoslovakia, he received a BS in Chemical Engineering and an MA in Economics from Tufts University and a PhD from the University of Minnesota.

Paul Wachtel is Professor of Economics and Academic Director, BS in Business and Political Economy Program at the Stern School of Business, New York University, USA. He teaches courses in global business and economics, monetary policy and banking, and the history of enterprise systems. His primary areas of research include monetary policy, central banking, and financial sector reform in economies in transition. He has been a research associate at the National Bureau of Economic Research, a senior economic advisor to the East West Institute, and a consultant to the Bank of Israel, the IMF and the World Bank. Wachtel is the co-editor of *Comparative Economic Studies* and serves on the editorial boards of several other journals. He received his undergraduate degree from Queens College, CUNY, and his MA and PhD degrees from the University of Rochester.

Dennis Tao Yang is Dale S. Coenen Professor of Business Administration at the University of Virginia, Darden School of Business, USA. His research focuses on economic development and growth and labor economics, especially in the context of China and economic transition. He is also President of the Association for Comparative Economic Studies. Yang is a senior research fellow at the Chinese University of Hong Kong, Peking University, Tsinghua University, and the Institute for the Study of Labor (IZA) and holds the Chang Jiang Visiting Professorship at Shanghai Jiao Tong University. He has been a consultant to international organizations such as the World Bank and The Conference Board as well as multinational companies. A native of China, Yang obtained his undergraduate degree from UCLA and his PhD in economics from the University of Chicago.

1
Introduction

Josef C. Brada[1], Paul Wachtel[2], and Dennis Tao Yang[3]
[1] *Arizona State University, USA;* [2] *Leonard N. Stern School of Business, New York University, USA; and* [3] *Darden School of Business, University of Virginia, USA*

Over the past three and half decades, since the inception of economic reforms in the late 1970s, the Chinese economy has experienced great success, both in terms of its rate of economic progress as measured by the growth of per capita income and in terms of China's ability to introduce extensive changes to its economic system in a way that has supported its development. The chapters in this book are compiled from *Comparative Economic Studies*, a leading journal dealing with economic systems and their evolution. The chapters, written by noted experts in the field of China studies, document and analyze the key aspects of China's institutional development and the strategies and policies that have been used to move the economy from rigid central planning toward an economy that is a unique blend of market and planned economy institutions and mechanisms that have delivered unprecedented economic growth and that continue to evolve over time.

Chapter 2 in this book, perhaps paradoxically, examines the nadir of China's economic fortunes, the famine of 1959–1961, one of the greatest catastrophes in human history. As Dennis Yang shows in his survey of the famine's causes, a great deal, though not all, the blame could be placed on bad economic policy and failures in planning. Nevertheless, the famine had some important lessons for the leadership. One was to exercise greater caution in formulating policies for China's economic development and the other was to focus greater attention on the agricultural sector.

One outcome of the greater emphasis on agriculture was the development and spread of the household responsibility system, which created more rational incentives to improve productivity in agriculture. Another outcome was the decision to harness surplus rural labor into increasing industrial output through township-village enterprises (TVEs), small firms located in the countryside, rather than through massive state investment programs. As Chapter 3 shows, TVEs were small and used relatively simple technologies but they were able to supply a wide range of consumer goods. The authors,

Enrico C. Perotti, Laixiang Sun, and Liang Zou, also show that some of the seeming greater efficiency of TVEs relative to large state-owned enterprises (SOEs) was due to the fact that the latter provided a wide range of social services and economic benefits to their employees, benefits often referred to as the "iron rice bowl," which ensured the well-being of the urban work force. They also note that the further progress of TVEs would require grass-roots democratization and the liberalization of the central planning system because the TVEs brought about local control over productive resources and, given their numbers and small size, their inclusion in the central planning process was infeasible, necessitating a greater reliance on price signals to guide their decisions. Thus, the process of structural change may be seen as having started with the responses to the famine caused by Mao's Great Leap Forward.

Perhaps the most daring of the Chinese reforms was the introduction of the dual-price system, whereby SOEs fulfilled planners' output targets based on state-set prices but could sell above-plan production at market-determined prices. Critics of the system argued that these market prices would reflect the shortages and surpluses that occurred in the production of planned goods rather than the costs and value of the above-plan output and thus would do little to improve the allocation of resources. In Chapter 4, Anthony Koo and Norman Obst argue that the dual-pricing scheme did in fact allow China's SOEs to move toward a market economy, and they construct a simple model that shows why the scheme worked to improve efficiency in the state-owned sector. Putting the SOEs on a more market-oriented basis also meant that the job security of workers in SOEs had to be abridged in order to allow firms to adjust staffing to their needs. In Chapter 5, Margaret Maurer-Fazio describes the care with which labor market reforms were executed to avoid unrest among urban workers who now had to face a labor market that did not guarantee them the security they had enjoyed under central planning.

Chapters 6 and 7 summarize the effects of these reforms on the performance of China's industry. Alberto Gabriele argues that, despite the proliferation of TVEs, SOEs continued to be the lynchpin of Chinese industrial development, in part due to their ability to improve performance by taking advantage of the reforms enacted in the 1990s. The proliferation of new types of firms and the entry of foreign investors into China has provided extensive data on the effects of the reforms and the relationships between corporate structure and firm performance. In Chapter 7, Weiye Li and Louis Putterman review the extensive literature on the effects of the reforms on the performance of SOEs and other types of firms. The studies they review conclude that the reforms did improve productivity and that they also reduced productivity differences between SOEs, TVEs, and foreign-owned firms.

Gains in the autonomy of SOEs and the growing role of TVEs required changes not only in the price system to allow for a greater role for the market but also in the China's monetary system. In Chapter 8, Carsten Holz explains that the monetary system that existed under central planning was designed to use monetary flows as a means of verifying SOEs' adherence to the plan and to balance household incomes and expenditures. Thus the role of money was entirely passive; deposit balances were accounting entries determined by the plan. Firms with deposit balances could not purchase industrial goods unless the plan called for such purchases. When SOEs gained the right to buy and sell above-plan output, the role of money had to change to one where the willingness of SOEs to spend, rather than the dictates of central planning, initiated transactions between firms. Holz explains the emerging role of banks in promoting financial intermediation to finance investment and to maintain a balance between household incomes and the availability of consumer goods. Of course, with money, and, therefore, bank credits, now driving the effective demand of firms for investment goods and of households for consumer goods, the role of China's central bank, the People's Bank of China, became central to controlling the volume of investment and maintaining price stability. Given China's rapid growth and the growing demand for money due to financial deepening, meaning the broader use of financial instruments, the central bank faced a difficult task. In Chapter 9, Aaron Mehrotra and José R Sánchez-Fung show how the bank used information about the inflation and output gaps to steer monetary policy during the reform period.

China's opening to the global economy has had major, and often controversial, impact on the pattern of international trade. Less well understood is the impact of China's opening to the world economy on the Chinese economy. In Chapter 10, Aimin Chen examines the likely effects of China's joining the World Trade Organization (WTO) in 2001 on the Chinese economy. Because China will gradually have to open its economy to foreign competition, Chen sees two likely effects. The first is a systemic one, where the entry of foreign competitors will shrink the size of the SOE sector, especially in industry, and will thus promote the growth of the non-state sector. The second is that greater trade openness will promote the reallocation of productive resources within China. The agrarian sector as well as services such as banking and finance are facing growing competition from foreign suppliers.

A major source of labor for China's emerging industries, mainly located in coastal cities, is the millions of migrant workers from rural inland areas who, despite various institutional barriers, provide much of the labor supply for the growth of the economy. At the same time, this leaves many rural areas populated by older people who have to take care of the children of the migrants. A major concern in the migration literature is that the educational performance of the children of migrants suffers from the absence of parental involvement. Research by Xinxin Chen, Qiuqiong Huang, Scott Rozelle, Yaojiang Shi, and Linxiu Zhang in Chapter 11 suggests that this does not seem to be the case; children of migrant families do not perform worse in their schooling outcomes than do children in households where the parents do not migrate; in fact in some cases they perform better. This means that policies that limit workers' ability to establish residency in cities may not be as costly in terms of the future skills of the labor force as is often thought.

In Chapter 12, Garry Jefferson reviews the entire Chinese experience with economic reform and growth from the perspective of modern economic theory. He notes that China did not always follow either the policy recommendations of international organizations such as the Indian Monetary Fund (IMF) or the emphasis of the modern growth literature on the need for strong institutions that support the rule of law and provide clear property rights. Nevertheless, China's exemplary growth performance does confirm conventional wisdom regarding the sources of economic growth, the intersection of politics and economics and the role of incentives, themes that are developed in the other contributions to this volume. This wide-ranging essay is worth reading for those beginning their study of the Chinese economy and, for those who have studied the Chinese economy extensively, reading this chapter will help them to put China's experience into a broader perspective.

2

China's Agricultural Crisis and Famine of 1959–1961: A Survey and Comparison to Soviet Famines

Dennis Tao Yang
Darden School of Business, University of Virginia, USA

China's Great Leap Forward (GLF) of 1958–1961 ended as a catastrophe as wide-spread famine claimed millions of human lives. This paper reviews the literature on this historical crisis. The collapse of grain production was primarily attributable to failures in central planning that diverted agricultural resources to industry and to malnutrition among peasants, which lowered their productivity. The resulting decline in grain availability and the urban bias in China's food distribution system were the main causes of the famine. This paper also compares China's experience with the Soviet famines of 1931–1933 and 1947.

Introduction

The Great Leap Forward (GLF) campaign of 1958–1961, which aimed at quickly transforming China into a powerful industrial state, involved dramatic turns of events, but ended as a national catastrophe. In the 1958 New Year's editorial of the *People's Daily,* the Chinese Communist Party proclaimed the GLF goal of surpassing the United Kingdom in industrial production in 15 years and the United States in 20–30 years. The nation was soon elevated to a state of euphoria, as news of exaggerated production miracles spread throughout the country like wildfire. However, dreadful reality quickly set in. In 1959, China's grain output suddenly declined by 15%, and in the following 2 years, food supply plunged further, to 70% of the 1958 level. During the same period, a widespread famine raged across China. Years later, based on population census and fertility survey data, demographers were able to estimate that the total excess mortality during the GLF crisis ranged from 16.5 (Coale, 1981) to 30 million people (Banister,

---

Reprinted with permission from Association of Comparative Economic Studies. All rights reserved. *Comparative Economic Studies* (2008) 50, 1–29.

1987). This monumental scale of the famine makes it arguably the largest in recorded history.

However, during the two decades after the famine ended, there was no public recognition of its existence outside of China. Even within China, despite awareness of severe hardship during the crisis years, the magnitude of the famine was largely unknown because the Chinese government prohibited scholarly inquiries into the subject. The public in China and the West began to realise the full severity of the Chinese famine only in 1980, when demographers and Sinologists released systematic research findings.[1] Since the publication of a complete time series of crude mortality rates in the 1983 *Statistical Yearbook of China,* and the subsequent release of population census and fertility surveys, this catastrophe has received increasing attention among social scientists. Initially, academic research was focused on reliable estimation of excess deaths and delayed births associated with the famine. Then, following the seminal work of Lin (1990) on agricultural collectivisation and performance in China, economists intensified research effort on the causation of the collapse in production as well as the concurrent famine. Research findings include a 1993 special issue of the *Journal of Comparative Economics* and a 1998 symposium issue of *China Economic Review.* Thanks to recent progress made possible by retrospective surveys and the collection of archived data, researchers are able to conduct rigorous econometric studies assessing the joint significance of various factors contributing to the GLF crisis. Much has been learned about what caused the precipitous decline in grain output, why mortality climbed to the colossal scale, and why the catastrophe lingered so long.

This article offers an overview of the growing literature on the economic analysis of China's GLF.[2] To establish a reliable factual basis for subsequent discussion, the next section documents the estimates of existing studies on the scale of excess mortality and the magnitude of decline in grain production during the crisis. Relying on Sen's entitlement approach to famine (Sen, 1981), we clarify several conceptual issues that are important for the analysis

---

[1] The Chinese government did not publish mortality statistics for the years 1959–1961 for two decades. Isolated, yet important, mortality data were published in 1980 by two Chinese demographers, Zhu (1980) and Liu (1980), who inferred the total famine deaths of 14–16.5 million people in China in the crisis years. A Chinese economist, Sun (1981), provided an estimate of 15 million extra deaths for the Great Leap famine. Parallel to these studies, Western demographic researchers also suggested the occurrence of a large-scale famine (Coale, 1981; Aird, 1982), which was mentioned in popular media as well (eg, Sterba, 1981). Soon after, scholars of China carried out systematic and detailed analysis of the disaster (Bernstein, 1984; Walker, 1984).

[2] See Yang (1996) and the references therein for the analysis of the calamity from the perspective of political science. Becker (1996) presents a historical account of the tragedy based on hundreds of interviews and years of painstaking detective work that uncovered facts and personal experiences related to the famine.

of China's GLF, particularly with regard to the role of central planning and the relationship between aggregate food supply and the causation of famine. The subsequent section examines the determinants of the decline in output, while the penultimate section analyses the determinants of extra mortality. In each section, brief expositions of economic hypotheses are followed by discussions about data issues and econometric strategies for estimation. We also report up-to-date empirical findings.

Subject to qualifications, the existing research supports the hypothesis that a sequence of failures in central planning was mainly responsible for the sharp declines in China's grain output between 1959 and 1961. At the inception of the GLF, wishfully hoping for a jump in agricultural productivity from collectivisation, the Chinese government implemented an infeasible industrialisation timetable. The diversion of massive amounts of agricultural resources to industry and excessive grain procurements from the peasants, which led to malnutrition and decimation of labour productivity, were both responsible for the collapse of grain supply. The time lag between heavy grain procurement in 1 year and the nutritional deficiency in rural workers in the subsequent year contributed in part to the prolonged decline in production. Bad weather also exacerbated the mistakes of economic planning. The associated famine has multiple determinants. In addition to grain availability decline, during normal years as well as periods of national food emergency, China's food distribution system under planning gave only urban residents legally protected rights for acquiring a certain amount of food. The lack of food entitlement to the rural population due to the urban-biased allocation rule, together with political radicalism and grain exports during the crisis, contributed to the enormous death toll.

Agricultural crisis and famines have long occupied the attention of scholars. The traditional approach to famine analysis, which dates back to the writings of Adam Smith and Thomas Malthus, proposes that famines are primarily caused by a sudden decline in food availability (FAD). From the late 1970s onward, a new literature on famines emerged. The intellectual foundation of this new literature is Sen's entitlement approach, which goes beyond FAD explanations and emphasises a broader set of causal factors that influence hunger and welfare, including food distribution, ownership patterns, relative prices, and famine policies (Sen, 1981; Dreze and Sen, 1989).

However, despite substantial progress in developing a richer conceptual framework and improving empirical knowledge for the new literature, the understanding about famines in socialist economies had long remained rudimentary (see Ravallion, 1997; O'Grada, 2007). This void in research was due in part to the fact that socialist institutional arrangements differed from standard market settings of the entitlement approach, in which private wealth and relative prices could explain a large part of hunger and starvation. In contrast, governments under central planning set commodity prices and controlled food production and distribution. Hence, research findings from the Chinese GLF crisis contribute to our understanding about famine causes under alternative economic systems. A key insight is that central planning embodied a systemic risk. If erroneous policies were made at the top and implemented with dogmatic confidence, policy failures would have nationwide repercussions, resulting in a monumental disaster and an enormous death toll (Li and Yang, 2005). Perhaps this finding provides a partial answer to a perplexing contrast between two large developing countries that was raised by Sen (1983) more than two decades ago: the inability of China to avoid large-scale famines, while achieving a much better record of eradicating regular malnutrition and hunger than that of India. The research findings on China also have implications for analysing the Soviet famines under planning in which overambitious production plans, excessive grain collections, and biases in food distribution were important causal factors. While the major focus of this article is on Chinese government policies as they relate to the GLF, in the last section of the paper, significant parallels will be drawn to the Soviet famines of 1931–1933 and 1947. These correlations corroborate and bring into relief the research findings on China.

Factual and conceptual issues

Existing studies generally agree with the severity of production shortfalls during the Great Leap crisis. The national grain output figures reported in Table 2.1 indicate yearly grain productions of 195, 200, 170, 143, 148, 160, and 170 million metric tons for the period 1957–1963. The 15% and 16% sudden declines in grain output in the two consecutive years 1959 and 1960, when China was barely self-sufficient in food supply, were catastrophic. These official figures of grain output are broadly consistent with other output estimates based on independent data sources (see Ashton et al., 1984),[3] despite the serious disruptions to the operation of government agencies, including the State Statistical Bureau, during the GLF.

The extent of the demographic catastrophe was not known to Chinese and Western scholars for almost two decades after the event. For years after the GLF, some Western scholars actually praised the ability of the Chinese government to avoid a famine in spite of a sharp production shortfall during

---

[3] The output figure for 1958 is perhaps most unreliable because it has been revised several times. In 1958, the *People's Daily* (10 September 1958) forecasted a total grain output of 525 million metric tons for that year, or more than 2.6 times the grain output in 1957 (see Table 2.1). The 'actual' output was estimated to be 375 million metric tons, before it was revised downward to 250 million metric tons in 1959. The last revision of 200 million tons was published in the 1980 Statistical Yearbook of China.

Table 2.1 China's grain output and agricultural inputs: 1952–77

Year	Grain output (million tons)	Grain procurement (million tons)	Retained grain per capita (kg/person)	Rural labour (million)	Area sown to grain (million heads)	Draft animals (million heads)	Farm machinery (million HPs)	Chemical fertiliser (million tons)	Sown area hit by calamity (%)
	(1)	(2)	(3)	(4)	(5)	(6)	(7)	(8)	(9)
1952	164	33	270	173	124	76	0.3	0.08	2.9
1953	167	47	257	177	127	81	0.4	0.12	4.9
1954	170	51	265	182	129	85	0.5	0.16	8.5
1955	184	48	278	186	130	88	0.8	0.24	5.2
1956	193	40	306	185	136	88	1.1	0.33	8.2
1957	195	46	295	193	134	84	1.7	0.37	9.5
1958	200	52	286	155	128	78	2.4	0.55	5.2
1959	170	64	223	163	116	79	3.4	0.54	9.7
1960	143	47	212	170	122	73	5.0	0.66	15.3
1961	148	37	229	197	121	69	7.1	0.45	18.6
1962	160	32	241	213	122	70	10	0.63	11.9
1963	170	37	245	220	121	75	12	1.0	14.3
1964	188	40	270	228	122	79	13	1.3	8.8
1965	195	39	271	234	120	84	15	1.9	7.8
1966	214	41	287	243	121	87	17	2.3	6.7
1967	218	41	287	252	119	90	20	2.4	…
1968	209	40	265	261	116	92	22	2.7	…
1969	211	38	266	271	118	92	26	3.1	…
1970	240	46	289	278	119	94	29	3.4	2.3
1971	250	44	298	284	121	95	38	3.8	5.1
1972	241	39	286	283	121	96	50	4.3	11.6
1973	265	48	303	289	121	97	65	4.8	5.1
1974	275	47	307	292	121	97	81	5.4	4.4
1975	285	53	315	295	121	98	102	6.0	6.7
1976	286	49	317	294	121	95	117	6.8	7.6
1977	283	48	313	293	120	94	140	7.6	10.2

Data source: Columns (1)–(2), (4)–(6), and (9) are from MOA (1984); (3) = (1)–(2) + (grain resales from rural to rural areas) divided by rural population, grain resale data are from Lardy (1987) and NBS (1983); and, (7)–(8) are from Wen (1993).

the GLF (eg, Perkins, 1966). However, based on 1964 and 1982 Chinese population census and other fertility surveys released since the early 1980s, Western demographers have discovered that the total premature deaths between 1959 and 1961 were astonishing. Among this wide range of estimates, Coale (1981) provides the lower bound of 16.5 million, while Banister (1987) gives the higher bound of 30 million. Because of differences in methods of estimation and data sources, other estimates are reported at 18.48 (Yao, 1999), 23 (Arid, 1982; Peng, 1987), and 29.5 million (Ashton *et al.*, 1984). Total lost or delayed births are estimated at 33 million by Ashton *et al.* (1984) and 30.79 million by Yao (1999). As Table 2.2 shows, 1960 registered the highest death rate: 25.4 per thousand.

These mortality estimates identify China's Great Leap crisis as the worst famine in recorded history, measured in absolute number of lives lost. The enormous number of deaths dwarfs the other major historical famine in China between 1876 and 1879, which, due to drought, claimed the lives

Table 2.2   Death rates of the Chinese provinces: 1954–1966 (unit = 0.1%)

Province	1956–1957 Average	1958	1959	1960	1961	1962–1963 Average
Anhui	11.7	12.3	16.7	68.6	8.1	8.1
Fujian	8.2	7.5	7.9	15.3	11.9	7.9
Gansu	11.1	21.1	17.4	41.3	11.5	9.4
Guangdong	9.8	9.2	11.1	15.2	10.8	8.5
Guangxi	12.5	11.7	17.5	29.5	19.5	10.2
Guizhou	8.2	13.7	16.2	45.4	17.7	9.9
Hebei	11.3	10.9	12.3	15.8	13.6	10.2
Heilongjiang	10.3	9.2	12.8	10.6	11.1	8.6
Henan	12.9	12.7	14.1	39.6	10.2	8.7
Hubei	10.2	9.6	14.5	21.2	9.1	9.3
Hunan	11.0	11.7	13.0	29.4	17.5	10.3
Inner Mongolia	9.2	7.9	11.0	9.4	8.8	8.8
Jiangsu	11.7	9.4	14.6	18.4	13.4	9.7
Jiangxi	12.0	11.3	13.0	16.1	11.5	10.4
Jilin	8.3	9.1	13.4	10.1	12.0	9.7
Liaoning	8.0	6.6	11.8	11.5	17.5	8.2
Ningxia	10.9	15.0	15.8	13.9	10.7	9.4
Qinghai	9.9	13.0	16.6	40.7	11.7	6.9
Shaanxi	12.2	11.7	12.8	14.2	12.2	11.4
Shandong	12.1	12.8	18.2	23.6	18.4	12.1
Shanxi	10.1	11.0	12.7	12.3	8.8	10.0
Sichuan	11.3	25.2	47.0	54.0	29.4	13.7
Yunnan	15.8	21.6	18.0	26.3	11.8	12.5
Zhejiang	9.4	9.2	10.8	11.9	9.8	8.3
Nation	11.1	12.0	14.6	25.4	14.2	10.0

Source: NBS (1990).

of between 9.5 and 13 million people (Bohr, 1972), the previously highest death toll. Even by the most conservative estimate, the GLF famine is more destructive than other well-known famines in the world. For instance, the great Irish famine of 1845–1851 destroyed 1 million lives; the Bengal famine of 1943, 2 million; and the Soviet famines of 1921–1922, 5–9 million, 1932–1933, 5–11 million, and 1946–1947, 1.2–5 million. The Ethiopian famine of 1984–1985 resulted in 0.6–1 million premature deaths (see Ravallion, 1997; O'Grada, 2007).[4]

Decline in grain production and massive starvation are two critical aspects of the GLF. Researchers face the challenge of determining the causal factors of each catastrophe despite their concurrent occurrence and the possible interrelationship between the two events.

Economists have long studied the causation of production crises in agriculture. While natural calamities and war are often blamed as the leading causes of crop failures, Rosen (1999) shows that bad human judgements can also be fatal. For the Irish famine that Rosen studies, erroneous expectation of the productivity of seed potatoes provoked 'oversaving', which delayed possible substitution of other crops and led to a sharp reduction in the next year's food supply.[5] Acknowledging the relevance of weather and intertemporal decisions, there is little doubt that China's collapse in grain output was also influenced by the dramatic changes in institutions and policies that are commensurate with the central planned economy of the GLF period.

Severe crop failures are neither a necessary nor a sufficient condition for famines to occur. This is the view of modern economic analysis associated with Sen's entitlement approach (see Osmani (1995) for elaborations). For China's GLF, there was a dramatic decline in grain production and a concurrent famine; the causes of each event are worth careful investigation. One important point is to determine the importance of the decline in food availability among other possible causes of the famine. If the decline in grain output did not contribute significantly to excess mortality, as in Sen's

---

[4] While the total excess mortality of the GLF crisis was the highest among all recorded famines its excess death rate of less than 20 per thousand is modest compared to other worst famines in history, such as those of 120 per thousand in Ireland in the second half of the 1840s and 60 per thousand during the 1921–1922 famine in the USSR. O'Grada (2007) presents the estimated death tolls of many major historical famines in both relative and absolute terms.

[5] In 1985, the fungus *p. infestans* made its appearance in the Irish potato crop; potato output fell by half in that year. Potato growers mistakenly believed that the drop in output was temporary, but in fact the productivity of seed potato due to the fungus was permanent. In the second year, there was no significant decline in the planting of seed potato relative to the previous year, yet output fell by 80%. See Mokyr (1983), O'Grada (1989), and Bourke (1993) for additional economic analysis of the Irish famine.

analysis of several well-known historical famines, the causes of the production crisis, such as bad weather, would be irrelevant factors in explaining the famine. Failures in entitlement relationships, institutions, and policies would be the main causes. However, if the decline in grain output was a significant factor responsible for the excess deaths, all causes of the production shortfalls would be indirect contributors to the famine, that is, through their negative effects on food availability.

The collapse in grain production

Economists have analysed multiple factors that were responsible for the precipitous declines in grain output between 1959 and 1961. We briefly discuss these causes and the empirical strategy suitable for testing the proposed hypotheses. Existing evidence suggests that the main culprit of the collapse in production was a series of mistakes in central planning.

Hypotheses on casual factors

The postmortem official explanation for the drop in grain output puts the blame mainly on bad weather (CCP, 1981) and refers to the period 1959–1961 as the 'three years of natural calamities' (Hypothesis 1). According to official weather records, the average percentage of sown areas affected by natural calamities during that period was 14.53%, which compares with an average of 7.63% disaster areas in the 3 years before the crisis (see column (9) of Table 2.1). Using meteorological data collected independently, Kueh (1995) confirms that bad weather was indeed a contributing factor to the poor harvests (see also Peng, 1987). Although inferior climate could severely damage agricultural production, researchers are cautious about the magnitude of its negative impact. As Kueh notes, bad weather of similar magnitudes did occur in the past, but they did not result in such serious reduction in aggregate grain output as observed in 1959–1961. A closer examination of the official statistics yields a similar conclusion. For instance, the proportion of disaster-hit areas in 1962 and 1963 were 13.1%, comparable to the crisis period, but the negative impact on grain supply was minimal (see Table 2.1). Another reason not to trust the official measure of meteorological conditions is that the disaster areas are defined as the sown acreage that is hit by flood, drought, and other natural calamities, and that has 30% or more reduction in yield compared to normal yield. By this definition, and given the party line explanation of the GLF disaster, it is plausible that the crop failures caused by other factors, such as the GLF policies, may have been attributed to bad weather. Despite these caveats, scholars generally agree that natural calamities were responsible for a fraction of the decline in grain production during the GLF, although other factors must have played important roles.

Incentive problems due to the unwieldy size of the communes could result in lower production efficiency (Hypothesis 2; see Eckstein, 1966;

Perkins and Yusuf, 1984). When 'people's communes' were established in 1958, the average size of the basic production unit in rural China increased dramatically. Since the work-point system practiced in rural collectives rewarded individual workers based on average team performance, the rise in the scale of the production unit would reduce the marginal returns to individual work effort, leading to a decline in peasants' work incentives. To assess this negative effect of collectivisation on agricultural labour productivity, one could approximate the incentive effort by using the size of the basic production unit that had independent accounting. Based on information from retrospective surveys, the provincial average production unit grew from a size of 22 households in 1954 to 176 households in 1957 and then jumped to 2,675 households in 1958. The size of the organisation declined sharply to 41 households in 1962 (Li and Yang, 2005).

Lin (1990) develops a game theoretical explanation, arguing that the main cause of the agricultural collapse was the deprivation of the peasants' right to withdraw from people's communes (Hypothesis 3), which were established in the fall of 1958. Prior to 1958, with voluntary participation in rural cooperatives, the peasants had a self-enforcing agreement to work hard because otherwise, hard-working members would exit the cooperatives. As Lin argues, the switch in organisation to compulsory participation changed the incentive structure so that peasants were prone to shirk within the communes. The total factor productivity (TFP) index estimated by other researchers (eg Wen, 1993) indicates a sudden decline in TFP in 1959, and the index remained at a low level for the entire collectivisation period 1958–1978, giving support to Lin's exit right hypothesis. Since productivity is an important determinant of output, the removal of exit rights may indeed have contributed to the sharp decline in total output.[6]

A number of factors clearly contributed to the sudden decline in food production during the GLF (see Johnson, 1998; Riskin, 1998). But, as Li and Yang (2005) argue, the centerpiece of the puzzle is a systematic failure in central planning (Hypothesis 4). To analyse the relationship between several key variables and obtain a better understanding about the sequencing of GLF events, Li and Yang have formulated a dynamic model of central

---

[6] Lin's explanation for the abrupt collapse of Chinese agriculture provoked a heated debate over the nature of incentives within agricultural collectives. The articles that appeared in the 1993 symposium issue of the *Journal of Comparative Economics* were, in effect, criticisms and comments on Lin's paper. The debate focuses on two critical issues: (a) theoretically, whether the right to exit is necessary for high effort-supply among cooperative members, and (b) historically, whether there was voluntary participation during the collectivisation movement before the GLF movement (see additional evidence on this issue by Kung and Putterman (1997)). Although the symposium did not fully resolve the disputes, there was convergence on a key issue: that the elimination of exit right caused a decline in agricultural productivity during the collectivisation period of 1958–1978.

planning that consists of an agricultural sector and an industrial sector. The objective of the planner is to maximise a discounted flow of industrial output into the future, subject to the constraint that there must be enough grain to feed the industrial work force and function as an intermediate input for industrial production in each year.

In the model of these researchers, two parameters play a crucial role in determining the equilibrium allocation of production inputs between the industrial and agricultural sectors. One is the government's time discount factor, which reflects its preference for speed in achieving industrialisation for China. Another parameter is agricultural productivity, which generally depends on available technology and the form of farming organisation. If the government assigns high priority to rapid industrialisation, it would extract more resources from agriculture to support the industry, but if agriculture has high productivity, less inputs are needed in order to produce sufficient agricultural output to feed the labour force and provide material inputs for the industry. In addition, as a key feature of the model, the physical capacity of agricultural labourers depends on their nutritional status, which increases with food consumption.

Li and Yang argue that on the eve of the GLF movement, two factors acted as the catalysts for a series of policy mistakes that were responsible for the subsequent catastrophe: (a) the central planner became impatient with the slow pace of China's industrialisation and (b) the government formed an erroneous expectation that agricultural productivity would jump to a very high level with the formation of the people's communes. The model predicts that these two changes, which reflect on the central planner's time discount and agricultural productivity parameter, would induce the government to divert large amounts of labour and other resources from agriculture to industry and sharply raise grain procurement from the rural population. Resource diversion reduces agricultural output directly. Excessive procurement, when combined with an actual reduction in productivity due to commune formation, significantly reduces food available for consumption in rural areas, which would lead to a severe nutritional deficiency among rural workers. The resulting reduction in physiological capacity to carry out manual labour would in turn reduce the quality of labour input in growing next year's crops, leading to an additional decline in production. Numerical simulations of the dynamic model suggest that grain output would decline sharply at the onset of these policies, and nutritional deficiency, which realises its effects through intertemporal linkages, could suppress grain production for multiple years. Grain production would not begin to recover until resource allocation and procurement policies are reversed.

Table 2.1 reveals the extent of resource diversions, heavy procurement, and sharp reduction in food availability in rural areas during the GLF crisis. As shown in column (4), the agricultural labour force was reduced by 38 million between 1957 and 1958, when a large number of workers were mobilised to participate in industrial production.[7] Since the labourers who left agriculture were usually the best workers, there was a decline in both the quantity and the quality of the agricultural labour force.

Under the illusion that the collectivisation drive had solved China's food problem, the government advocated a 'three-three system' of agricultural land use under which only a third of the arable land would be needed for grain cultivation, a third would be allocated for growing cash crops and planting trees, and a third would lie fallow (Walker, 1984; Peng, 1987; Yao, 1999). Another official policy was 'sow less, harvest more'. Table 2.1 shows that the area sown with grain was reduced by more than 13% between 1957 and 1959.

Influenced by the 'wind of exaggeration' in production forecasts, the government increased the procurement of grain at the onset of the GLF. Table 2.1 shows that state grain procurement increased from 46 million metric tons in 1957 to 64 million in 1959, despite a sharp decline in grain output in 1959. Consequently, grain retained in rural areas declined sharply from 295 kilograms (kg) per person in 1957 to 223 kg in 1959, and further down to 212 kg in 1960. Since grain was the primary source of food energy in China at the time, the decline in per capita food availability would sharply reduce the physical capacity of carrying out manual work, therefore adversely affecting the labour productivity of rural workers.

Regional innovations in radicalism, as exemplified by the establishment of communal kitchens, may have wasted a substantial amount of food and hence compounded the nutritional effects of excess procurement on peasants' work capacity (Hypothesis 5). In the fall of 1958, local governments established more than 2.65 million communal kitchens (Chang and Wen, 1997). By the end of 1959, the participation rate of peasants in communal mess halls reached an average of 64.7% across the Chinese provinces, with a range from 16.7% to 97.8% (see Table 2.3). In addition to food waste, Yang (1996) argues that the extent of communal dining reflected in large part the degree of radicalism of local political leaders. The more radical the leaders, the more it was likely that local governments would engage in GLF-related non-agricultural activities, such as the construction of mass irrigation and land reclamation projects. These radical initiatives were likely to interfere with grain production in the short run; their negative effects can also be assessed empirically.

---

[7] Riskin (1987) gives a similar estimate of 41 million workers, or 21% of the agricultural labour force, who left farming between 1957 and 1958. Among these workers, approximately 17 million worked in the iron, steel, and other heavy industrial undertakings in the countryside, while close to 16 million migrated into cities, working in state industrial enterprises. See Ashton *et al.* (1984), Walker (1984), and Bernstein (1984) for additional information on sectoral labour allocation during the GLF, including the corrective policies of sending workers back to their rural homes for reducing urban food demand and increasing agricultural labour inputs.

Table 2.3 Mess hall participation rate, party membership density, and time of liberation

Province	Mess hall participation rate at end of 1959 (%)	Density of party membership in 1956 (%)	Time of liberation (month/year)
Anhui	90.5	0.83	01/1949
Fujian	67.2	1.06	08/1949
Gansu	47.7	1.54	08/1949
Guangdong	77.6	0.93	11/1949
Guangxi	91.0	0.85	11/1949
Guizhou	92.6	0.86	11/1949
Hebei	74.4	3.14	11/1947
Heilongjiang	26.5	1.38	10/1948
Henan	97.8	1.08	06/1948
Hubei	68.2	0.77	05/1949
Hunan	97.6	0.80	08/1949
Inner Mongolia	16.7	1.78	09/1949
Jiangsu	56.0	1.37	04/1949
Jiangxi	61.0	1.39	05/1949
Jilin	29.4	1.62	10/1948
Liaoning	23.0	1.75	11/1948
Ningxia	52.9	N.A.	09/1949
Qinghai	29.9	1.04	09/1949
Shaanxi	60.8	1.15	05/1949
Shandong	35.5	2.14	09/1948
Shanxi	70.6	2.92	10/1948
Sichuan	96.7	0.71	11/1949
Yunnan	96.5	0.98	12/1949
Zhejiang	81.6	0.78	05/1949

Source: the first two columns are from Yang (1996, p. 57); the last column is from Kung and Lin (2003).

Empirical findings

Although there has been general awareness about the causes of the production shortfalls analysed in the previous section, for a long time, scholars of the Chinese economy only provided descriptive evidence in support of their individual arguments. Descriptive analyses are helpful in identifying the causal factors and informative of related institutions, but they do not offer quantitative assessments on the effects of the causal factors on output, thus leaving a significant gap in our understanding of the decline in food supply. The paucity of rigorous empirical research is due to several reasons, including the absence of data for several key variables, the need for a unified strategy of testing alternative theories, and the lack of a consistent framework for analysing GLF policies.

In a recent article, Li and Yang (2005) propose a unified framework to assess the relative contributions of the above-mentioned factors to the production shortfalls during the GLF. Their empirical framework adopts a production function approach, in which variations in agricultural output in the Chinese provinces are determined by variations in the quantity and quality of inputs in those provinces. More specifically, the production analysis first takes into account the quantities of conventional inputs – such as land, capital, labour, fertiliser, irrigation, and weather conditions – as determinants of grain output. Then, the framework also takes into account the quality dimensions of the inputs, which depend on factors such as the nutritional status of the rural workers, size of basic production unit, and whether peasants had the right to exit from rural collectivisation. This production function framework is capable of testing not only the hypothesis that the GLF policy package – diversion of agricultural resources and excessive procurement – was responsible for a significant fraction of the collapse in grain output but also other complementary hypotheses on the role of bad weather, labour incentive problems, exit right, and GLF radicalism in causing the production shortfall.

Given the proposed hypotheses, there is still the challenging task of constructing key variables before econometric testing. Li and Yang use a mix of their own constructions as well as innovative measurements suggested by other researchers. The yearly incremental steel and iron output for the period 1954–1964 is used as a proxy for the unobserved diversion of rural labour to nonagricultural GLF projects, as the upheaval associated with the proliferation of backyard steel mills during the crisis absorbed many agricultural labour inputs in rural China. Although yearly food consumption of the peasants was not recorded directly, the retained grain (total grain output minus total grain procurement of the previous year) per person in a specific region is used as a proxy for the nutritional status of local peasants. Collection of historical weather data provides a five-level climate quality index, which is independent of the potentially problematic official weather records. Moreover, the communal dining participation rate at the province level measures the degree of GLF radicalism in local regions (Yang, 1996; Chang and Wen, 1997).

It is also worth noting the unit of observation for empirical analysis. To assess the determinants of grain production, regression analysis requires sufficient variations in agricultural input-output data, either from cross-section units or time series records. This data requirement presents difficulties for studying historical agricultural crises in many parts of the world because detailed data were not available. A unique research opportunity exists for analysing the GLF crisis because China has 25 provinces from which there is systematic historical information on agricultural production. Li and Yang (2005) have compiled a province-level panel data set for the period 1952–1977 consisting of information from published sources and a retrospective survey, which contains additional statistics from local data archives and agricultural experts. The data are rich for estimating econometric models.

The empirical analysis of Li and Yang pays particular attention to two GLF policy variables: food consumption of rural workers and incremental output of steel. Having grain output specified as the explained variable in the regression, the coefficient on the explanatory variable food consumption – a measure of nutritional intake that affects the physical capacity of peasants – enables one to assess the effect of heavy state grain procurement on the collapse in production. The coefficient on the other explanatory variable steel output – a measure of diversion of labour away from farming – enables one to assess the effect of inefficient activities on grain output during the GLF. The estimation results suggest that, *ceteris paribus*, a 10% reduction in retained grain from the previous year would substantially lower the work capacity of peasants, causing a 2.67% decline in grain output in the current year. Similarly, a 10% increase in the change of steel output, *ceteris paribus*, would reduce the quantity and quality of agricultural labour and hence result in a 0.99% decline in grain output. Therefore, given the severe decline in food availability in rural areas (see Table 2.1) and sharp increases in steel and iron output during the GLF,[8] these two factors were important causes of the collapse in gain output.

Through a decomposition analysis, Li and Yang quantitatively assess the contributions of the identified factors to changes in grain output during the GLF crisis beginning in 1958 and ending in 1961. Their findings show that the diversion of agricultural resources to industry was the most important causal factor, responsible for 33% of the observed grain output decline. The intertemporal effect of excessive procurement and nutrition was the second largest contributor to the decline, accounting for 28.3% of the production shortfall. Adverse weather conditions also played a significant role, reducing food supplies by 12.9%. However, despite noticeable effects of other causal factors on output in specific years, none of them had a major impact on the shortfall in grain production for the entire crisis period.

The famine

Sen's entitlement approach provides the insight that decline in food availability is only one possible cause of famine. To understand massive starvation, analysts often need to explore factors beyond a shortage in food supply, which is the focus of the last section. Moreover, since the entitlement approach is built primarily on a market system in which commodity

---

[8] The national output of pig iron and steel was 11.3 million tons in 1957. It increased dramatically to 21.7, 35.8, and 45.8 million tons in the next 3 years, before it returned to the trend level of 14.7 million tons in 1962. Most of these increases in steel output were produced in China's rural areas.

prices and rights to private properties are central ingredients of analysis, its application to the Chinese famine must take into account factors unique to China. First, China had a central planning system in which the government set commodity prices and controlled the procurement and distribution of food. Second, the Chinese famine occurred in the chaotic GLF period when radical policies other than food distribution may have aggravated hunger and starvation. Third, unlike many famines examined by Sen in which aggregate food availability did not decline, China indeed experienced severe shortages in food supplies at the national level. The challenge to researchers is to assess the importance of food availability decline, failures in entitlement arrangements, and other institutional and policy factors to the enormous loss in human lives.

Hypotheses on causal factors

Applying Sen's entitlement approach, Lin and Yang (2000) present a framework that considers FAD and urban bias in China's food distribution system as joint determinants of the GLF famine (Hypothesis 1). Under central planning, China had an effective, urban-biased rationing system in which city residents were given protected rights to acquire certain amounts of food. On the other hand, compulsory quotas of grain procurement were imposed on the peasants. As a result, peasants were entitled only to the residual grain output. In years of poor harvests, particularly during the GLF period when there were sharp declines in food production in many rural regions, delivery of production quotas set in the beginning of a year would leave insufficient food supplies for farmers in the following year, causing the caloric intake of some peasants to fall below the minimum threshold required for survival. Hence, urban bias in food procurement and distribution may directly cause excess mortality in the presence of negative shocks on grain production.

Admittedly, dramatic declines in food supply may directly cause starvation and hunger. During the GLF, national grain output declined abruptly by 15% in 1959 and aggregate food availability reached only 70% of the 1958 level in 1960–1961. Lin and Yang argue that the sudden collapse in grain supply, along with urban-biased food allocation, were both likely responsible for the massive death toll. The empirical question they attempt to answer is the relative importance of the two factors in causing the variations in death rates across Chinese provinces.

Factors other than FAD and legal rights to food may also contribute to the severity of the famine. Yang (1996) and Chang and Wen (1997) argue that wasteful preparation and consumption of food associated with communal dining, which led to the depletion of grain before next year's harvest, were the primary causes of the Great Leap famine (Hypothesis 2). Yang (1996) considers wasteful food consumption in communal kitchens as a tragedy of the commons: when meals were freely supplied in communal mess halls, the pursuit of individual gains led to excessive food consumption, a result that was detrimental to all commune members. Yang further argues that agrarian radicalism, of which commune dining is an example, is the more fundamental cause of the catastrophe. He proposes a 'loyalty compensation' hypothesis: that provinces with lower ratios of communist party members would implement radical policies of the GLF more enthusiastically than the provinces with higher ratios of party members. This is because those who wanted to join the party would try hard to gain their party membership by showing unshakable loyalty to the centre, a classic case of overcompensation for the sake of a cause. Therefore, the provinces that had lower ratios of party members were expected to have higher mess hall participation rates, and consequently, higher levels of mortality.

In a related study, Chang and Wen (1997) single out the communal dining system as the primary cause of the famine. While admitting that multiple factors contributed to the catastrophe, they placed emphasis on one piece of evidence: the national death rate started to rise in 1958, when there were good harvests and abundant food supplies. Since many communal dining halls were established in the second half of 1958 and there was over-consumption and waste of food in the kitchens, they argue that communal dining must be the culprit that first started, and then greatly aggravated, the famine. The paper presents much anecdotal evidence and draws inference from the sequencing of events. Their conclusion is also supported by a positive correlation between 1960 excess death rates and the 1959 dining hall participation rates across the Chinese provinces.

The study by Chang and Wen gives the impression that famine started in 1958. However, on the basis of China's provincial mortality statistics, Lin and Yang (1998) point out that widespread famine did not occur until 1959. Table 2.2 shows that China's death rate increased to 12.0 per thousand in 1958, from an average of 11.1 per thousand in 1956–1957. However, this increase was driven by dramatic increases in mortality in three provinces: Sichuan's death rate increased from 11.3 to 25.2 per thousand, Yunnan from 15.8 to 21.6, and Gansu from 11.1 to 21.1. In fact, using the 1956–1957 average as a reference, the death rates in 1958 actually declined in 16 out of 28 provinces; therefore, rising mortality was not a widespread phenomenon across the Chinese provinces in 1958. In 1959, the national average mortality jumped to 14.6 per thousand and higher mortality rates are found in 27 out of 28 provinces, marking the beginning of widespread starvation. Since most provinces started communal dining halls in 1958, but rising mortality rates were concentrated in three provinces, these facts do not support the claim that communal dining initiated the famine in that year.[9]

---

[9] Anecdotal evidence used by Chang and Wen (1997) suggests that the total waste of food was enormous in some rural areas. For instance, 'in some rural areas the grain consumed by peasants in a three-month period amounted to what usually sufficed for six months' (Peng, 1987). 'In some places, three months' supply of grain was

The timing of the 1958 harvests and the creation of communal kitchens also suggests that public dining was an unlikely cause of the excess mortality in 1958. Communal mess halls emerged after the formation of the communes. The first commune appeared in August 1958; most others were established in October or November 1958. Therefore, many communal kitchens did not start until the end of that year. It is well known that in most places in China, crops were not harvested until October or November. For areas with single-crop production, the harvested grain should provide sufficient consumption for 12 months, while in double-crop areas the supply should last for 6 months. Based on the above information, it is highly unlikely that people who participated in communal kitchens consumed all the food in one or two months and went on to hunger and starvation in 1958. The rise in mortality rates in the few provinces was likely due to factors other than food waste and overconsumption.

There is little doubt that overconsumption and waste of food in communal mess halls during the GLF could have reduced food availability in local regions and magnified the severity of famine. The relevant empirical questions are: how does one reliably measure the quantity of food waste resulting from the public dining arrangements,[10] and how does one assess its impact on excess deaths relative to other causes? The information available to approximate the extent of food waste associated with communal dining is the province-level mess hall participation rate (MHPR) at the end of 1959 (see Table 2.3). Chang and Wen (1997) use MHPR as a proxy for consumption inefficiency; they find a positive correlation with the 1960 provincial excess death rates. This result is taken as empirical support for the hypothesis that consumption irrationality led to famine. However, since only 24 sample points are used in the regression and the specification does not control for other possible causes of famine, the correlation can hardly represent reliable evidence on causality.

The political attitude of provincial leaders may have strongly influenced local policies and economic activities during the GLF, which could in turn have contributed to the excess mortality (Hypothesis 3). As Yang (1996, p. 58) observes, mess hall participation rates varied from over 90% for Henan,

---

consumed in merely two weeks' (Yang, 1996). There is also anthropological evidence from Potter and Potter (1990): 'According to one peasant, everyone "irresponsibly" ate whether they were hungry or not, and in 20 days they had finished almost all rice they had, rice which should have lasted for six months'. While these descriptions could be true as isolated events, they cannot be used as scientific evidence to support the hypothesis that communal dining was a major cause of the famine.

[10] Chang and Wen (1997) provide a quantitative estimate made by a Chinese economist Xue Muqiao that the over-consumption of grain by peasants in 1958 amounted to 17.5 million tons, which was 8.78% of the total domestic production in that year. However, the authors did not explain the method used to derive this estimate.

Hunan, Sichuan, Yunnan, Guizhou, and Anhui to under 50% for provinces such as Liaoning and Heilongjiang (see Table 2.3). He also notes that the seven provinces with the highest mess-hall participation rates (Shanghai as a municipal city is not included in the table) either were under the influence of the most zealous leaders of the time or had just gone through a political purge. These observations corroborate the view that radical leaders were more responsive to the calls from the party centre in Beijing for achieving high levels of participation in communal kitchens. Since communal dining caused overconsumption and waste of food, the radical provincial leaders and their policies are likely partly responsible for the subsequent death toll.

Another mechanism through which agrarian radicalism may contribute to excess mortality is the exporting of grain from provinces to the central government by zealous provincial leaders who were most enthusiastic to show their loyal support for the GLF policy (eg, Lin and Yang, 1998). For instance, provincial leaders in Sichuan and Hunan, who were among the most cooperative and obedient to the centre, managed to deliver large quantities of grain to the state despite their own shortages (Walker, 1984). In 1959–1960, each of the provinces submitted 2.24 and 0.44 million tons of grain to the centre, while starvation prevailed in their own provinces. As early as 1958, a procurement slogan was propagated in Sichuan: 'First the center, than the locality; first external (commitments), then internal (commitments)'. The province organised 5 million people to transport grain for export, and the procurement reached the highest historical level of 2.595 million tons. Because of heavy extractions, food availability in Sichuan and Hunan fell to dangerously low levels, ultimately causing high levels of mortality. In contrast, provinces such as Guangdong and Jilin only experienced mild increases in excess deaths during the crisis, partly because these provinces successfully reduced their grain export burdens (Walker, 1984).

Finally, provinces with zealous leaders were prone to deeply involve themselves in the radical GLF campaigns, such as backyard steel production, massive irrigation work, land reclamation tasks, and other labour-intensive projects. These energy-consuming projects in nonagricultural activities often increased the demand for calories among participating labourers, leading to faster exhaustion of food supplies before the next harvest and thus malnutrition and starvation (Johnson, 1998; Kung and Lin, 2003). Moreover, since these physically demanding projects may be detrimental to health, and the zealous devotion to these campaigns may also have led to the neglect of health care, both situations could lead to higher mortality (Lin and Yang, 1998). This health-related factor, plus the large quantity of grain outflow from the provinces, could be important factors in explaining the sharp rise in mortality rates in Sichuan, Yunnan, and Gansu in 1958.

With the agreement that GLF radicalism could aggravate the famine, researchers have used two different proxies to measure the degree of radicalism for empirical analysis: (a) the density of party membership (DPM) in individual provinces, as measured by the proportion of the rural population who were communist party members;[11] and (b) the revolutionary history of a province, as measured by the time order of liberation for individual provinces (see Table 2.3). Measure (a) is based on the idea of Yang (1996) that low-level cadres not yet joining the party were usually the most zealous because they were eager to show strong loyalty to the party centre. Therefore, as he argues, a lower density of party membership in a province implies a higher degree of agrarian radicalism. However, because of noticeable limitations of the party density measure,[12] researchers also use (b) to measure radicalism, which is an index known as the time of liberation (TOL) according to the actual month and year when a province was declared 'liberated' by the government (Yang, 1996; Kung and Lin, 2003). The rationale behind this measure is based on the historical fact that newly liberated provinces were more likely to be appointed with zealous leaders, who would in turn pursue more radical GLF policies, leading to higher mortality in those provinces during the GLF.

It is ironic that China's net grain export reached a historical record of 4.2 million tons in 1959 and remained at 2.7 million tons in 1960 when the nation suffered from the horrific death rate of 25.4 per thousand. The bulk of those grain exports functioned as payments to the USSR in exchange for machinery and equipment for the GLF, which peaked in 1959 (Riskin, 1987, p. 132; Lardy, 1987). Since the quantities of China's total grain output were 170 and 143.5 million tons in those 2 years, net grain exports accounted for 2.47% and 1.88% of the total production. Hundreds and thousands of lives could have been saved without those grain exports (Hypothesis 4; eg, Johnson, 1998). Moreover, the combined effects of closing down rural commodity markets and the decline in government coordinated interregional grain trade during the GLF may have contributed to the severity of the famine (Hypothesis 5; Lardy, 1987). The reduction in food trade across provinces was caused in part by the government initiative of establishing local self-sufficiency with the communes. It also reflected the political incentives of local cadres who often concealed food shortages within their jurisdiction and the need for outside help because of their earlier exaggerated production

---

[11] Since information on the density of party membership is available only for 1956, the data are used for the analysis of the GLF period, with the implicit assumption that the ratio did not change much in the period of several years.

[12] As Lin and Yang (1998) and Kung and Lin (2003) point out, the range of variations in DPM was very narrow, with a low of 0.71 and a high of 3.41%, which raise the question of whether 1%–2% differentials in non-party membership would lead to significant differences in the degree of radicalism. Second, it is not clear whether party or non-party members were more zealous and loyal to the party centre. Third, it is likely that top provincial leaders played a much more influential role than low-level cadres in formulating local GLF policies.

forecasts. There is evidence that mortality was particularly high in rural areas that specialised in non-grain production, where the starvation would have been less severe if there were effective markets and regional redistribution. Lastly, as Sen (1983) emphasises, the lack of news distribution systems and pressure groups within China may have obstructed information flows to provide necessary famine relief or international aid (Hypothesis 6), which could have significantly reduced famine deaths.

Empirical findings

In famine analysis, researchers often rely on case studies to investigate the cause of specific famine events, emphasising either food availability or entitlement as a crucial factor. The lack of econometric analysis reflects in part the difficulty of measuring spatial and/or time series variations in entitlement arrangements and food availability decline. In the Chinese famine of 1959–1961, food availability and entitlements to food were both important factors. Moreover, data are available that reveal variations in mortality rates, food availability, entitlement arrangements, communal dining, and the degree of radicalism in the Chinese provinces in specific years and over time. These rich data sources permit researchers to test Hypotheses 1–3 discussed in the last section. Applying Sen's entitlement approach, Lin and Yang (2000) develop a framework that is amenable to empirical testing and that simultaneously considers per capita food supply and the right to food as determinants of famine. The paper is the first econometric study to directly assess the importance of famine causes using the entitlement approach.

Lin and Yang use a panel data set of 28 Chinese provinces for the period 1954–1966 for empirical analysis. They use the percentage of rural population and per capita grain output in a province as, respectively, proxies for the degree of urban bias and the extent of food availability in that province, and assess the contributions of these factors to observed cross-province differences in death rates. Their basic estimation function controls for year and provincial fixed effects. The main hypothesis to be tested is whether during a famine in China, the death rate in a province is positively related to the proportion of rural population in that province (urban bias hypothesis) and negatively related to per capita grain output in that province (food availability hypothesis).[13]

---

[13] Note that the percentage of rural people in a province measures the percentage of people who did not have legally protected rights to food in that province. An alternative entitlement measure would be the state grain procurement and transfers from rural areas of a province, representing the deprivation of food entitlement of that province. However, the procurement and transfer information was not available to the authors at the time of their research.

Lin and Yang's empirical results show that in normal years, the cross-province differences in the urban bias and food availability variables did not result in cross-province differences in death rates. However, in the famine period of 1959–1961, both variables contributed significantly to the observed inter-provincial differences in mortality rates. In fact, the Chinese food entitlement system, which was dominated by urban-biased distribution, explains a greater part of the inter-provincial variation in mortality rates than does food availability, providing support to Sen's entitlement approach.

More specifically, estimation results indicate that a 10% increase in the proportion of rural population in a province would result in a 7.19% increase in the provincial death rate. By contrast, a 10% decline in per capita food availability would result in a 4.17% increase in mortality rate. Therefore, the effect on excess death rate from a given percentage change in entitlement is about 72% bigger than from the same percentage change in food availability. Another method of evaluating the relative importance of the two famine causes lies in their power to explain variations in provincial death rates. Using measures of partial correlation coefficients, Lin and Yang show that, among the variations of inter-provincial death rates explained by the two famine causes, 69.5% of the total was attributable to urban-biased food entitlements and the remaining 30.5% was attributable to grain availability. The findings from both methods confirm that urban bias in food allocation, as well as shortages in food supply, played central roles in causing the famine.

In a recent study, Kung and Lin (2003) expand the above framework to also examine the effects of communal dining and the Leap's radical policies on death rates across provinces. They use mess hall participation rate (MHPR) as a proxy for food waste and two other variables, the density of party membership (DPM) and time of liberation (TOL), as alternative proxies for GLF radicalism. This specification improves upon the earlier empirical analysis by Chang and Wen (1997), who examine the correlation between provincial death rates and dining participation rates, without controlling for other key causes of the famine. The findings confirm the importance of food availability decline and urban bias in food distribution in causing the famine. Political radicalism was also an important factor that helps account for variations in the death rates across provinces.

However, empirical evidence fails to support the hypothesis that food waste and overconsumption in communal dining was an important cause of the GLF famine. When either DPM or TOL is included in the regression, the coefficient estimate on MHPR is no longer statistically significant, suggesting that food waste *per se* did not contribute to provincial variations in death rates, although other aspects of radicalism raised the death toll. To explain why communal dining fails to affect death rate negatively, Kung and Lin present additional evidence. Based on information collected from provincial newspaper archives, they report that food was generally rationed to peasants in the mess halls, a fact that is inconsistent with the popular perception of mess hall operations, as in the political slogan 'opening up your stomach and eating as much as you can'. Moreover, official sources also reveal that communal dining became unpopular in many rural regions as early as the spring of 1959. Local adaptive policies also permitted peasants to cook at home or to open communal kitchens on a seasonal basis. These corrective actions must have mitigated some potential damage of the mess halls in the people's communes.

Remarks on the Chinese and Soviet famines

China's agricultural crisis and the associated famine of 1959–1961 were among the worst catastrophes in human history, but for a long time they were also the least studied and understood of human calamities. This paper reviews a growing economic literature on this historical crisis. Existing evidence suggests that the collapse in grain production was largely attributable to two fallacious GLF policies. Encouraged by expectations of a great leap in agricultural productivity from collectivisation, the government diverted massive amounts of agricultural resources to industry and sharply raised grain procurement from the peasants, eventually leading to malnutrition among peasants and decimation of their labour productivity in growing next year's crops. The consecutive years of bad weather also aggravated the fatal economic policies. The decline in food availability was indeed a cause of the GLF famine. But other institutional factors, including urban bias in China's food distribution system, radical local policies, and grain exports, were also major contributors of the excess mortality. By and large, the GLF catastrophe was the result of a series of failures in central planning.

The literature on the Great Leap crisis not only provides insights into the relationship between economic system and economic performance in China but also suggests a framework to help understand the cause of famine in other centrally planned economies. Under collective agriculture, the USSR experienced two major famines: one in 1931–1933, with 4.5–8.0 millions of excess mortality (eg Davies and Wheatcroft, 2004, pp. 402–403), and the other in 1947, with 1.0–1.5 millions of famine deaths (Ellman, 2000).[14] Lively scholarly debates on the cause of these famines, especially

---

[14] Prior to agricultural collectivisation, two other large-scale famines also occurred in the Russian Empire and the USSR in recent history. The 1891–1892 famine resulted in 0.4–0.5 million excess deaths; the death toll in the 1918–1922 famine reached as many as 10–14 million. These two famines, which were primarily attributable to natural calamities, rural revolution, civil wars, and famine-related infectious diseases (Davies and Wheatcroft, 2004, pp. 402–406), are not covered in the subsequent discussion.

the 1931–1933 disaster, have continued for several decades. In his book *The Harvest of Sorrow,* Conquest (1986) advocates that the 1931–1933 famine was 'man-made' and 'deliberate', orchestrated by Stalin, who imposed the famine to suppress the nationalist aspirations of the Ukraine and peasant resistance to agricultural collectivisation. Alternatively, Tauger (2001) – who investigates in detail the weather conditions and agricultural performance in the crisis years – concludes that the famine was 'the result of the largest in a series of natural disasters'. Between these polar views, researchers have compiled and analysed a large body of historical evidence on the development of events surrounding the two disasters.[15] A comparison with the Chinese experience reveals that policy failures of central planning were also critical for causing the production catastrophe and the famines in the USSR.

Resembling the Chinese GLF campaign was the USSR's first five-year plan in 1928, a superindustrialisation drive that aimed to achieve lofty production and accumulation goals. Soviet capital stock was to double in 5 years, and even light industry was expected to expand by 70% (Gregory and Stuart, 2001). To support the big push, industry needed an expanding labour force, ample supplies of raw materials, and agricultural export earnings to exchange for machinery and equipment imports for all sectors. There was also an urgent requirement for securing grain from the countryside because of forecasted increasing demand for food during the plan. Such a requirement was also influenced by the earlier grain procurement crisis of 1927–1928, during which Stalin believed that peasants intentionally withheld grain from markets, which resulted in food shortages in cities. Agricultural collectivisation was the proposed solution to these concerns and problems: as the government believed, collectivisation would enable the state to acquire grain more easily and cheaply, and large-scale mechanised farming would quickly transform traditional peasant cultivation into modern and productive agriculture. Based on the false premise of a leap in agricultural productivity, the Soviet government forcefully carried out rural collectivisation in a sweeping fashion. In 1929, only 3.9% of peasant households participated in collective farming; by 1932, 61.5% of peasant households worked under central planning (Volin, 1970, p. 211).

Wishfully expecting a surge in agricultural productivity from technological and organisational innovations with collectivisation, the Soviet government proposed to raise grain collection dramatically in the first 5-year plan. While actual acquisitions encountered fierce resistance from the peasants, total grain collection still increased sharply, from 10.8 million tons in 1928 to 16.1, 22.1, 22.8, 18.5, and 22.6 million tons between 1929 and 1933. Since total grain outputs were at 73.3, 71.7, 83.5, 69.5, 69.6, and 68.4 million tons in those individual years (Clarke and Matko, 1983, p. 149),

---

[15] See O'Grada (2007) for a survey of the major studies and their findings.

both production and retained food grain in rural areas declined to very low levels in 1931, 1932, and 1933.[16]

These figures and related data suggest that malnutrition among peasants due to excessive grain procurements and diversion of agricultural resources to industry – the two most important causal factors of the Chinese agricultural crisis – were also critical to the decline in grain production in the USSR. Under the superindustrialisation drive, there were large flows of labour from rural to urban areas: Soviet urban population increased by 12.7 million between 1929 and 1933, while the rural population declined from 126.7 to 125.4 million (Clarke and Matko, 1983, p. 2). Within agriculture, resources were also diverted away from grain production; emphasis was placed on industrial crops instead. For instance, home-produced cotton consumption jumped from 168,400 tons in 1926–1927 to the same as above: 394,800 tons in 1933 (Wheatcroft *et al.*, 1986). Grain production was further undermined by a disastrous decline in the number of draft animals. In 1933, the total heads of cattle declined to 54% of the 1928 level, and the number of work horses declined from 23.4 million in the spring of 1929 to 12.8 million in July 1934. The slaughter of animals on the eve of collectivisation, and the reduction in fodder due to heavy grain procurements during the crisis years, were largely responsible for the destruction of much-needed draft power in agricultural production. The reduction in resources for grain production and the destruction of peasants' labour capacity due to insufficient food consumption must have contributed to the production shortfalls, although their quantitative effects on output are not yet estimated for Soviet agriculture.

As with the Chinese experience, consecutive years of bad weather also contributed to the Soviet production crisis. Following the adverse climate conditions that resulted in the loss of half of the entire winter-sown crop in 1927–1928 and one-third of the winter crop of 1928–1929 in the Ukraine, severe dry weather spells occurred over a large part of the major grain-production regions in the USSR in the early 1930s, especially in 1931 (Wheatcroft *et al.*, 1986). During certain periods in 1932, extremely wet and humid weather hit the USSR, giving rise to severe plant disease infections, smut and rut, in particular, which resulted in the loss of 7.1 million tons of grain, equivalent to 13% of the official harvest figure (Tauger, 2001). Although the quantitative effect of unfavourable weather on output is not yet evaluated statistically, scholars generally agree that natural calamities were important determinants of these production shortfalls.

---

[16] See Davies and Wheatcroft (2004, pp. 432–433) for a summary of the estimates of substantial decline in rural food availability from several independent sources. They also point out a more severe decline in the consumption per head of meat and diary products during the famine years.

Taking as given the decline in food supply, policies and institutions of the Soviet planning system were also important causal factors that aggravated hunger and starvation. Closely resembling China's food ration system, employment in industry and other nonagricultural sectors in the USSR generally had legally protected rights for certain amounts of food, while collective farmers were paid out of what was left over after compulsory deliveries. In effect, the state and the urban population were the primary claimants of food grain through the use of compulsory state acquisitions, while the rural population was essentially a residual claimant. Therefore, during the periods of severe food shortages, peasants were the most vulnerable to mortality risks. In fact, when starvation became widespread in 1932 and 1933, the Politburo of the USSR made the decision that state-collected grain must be supplied to the hungry towns; no allocations could be made available to the countryside for seed, food, or fodder (Davies and Wheatcroft, 2004, p. 440). Like China, the USSR also exported grain during the crisis years. Insisting on the priority of industrialisation, the Soviet government continued to export large quantities of grain – 5.83, 4.79, 1.61, and 2.32 million tons in each of the individual years between 1930–1931 and 1933–1934 – in exchange with other European countries for machinery and equipment to achieve the intended goals of capital accumulation, even as famine devastated the country (Davies and Wheatcroft, 2004, p. 471). There is little doubt that countless lives would have been saved if the Soviet government had stopped exporting grain and used this grain for famine relief.

History repeated itself during the 1947 Soviet famine, which was triggered by long periods of bad weather, especially a serious drought in 1946 that led to a sharp decline in grain production. Given the output shortages, urban bias in food rationing and exports of grain during the crisis emerged again as major causes of massive starvation. As Ellman (2000) documents, the total quantities of grain exports were 1, 0.3, and 2.4 million tons in the three years from 1946 to 1948. The bulk of grain exports went to Poland and East Germany as the Soviet government strove to consolidate the New Soviet bloc (Hanson, 2003, p. 38). The government also started building a state grain reserve after the harvest of 1947, the purpose of which was to deal with future food emergencies and strengthen national food security (Ellman, 2000). Corresponding heavy grain procurements suppressed food availability in rural areas. As a result, policy mistakes of the central planner became critical factors in causing a large number of the rural population who did not have entitlement to food under the Soviet ration system to become famine victims.

These famines in China and the USSR were the worst catastrophes in the loss of human lives in the last century. These famines, each of which lasted for several years, were accompanied by precipitous declines in grain production. The research findings reported in this paper suggest that policy errors and institutional failures of central planning are significant factors in explaining the origin and mechanism of these production and demographic disasters. The blind pursuit of rapid industrialisation at the expense of agriculture sowed the seeds of tragedies for China's GLF campaign of 1959–1961 and the Soviet superindustrialisation drive of 1928–1932. Through a chain of interrelated human actions consisting of agricultural collectivisation, overoptimistic expectations on productivity change, the diversion of agricultural resources to industry, excessive grain procurements, and malnutrition among peasants, both economies experienced sudden declines in aggregate grain production. Compounding the shortages in food supplies, urban bias in the food distribution systems and grain exports during the crisis both contributed significantly to the enormous death tolls. Therefore, central planning was the main culprit of the catastrophes, as the governments acted on false premises, imposed aggregate risks through the implementation of nationwide economic plans, and insisted on deleterious policies with dogmatic certainty. The amplifying effects of central planning on natural calamities can explain much about the long duration and the monumental scale of the catastrophes. Hence, the research reviewed in this article provides additional evidence on the weaknesses of central planning through the perspectives of agricultural crises and famines as economic transition continues to progress in China and the former USSR.

Acknowledgements

I thank Meg Gottemoeller, James Kung, Ryan Monarch, James Wen, and two anonymous referees for making constructive suggestions and comments on earlier versions of this paper. I am also grateful for the financial support from the Center for China in the World Economy (CCWE) at Tsinghua University, where I carried out much of the research of this paper while serving as Senior Research Fellow at the CCWE.

References

Aird, JS. 1982: Population studies and population policies in China. *Population and Development Review* 8: 85–97.
Ashton, B, Hill, K, Piazza, A and Zeitz, R. 1984: Famine in China, 1958–61. *Population and Development Review* 10: 613–645.
Banister, J. 1987: *China's changing population.* Stanford University Press: Stanford.
Becker, J. 1996: *Hungry ghosts: Mao's secret famine.* Henry Holt and Company: New York.
Bernstein, TP. 1984: Stalinism, famine, and Chinese peasants. *Theory and Society* 13: 339–377.
Bohr, PR. 1972: *Famine in China and the missionary: Timothy Richard as relief administrator and advocate of national reform, 1876–1884.* Harvard East Asian Center: Cambridge.
Bourke, A. 1993: *The visitation of god? The potato and the great Irish famine.* Lilliput Press: Dublin.

CCP, Central Committee of Chinese Communist Party. 1981: *Decisions on several historical issues of the Communist Party of China since the founding of the Republic.* People's Press: Beijing.

Chang, GH and Wen, GJ. 1997: Communal dining and the Chinese famine of 1958–1961. *Economic Development and Cultural Change* 46: 1–34.

Clarke, RA and Matko, DJI. 1983: *Soviet economic facts 1917–81.* Macmillan Press: London.

Coale, JA. 1981: Population trends, population policy, and population studies in China. *Population and Development Review 7:* 261–297.

Conquest, R. 1986: *The harvest of sorrow: Soviet collectivization and the terror – famine.* Oxford University Press: New York.

Davies, RW and Wheatcroft, SG. 2004: *The years of hunger: Soviet agriculture, 1931–1933.* Palgrave Macmillan: London.

Dreze, J and Sen, AK. 1989: *Hunger and public action.* Clarendon Press: Oxford.

Eckstein, A. 1966: *Communist China's economic growth and foreign trade: Implications for US policy.* McGraw-Hill: New York.

Ellman, M. 2000: The 1947 Soviet famine and the entitlement approach to famines. *Cambridge Journal of Economics* 24: 603–630.

Gregory, PR and Stuart, RC. 2001: *Russian and Soviet economic performance and structure,* 7th edn. Addison Wesley Longman: Boston.

Hanson, P. 2003: *The rise and fall of the Soviet economy: An economic history of the USSR from 1945.* Pearson Education Limited: London.

Johnson, DG. 1998: China's great famine: Introductory remarks. *China Economic Review* 9: 103–109.

Kueh, YY. 1995: *Agricultural instability in China, 1931–1991.* Clarendon Press: Oxford.

Kung, J and Lin, JY. 2003: The causes of China's Great Leap famine, 1959–1961. *Economic Development and Cultural Change* 52: 51–73.

Kung, J and Putterman, L. 1997: China's collectivization puzzle: A new resolution. *Journal of Development Studies* 33: 741–763.

Lardy, N. 1987: The Chinese economy under stress, 1958–1965 In: MacFarquhar, R and Fairbank, JK (eds) *The Cambridge History of China.* Cambridge University Press: New York.

Li, W and Yang, DT. 2005: The great leap forward: Anatomy of a central planning disaster. *Journal of Political Economy* 113(4): 840–877.

Lin, JY. 1990: Collectivization and China's agricultural crisis in 1959–61. *Journal of Political Economy* 98: 1228–1252.

Lin, JY and Yang, DT. 1998: On the causes of China's agricultural crisis and the Great Leap Famine. *China Economic Review* 9: 125–140.

Lin, JY and Yang, DT. 2000: Food availability, entitlements, and the Chinese famine of 1959–61. *Economic Journal* 110: 136–158.

Liu, Z. 1980: The recent selection and development of China's population. Paper presented at Beijing International Round Table Conference on Demography.

MOA, Ministry of Agriculture. 1984: *Nongye Jingji Ziliao, 1949–83 (Agricultural economic data, 1943–83).* Ministry of Agriculture: Beijing.

Mokyr, J. 1983: *Why Ireland starved: A quantitative and analytical history of the Irish economy, 1800–1850.* Allen and Unwin: London.

NBS, National Bureau of Statistics. 1983: *Statistical yearbook of China.* China Statistical Press: Beijing.

NBS, National Bureau of Statistics. 1990: *A compilation of historical statistical data of provinces, autonomous regions, and municipalities, 1949–1989.* China Statistical Press: Beijing.

O'Grada, C. 1989: *The great Irish famine*. Macmillan: Houndmills, UK.

O'Grada, C. 2007: Making famine history. *Journal of Economic Literature* XLV: 3–36.

Osmani, S. 1995: The entitlement approach to famine: An assessment In: Basu, K, Pattanaik, P and Suzumura, K (eds) *Choice, Welfare, and Development: Essays in Honor of Amartya Sen*. Clarendon Press: Oxford.

Peng, XZ. 1987: Demographic consequences of the Great Leap forward in China's provinces. *Population and Development Review* 13: 639–670.

Perkins, DH. 1966: *Market control and planning in communist China*. Harvard University Press: Cambridge.

Perkins, DH and Yusuf, S. 1984: *Rural development in China*. The John's Hopkins University Press: Baltimore and London.

Potter, S and Potter, JM. 1990: *China's peasants – Anthropology of a revolution*. Cambridge University Press: Cambridge.

Ravallion, M. 1997: Famines and economics. *Journal of Economic Literature* 35: 1205–1242.

Riskin, C. 1987: *China's political economy: The quest for development since 1949*. Oxford University Press: Oxford.

Riskin, C. 1998: Seven questions about the Chinese famine of 1959–61. *China Economic Review* 9: 111–124.

Rosen, S. 1999: Potato paradoxes. *Journal of Political Economy* 107: s294–s313.

Sen, AK. 1981: *Poverty and famine*. Clarendon Press: Oxford.

Sen, AK. 1983: Development: Which way now? *Economic Journal* 93: 745–762.

Sterba, J. 1981: China believed to have understated scale of drought and flood. *The New York Times,* 25 April.

Sun, YF. 1981: Consolidate statistics work and reform the statistics system. *Jingji Guangli (Economic Management)* 2: 3–5.

Tauger, M. 2001: Natural disasters and human actions in the Soviet famine of 1931–1933. The Carl Beck Papers, No. 1506, University of Pittsburgh.

Volin, L. 1970: *A century of Russian agriculture*. Harvard University Press: Cambridge.

Walker, KR. 1984: *Food grain procurement and consumption in China*. Cambridge University Press: Cambridge.

Wen, GJ. 1993: Total factor productivity change in China's farming sector: 1952–1989. *Economic Development and Cultural Change* 42: 1–41.

Wheatcroft, SG, Davies, RW and Cooper, JM. 1986: Soviet industrialization reconsidered: Some preliminary conclusions about economic development between 1926 and 1941. *Economic History Review* (2nd ser.) 39(2): 264–294.

Yang, DL. 1996: *Calamity and reform in China: State, rural society, and institutional change since the Great Leap Famine*. Stanford University Press: Stanford.

Yao, SJ. 1999: A note on the causal factors of China's famine in 1959–1961. *Journal of Political Economy* 107: 1365–1369.

Zhu, ZZ. 1980: China's population problem at present and its development trend. *Jingji Kexu (Economic Science)* 3: 54–58.

3

State-Owned versus Township and Village Enterprises in China

Enrico C. Perotti[1], Laixiang Sun[2], and Liang Zou[3]
[1]*University of Amsterdam, Netherlands;* [2]*University of Maryland, USA; and*
[3]*University of Amsterdam, Netherlands*

This paper presents an up-to-date survey of the comparison issue between state-owned enterprises (SOEs) and township-village enterprises (TVEs) in China. Although TVEs are at a disadvantage in areas such as technology, labor skills, education levels of staff, access to bank loans and government supports, they have important advantages in ownership and governance structures, personnel systems and labor relations, and conditions of institutional arrangement. These advantages apparently have outweighed the disadvantages, allowing the TVEs to outperform SOEs and successfully expand their market shares that previously belonged to the SOEs. However, our analysis also reveals that SOEs may not have performed so badly if their broad social contributions other than reported profits are also taken into account. In conclusion, we argue that both SOEs and TVEs need to reform their ownership and governance structures. In particular, if TVEs are to develop further during the next century, they cannot avoid the grassroots democratization.

1 Introduction

While China's overall economic reform has resulted in considerable achievements in the past two decades, some deep structural problems remain, one of which is the long-lasting inefficiency of the state-owned enterprises (SOEs). Although there have been disputes over the total factor productivity of SOEs, it is widely acknowledged that a growing proportion of SOEs are losing money. According to a recent World Bank (1997) report, about half of industrial SOEs made a loss in 1996, up from one-third just two years ago. The SOE share in national total industrial output has fallen from 77.6 percent in 1980 to 28.5 percent in 1996 (SSB, 1997, p. 413), and estimated to decline further to 25 percent by the year 2000.

The statistics seem to indicate that despite persistent enterprise reforms, the situation of SOEs is worsening, or at least has had little improvement.

Reprinted with permission from Association of Comparative Economic Studies. All rights reserved. *Comparative Economic Studies* (Summer/Fall 1999) 41(2–3), 151–179.

Is this completely true? Or how bad is the performance of SOEs and why? This paper will show that official statistics do not provide a complete picture of the performance of SOEs. Moreover, where they underperform non-SOEs, their underperformance relative to commercial measures can be partly explained by their attention to certain social objectives.

In contrast, township and village enterprises (TVEs), which are either collectively established by or initially based on and closely associated with rural communities such as townships and villages, have developed rapidly and become engines of China's rapid economic growth.[1] In 1995, the TVE sector produced nearly 30 percent of China's gross domestic product (GDP). In the same year, industrial TVEs produced about half of the total industrial value added, profit, and output.[2] In 1980, there were 1.4 million TVEs with 30 million employees. By 1996, there were 23.4 million TVEs with 135 million workers (SSB, 1997, pp. 399-400). Their real total output increased by an average rate of 21 percent per annum from 1978 to 1995 (SSB, 1996, pp. 389 and 403), and the growth rate of their real value added remained over 18 percent in 1996 and 1997 (*People's Daily*, 28 February 1998). The TVE exports increased from US$8 billion in 1988 to US$84.3 billion in 1997. The TVE shares in the national total export rose from 16.9 percent in 1988 to 46.2 percent in 1997 (see, Table 3.2).

The TVE miracle brings about a series of interesting questions. Typically, the core TVEs are collectively owned by the citizens in rural communities such as townships and villages. In this sense, TVEs are also public enterprises like SOEs. In addition, TVEs are usually competitively disadvantaged in comparison with SOEs in such areas as technology, labor quality and skills, accesses to bank credit, information flows within the government hierarchy, distribution of key materials through official channels, and other proxies for market intermediaries. How can TVEs do so much better than SOEs? What are the real causes for the difference? Is there anything SOEs can learn from TVEs? Although some of the TVE experiences may be useful for the reform of small and medium SOEs, a careful examination of the management conditions has led us to conclude that TVEs actually have disadvantages in some crucial aspects as well. In other words, the ownership and governance structures of both TVEs and SOEs need to be reformed. Such reforms have already been taking place since the mid-1990s (Sun, 1999), and we expect to see more innovative structural changes in both sectors.

---

[1] TVE in this paragraph is interpreted in the broader sense, i.e. including household-run and jointly owned private enterprises, which accounted for 33 percent of output and 51 percent of employment in the broader TVE sector in 1994 and tend to be much smaller in scale (Sun, 1997, p. 28). In the discussion which follows, TVEs are understood in the narrower sense of those with dominant community ownership only. We may call TVEs in the narrower sense "core TVEs" when it is necessary.

[2] Sources: "Selection from the 1995 National Industrial Census", published in *People's Daily*, 19 February 1997; and Ministry of Agriculture, 1997.

This paper attempts to present a comprehensive survey of the SOE-TVE comparative literature, incorporating our first-hand data and some original analyses. We shall argue that the SOE performance may not have been as bad as statistics indicate, despite the fact that they have, in general, under-performed. Our viewpoint is based upon both external and internal perspectives, where the external factors refer to those beyond, and the internal factors those closely associated with, the notions of property rights, governance structure, and labor relations.

The paper is organized as follows. In section 2, we summarize the external causes for SOE underperformance, which include their heavy social burdens, unfavorable position in taxation and pricing, and rapid de-capitalization in recent years. The failure of China's state investment system and defective statistics have indeed contributed to the SOEs' underperformance. Section 3 explains why TVEs have been so successful, with focus on the factors extrinsic to ownership. In sections 4 and 5, we focus on the internal factors that lead to the different performances of SOEs and TVEs. Section 4 highlights the differences of the governance structure between SOEs and TVEs. Section 5 examines the personnel systems and labor relations in TVEs and SOEs, comparing the incentive and supervision mechanism of managerial and labor behavior. The last section contains some concluding remarks.

2   External Causes for SOEs' Underperformance

Undoubtedly, the development pace of the SOE sector has lagged behind that of the non-state sector. However, as we shall show, the SOEs' performance may actually not be as bad as statistics or the coverage by the Western media have indicated. While arguing that SOE underperformance may be partly justified by their considerable contribution to the overall social security, we have no intention of joining the debate over the measurement of efficiency or productivity of SOEs. We agree that SOE performance has not been, at least, as good as that of TVEs during the reform period. Many external factors have contributed to the reported poor performance of SOEs, among which we identify four of them that we consider most important.

2.1   Social Responsibilities beyond Profit-Seeking

The heavy social burden may be one of the predominant factors undermining the economic efficiency of SOEs. An SOE has never been a pure economic actor. It has historically had many other functions beyond profit-seeking. These include political support to the government, expansion of employment, and provision of various social services and securities, such as housing, education, health insurance, and pensions. What distinguishes the Chinese SOEs from their counterparts in Eastern Europe is that in China each SOE, particularly large and medium sized, forms a resident community or small society in which all kinds of social services and facilities are provided by the enterprise. The manager of the SOE is more like a mayor or tribal chief. Traditional Chinese family values and employment pressure may have strengthened such welfare obligations, making them difficult to change. The increasing burden for providing a large set of public goods to its community members has severely hindered the development of SOEs.

Taking pension provision as an example, as the urban population ages, SOE pension payments have been mounting rapidly in terms of both absolute amount and relative share in the total wage payment. In 1980, the SOE sector had about 6.3 million retired employees and the ratio of the retired over the in-post was 1/13. By 1996, the retired in the SOE sector had reached 25.2 million and the ratio of the retired over the in-post rose to 1/6. Accordingly, the proportion of pension expenditure in the total wage payment increased from 6.9 percent in 1980 to 22.6 percent in 1996 (SSB, 1997, pp. 121, 749–750). While the newly established SOEs have been relatively free of the pension burden, older SOEs have become weighed down by the increasingly heavy pension provision.

To what extent is the SOEs' efficiency directly affected by their provision of the large set of public goods to the urban population? It has been estimated that about 40 percent of the difference in profitability between SOEs and TVEs can be attributed to social welfare provision of this kind (Xiao, 1991). In addition to the direct contribution, while functioning as a small society, an SOE has *de facto* provided unemployment insurance payment to its redundant employees (on-the-job unemployment). It is estimated that about 20 percent of employees in the SOE sector are in fact redundant (Bell, 1993).

The above facts indicate that these heavy social burdens may justify a large part of SOE losses in a society where a functional social security system is absent. Without SOEs many of these social costs would go to the governments at different levels.

2.2   Unfavorable Position in Taxation and Pricing

Along with the marketization reform, the traditional advantages that SOEs have enjoyed, such as easy access to key materials, credit, and captive markets, have gradually diminished. However, many disadvantages have persisted and two of them are critical.

The first one is the SOE's unfavorable taxation position. Although many tax reforms conducted in the past two decades were intended, with different degrees, to reduce the SOE heavy tax burden, taxes collected from the SOE sector have accounted for more than 70 percent of the total government revenue (SSB, 1997, p. 238). By 1995, the SOE sector produced about 44 percent of GDP, but contributed 71 percent of national fiscal revenue.[3] Before

---

[3] The GDP share of SOEs in 1995 is estimated as follows. In 1995, the agricultural sector (dominated by peasant households) produced 21 percent of GDP (SSB, 1997, p. 42), the broader TVE sector contributed 30 percent of GDP (Ministry of Agriculture, 1997), and the urban collective, private, and foreign sectors could have produced 5 percent of GDP.

the 1994 tax reform, the nominal tax rate of corporate income for large and medium-sized SOEs was 55 percent, 35 percent for private enterprises, 33 percent for foreign-invested enterprises, and progressive tax rates ranging from 7 percent to 50 percent levied on small SOEs and collective enterprises, including TVEs. The reform unified the corporate tax rate to 33 percent for all kinds of domestic enterprises *(Beijing Review,* 14–20 March 1994, p. 11). However, except for these shifts in the nominal tax rate, the SOE's contributing share to the government revenue remained unchanged (see Table 3.1).

The large difference between nominal and actual tax rates can be explained by three factors. First, there has been room for negotiating tax reduction between firms and local tax authorities (Guo, 1992). Second, tax evasion is much less difficult for those enterprises outside the state sector. According to a statistical analysis conducted by Chinese statistical officials, the accumulated sum of verified evasions of industrial and commercial taxes from 1985 to 1992 amounted to 98.27 billion yuan, being equal to about 4 percent of total taxation income in each of these years *(China Economic News,* 23 Aug. 1993, p. 1). The evasion of enterprise income tax is much more difficult to verify and therefore, may be used more effectively by numerous small firms in the non-state sector. The easier access to tax evasion enjoyed by the non-state firms puts SOEs at a relatively unfair position. And third, unlike for TVEs, wage expenditure is not counted as a business cost for SOEs and must be deducted from their net profit (after sales tax). It substantially expands the income-tax base of the SOEs (Guo, 1992).

The second disadvantage is associated with the so-called policy losses induced by the remaining price control of the state. According to Zhou (1993, p.70), of the 51 billion yuan of subsidies to loss-making SOEs in 1991, one-quarter was used to subsidize the energy producers who had to bear the very low controlled prices of their products. And another quarter was used in exchange for supplying other necessities at low state prices. In fact, many SOEs in the red are engaged in energy production (mainly coal mining), grain storage and processing, and the weapons sector.

Table 3.1 The contribution shares to government revenue by ownership, 1985–1995 (present)

	1988	1990	1993	1994	1995
State-owned firms	71.6	71.3	71.6	71.4	71.1
Collective firms (including TVEs)	19.7	18.6	17.3	17.3	17.2
Households	5.8	4.7	5.5	5.6	6.1
Other ownership	2.9	5.4	5.6	5.7	5.6

Note: Revenue from both domestic and foreign debts is excluded.
Source: SSB (1997, p. 238).

2.3   New Losses from New Investment Projects

Many newly established projects in the SOE sector often become new sources of loss. These projects are typically established by local governments or industrial ministries and bureaus. The failures of these projects are the failure of China's state investment system, which has been characterized by bureaucratic co-ordination and has not yet been reformed successfully (Sun, 1997a, 1998).

As pointed out in Sun (1998), the process of investment decisionmaking in the state sector is a distribution process of rights to possess and use certain scarce state assets, including budget funds, bank loans, land, quotas of power, oil, and other key materials. The very first intention of local governments, ministries, and SOEs is to obtain and occupy as much investment and property from the distributive negotiation process as possible, so that they can reap future benefits and justify their power base. For example, if an SOE was initially assigned premises in a commercial part of a city (be it by negotiation or only by chance), then its employees can get more bonuses simply by renting out the building. Often the consequence is that when trying to establish new investment projects, the decision-makers do not care much about whether or not the project will be profitable in the future. It is good if the project is profitable, but if it is not the loss will be born by the state anyway. Such an investment expansion drive, combined with the persistent soft-budget constraint, inevitably induces investment hunger and leads to inefficient investment projects (Zou and Sun, 1996).

Before the reform, the inefficiency of the state investment system was manifested in subjective decisions of the central leaders, poor preparation and monitoring, and widespread waste of scarce resources. In the reform era, following the increase of local autonomy, the inefficiency of the state investment system has been characterized by lasting and large-scale duplication of construction at the national level, and the initiation of too many new projects at the expense of technical updating of existing assets. In the end, many projects have little value once their products face weak market demand and strong competition. There are numerous examples of this in almost all industrial sectors. For example, by the end of 1990 China had built up 167 production lines for color television sets with an annual production capacity of 20 million sets. The annual real output was only 10 million, thus half of the production capacity was idle. In 1993, China had 126 automobile factories and 5,000 re-equipping automobile factories with a theoretical capability of producing 1 million automobiles per year. However, most of these factories had no economy of scale by any standard and the average utilization ratio of capacity was less than 50 percent (Sun, 1997a, p. 214).

The lasting and severe investment inefficiency has caused continuous worsening of SOE capital productivity, which can be clearly revealed by the change in the incremental capital-profit ratio. During 1985–1992, the net value of fixed assets of industrial SOEs with independent accounting systems increased from 398 billion yuan to 1,098 billion yuan, an increase of 700 billion yuan. While their realized pre-tax profits increased by only 61 billion yuan, from 133 billion yuan to 194 billion yuan. The incremental ratio of fixed assets to pre-tax profit is 11.5, indicating that every 11.5 yuan increase in fixed assets (net of depreciation) resulted in only one yuan increase in pre-tax profits. The fact that the ratio of pre-tax profits to total capital decreased from 23.8 to 9.7 percent during this period (SSB, 1993, pp. 430, 437) can be, to a large extent, attributed to the failures of the state investment system.

2.4 Capital Diversion and Statistics Bias

Whether the official Chinese statistics are capable of providing a reliable account of SOE performance is an open question. One of the basic requirements for official statistics in any economy is to provide standardized and relatively stable data. These requirements may not allow the official statistics to capture tactical activities used by firms in a rapidly changing economy. Among these tactical activities, several have significantly contributed to the under-reporting of SOE performance. These include implicit diversion of assets and profits from SOEs, the SOE-foreign joint venture, and the SOE's incentives to under report their profit potential owing to the so-called ratchet effect.

The implicit diversion of assets and profits from the SOE sector to the collective sector is induced by SOE social responsibilities. In order to create jobs for the children of their employees, most SOEs have to set up some new branches, making use of technologies and equipment of the parent SOEs, often free of charge. These branches are officially independent identities, which are usually registered as collective firms. In fact, these firms typically depend on the parent SOEs for survival and development. Once discovering such diversion as a convenient channel to avoid tax and to increase the incomes of the managers and employees, many SOEs also transfer part of their profits to these daughter firms in the name of subsidies and employment creation (Qian, 1995).

A survey (conducted in 1992) on 760 collective enterprises set up by SOEs in Shandong province showed that 54 percent of them were using 6.07 million yuan of parent SOE assets freely. Some SOEs tend to transfer profitable products and technologies to their daughter subsidiaries (Guo, 1992, p.49). Often such subsidiary companies make profits by simply selling the low-price planned goods from the parent SOEs at going market prices.

Thanks to many preferential policies for Sino-foreign joint venture and their own expansion drive, SOEs have had strong incentives to set up joint ventures with foreign firms. Such ventures are not counted as a part of the SOE sector in official statistics, although the SOE in such a joint venture is often the *de facto* majority investor or controller. In addition, many of the (more successful) SOEs have been transformed, partly or fully, into joint stock companies, which is classified into the category of "other ownership firms" despite the state holding the majority share. In 1994, for instance, the output value of these state share-holding companies was equal to 17.6 percent of that of the SOE sector (SSB, 1995, p. 375). Therefore, it is likely that the official statistics suffer selection bias in reporting the poor performance of the SOEs.

SOE management has been monitored by responsibility contract during the reform era. This monitoring system seems to have transferred the ratchet effect from output target to profit target. A higher profit achievement of any year means that a higher target will be set up for the next year, which has been vividly likened as "lashing the faster oxen". As a consequence, SOEs have a tendency of under-reporting their profitability to a certain degree, often reporting that they are just breaking-even allowing for a better negotiating position in setting future profit targets (Zhou, 1993, p.71).

In comparison, TVEs have few such concerns and, in fact, the contrary seems more likely. Local government officials tend to encourage their subordinates to exaggerate profits of TVEs, which can be used as achievements to speed up the promotion of their own administrative career and to compete for more bank loans. Though it is impossible to have an accurate picture, one recent news report may be informative: the director of the statistics bureau of Changzhou city in Jiangsu province, one of the areas with the highest level of TVE development, was arrested because he invented high figures for local TVEs to reach projected profit targets (*The Chinese Times*, June 15, 1995). Clearly, he might have been encouraged, even pressured by some higher level officials.

To sum up, considering all these factors as discussed above, we come to a conclusion that the actual performance or efficiency of SOEs may not have been as bad as indicated by the statistics. An additional observation is that it was SOEs, not TVEs, that typically operated at the frontier of new product development (Jefferson, 1993, p.3).

3   Conditions Contributing to the TVE Miracle

The TVE phenomenon is unique in the sense that the emergence of rural entrepreneurs and enterprises has not been experienced in any other country on such a large scale and at such a rapid rate. Its roots can be traced back to the late 1950s, but its development was not truly noticeable until the late 1970s when China began to carry out reforms and to open up to the outside world. The TVE development so far is not an outcome of any carefully designed policy or plan. The government policy changed from tolerance to encouragement during the 1980s, only after recognizing that the TVE was a vehicle to increase rural income, and more importantly, to absorb a large amount of rural labor surplus without much need for state investment — a serious problem which had been confronting the Chinese governments at all levels (see Jin and Qian 1998 for more details).

Generally speaking, there has been an overall favorable environment for TVE growth during the reform period, providing both incentives and disciplines for township and village governments and TVE managers in the process of TVE development.

3.1 Hard Budget Constraints Confronted by Township and Village Communities

In China, the central, provincial, municipal, prefecture, and county governments all have sufficient authority to regulate markets through administrative methods and to be involved in credit decisions through both vertical and regional accountability (dual coordination). *Ex ante,* governments at the level of the county or above are directly involved in the formulation of credit plans and can direct specialized banks to make loans. *Ex post,* governments have the authority to decide whether or not SOEs should pay back the loans.

Township and village governments (TVGs) have no such authority. A TVG cannot protect its TVEs by erecting trade barriers to keep out competition simply because the market within a community is both too small and limited. TVGs have no access to the state banking system, because all townships and villages are historically institutionalized as part of the traditional rural sector whereas the banking system is a part of the modern urban sector. Likewise, all staff members of state banks are registered in the urban residency registration system and have no links with the rural sector except through business dealings.

As a consequence, state banks have typically followed the commercial principles in making loans to TVEs. Often, they ask TVGs to act as guarantors of investment loans. If a township or village has a poor credit repayment record, state banks can refuse the loan application and, additionally, they can withhold interest payments and some of the principal from the bank accounts of the community or its TVEs. Each TVG well understands that a community may be able to delay debt repayments over the short term, but that it cannot delay them indefinitely. Meanwhile, a poor credit record implies that the community must depend on self-financing for future development and debt servicing. This is not possible even in agricultural communities, for which bank credits are needed seasonally for the purchase such inputs as seeds, chemical fertilizers and pesticides, etc.

The above facts force township and village communities to confront the pressure of market competition and a hard budget constraint. Though subsidizing across TVEs within a community is possible, the extent of such subsidies is very limited. Thus, in reaction to the economic austerity in 1989 and 1990, several million TVEs were closed down or taken over by other TVEs (Zou and Sun, 1998, Table 3.1). In contrast, the losses among SOEs soared, although only a handful actually went bankrupt. A 120 billion yuan credit relief operation was initiated in the fourth quarter of 1989 to write off non-performing inter-enterprise credits, mainly inter-SOE credits (Portyakov 1991).

3.2   Initiatives and Supports of Community Government

Core TVEs are typically initiated or directly established by TVGs. Motivated by revenue generation, employment creation, and the strong desire of the community for improving living standards and increasing wealth, TVGs have been strongly enthusiastic developing TVEs. This enthusiasm has been further strengthened by an increasing responsibility for improvement of local education, infrastructure, and social welfare, which have been gradually shifted from upper levels of government to TVGs.

Three critical contributions of TVGs to TVEs have been outlined by Chang and Wang (1994, pp. 443–44). First, because TVGs are part of a large governmental system with broad powers, and because of the long tradition of authoritarian government in China, the full support of TVG can provide community members and other TVE stakeholders with a sense of security which is needed to achieve long-term development. Second, TVGs can offer managerial inputs to TVEs in several ways. Because the market is in its infancy and ordinary citizens who have suitable market-oriented talents are a scare resource, TVGs are essential in the organization of major economic and political activities within their jurisdiction. Without a market or other social mechanisms, TVGs are often the only available local institutions with the authority to settle disputes which arise in the process creating TVEs. Third, TVGs can play an essential role in gaining access to outside resources, particularly bank loans. In addition to these three contributions, TVGs are not only the guarantors of TVE loans, but also the executors of the collective financing and debt repayment system. This collective financing and debt repayment system represents another support for TVE growth. All the funds required for the start-up of a new TVE can be borrowed from existing TVEs with the help of the TVG (Wong *et al.*, 1995). This system also offers TVGs the power to initiate and co-ordinate internal reorganizations or takeovers so that communities can avoid the social and economic costs of bankruptcy and of takeovers by outsiders (Sun, 1997b; Zou and Sun 1998).

3.3   Integration into World Economy

Geographically, TVEs are most developed in the coastal provinces of Guangdong, Fujian, Zhejiang, and Jiangsu. These provinces, both historically and today, have close links with the overseas Chinese in Hong Kong, Taiwan and Southeast Asia. TVE development in these provinces has well fitted in the requirement of international division of labor and in the considerable comparative advantages of rural China.

For overseas Chinese investors, the attractions of TVEs in the coastal areas manifest themselves in (a) a large number of cheap and well-disciplined

Chinese rural laborers released from the successful agricultural reform and development in the early 1980s; (b) various preferential treatments in tax exemption, currency conversion and remission of profit granted by the open-door policy; (c) flexible and relatively convenient approval procedures for their investment projects in the rural society; (d) proximity to their bases; and (e) cultural convenience and traditional family or kinship network. It is also conceivable that (a), (b) and (c) are attractive to other foreign investors.

Foreign investments have played an important role in TVE development. Foreign investors have brought in scarce foreign capital and relatively advanced technology and management skills, and their marketing networks abroad provide easy access to international markets. Compared with domestic buyers, there are less problems of the (widely spread) inter-enterprise debts, because exports also guarantee payment, as it is due mostly upon delivery.

Thanks to the compatible incentives and comparative advantages, TVE achievement in exports has been most impressive. Table 3.2 presents TVE export growth in terms of both total scale and relative share. It can be seen that during the ten year period of 1988–97, the TVE's shares in the total national export increased from 16.9 to 46.3 percent. The TVE's total export value increased from US$8.02 to 84.6 billion. This is equivalent to an annual growth rate of 26.5 percent in terms of US dollars, despite the devaluation of yuan from 3.7 to 8.3 yuan per US dollar. It is worth mentioning also that the TVE's export growth has been largely contributed by the TVEs with dominant community ownership *(People's Daily, 6 Feb. 1998).*

3.4 Unique Market Opportunities

To a large extent, TVE success also depends on the unique opportunities created by China's market liberalization especially relaxation of state monopoly over industry. The protected industrial sector was effectively opened to new entrants beginning in 1979. A large number of TVEs started up and rushed to take advantage of sharing the monopoly profits in the industrial sector. For these early entrants, the average rate of net profit on capital was

Table 3.2 The growth of TVE export, 1988–1997

	1988	1991	1993	1995	1997
TVE export (billion US dollars)	8.02	14.8	38.1	64.5	84.6
TVE share in total export (%)	16.9	20.6	41.5	43.3	46.3
Average exchange rate (yuan/$1)	3.718	5.327	5.761	8.369	8.270

Note: TVE export includes direct and indirect (e.g. in the form of subcontracting with SOEs and foreign companies) exports, and charges on processing for foreign firms *(TVE Yearbook,* 1996, pp. 122–123).
Sources: TVE Yearbook (1990, p. 20; 1996, pp. 102–103), SSB (1993, p. 633; 1997, p. 587), and *People's Daily* (5 Feb and 22 March 1998).

32 percent and the total rate of profit and tax per unit of capital was 40 percent (SSB, 1993, pp. 396–397). Of course, continued TVE entry gradually created and intensified competition, inducing monopoly profits to decrease and finally to vanish. However, the windfall profits enjoyed by early entrants in the late 1970s and early 1980s greatly contributed to the TVE takeoff.

In the early years of TVE development, there were many empty niches in the consumer goods market (processed foods, clothes, etc.) and primarily processed products markets, mainly owing to lasting shortages induced by the inefficient command economy. Not surprisingly, TVEs jumped to meet demands of these markets. Moreover, the rapid economic development in both urban and rural areas has created a whole series of new markets – a good example is building construction and building materials production in both urban and rural areas, where TVEs have dominated these industries since the mid-1980s (Naughton, 1996, pp. 150–151).

Meanwhile, the two-track system of market and planning has also eased constraints, providing TVEs with access to raw materials and market shares outside the state plan. They can afford higher input prices by setting up higher prices for outputs, or by simply using low quality input to produce cheap and poor quality goods to meet the corresponding demands.

3.5   Flexibility due to Size and Accounting System

Most TVEs are small in size and engage in labor intensive industries with low asset specificity. By 1996, the average size of township enterprises was 73 employees per firm and that of village enterprises was 26 employees per firm. In the earlier years, the average TVE size certainly was smaller (SSB, 1997, pp. 399–400). This makes them very flexible to react to market changes, to switch products, and to catch new market opportunities.

The accounting system in TVEs has been much less standard and strict than in SOEs. Only the TVE owners are accountable for bookkeeping, and not all of the income and expenditure need to go through banks. Thus, they can use such flexible financial and bookkeeping systems to develop their business. TVEs typically pay the highest salaries to their marketing staff, which can be more than ten times an average worker's income. TVEs have enjoyed the flexibility to pay higher commission, send gifts, or even offer bribes to government or SOE officials so as to get low-price inputs or materials in shortage and to expand market shares of their products.

In contrast, these conveniences have rarely been possible for SOEs. The accounting systems of SOEs have been much more standardized, and is controlled by a nationally uniform accounting inspection system – with careful supervision of such items as wages and travel expenses.

3.6   Support from SOEs

The growth of TVEs in peri-urban areas has been facilitated by direct co-operation between urban SOEs and rural TVEs, mainly in the form of subcontracting. In the suburban areas of Beijing, Tianjin and Shanghai, an estimated 60-80 percent of TVE output was produced by firms subcontracting with large urban SOEs in the early 1980s (*Industrial Almanac*, 1949–1984, p. 50). In Jiangsu and Zhejiang provinces, where TVEs have dominated the local economies since the mid-1980s, the proportions were only slightly lower in the mid-1980s. Linkages with Shanghai SOEs in these two provinces have played a decisive role in their TVE development (Tao, 1988, p. 100).

Why are urban SOEs motivated to cooperate closely with TVEs? Naughton (1996, pp. 155-156) gives three plausible reasons, namely diversified supply, cheap labor and land use, and the flexibility to escape some rigid controls of the state sector.

4   Ownership and Governance Structures of SOEs and TVEs

It has become popular to view ownership as a bundle of rights and the firm as a nexus of contracts among various owners of different production factors (Alchian and Demsetz, 1972). Ownership structure involves many dimensions, among which the most important are the allocations of residual control rights and rights to residual benefits. An ownership structure that is consistent with the objective of firm-value maximization may require that the residual claimants, who contract for the residual benefits, bear the residual risks, the "risk of the difference between stochastic inflows of resources and promised payments to agents" (Fama and Jensen, 1983, p. 302).

The governance structure of a firm refers to "the ways in which suppliers of finance to [the firm] assure themselves of getting a return on their investment." (Shleifer and Vishny, 1997). The governance structure of the SOEs is weak because the state, in the role of financing SOEs, has no assurance to get adequate returns on the investments. The governance structure of the TVEs is better defined and appears to be much more effective. The main suppliers of finance to the TVEs are the township or village households and outside creditors. Acting on their self-interests, these finance suppliers have all the incentives to make sure that their investments will not be appropriated. Alternatively, without an adequate governance structure, a TVE would find it very hard to get any project financed by outside creditors.

Separation of ownership and control, or, in more intuitive terminology, of finance and management, is likely to lead to agency problems. This refers to self-interested managerial behavior that imposes agency costs on the firm or on the absentee owners' welfare. Optimal incentive contracting may ameliorate some of these costs, but owing to informational asymmetries, monitoring costs, or other market imperfections, agency problems are in most cases inherent in the separation of ownership and management.

As with China's SOEs, the agency problems are further aggravated by the conflicting roles assigned to the managers and to the supervising bodies, and by the fact that SOEs' assets are akin to public goods that suffer from free-riding problems (Jefferson, 1998). On the other hand, TVEs are much less affected by these problems. The TVG usually has close relationships with the managers of the TVEs. Monitoring costs are lower, and thanks to their close relationships, information could be shared by the member firms within the community. Furthermore, incentives can be aligned more easily because of member firms' common interests and the fact the TVEs share financial risks under the umbrella of the TVG (Zou and Sun, 1998). However, along with the expansion of the TVEs as they become more successful, the traditional close ties among the community member firms may be loosened. Powerful TVEs may eventually free themselves from the control of the TVG, and new conflicts among the TVEs or between TVEs and the TVG could emerge. These would likely result in more serious agency problems as well.

4.1 Problems Inherent in SOE Ownership and Governance Structures and Choices for SOE Reform

An SOE is, by legal definition, owned by the Chinese people. Being owned by 1.2 billion people inevitably means nobody directly owns the firm. As analyzed in Jefferson (1998), this widely dispersed and ambiguous ownership structure induces the excludability problem. In different periods and following the policy shifts, SOEs have been subject to opportunistic behaviors and appropriations by those who have direct control of or influence on the firms' assets. These appropriations may include, e.g., asset stripping by managers and other insiders; shirking by workers; predatory taxes, fees and bribes levied by government officials; and non-pecuniary benefits for employees and their relatives in the forms of housing and social services.

While the 1.2 billion people have no way to exercise direct control over SOEs, the real control rights are delegated by the central government to ministries, local governments at different levels and their industrial bureaus. In order to limit the opportunistic behaviors of managers and officials at lower levels, the governments at higher levels have sufficient reasons to keep tight control over SOE operation. Thus government interventions become inevitable. On the other hand, the state has to bear the losses made by SOEs in return, assuming an unlimited liability for SOEs. The asymmetry between lower jurisdictions that are interested in extracting value from the SOE pool and higher jurisdictions that replenish value, through either direct subsidies or the state bank system, creates a serious moral-hazard problem for opportunist local officials. It has induced an accumulation of bad loans and non-performance debt within the SOE sector that renders the financial system vulnerable to external shocks and crises (Jefferson, 1998).

How should China reform the ownership and governance structures of SOEs? Diversified alternatives have been proposed by scholars and experimented with in China, which include selling, leasing, and management and employee buyout (MEBO) of small and some medium SOEs, SOE equitization through equity joint venture with foreigners, and restructuring SOEs into shareholding companies. It is widely acknowledged that China's enterprise reform is a progressive process of reassigning property rights, reducing transaction costs, and exchanging these rights among officials, managers within the firm, and outside entrepreneurs and firms in search of sales, mergers, and acquisitions (Sun, 1997b, pp. 16–23; Gu, 1997; Jefferson *et al.*, 1998). Though SOE property rights are not well-defined, the entering of SOEs into an economy where market-mediated exchanges of property rights are possible does define the opportunity cost of state ownership (Jefferson, 1998). The increasing opportunity costs of SOEs have motivated and will further stimulate the SOE reform in China.

4.2 Relative Advantages of TVE Ownership and Governance Structure

TVEs are under the direct jurisdiction of their TVGs. The government-enterprise relationship is much simpler and more direct than that of SOEs. In terms of the owner-management relationship, community members as owners do have incentives to monitor the TVG officials and TVE management, though the real effectiveness varies across different communities. Because community members, as owners, possess the right to derive both short-run and long-run residual benefits from the TVE's operation, when necessary they are willing to give up short-run benefits, such as dividends, in exchange for long-run more profitable benefits. Here, the term "benefits" can be broadly defined as including job opportunities and security, pension funds, and communal welfare programs in housing, health care, irrigation, road construction, and other infrastructure (Chang and Wang, 1994; Sun, 1997b).

Although the residual control rights exercised by TVG may imply a certain risk of bureaucratization, the control by the government over implementation and coordination of internal reorganization, or over the takeover process, does sidestep the social and economic costs of bankruptcy through court action or of takeover by outsiders. This control is quite similar to that exercised by the main bank in a Japanese *Keiretsu*.

Because the residual control rights of TVEs within a community is held by TVGs, the community becomes a *de facto* corporation or "mini conglomerate", facing a hard budget constraint (Section 3.1). Under the pressure of intense competition, this arrangement can facilitate a consensus among community members, TVG officials and TVE managers and workers to maximize profits even by sacrificing all or part of wage income. Moreover, because a community is diversified in an economic sense, it can diversify the business risk. A township or village can rather easily create several small-scale TVEs in manufacturing, agriculture, commerce, construction, and transportation and then expand the size of these TVEs (Zou and Sun, 1998).

A community can be seen as a small society, in which the citizens/owners can vote by a show of hands in semi-competitive elections for community officials. In wealthier villages and villages that enjoy a large TVE economy, this is particularly true (O'Brien, 1994, pp. 47 and 51; *The Economist*, 2 Nov. 1996, pp. 81–83; Howell, 1998). The villagers may also directly participate in discussions with community leaders. These avenues contribute to the resolution of the agency problems and help reduce costs of organization.

A community can also be seen as a corporation, governed by, e.g., a system of responsibility contracts or subcontracts. Such a system can be arranged between the community representative assemblies and the community government, between the government and the TVEs, and within the TVEs. These contracts and subcontracts have facilitated the solution of monitoring problems within the community and within the TVEs (Lin, 1995; Wong *et al.*, 1995).

For the large-scale TVEs requiring access to domestic and international capital markets, a further clarification of property rights is necessary. However, this does not mean that the only alternative is the distribution of shares among individuals. The community as a collective equity holder and the TVG as the executive equity holder may still possess comparative advantages. Even if each citizen becomes a shareholder, it may still be more efficient if the TVG can act as the representative of local shareholders in the exercise of their residual control rights over the TVEs (Vermeer 1996). In this connection, the democratization recently exercised in China's villages is of decisive importance for future TVE development.

4.3   Disadvantages Inherent in TVE Property Rights Arrangement

The so called "mechanism degeneration" of TVEs has been widely reported since the early 1990s (see, e.g. Ministry of Agriculture, 1997). Many aspects of mechanism degeneration can be linked to the problems inherent in TVE ownership and governance structures. Among them, two are often pointed out.

First, TVGs are not purely economic actors. As TVEs mature, the objectives of TVG officials are coming increasingly into conflict with those of TVE managers, although initially these two sets of objectives were quite similar (Ren et al., 1990; Wang 1990; Shi and You, 1997). TVGs have assigned priority to raising employment, local prosperity and financial revenue. This could hinder the stable, long-term development of TVEs. The powerful control rights of TVGs could thus lead to unfavourable interference into TVE management. TVGs also seem to be shifting the responsibility for the overall development of rural communities onto TVEs. As a result, many TVEs are now also experiencing redundant employment and increasingly heavy social burdens. In this, they are becoming quite similar to SOEs in many ways (Byrd and Lin 1990, pp. 125, 304 and 351, Shi and You, 1997; Xu and Zhang, 1997).

Second, bureaucratization and corruption among TVG officials and TVE managers are growing. In those townships and villages where the development of grassroots democratization has lagged behind, the problem of who monitors the monitors becomes increasingly serious. This is because there is a lack of effective checking and restraint devices to curb corruption behavior of those increasingly powerful TVG officials. For example, many TVEs are becoming "purses" of their TVGs, required to pay all sort of expenses for TVG officials. And many TVE managers are stripping TVE assets for their own interests (Shi and You, 1997).

Although there have been supervisions from county governments as highlighted in Che and Qian (1998), this kind of monitoring may be limited due to the problem of information asymmetry. The restraints from county governments are mainly based on disciplines of the Communist Party. This may not make sense for most officials at grassroots level, because the probability for them to get promotion into a formal bureaucrat is tenuous. Indeed, compared with the economic and social rents they enjoy from the TVEs, the career of being a low-rank bureaucrat is not that attractive. In addition, this monitoring is bound to be weak because of the communication difficulty in rural areas and there being usually a large number of TVEs and TVGs in a county.

The existence of these problems calls for further reforms of TVE ownership and governance structures and for grassroots democratization (Sun, 1999).

5 Differences in Personnel Systems and Labor Relations

Another important reason for the different performance of SOEs and TVEs lies in the different personnel and employment systems, which assigns the roles of managers and shapes the basic labor-management relations in SOEs and TVEs. Generally speaking, unlike in the TVE sector, there is no significant labor market for both SOE managers and workers. An SOE manager is not just an entrepreneur but also a bureaucrat and the chief of the SOE community. He/she has to cope with and co-ordinate conflicting interests among different stakeholders, inside and outside the SOE, and within the community. SOE employees, as the inside stakeholders of their SOE, have enjoyed a special set of social privileges, are more influential in certain areas, and are more difficult to manage than their counterparts in TVEs.

5.1 Urban versus Rural Social Status

China has practiced a very strict personnel control system. People are divided into different social statuses, among which the most significant differentiation is between urban and rural ones. Each Chinese citizen is registered either as urban or rural resident under a household residence registration system. The registration status depends on one's mother's status at birth. This status can only be changed due to a promotion to certain level in military service, university enrollment, or marriage plus a repeated change-of-status application and waiting for many years. As urban citizens, their food supply is subsidized and employment is guaranteed by the state. Furthermore, whether a citizen is employed in a SOE or in an urban collectively owned enterprise (COE) will further determine the different levels of his or her employee benefits. Only are urban citizens entitled to work in SOEs and to the associated welfare benefits, such as subsidized low-rent houses, life-time employment, health care, retirement pension, children's schooling and employment, and so on. This systematic arrangement is why Chinese peasants often say that the socialism has been realized only in urban China and in the state sector. This arrangement establishes a specific incentive structure for urban Chinese and SOE employees, allowing them to enjoy benefits and costs packages that are different from those for the rural Chinese.

A positive externality of this arrangement, though, is that by restricting the employment opportunity of rural citizens in cities, this system helps create a more competitive rural labor market for TVEs.

5.2   Personnel/Employment System in the SOE Sector

For both SOE managers and workers there has been no pressure or threat from the labor market until significant layoffs took place in 1996.[4] The long-lasting reform over the lifetime employment system has had a limited effect. The system of contract employment was adopted in 1986, but is only applicable to the newly recruited workers. Before 1989, almost 90 percent of the employees in the state sector had permanent job tenure. Until 1994, only 26 percent of SOE employees were on employment contracts (SSB, 1997, p. 113). It is also widely reported that there has been little real difference between permanent employees and those contracted prior to 1996. One may argue that the lifetime employment may not necessarily result in lower efficiency with reference to the evidence from Japan, but the difference is that Japanese firms are constantly facing pressure from market competition and the threat of takeover and bankruptcy whereas Chinese SOEs can depend on the ultimate protector, the state, for solving their troubles.

---

[4] By the end of 1996, there were about 9 million SOE lay-offs in urban China (SSB, 1997b, p. 31). These workers continued to be identified as SOE employees rather than unemployed. Their cash salaries are reduced by a large margin, but other non-pecuniary benefits basically remain. In addition, governments at different levels have promised and conducted programs to help them find new jobs. Because they have maintained and expect to maintain their favorable urban plus SOE social status in the future, they usually resist joining TVEs or entering the huge emerging urban labor market that has attracted tens of million rural laborers since the late 1980s.

Managerial appointments in the SOE sector have been tightly controlled by the Party committees at different levels. Although an increasing number of technicians have been appointed as SOE managers in recent years, political consideration is still an important factor in promotion, and the dominant feature of heads of Party committees is that they have either an administrative or military background (Qian, 1995, pp. 228-230).

Although an evolving managerial labor market seems to emerge in the SOE sector (Groves, *et al.*, 1995), its significance should not be overestimated because of the following two reasons. First, the entry to the market is far from free. According to an official survey conducted in 1995, about 80 percent of SOE managers, especially those of large and medium SOEs, are appointed through political and administrative channels (Window, March 10, 1995, p. 10). The social status of SOE managers has been continuously defined by their ranks within the hierarchy of Party and government. For instance, some managers of large SOEs enjoy the rank of vice-minister. Second, dismissals rarely happen. It is a well-known practice in China for government officials or SOE managers usually to only be promoted and not demoted unless they commit important economic crimes or political mistakes. Usually, those managers who suffer certain difficulties in their SOEs will be transferred to work in other SOEs with a similar position as before. Only an early retirement results in an effective exit. Such a turnover cannot form real pressure or be a threat to most managers. Quite ironically, the competence of an SOE manager may be judged in an adverse way according to the turnover numbers: the more firms he has managed, the less professionally competent he may be. The selection of managers through bidding is only used in some small SOEs. These facts indicate that there are still both severe entry and exit barriers to the SOE managerial labor market.

5.3 Employment System in the TVE sector

For TVE employees, there is no guarantee of lifetime employment, the so-called "iron rice bowl". There have been an increasing number of rural surplus laborers who are released by agricultural development and pushed by regional development imbalance. Therefore, the rural labor market for TVEs has been highly competitive. TVEs can employ workers from both local communities and other places outside their communities. Thanks to the competition, there are no generous welfare benefits, housing in particular, for TVE employees. The unemployment and retirement insurance typically lies on their contracted land in their home villages. As a consequence, TVEs have enjoyed low labor cost and a clear management objective. In the meantime, a competitive labor market plus a land contracting system induces high labor mobility, the opportunity cost of unemployment for TVE workers being much lower than for SOE workers. If unemployed, the worst thing for them is to return to farming. This mobility combined with the bottom-line insurance may help reduce the problem of labor-management conflicts.

5.4   Triple Role of SOE Managers

An SOE manager not only has to be an entrepreneur but also a government official and the chief of the SOE community. The manager is a government official because he/she is assigned by the government bodies to be an agent of the state to manage the business of the SOE and to protect the interest of the owner, the state. As government officials, managers are likely to be motivated by administrative promotions, respected social statuses, and the associated fringe benefits. Although the cash salary for an SOE manager is typically fixed to be no more than three times the average salary of regular workers, he/she can be compensated by many non-pecuniary benefits such as an elevated social status, large house, and other luxurious on-the-job consumption. The levels of these non-pecuniary benefits are mainly determined by his/her official rank in the bureaucratic hierarchy. This incentive structure serves the purpose of inducing SOE managers to identify themselves with the government and the state, and to protect the interest of the state in their SOEs.

The role of bureaucrat is bound to conflict with the role of entrepreneur in any economy, because politicians or bureaucrats have to, in most cases, give priority to political control, job generation, and complaints of their constituencies rather than to profit maximization of SOEs under their control (Boycko *et al.*, 1996).

As we analyzed in Section 2.1, each SOE, in particular large or medium sized, lives as a resident community or small society, and the manager naturally assumes the role of the mayor or chief of the community. Within a community, the power balance appears to have been well established. The Party Committee has played a key role in the appointment of upper level personnel, particularly the assistant directors and mid-level cadres. The Employees' Congress has played a dominant role in dismissal decision of workers and in distribution of social welfare. Employees also have a large influence over the decision concerning wage and bonus differentials (Jefferson *et al.*, 1998). For the community members, the top concern is their employment security and welfare maximization, which is in conflict with profit maximization.

By way of a compromise between the roles of bureaucrat and entrepreneur, SOE managers prefer to develop smooth relationships with their superiors. These managers tolerate many kinds of predatory demands from their superiors, and pay various bills and unauthorized charges imposed by these above, thereby adding to the losses of SOEs. Table 3.3 presents a comparison of initial distribution patterns of 769 surveyed SOEs in 1981 and 1989. We see in the table that there is a category of "other expenses", the share of which almost doubles from 1981 to 1989. Among the other expenses, the unauthorized fee imposed by superior bodies is a major component (Tang, 1992, p. 9).

Table 3.3   Initial distribution of net revenue in 769 surveyed SOEs in Sichuan province (percent)

	1981	1989
Profit (after sale tax)	46.23	33.03
Sales tax	24.34	24.69
Interest payment	2.13	9.24
Wages	20.28	24.70
Other expenses	4.50	8.50
Total net revenue	100.00	100.00

Note: This survey is conducted by Economic Institute of China Academy of Social Sciences. The sum of shares is not equal to 100 because of rounding and compiling errors in the raw data.
Source: Tang (1992).

Driven by the interest of the SOE community and thanks to the increasing autonomy along with the reform, SOE managers now have more discretion to increase wages, bonuses, and other community welfare at the expense of earnings. It is reported that during 1986–90, the realized pre-tax profit of those SOEs within the state budget (key large and medium SOEs) increased by only 3.2 percent while the total wages and bonuses of their employees went up by 91 percent (Survey Report, 1992, p.4). It is also frequently reported that some loss-making SOEs continuously pay bonuses to their workers by using bank loans.

The unbalanced increase of employees' benefits have failed to result in better performances, because of the effective "lower level bargaining between managers and workers at the factory level," both of whom seek to maximize profit retention while distributing it as equally as possible within the firm (Walder, 1987, p. 41).

5.5   Simple Role of TVE managers

By contrast, the role of TVE manager is simple. A bureaucratic career has very limited possibility, and thus is hardly attractive, especially for those in rich regions. The tasks and objectives of a TVE manager or management team are typically well specified in a contract between them and their TVG. They only need to report to the TVG. This simple principal-agent contract also makes their work considerably easier and more efficient.

The major compensation for TVE managers includes direct pecuniary benefits in various forms such as higher wages, year-end bonuses and contract fulfillment bonuses. These bonuses are closely linked with the TVE performance and thus can be considered as a kind of sharing scheme of residual benefits. Typically, the bonuses of TVE managers are not only related to their own TVE performance but also decided through comparison with the performance levels of other TVEs in the same township or village. This horizontal comparison has generated competition pressure among managers of different TVEs (Wu *et al.*, 1990, p. 332).

TVE managers also face competition and threat from the managerial labor market. They are not guaranteed lifetime status, and their terms are fixed for a limited period. As a result, over time, entrepreneurship has developed in the TVE sector. TVE managers are becoming more experienced and professionally competent, and more capable to deal with market competition.

The evaluation practices are also different in the SOE sector and TVE sector. TVE managers are evaluated mainly by fulfillment of profit targets. But in the SOE sector, under the current institutional arrangement and market conditions, it is hard for the superiors to figure out which losses are caused by external factors, which are inherited problems of the SOE, and which are resultant from the incapable mangers. For an SOE manager, it is easy to list a number of objective reasons that can serve as excuses for poor performance.

5.6   Labor-Management Relations in SOEs and TVEs

For SOE workers, there has been a lack of incentives and pressure to work hard because of the lasting egalitarian practice of income distribution, the lifetime employment system, and the public goods property of SOE assets.

In comparison with TVE workers, SOE workers are less disciplined and may be more difficult to manage. The labor-management conflict can turn into a personal one. For instance, if the manager decides to penalize an undisciplined worker, the worker may take it personally and make trouble or brandish threats to the manager and even the manager's family. The worker believes that any loss of the enterprises caused by his undisciplined performance will be borne by the state while any personal punishment against him will have to be borne by him individually. This adds to Jefferson's (1998) list an additional manifestation of nondiminishability property of the SOE public goods, which indicates that one person's overconsumption need not seriously constrain the ability of others to extract value from the SOE. Because of this nondiminishability, the undisciplined worker has a rational reason to think that if the manager decides to punish him then it must be out of the manager's personal intention. There is nearly a consensus among workers and managers about this. Moreover, because of such obvious nondiminishability, the punished worker can often get sympathy from other workers. There have even been examples where managers were injured or even killed, by workers during reforms in some places. Meanwhile, managers have no incentive to place the workers under strict disciplines at all. As a consequence, pervasive shirking and free riding become inevitable and widespread in the SOE sector.

TVE workers are much easier to disciplined and to manage. They have sufficient motivation and face strong pressure to work hard. They are motivated by the close link between their wages and performance. Piece-rate and team-responsibility-wage systems are common in the TVE sector. As for pressures, TVE employees are almost without exception contract workers, hired for the year or the season with no job security as there are many others waiting for jobs. They often work longer hours and much harder than SOE workers do, because if their performance is not satisfactory, their job contracts may not be renewed or even terminated in advance (Ho, 1994). Collectively, if business goes wrong, everybody in the firm will lose their job. Therefore, TVE workers well understand that their own future is closely tied with that of the firm, with which they have to share the risk.

The outstanding performance of TVE workers may be further explained by a kind of group or mutual monitoring at the horizontal level. This mechanism is induced by the threat of collective unemployment caused by the failure of their enterprise, in academic words, by a "cooperative culture" within a small commons (Weitzman and Xu, 1994; Jefferson, 1998).

6 Concluding Remarks

In this paper we have presented a comprehensive account of the issue of SOE-TVE comparison in China. The account is based on a major survey on the literature as well as first hand analysis. It is concluded that though TVEs have been confronted with comparative disadvantages in the areas of technologies, labor skills and education levels, accesses to bank loans, official channels of information and key material distribution, they have enjoyed and established more important advantages over SOEs. These can be summarized in the following major points: (a) Hard budget constraints to TVEs in general and to each township and village community in particular, whereas SOE budget constraints remain soft. (b) Relatively compatible interests and incentives within a TVE community, constantly reinforced by competitive pressures from markets and other communities, whereas SOEs have continuously shared the properties of public goods and faced conflicts of interest in many aspects. One example is the conflicting roles of SOE managers, who have to be simultaneously a government bureaucrat, chief of the SOE community, and entrepreneur. (c) Flexibility due to small size, diversified community economy, and far from strict bureaucratic control, which give TVEs an advantage to capture opportunities emerging in all markets of products, labor, capital, and the domestic and international. And (d) simpler principal-agent tier, personnel and employment system, and labor relations, which are induced by the historical institutional arrangements in rural China and subject to the adjustments required by competition. As a consequence, TVEs have out-performed SOEs and replaced SOE positions in many areas. The TVE sector has become the number one sector in China's industrial production and export. In the near future, it will become number one sector in China's GDP generation.

In contrast, though having enjoyed advantages in technologies, government financing and supporting, SOEs have suffered from many problems inherent in SOE institutional arrangements and their ownership and governance structures. Due to the widely dispersed and ambiguous SOE ownership structure and the multiple principal-agent tiers, the SOE sector has suffered most serious agency and asymmetric information problems. There are large numbers of stakeholders around each SOE, all having sufficient incentive to extract value from the SOE but with much less incentive to put their efforts into the SOE. This is the essential reason why the SOE financial situation increasingly becomes worse while their output expansion continues – although the real performance of the SOE sector is better than what is indicated by official statistics if the SOEs' broad social contributions are taken into account. However, much of SOE social contributions may have been transferred into bad loans and non-performing debts in the state banking system, when the SOE sector has continued to consume about 80 percent of state bank credit funds but creates less than 45 percent of China's GDP.

Due to the broad institutional arrangements and cultural environments around and within SOEs are so remarkably different from those around and within TVEs, there seems to be no partial solution for SOEs to learn from TVEs. Facing a hard budget constraint, a survival urge placed by tough market and inter-jurisdiction competitions, and the self-initiated adaptive innovations induced by the competition and hard budget constraint may be the basic lessons TVEs can offer. These basic lessons have been appealing to not only SOEs but also TVEs to reform their ownership and governance structures, because both SOEs and TVEs have appeared to face similar problems while the initially favorable market and environmental conditions enjoyed by TVEs have gradually dissolved. Following the expansion of TVE scale and market shares, TVE mechanism degeneration has become increasingly serious in those township and villages where grassroots democratization has lagged behind. It has generated serious consequences in TVE performance since the mid-1990s (Sun 1999, Section 4.3). The central issues here are, once again, the increased agency costs and the question of who monitor the monitors. In this connection, SOEs and TVEs face the similar challenge and need to conduct similar reform on their ownership and governance structures. Interestingly, collective ownership within a small community which faces competition and hard budget constraint is more akin to the small commons such as the small fisheries in Maine, where a self-initiated effective property-rights arrangement has evolved (Jefferson, 1998). In fact, many Chinese rural communities initiated "joint stock cooperative" reform even in the 1980s. Such a self-initiated, innovative property rights reform appeared well-fitting in local conditions in most cases and has become widespread in both the SOE and TVE sectors since 1992 (Sun, 1999).

China's ambitious and radical SOE reform plan has been delayed by the problem of a large number of layoffs and the shock of Asia's financial crisis. But the scenario is clear. The plural ownership structures and diversified governance structures have emerged and will become widespread in the near future, which include pure private ownership, employee stock ownership, joint stock partnership or cooperative, leasing, joint ventures, shareholding company and hybrid forms of shareholding company, and a small proportion of reformed state ownership in certain industries.

Acknowledgments

Part of this paper was written and revised while Laixiang Sun was visiting the World Institute for Development Economics Research (UNU/WIDER) in Helsinki and Liang Zou was visiting the Hong Kong Baptist University. They gratefully acknowledge the gracious support of their hosts. While fully responsible for any remaining errors, all the authors wish to thank Robert C. Stuart, the editor, and an anonymous referee of this journal for their comments and advice.

References

Alchian, Armen and Harold Demsetz. 1972. "Production, Information Costs, and Economic Organization," *American Economic Review,* 62: 777–795.

Beijing Review (weekly periodical, in English).

Bell, Michael W., Hoe Ee Khor, and Kalpana Kochhar. 1993. "China at the Threshold of a Market Economy," IMF Occasional Paper, No. 107, Washington DC: IMF.

Boycko, Maxim, Andrei Shleifer, and Robert W. Vishny. 1996. "A Theory of Privatization," *Economic Journal,* 106 (March): 309–319.

Byrd, William and Lin, Qingsong (eds.). 1990. *China's Rural Industry: Structure, Development and Reform,* Oxford: Oxford University Press.

Chang, Chun and Yijiang Wang. 1994. "The Nature of the Township-Village Enterprises," *Journal of Comparative Economics,* 19, 3: 434–452.

Che, Jiahua and Yingyi Qian. 1998. "Institutional Environment, Community Government, and Corporate Governance: Understanding China's Township and Village Enterprises," *Journal of Law, Economics, and Organization,* 14, 1 (April): 1–23.

The Chinese Times (Huaren Shibao in Chinese), published in Japan, 1995.

Fama, Eugene, and Michael Jensen. 1983. "Separation of Ownership and Control," *Journal of Law and Economics,* 26, 2 (June): 301–326.

Groves, Theodore, Yongmiao Hong, John McMillan, and Barry Naughton. 1995. "China's Evolving Managerial Labor Market," *Journal of Political Economy,* 103, 4 (Aug.): 873–892.

Gu, Edward X. 1997. "Foreign Direct Investment and the Restructuring of Chinese State-owned Enterprises (1992-1995)," *China Information,* 12, 3 (Winter 1997–1998): 46–71.

Guo, Zhengying. 1992. "On Problems of China's Ownership Structure," *Economic Research* (Jinji Yanjiu, in Chinese), No. 2.

Ho, Samuel. 1994. *Rural China in Transition,* Oxford: Clarendon Press.

Howell, Jude. 1998. "Prospects for Village Self-Governance in China," *Journal of Peasant Studies*, 25, 3 (April): 86–111.

Industrial Almanac – *Almanac of China's Industry: 1949–1984*. Beijing: China Labor Publishing House, 1986 (in Chinese).

Jefferson, Gary H. 1993. "Are China's Rural Enterprises Outperforming State-owned Enterprises?" Research Paper Series, Number CH-RPS#24, Transition and Macro Adjustment Division, Policy Research Department, Washington, DC: World Bank.

———. 1998. "China's State Enterprises: Public Goods, Externalities, and Coase," *American Economic Review*, 88, 2: 428–432.

Jefferson, Gary, John Zhiqiang Zhao, and Mai Lu. 1998. "Reforming Property Rights in Chinese Industry," in G. Jefferson and I. Singh (eds.), *Reform, Ownership, and Performance in Chinese Industry*, New York: Oxford University Press.

Jin, Hehui and Yingyi Qian. 1998. "Public versus Private Ownership of Firms: Evidence from Rural China," *Quarterly Journal of Economics*, 113, 3 (Aug.): 773–808.

Lin, Nan. 1995. "Local Market Socialism: Local Corporatism in Action in Rural China," *Theory and Society*, 24, 3:301–354.

Ministry of Agriculture. 1997. "The Status of China's TVEs and the Suggestions for TVE Reform and Development in the Future," in *People's Daily*, 24 April 1997 (in Chinese).

Naughton, Barry. 1996. *Growing out of the Plan: Chinese Economic Reform 1978–1993*. Cambridge: Cambridge University Press.

O'Brien, Kevin J. 1994. "Implementing Political Reform in China's Villages" *Australian Journal of Chinese Affairs*, No. 32 (July): 33–59.

People's Daily (Renmin Ribao, in Chinese).

Portyako, Vladimir. 1991. "The Financial Market in China," *Far Eastern Affairs*, No 2.

Qian, Yingyi. 1995. "Reforming Corporate Governance and Finance in China," in Masahiko Aoki and Hyung-Ki Kim (eds.), *Corporate Governance in Transitional Economies: Insider Control and the Role of Banks*, Washington, DC: The World Bank.

Ren, Qi, Ying Du, Jicheng Qiu, and others. 1990. "An Initial Analysis of TVE Survey in Ten Provinces," *Development Research* (Fazhan Yanjiu, in Chinese), March, pp. 265–288. Beijing: Beijing Normal College.

Shleifer, Andrei and Robert W. Vishny, 1997. "A Survey of Corporate Governance", *Journal of Finance*, 52, 2: 737–783.

Shi, Xiongru, and Jinbo You. 1997. "An Analysis of the Heavy Debt in Rural Enterprises of Southern Jiangsu," *China Rural Economy* (Zhongguo Nongcun Jingji, in Chinese), No. 1 (Jan.): 10-16.

SSB (State Statistics Bureaus), *China Statistical Yearbook*, various issues, Beijing: China Statistical Publishing House.

———. 1997b. *A Statistical Survey of China*. Beijing: China Statistical Publishing House.

Sun, Laixiang. 1997a. Aggregate Behavior of Investment in China: An Analysis of Investment Hunger and Fluctuations, PhD Dissertation, Institute of Social Studies, The Hague, London: Macmillan Press (forthcoming).

———. 1997b. "Emergence of Unorthodox Ownership and Governance Structures in East Asia: An Alternative Transition Path," Research for Action Series RFA38, United Nations University, WIDER, Helsinki, Finland, July. ISBN 952-9520-62-X.

———. 1998. "Estimating Investment Functions Based on Cointegration: The Case of China," *Journal of Comparative Economics*, 26, 1 (March): 175–191.

———. 1999. The Evolutionary Dynamics of China's Small and Medium-Sized Enterprises in the 1990s. *World Development Studies Series* (forthcoming), UNU/WIDER, Helsinki.

Survey Report, by the Research Group of Policy Orientation in Vitalizing Large and Medium SOE. 1992. Published in China Social Sciences (Zhongguo Shehui Kexue, in Chinese), No. 3.

Tang, Zongkun. 1992. "Profit Transfer of SOEs and Their Reproduction Capability," *Economic Research* (Jinji Yanjiu, in Chinese), No. 7 (July).

Tao, Youzhi. 1988. *The Southern Jiangsu Model and the Road to Prosperity*. Shanghai: Shanghai Academy of Social Sciences (in Chinese).

TVE Yearbook – *Statistical Yearbook of China's Township and Village Enterprises*, various issues, Beijing: China Agriculture Press.

Vermeer, Eduard B. 1996. "Experiments with Rural Industrial Shareholding Cooperatives: The Case of Zhoucun District, Shandong Province," *China Information*, 10, 3/4 (Winter 1995/Spring 1996): 75–107.

Walder, Andrew. 1987. "Wage Reform and the Web of Factory Interest," *China Quarterly*, March.

Wang, Xiaolu. 1990. "Capital Formation and Utilization," in W. Byrd and Q. Lin (1990).

Weitzman, Martin L. and Chenggang Xu. 1994. "Chinese Township-Village Enterprises as Vaguely Defined Cooperatives," *Journal of Comparative Economics*, 18, 2: 121–145.

Window of Hong Kong (published in Hong Kong), March 10, 1995.

Wong, John, Rong Ma and Mu Yang. 1995. *China's Rural Enterprises: Ten Case Studies*. Singapore: Times Academic Press.

World Bank. 1997. *China's Management of Enterprise Assets: The State as Shareholder*. Washington DC: World Bank.

Wu, Quhui, Hansheng Wang and Xinxin Xu. 1990. "Non-economic Determinants of Workers Incomes," in W. Byrd, and Q. Lin (1990).

Xiao, Geng. 1991. "Managerial Autonomy, Fringe Benefits, and Ownership Structure," Research Paper Series, No 20, Socialist Economies Reform Unit, Country Economics Department, World Bank

Xu, Zhimin and Jianliang Zhang. 1997. "Rapidly Increased Capital versus Decreased Capital Efficiency in Township and Village Enterprises: Survey over TVEs in Suzhou of Jiangsu Province," China Rural Economy (Zhongguo Nongcun Jingji, in Chinese), No. 3 (March): 51–58.

Zhou, Xiaochuan. 1993. "Privatization versus Minimum Reform Package," *China Economic Review*, 4, 1 (Spring): 65–74.

Zou, Liang and Laixiang Sun. 1996. "Interest Rate Policy and Incentives of State-owned Enterprises in the Transitional China," *Journal of Comparative Economics*, 23, 3 (Dec): 292–318.

———. 1998. "A Theory of Risk Pooling and Voluntary Liquidation of Firms: With an Application to Township and Village Enterprises in China," Tinbergen Institute Discussion Paper, TI 98-123/2, Amsterdam: Tinbergen Institute. ISSN 0929-0834.

4
Dual-Track and Mandatory Quota in China's Price Reform

Anthony Y. C. Koo and Norman P. Obst
Michigan State University, USA

China's price reform has been progressing through the mandatory quota (MQ) and dual-track schemes; a unique characteristic of China's gradualist approach to economic transition. The purpose of this paper is to show how MQ, properly modified, has been a bridge from a planned to a market-oriented price system. We analyze six criteria: industry output, average price, excluded buyers, buyers' surplus, producers' surplus and deadweight loss (not necessarily all independent) in our welfare comparison of a competitive market, monopoly and MQ form of market structure. A more general analytic formulation of our model and a graphic representation of the process are shown in the Appendix.

China's transition from socialist central planning to a market-oriented economy is historically unprecedented. With neither a benchmark in past experience, nor a well-formulated theoretical framework, China has proceeded in a trial-and-error manner one step at a time. Despite the recent expanding literature focusing largely on how economic reform should proceed,[1] what has actually happened in China as well as other former socialist economies is still far from being understood and its underlying complexity far from being fully appreciated.

Despite the numerous plans which have been drawn up,[2] economic reform in China has not followed a well-designed blueprint. Many reform measures have been cancelled or interrupted simply because reformers

---

[1] See, among others, Murrell (1991), Murrell and Olson (1991), Dewatripoint and Roland (1992a, 1992b), McMillan and Naughton (1992), Murrell and Wang (1993), and Sachs and Woo (1993).
[2] Up to 1988 there were 14 blueprints drawn up by the State Commission for Restructuring Economic Systems (Zhang and Yi 1994).

Reprinted with permission from Association of Comparative Economic Studies. All rights reserved. *Comparative Economic Studies* (Spring 1995) 37(1), 1–17.

perceived their risk of failure as too great. This is especially true for price reform. Under the planning system, centrally administered pricing was a major policy instrument of government revenue collection and of income redistribution between sectors and regions. In the transition to a market-oriented economy, price reform constitutes a core element. Risk averse reformers have contributed to many distinct features of China's economic reform including "easy to hard reform sequence," its experimental nature of approach, and the key role played by the local governments. For example, the Chinese structure of authority is split not only just between top leaders, but also between different level bureaucrats. It is in reality governed by a fragmented bureaucracy in which state enterprises and local governments pursue their own interests at the expense of the state. To a certain extent, this calibration seems more promising for explaining why major policy initiatives require not only a concensus among the top leaders, but also the active participation and support of many bureaucrats who have vested interests and the power to block or manipulate any policies which are not in their interests.[3]

China's economic reforms have been progressing through the mandatory quota (MQ) and dual-track system—a unique characteristic of China's gradual reform. In this system most products have two prices: goods subject to quota are allocated at the official prices; above-quota products are sold at market prices.[4] It is a transitional approach to a market-price system, respecting the status quo of most agents in the former planning system. The key point is not the co-existence of the quota and market tracks, but that market track was introduced at the margin, paralleling the plan track. For example, market transactions were created not by downsizing state enterprises and limiting their outputs, but by quota allocation. Similarly, the non-state sector was created not by privatizing the state sector, but by freeing the entry of new enterprises. Bureaucrats generally have been assumed to be the major losers since most of their privileges and rent-seeking activities will be reduced or eliminated by reform. If the success of reform depends heavily on how to mitigate the resistance from the powerful bureaucrats, then the dual-track served the purpose well. Their "insider information" and past connections are now more valuable as ex-bureaucrats become entrepreneurs, stockholders and managers of business ventures after price reform. This is the reason why it emerged spontaneously from the very beginning of reform without much resistance. The system's success deserves careful analysis.

Many state enterprises in China enjoy the privileges of priority allocation of factors and raw materials on the cost side, and monopoly power on the output side. They frequently are dominant suppliers of "bottleneck"

---

[3] Liu (1992).
[4] Putterman (1992).

products because of location, regional protectionism,[5] and lack of competing sources of supply from domestic or foreign sources. Thus, prices immediately after deregulation can be monopolistically high and output correspondingly restricted.

Few would deny that the two-track system with mandatory quota (MQ) is a source of numerous distortions.[6] What may have been overlooked, however, is that under a monopoly system, a form of rent seeking, the size of the obligatory quota, and the practice of selling goods at various prices may result in vast differences in average market prices, in total output of an industry, and in buyers' and producers' surplus. Differences also may occur in deadweight loss and in the extent of discrimination against groups of buyers from two limiting cases of market structures: monopoly and competitive markets. Far-reaching welfare consequences are to be expected.

The purpose of this paper is to show how the mandatory quota system (MQ), properly modified, was a bridge from a centrally controlled to a market-oriented price system. In contrast to Byrd's general equilibrium model (1989), ours is a partial equilibrium approach within a time framework. Our purpose is a limited one; we seek to assure and analyze some measure of price determination by market forces under MQ and, particularly, gradual output expansion in the transition to market pricing to minimize social conflict. Our hypothesis is that, given time, as new firms enter a monopolized industry, MQ could be reduced by degrees and finally abolished when a competitive market price is achieved.

In the sections that follow we view instantaneous price deregulation as an alternative to MQ. In section I we examine a monopoly with constant marginal cost. This constant marginal cost assumption is relaxed in section II. Appendix A offers the general analytic formulation of the model.

I   Price Deregulation

To serve as a benchmark, let *Dd* and *S* in Figure 4.1 stand for the demand and supply functions (or marginal cost function of a monopolist) of a product under consideration. For simplicity in this first case, we assume *S* to be linear and horizontal. Demand and supply intersect at price *p* under competitive market conditions. Suppose two units of the product acquired by the government are to be disposed of at a prespecified set of prices. What are the effects of these sales on the shape of *Dd*? We adopt here a graphic method of analysis used by trade theorists to demonstrate the equivalence or nonequivalence of tariffs and import quota restrictions.[7]

---

[5] Wong (1987) and Naughton (1992).
[6] Wu and Zhao (1987).
[7] See contributions by Bhagwati, Johnson, Sweeney and others.

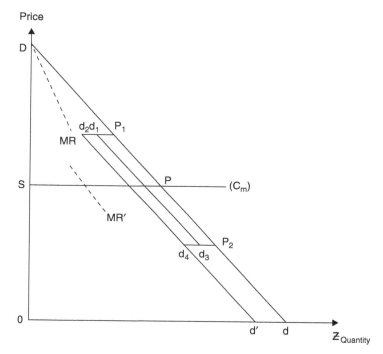

Figure 4.1   Demand and supply in a market for one good

Consider as an example that both units are sold to a buyer (or buyers) who paid price p_1. At that price the new demand curve shifts two units to the left, and its remaining portion runs parallel to Dd, something like $Dp_1d_2d_4d'$. Examine the second case, in which each unit is sold to a buyer (or buyers) who paid prices p_1 and p_2. Then the Dd curve shifts to the left by one unit at p_1, and two units at p_2, to look like $Dp_1d_1d_3d_4d'$. In short, the shape and extent of the shift of the original demand curve depends upon total units to be disposed of and the price(s) at which each unit is sold. In this illustration, following the tradition of such analysis in trade theory, the income effect is ignored.

Consider the price response of monopoly enterprises at the time of price deregulation. A monopoly will not supply in accordance with the intersection of Dd and S. Instead, it will equate marginal cost with marginal revenue under the assumption of profit maximization. A word should be added concerning the validity of this assumption. Chinese managers of state-owned enterprises are subject to numerous policy constraints[8] and if

---

[8]   Koo (1990).

these are not taken into account, the manager's action may mistakenly be viewed as reflecting differences in goal functions rather than differences in policy constraints. Instead of attempting to identify the objective function based on revealed behavior, we assume that Chinese managers, like their counterparts in other economic systems, seek to maximize net revenue or resources at their disposal.

For example, in Figure 4.2 we draw a marginal revenue curve *MR*, corresponding to *Dd*. It intersects *S* at *b'*. Consequently, the monopolist will charge a price, *p''*, higher than the competitive price, *p*. We relegate the static welfare comparison of the pricing systems under MQ versus the monopoly and competitive cases to Appendix A for the interested reader.

Based on Figure 4.2, is it possible for the government to set price at *p* and let the industry supply *oz* to achieve the competitive outcome immediately? The answer is that the government needs to know the right price and it might not have that information. Besides, if one were to follow this price-setting course for the industry, no market institutions would be built and buyers and sellers would not learn how the market functions (where the

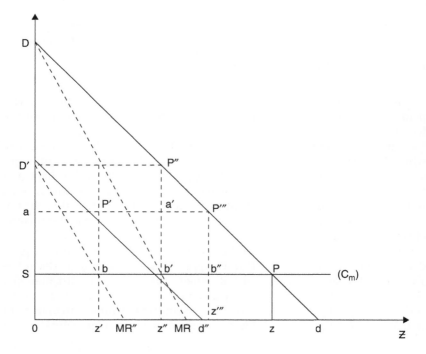

Figure 4.2   Demand and supply with a monopoly

forces of supply and demand determine prices). Thus, the economy would not move closer to a market-oriented structure.

"The two-tier price system has contributed substantially to the improvement in the market supply and demand situation over the recent years. The crux lies in the lifting of control. It was through this that market prices made their appearance. Without real market prices, there would be no standard whatsoever to go by in the readjustment of prices to market prices."[9] In other words, there is no practical way to go directly from the planned system to market prices. There is need for MQ, an intermediate step, to smooth the transition.

Consider the case in which the policy of MQ is to set the monopoly output Oz'' (= $D' p''$) in Figure 4.2. At the same time the monopolist will be informed that the MQ will be sold by the government at prices equal to what the monopolist will charge for its own output in excess of MQ.[10] Thus, the monopolist will be convinced that the residual demand curve it faces is $D' d''$. Draw a marginal revenue curve MR'' corresponding to $D' d''$. Since MR'' intersects S at b, the monopolist's output will be oz' at a price equal to p'. The total industry output will be the sum of Oz'' and Oz' (= od''). In order that the price at which the government compensates the monopolist for output not be taken as a factor entering into the monopolist's profit maximization calculus, we set the acquisition price at the level of unit marginal cost, that is, OS. Consider that the monopolist first delivers Oz'' at cost to the government. Next, the monopolist will sell an additional quantity of Oz' beyond z'', say, $z''\ z'''$. The government should be able to sell MQ at price p' set by the monopolist for its output in excess of MQ for the following reasons: (1) quantity $D' p''$ is exactly equal to quantity $p' p'''$ because graphically the distance between two parallel lines (*Dd* and $D' d''$ is always the same; and (2) at p' the total quantity demanded is ap''' (= Oz'''). We label this outcome MQ. Total output for the industry will be the sum of Oz' and $z'z'''$ or Oz''' (= od'').

The steps just outlined are similar to what Lerner called "the device of counter speculation by government," that is, if a government agency estimates the demand functions, sets the size of MQ, and guarantees

---

[9] Diao Xinshen, in Reynolds (ed.) (1987), p. 45.

[10] Selling an intermediate product at an arbitrarily set price is not uncommon in China. For example, in a 1978 report on the pricing of Wulitun Chemical Fertilizer Plant at the Daqing oil field, a profit of 133% was made on the basis of production cost. According to that report, the selling price was reached as follows: "Production costs per ton at the plant were 150 yuan while industrial profit was set at 200 yuan, resulting in an ex-factory price of 350 yuan (no tax was mentioned in this case). Selling costs added another 100 yuan (including 46 yuan for transportation, loss, and capital interest; 18 yuan for management; with the balance as profit for the wholesaler and retailer). The retail price per ton was set as 450 yuan." See Tong Dalin and Bao Tong, "Some Views on Agricultural Modernization," *Remin ribao*, December 8, 1978, p. 3, as quoted in Cheng (1982), p. 230.

appropriate prices to buyers (but not by legislative interference with the price mechanism), then it prevents price manipulations by the monopolist (or speculator).[11] Lerner omitted the government mechanism for guaranteeing the price. MQ fills this gap as it varies in accordance with a price-MQ trade-off curve (to be specified in Appendix A).

II   Comparing Welfare Effects

In section I, we arrived at several results, but to generalize these we must relax several simplifying assumptions. The foremost assumption is the constant marginal cost function. If the marginal cost curve is upward sloping, the cost of output will vary from unit to unit. Thus, the larger the MQ, the higher the marginal cost for each additional unit of output beyond MQ. The point is illustrated by Figure 4.3, a duplication of Figure 4.2 except for the shape of the supply (marginal cost) curve, which is upward sloping S_o (c'_m). Suppose S_o (c'_m) intersects marginal revenue MR at b', determining the size of MQ, that is, Oz'' Any output beyond Oz'' by the monopolist for its

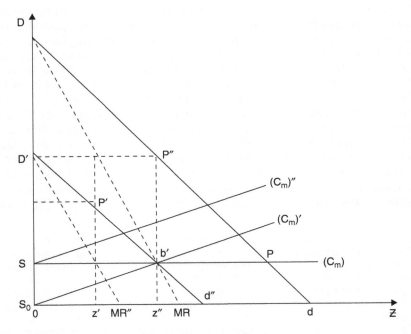

Figure 4.3   Demand and supply with increasing marginal cost

---

[11] Lerner (1944), pp. 94–95.

own would have to start from a point to the right of b'. To illustrate the new situation, we map b' on line c'_m into S_0, and $S_0(c'_m)$ becomes $S(c''_m)$ in Figure 4.3. We can then compare the welfare effects under a competitive market, a monopoly, and MQ in Figure 4.3. The upward-sloping marginal cost may be so steep that no additional output will be produced because of lack of profit or, even worse, a loss. Our model needs conditions on both demand and cost functions and on the policy of paying the monopolist for MQ so that some output will be produced after MQ delivery under an upward-sloping $S_0(c'_m)$.

There is no assurance that suppliers under MQ will not take advantage of their monopoly power and seek rent. In that case, a new problem emerges when we draw the kinked marginal revenue curve MR' corresponding to demand curve $Dp_1d_2d_4d'$, as was shown in Figure 4.1. The marginal revenue curve has a gap between MR and MR'. There will be many such gaps if the government disposes of its acquired units at various prices, as illustrated by the residual demand curve in Figure 4.1. This means that when the marginal cost curve of the monopolist shifts, the monopoly price may remain unchanged if it intersects within the gap between marginal revenue curves both before and after its shift. Thus, the welfare effect of MQ would be difficult to analyze and to generalize. Under the prevailing MQ system of delivery in China, even orderly disposal is unlikely to serve as a bridge of transition because MQ is arbitrarily set and generally disposed of at prices below market-clearing levels. Consequently, the residual demand function confronting the monopolist will be the higher portion of original function, given a firm the opportunity to explore market power. This largely accounts for the failure of MQ to speed the transition from a planned to a market system under current practice.

To derive the welfare implications of MQ which we propose, we list below six criteria based on Figure 4.2, not necessarily all independent. These represent different ways of judging and ranking various policy options: total industry output, average price, buyers' surplus, producers' surplus, the number of excluded buyers, and deadweight loss. Suppose we start with instant deregulation under a competitive market. The demand curve Dd and supply curve S (marginal cost) intersect in Figure 4.2, determining price p and total output oz. There is neither producers' surplus nor deadweight loss because of the competitive price and the horizontal supply curve. After instant deregulation, if the market is composed of a single firm, a marginal curve corresponding to Dd is in Figure 4.2. Output will be determined by the intersection of MR and S, that is, at oz'', and the price will be p''. Buyers' surplus under monopoly will be the area $DD'p''$. Under competition it will be area DSp. Consequently, the difference between total revenue $OD' \times Oz''$ and cost $Oz'' \times OS$, that is, $D'Sb'p''$, is producers' surplus, as illustrated in Figure 4.2. Deadweight loss equals the area $p''b'p$. Under competition, if no buyer is ready to pay price p, the marginal cost of production (on the assumption of zero fixed costs) will be excluded from the market. Under a monopoly system, buyers prepared to buy in the price range between p'' and p would be excluded.

The above three cases, based on Figure 4.2, are summarized below in accordance with six welfare criteria (see Table 4.1).

On these six welfare indicators, the competitive market ranks best and monopoly the worst; MQ lies in between.

Appendix A

The following notations will be used. Start with the demand function faced by the monopolist:

$$z = A - Bp,$$

or

$$p = \frac{A}{B} - \frac{z}{B}, \tag{1}$$

where p stands for price, z output, and A and B are positive constants. Marginal revenue corresponding to (1) is:

$$MR = \frac{A}{B} - \frac{2}{B}z \tag{2}$$

Next consider the total cost function of the monopolist:

$$TC = mz + \frac{nz^2}{2} + k, \tag{3}$$

where m and n are positive constants, and k is fixed cost. To get marginal cost functions, take the derivative of the total cost function with respect to z, to obtain

$$MC = nz + m,$$

Table 4.1 Market structure

	Market structure		
	(I) Competitive	(II) Monopoly	(III) MQ
1. Industry output	Oz	Oz''	$Oz'' + oz' = oz'''$ (od'')
2. Average price	p	p''	p'''
3. Excluded buyers	none	between p'' and P	between p''' and p
4. Buyers' surplus	DSP	$DD' p''$	Dap'''
5. Producers' surplus	zero	$D' Sb' p''$	$a' b' b''p''' = asbp''$
6. Deadweight loss	zero	$p'' b' p$	$p''' b' p$

or

$$z = \frac{MC - m}{n}. \tag{4}$$

Equal marginal revenue to marginal cost to get optimum output for the monopolist:

$$\frac{A}{B} - m = \left(n + \frac{2}{B}\right)z; \tag{5}$$

$$z'' = \frac{A - Bm}{2 + Bn}. \tag{6}$$

Note in our model that MQ is set at monopoly output

$$\frac{A - Bm}{2 + Bn} = z''.$$

z'' can be arbitrary, however, and may not always be equal to monopoly output, yet the same analysis will apply. (1) The truncated demand function (depending on the quota) is derived after quota delivery, and (2) the extent of the upward shift in the marginal cost function (depending on the quota) will start again at $z = 0$ after quota delivery.

We shall illustrate.

After delivery of the mandatory quota z'' to the government, the truncated demand function confronting the monopolist will be:

$$z = A - BP - z'',$$

where P should have an upper bound such that $A - BP > 0$, or

$$p = \frac{A}{B} - \frac{z}{B} - \frac{z''}{B}. \tag{7}$$

and the corresponding marginal revenue function is:

$$MR' = \frac{A}{B} - \frac{2z}{B} - \frac{z''}{B}. \tag{8}$$

After the MQ, z'', marginal cost at z equals zero, which is at the same level of marginal cost at z'' before MQ. Since the shift is constant, we have:

$$MC' = n(z'' + z) + m. \tag{9}$$

For optimum output after MQ, equate marginal revenue and marginal cost:

$$\frac{A}{B} - \frac{2z}{B} - \frac{z''}{B} = n(z'' + z) + m. \tag{10}$$

Simplifying,

$$z = -z'' \frac{(1 + nB)}{2 + nB} + \frac{A - mB}{2 + nB} \qquad (11)$$

Here z'' represents an arbitrary MQ and

$$\frac{A - mB}{2 + nB},$$

the monopoly output.

To determine the relationship between p and z'' we use (7):

$$p = \frac{A}{B} - \frac{z}{B} - \frac{z''}{B},$$

and then substitute (11). We have

$$p = \frac{A}{B} - \frac{z''}{B} - \left[\left(\frac{A - mB}{2 + nB} \right) \Big/ B \right] + \left[\frac{z''(1 + nB)}{2 + nB} \Big/ B \right]. \qquad (12)$$

Simplifying,

$$p = \frac{1}{B} \left\{ A - \left(\frac{A - Bm}{2 + nB} \right) \right\} - \frac{1}{B} z'' \left(\frac{1}{2 + nB} \right). \qquad (13)$$

In words, prices to be set by the monopolist will be negatively related to the size of the quota. This is illustrated graphically in Figure 4.4, where

$$\frac{1}{B} \left[A - \frac{A - Bm}{2 + nB} \right]$$

is the intercept, and the slope is

$$-(1/B) \left(\frac{1}{2 + nB} \right).$$

If there should be no quota ($z'' = 0$), then

$$P = \left[\frac{A}{B} - \left(\frac{A - Bm}{2 + nB} \right) \Big/ B \right]$$

is demand equation (1) with monopoly output

$$\frac{A - Bm}{2 + nB},$$

as shown in (6) after letting

$$z = \frac{A - Bm}{2 + Bn}$$

in (1). Accordingly, the monopoly price is the result.

Our model assumes that when there is more extensive or effective dissemination of market information and a longer adjustment time frame in order for more new firms to enter, the more the industry supply will increase. This is not an unrealistic assumption. According to the report of the American Economists Study Team (B. Naughton in Cady, ed., 1984): "There are no restrictions on the entry of producers into profitable, or potentially profitably product lines, and there is an excess of financial resources available to local agents for investment" (p. 25). Thus, we hypothesize that the supply function of the product would be affected in two ways. First, the supply (combined marginal cost) function will shift to the right, taking the form of lowering the intercept coefficient m in (12). Second, with m remaining unchanged, the curve becomes flatter (more elastic), resulting in a smaller value for n in (12). To investigate the effect of above-parametric change on price, take the partial derivatives of (13) with respect to m and n.

$$\frac{\delta p}{\delta n} = \frac{-1}{B}\left(\frac{-B}{2 + nB}\right) = \frac{1}{2 + nB} > 0; \tag{14}$$

$$\frac{\delta p}{\delta n} = \frac{\frac{1}{B}(A - Bm) - z''}{(2 + nB)^2} > 0, \tag{15}$$

for all small z''. In words, with a decrease in m or n, the market price of the product affected would decrease.

If

$$z'' = \frac{A - Bm}{2 + nB},$$

then

$$\frac{\delta p}{\delta n} = \left[(A - Bm)\left(\frac{1}{B} - \frac{1}{2n + B}\right)\bigg/(2 + nB)^2\right].$$

This is positive if

$$\frac{1}{B} - \frac{1}{2 + nB} > 0.$$

Simplifying,

$$\frac{\delta p}{\delta n}$$

is positive if

$$2 + B(n - 1) > 0, \tag{16}$$

where B and n are initial parameters imbedded in the demand and supply (cost) functions of our model.

Suppose the initial parameters of demand and supply (cost) are satisfied (equation (16) in the Appendix) is satisfied. Then, the door is open to synchronize MQ with changing values of m and/or n until MQ can be removed when market prices approach the competitive level. We name equation (13) in the appendix the MQ/market price trade-off curve and shall illustrate its working with various combinations of assumed numerical values of m, n and MQ in tables (a), (b), and (c) below. Assume $A = 6$, $B = 1$ for all three cases but choose specific values for m or n for each case. In Table (a) we assume $m = 2$, $n = \frac{1}{2}$. If MQ is set to zero, then $p = 4.4$; if MQ-1, $p = 4.0$; if MQ $= 2$, $p = 2.6$. The above three points are plotted and connected in Figure 4A.1 by a line labelled (a). In order not to clutter Figure A.1, only prices and MQ's in tables (a) and (c) are plotted since case (b) lies between them.

When the pric/MQ trade-off curve shifts from line (a) to line (c) because of changes in the shape of the supply function, that is, values of m and n, the government has the policy option of moving from the initial position y_0 on line (a), where MQ $= 1$ and $p = 4$, to a different policy combination of p and MQ on line (c). Take option y_1 where MQ remains unchanged at unity but price falls to y_1; or the government may choose option y_2 on line (c), where price is maintained at 4.0 and the size of the quota is reduced to less than 1. Option y_3 is a combination of y_1 and y_2. Alternatively put, if p falls because of keener competition in the market, the government could reduce MQ following the path of $y_0, y_3 \ldots$ in the direction of y_n.

	(a)			(b)			(c)	
	MQ	p		MQ	p		MQ	p
$m = 2$	0	4.4	$m = 1$	0	4	$m = 2$	0	4.23
$n = \frac{1}{2}$	1	4.0	$n = \frac{1}{2}$	1	3.6	$n = \frac{1}{4}$	1	3.79
	2	3.6		2	3.2		2	3.34

As the dual-track and quota prices move closer, the bridge can be shortened until completely abolished. It has served its purpose.

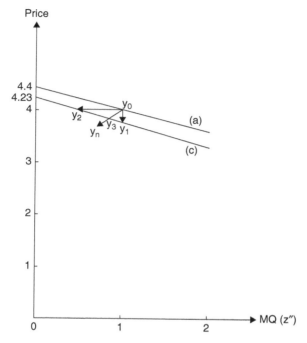

Figure 4.A1   Price-MQ trade off

Acknowledgments

We are grateful to our colleagues Professors Kenneth Boyer and Daniel Suits and an anonymous referee for comments and suggestions. Nevertheless, we are responsible for any shortcomings or errors that remain.

References

Bhagwati, Jagdish. 1969. "On the Equivalence of Tariffs and Quotas," in *Trade, Tariffs and Growth*, The MIT Press, Cambridge, MA, pp. 248–65.
Byrd, William A. 1987. "The Impact of the Two-Tier Plan/Market System in Chinese Industry," *Journal of Comparative Economics*, Vol. 11, No. 3, pp. 295–308.
———. 1989. "Plan and Market in the Chinese Economy: A Simple General Equilibrium Model," *Journal of Comparative Economics*, Vol. 13, pp. 177–204.
Chen, Nai-Ruenn. 1966. "The Theory of Price Formations in Communist China," *The China Quarterly*, July–September, pp. 33–53.
Dewatripoint, M., and G. Roland. 1992a. "The Virtues of Gradualism and Legitimacy in the Transition to a Market Economy," *The Economic Journal*, Vol. 102, pp. 291–300.

————. 1992b. "Economic Reform and Dynamic Political Constraints," *Review of Economic Studies*.

Johnson, H. G. 1966. "A Note on Tariff Valuation Bases, Economic Efficiency and the Effects of Preference," *Journal of Political Economy*, 74, No. 4, pp. 401–02.

Koo, A. Y. C. 1990. "The Contract Responsibility System: A Bridge of Transition from a Planned to a Market Economy," *Economic Development and Cultural Change*, 38, No. 4, July, pp. 797–820.

Lerner, Abba P. 1944. *The Economics of Control*, New York: The Macmillan Co.

Liu, Yia-Ling. 1992. "Reform from Below: The Private Economy and Local Rites in the Rural Industrialization of Wenzhou," *China Quarterly*, June, pp. 294–316.

McMillan, J., and Barry Naughton. 1992. "How to Reform Planned Economy: Lessons from China," *Oxford Review of Economic Policy*.

Murrel, Peter. 1991. "Public Choice and the Transformation of Socialism," *Journal of Comparative Economics*, Vol. 15, pp. 203–210.

————, and Mancure Olson. 1991. "The Devolution of Centrally Planned Economics," *Journal of Comparative Economics*, Vol. 15, pp. 239–265.

————, and Y. Wang. 1993. "When Privatization Should Be Delayed: The Effect of Communism Legacies on Organizational and Institutional Reforms," *Journal of Comparative Economics*, Vol. 17.

Murphy, K. M., Andrei Shleifer and Robert Vishny. 1992. "The Transition to a Market Economy: Pitfalls of Partial Reform," *The Quarterly Journal of Economics*, August, pp. 889–906.

Naughton, Barry. 1992. "Implications of the State Monopoly Over Industry and Its Relaxation," *Modern China*, Vol. 18, pp. 14–41.

Putterman, Louis. 1992. "Dualism and Reform in China," *Economic Development and Cultural Change*, Vol. 40, pp. 467–94.

Reynolds, B. L., ed. 1987. *Reform in China—Challenges and Choices*, M. E. Sharpe, Armonk, New York/London.

Sachs, Jeffrey, and Wing Thye Woo. 1993. "Structural Factors in the Economic Reforms of China, Eastern Europe and the Former Soviet Union," mimeo.

Sweeney, R. J., E. Tower and T. D. Willett. 1977. "The Ranking of Alternative Tariff and Quota Policies in the Presence of Domestic Monopolies," *Journal of International Economics*, 7, No. 4, pp. 349–62.

Wong, C. P. W. 1987. "Between Plan and Market: The Role of Local Sector in Post-Mao China," *Journal of Comparative Economics*, Vol. 11, No. 3, September, pp. 385–98.

Wu, Jinglian and Zhao Renwei. 1987. "The Dual Pricing System in China's Industry," *Journal of Comparative Economics*, Vol. 11, No. 3, September, pp. 309–18.

Zhang, Weiying, and Gang Yi. 1994. "China's Gradual Reform: A Historical Perspective," mimeo.

5

Labor Reform in China: Crossing the River by Feeling the Stones

Margaret Maurer-Fazio
Bates College, USA

Chinese economic reform appears to be following the path of outgrowing rather than jettisoning the central plan, perhaps to reduce the risk of considerable urban unemployment and its potential for social instability. How has this strategy affected the development of a labor market in China? Under the pre-reform labor system, urban workers were assigned to jobs, left there for a lifetime, and given nearly equal pay regardless of performance. Today, many redundant workers remain in state-owned enterprises. Housing and welfare reforms have proceeded slowly, leaving many obstacles in the path of job mobility. Despite the incomplete nature of the labor market reforms, change is profound. A labor market has emerged and, nascent as it may be, it is affecting behavior in significant ways.

It appears that Chinese reformers have decided not to dismantle the planning system, but rather to allow it to coexist with a market allocation system. This may reflect their strategy of "crossing the river by feeling the stones." Many observers suggest the primary motivation behind their decision to freeze the size of the state sector while allowing the non-state sector to grow rather than to simply jettison the central planning structure altogether sprang from widespread and strongly-held concerns about urban unemployment and social instability. The pre-reform labor market conditions and wage systems not only affected the pace of the reforms but also have been affected by the gradual and partial nature of the reforms.[1]

---

[1] An analogy can be drawn between the effects of labor reforms on labor allocations and that of implementing a dual-track pricing system on resource allocation. The dual-track pricing system assured continuity of supply while creating a situation where resources were allocated on the margin on the basis of market prices. The restriction on managers' rights to dismiss workers is akin to the continued production

---

Reprinted with permission from Association of Comparative Economic Studies. All rights reserved. *Comparative Economic Studies* (Winter 1995) 37(4), 111–123.

For example, the Chinese press reports large numbers of redundant workers (20–30% of the workforce) in state-owned enterprises. These and other reports suggest that market forces have not yet penetrated the workplace. This paper describes the extent to which market forces have replaced the pre-reform labor allocation system.

Under the pre-reform labor system, urban workers were bureaucratically assigned to enterprises, left in them for a lifetime, and given nearly equal pay regardless of performance. Enterprises hoarded labor to ensure fulfillment of production quotas. Fear of open unemployment caused enterprise overstaffing. Shirking, absenteeism, and carrying out personal affairs during work hours were common occurrences in China, as in the Soviet Union. Work units, especially in the state sector, took on many of the functions of a welfare state, including the provision of housing, education, medical care, and pensions. Job mobility was impeded by the need to surrender such benefits when changing jobs and by migration restrictions. The lack of choice, for both employers and employees, as to who would work where, the consequent mismatching of workers and firms, and the lack of material incentives led to tremendous losses of productivity, motivation, effort and initiative.

Pre-reform employment choices were non-existent for peasants who were organized into production teams which controlled the land and labor under their jurisdiction. Team members accrued earnings in terms of work points, the value of which was determined at the end of the year when the teams distributed earnings in cash and kind. The link between effort and reward was tenuous and problematic. The household registration system and the state's mandatory procurement of agricultural output kept peasants dependent on their teams for income and food supplies. The state's fear of urban unemployment led to the imposition of strict controls on rural to urban migration. The typical peasant's situation was little better than that of serfdom. Village production eams had virtually no choice over their constituents. Accidents of birth, rather than the exercise of preferences, matched agricultural workers to employers.

Labor and Wage Reforms

The industrial reforms of the 1980s included the adoption of managerial contracts which linked managers' pay to performance in terms of profits and sales. Profit considerations became important criteria. Managers, consequently, demanded the introduction of key labor market features to the workpalce. In particular, they wanted the authority to select workers and to dismiss redundant and incompetent workers. They also wanted to be allowed to use material incentives to elicit and reward productive behavior. Did the labor and wage system change in the direction managers desired?

---

of commodities under the plan. Just as the Chinese economy is growing out of the plan, so, too, are state enterprises slowly divesting themselves of redundant and incompetent workers.

The government, recognizing the inability of the egalitarian wage and rigid employment system to cope with the needs of employers, initiated a series of labor reforms. Two of particular note were adopted in 1986. First, a contract system for the hiring of labor in state enterprises was introduced nationwide in the fall of 1986. This system dictated that all new state employees be hired on the basis of 3- to 5-year contracts, at the end of which, either party could terminate the arrangement. The contract system represented a significant move away from the provision of lifetime employment—a crack in the "iron rice bowl."

Second, legislation intended to promote job mobility, or at least to lessen impediments to job transfers, was passed. Its implementation met with initial resistance from managers who were becoming aware of the benefits of keeping their skilled and well-trained staff in the increasingly competitive environment. Labor exchange centers were established. Individual and private-sector activity was sanctioned, promoted, and expanded rapidly. There were no plan allocations of labor for the entrepreneurial sector which was permitted to hire workers in a more-or-less deregulated fashion.

In 1989, a policy known as the Optimal Labor Reorganization Program was adopted to deal with the problem of severe underemployment in state enterprises. Its intention was to allow managers of state-owned enterprises to identify and reduce surplus workers. However, the state's deeply embedded concerns with open unemployment slowed the process. Attrition and retraining became the means of eliminating surplus labor. In 1992, regulations giving managers the right to hire and fire employees were drawn up, but, once again, the right to fire employees, resisted by local governments, was almost illusory.

Several creative new ways of dealing with redundant workers were developed. The first involved assigning surplus workers to service enterprises. These enterprises are gradually weaned from the financial resources of the parent enterprise. The second involved a type of limited-term, semi-unemployment called *xiagang* in which workers are placed on inactive status and sent home with partial pay and benefits, but no bonuses.

Wage plans were decentralized to local authorities, allowing employers to diverge from national wage scales. Coverage of the wage plan narrowed— private sector, township, and village enterprises were not subject to it. Bonuses, paid out of retained earnings, became an important component of workers' total monetary compensation, linking the wages of an enterprise to its profitability and productivity.

Effects of the Reforms

How have the reforms affected the work environment of China's 600 million employees? Is labor now allocated by market forces and at market wages? Are enterprises realizing efficiency gains of a labor market? There is a continuum of potential criteria one could apply in determining whether a labor market has come into existence in China. Perhaps the least stringent would be that people work, get paid, and that there is some degree of choice on the part of both employers and employees as to who works where. More stringent criteria would require that pay be determined by productivity,[2] that no major obstacles to job mobility exist, and that employers be given full flexibility in determining the optimal size and composition of their workforces.[3]

No doubt, the elements of the labor and wage reforms affecting urban areas enumerated above marked major changes from past labor policy. Wages were linked to productivity and profitability. Enterprises were delegated limited authority to make hiring and firing decisions. Individuals were allowed some degree of choice regarding their employment. Some of the restrictions on migration and job mobility were loosened. In recent years, over 13 million peasants settled in China's prosperous coastal cities with jobs and over 3 million people left urban homes for employment in township enterprises (Lu 1994). In 1993, job turnover rates were 3.2% for urban state enterprises, 3.8% for collective enterprises, and 6.3% for private sector enterprises (Lu 1994).

In rural areas, changes, which began with the adoption of the household responsibility system, snowballed. By the end of 1993, 123.5 million people, more than one-fifth of China's labor force, were employed by township and village enterprises (Lu 1994). Unfortunately, the opportunities provided by these enterprises still did not match the numbers of unemployed and underemployed peasants caused by the combination of the surge in new rural labor force entrants and the incentive to economize on labor on the part of now entrepreneurial farm households. The loosening of migration restrictions allowed large numbers of peasants to look for work in urban areas. Estimates of the total floating population vary from 70 to 100 million people. They work in state-run factories on limited-term contracts[4] as well as in collective-sector enterprises and private and foreign-funded firms.

---

[2] The efficiency wage literature demonstrates that involuntary unemployment can be consistent with both the profit-maximizing behavior of firms and the market determination of wages. Neither the absence of involuntary unemployment, nor the equalization of wages across firms, is required to determine the existence of a well-functioning labor market.

[3] Even more stringent criteria would be required to produce a perfectly competitive labor market: large numbers of employers and employees (both without access to collusive organizations) such that no player in the market could influence the wage; complete occupational choice with unimpeded access to funding for training; and full freedom of exchange such that any individual could work for any employer. Any attempt to apply such a strict market definition would border on the ridiculous—even the major market economies do not measure up to it.

[4] Peasant workers make up 5% of the workforce in state-owned enterprises (BBC Summary of World Broadcasts, 22 May 1995).

They also meet the demands of the construction industry. They peddle goods in the newly sanctioned free markets. They supply services of many types, from coal delivery to child care, for urban residents. The jobs they fill are, for the most part, those the privileged urban population disdain as being too dirty, dangerous, difficult, and demeaning. They find their own housing and demand few social services.

There is a surprisingly widespread belief that the labor reforms have failed to delivery their intended effects. Some observers admit the reforms have allowed a more flexible use of labor but claim the changes have not substantially increased market involvement. Many believe that successful reform of the labor system must await the completion of bankruptcy, housing, social security, and ownership reform. Harrold's (1992) assessment of the Chinese reform experience lauds its effectiveness in terms of output and welfare, productivity, the role of the state, and trade. However, he argues that no significant progress has been made in terms of labor reform (p. 34). Wilson (1990) focuses on labor policy in China, finds that the reforms intended "to incorporate features of a labor market into the Chinese system of labor allocation" were "highly circumscribed in their scope and impact" (p. 49). Christiansen (1992), using the Jiangsu labor market as a case study of market transition in China, claims that the "market is fragmented, marginal, and dependent on the command economy" (p. 73). Davis (1992), assessing the impact of the reforms in an article on job mobility in the post-Mao era, finds that the process by which "established urbanites" found or changed jobs in the late 1980s had "striking continuities with the recent past" (p. 1064).

If these authors are right, then the institutional changes described above must be only cosmetic, influencing relatively few workers. But this is not the case. The reforms introduced key labor market features to the urban workplace. They created the necessary conditions for a rural labor market to exist and allowed peasants to move to urban areas to participate in the urban sector's labor market. Anecdotal evidence abounds. (Of course, in a country the size of China, one can find anecdotal evidence in support of just about any claim.) A few cases, typical of many reports, some recent statistics, and important empirical work related to changing labor market conditions are reported below.

Employers are competing for skilled personnel. In one reported case, the mayor of Shenzhen went to Xian to offer high salaries to any senior technologist willing to move south to work for him. The mayor of Xian countered with similarly attractive deals to keep his technologists (*Economist*, 10 October 1992). At that time (1992), advertisements began to publish salary offers previously unheard of. Delegations from many provinces were sent out to scour the country for talent. The areas being raided for talent countered by going to Guangdong and Fujian to lure back needed specialists. The choice of terminology in the reports revealed fierce competition. Not only are "raids" and "counterattacks" reported but salary was claimed to be the "key weapon" in the competition for capable people (Huang 1993). Recruiters offered not only high salaries but spacious accommodation, commissions, and bonuses as incentives.

Recruiting is taking place not only through local and national job fairs and exchange centers, but also at the international level. The recruits are being selected according to criteria which match their education and experience with employers' needs. Recruiting efforts are no longer oriented only toward new labor market entrants but also very much toward experienced personnel. The reforms of the labor, personnel and wage systems have loosed a tide of interest in job transfers. The job exchange centers set up in major cities note remarkable increases in their business. In 1992, over 1 million technical and managerial personnel registered at local personnel exchange centers (Huang 1993). In 1993, 5 million, or 3.4% of the urban workforce changed jobs or resigned to find better employment on their own (Lu 1994). This situation represents a major change from 5 to 6 years earlier when any state sector employee requesting a transfer was viewed suspiciously as either being incompetent or having interpersonal problems. Now, in the recruitment process, new graduates are often passed over in favor of experienced personnel (Chan 1995). Many of the job transferees are moving to positions in foreign-funded enterprises, rural and township enterprises and private firms, who, together, employed 205 million people as of the end of 1994, an increase of 52 million over 1990 (Cao 1995).

Many of the transferees were formerly employees in the state sector. In an ironical turn of events, the large state-sector enterprises are decrying the "brain drain" from among their ranks and claiming that the township enterprises have unfair tax advantages. In one particularly well-publicized case, the resignations and transfer to a township enterprise of several managers and a group of engineers and technicians from a state-run machine tool factory provoked reactions across the nation (*FBIS*, 24 March 1993). The debate about the case brought to the fore the issue of how state-owned enterprises could prevent their staff from leaving. It appears the state sector has been forced to compete vigorously in terms of remuneration and benefits not only to attract the personnel they desire but also to keep the staff they have. In one example of this phenomenon,[5] a manager at the Central Iron and Steel Research Institute reported that losing staff is a big problem to the Institute. Staff members leave the Institute to work in companies in the southern zones and also to go abroad to work and study. When encouraged to stay at the Institute, those seeking work elsewhere argued that the government was endorsing the circulation of talent and that they would be working for China in their new position. To combat the outflow of talent, the wages and bonuses at the Institute were being increased year by year.

---

[5] T. G. Rawski's interview notes, 11 October 1993.

Another recent article reports that Chinese authorities are attempting to match the pay of outstanding bureaucrats to that of general managers in private firms. To attract and keep personnel, the bureaucracy is beginning to base promotions on performance rather than seniority and to use entrance exams to make recruiting merit rather than connection-based (Juan 1994).

Turning now to the empirical studies, I begin with my own work focusing on the returns to investments in education in China (Maurer-Fazio 1994). Using data gathered in 1989 to estimate earnings functions for a sample of over 17,000 working, urban residents, from 10 different provinces, I find that human capital accumulation is being rewarded in the workplace. Rates of return to education in the overall sample are quite low: in the neighborhood of 3% for males and 4.5% for females. However, when considering relatively new labor force entrants, those under age 30, 1 find rates of return to education of 6.4% for males and 6.8% for females. These results are remarkably similar to results I find for Taiwan, based on 1990 data where the returns are 7.0% and 6.9%, respectively for males and females under age 30. These returns also accord with general returns of 6.1% and 6.5% reported for Hong Kong and Japan. If these higher returns for young people indicate a move away from the administered wage system toward market rewards, then we would also expect to see higher returns in the areas which have more market influence. In this data, returns to schooling are highest in the private sector and higher in the non-state collective sector than the state sector. Yet, even in the state sector, returns to education are significantly higher for the youngest cohort. In comparing my results to those based on 1985 data (Gelb 1990, Jamison and Van Der Gaag 1957, Byron and Manaloto 1990), I find that returns to investments in education in 1988 exceed those obtained for comparable groups in the same countries in 1985. These results appear to lend some credibility to the claims that market forces are beginning to permeat the workplace and that wage determination is beginning to reflect market influence as early as 1988.

Jefferson, Rawski and Zheng (1992), in a study of growth, efficiency and convergence in China's state and collective industry, find some evidence of convergence in the marginal products of capital, and (of particular interest here) the marginal products of labor over the reform period. This suggests a move toward a more efficient reallocation of resources, one consistent with market influences.

Hussain and Zhuang assess the impact of the reforms on wage and employment determination in Chinese state enterprises from 1986 to 1991, a period in which managers made significant gains in their operational autonomy in exchange for contractual obligations to fulfill various performance targets. Their empirical work is based on a sample of 514 state-owned enterprises located in 20 of China's 30 provinces. In their sample, the share of bonuses increases from 21% in 1986 to 27% in 1992. They suggest that this increase could be interpreted as either an increase in performance-related incentives or an increase in workers' bargaining power. They argue that the increases in bonuses reflect increases in workers' ability to gain a greater share of the rents. Hussain and Zhuang (1994) also find that regular wages of the state-owned enterprises tend to move in tandem with others in the same province and that regular wages are unrelated to profitability. However, they do find that bonuses are much higher in profit-making enterprises than in loss-making enterprises. They find that the employment elasticity with respect to regular wages is negative, though smaller in magnitude than those found in market economies and suggest that the enterprises in their study respond in the same way to wages that firms in a market economy do, but less strongly. They report an elasticity of employment with respect to output, which is low relative to those found in market economies and interpret this result as both a confirmation of labor slack and a progressive reduction in the pool of surplus labor in the state-owned enterprises.

Concerning job mobility and turnover, a survey of the unemployed in Shanghai in 1989 revealed that 43% of the unemployed had previously held permanent positions. This study also revealed that the prohibitions on changing jobs are loosening—59% of the workers previously employed on contract had quit voluntarily (Fu *et al.* 1993). By mid-1994, 25.6 million out of the 109 million employees of state-owned enterprises were on contract, a further 7.4 million were deemed temporary (Lu 1993).

Fleisher, Dong and Liu (1995) carry out a study of productivity in 30 provincially, municipally and collectively owned enterprises (located in 9 provinces) in the Chinese paper industry. They pay special attention to the effects of schooling. They find rates of return to investments in both human and physical capital to be high; however, they also find that the divergence between the social and private returns to labor at all educational levels to be large. Perhaps their most astonishing result is the extent to which the marginal product of one additional college-trained engineer or manager exceeds the typical wage of such a person. The divergence between marginal product and wage rates implies, not only the lack of allocative efficiency, but also one of the costs of incomplete transition to a labor market. If the private and semi-private sectors are paying wages above those obtained in the state and collective sectors, they are likely to bid skilled and highly educated workers away from such employers. This distortion of signals could lead to a serious misallocation of workers—away from their highest productivity employment to higher-paying but less productive employment.

Conclusion

Using the criteria that people work, get paid, and that some degree of choice exists for both employers and employees as to who works where, one is unarguably led to conclude that, even in China's state sector, a labor market exists. Applying the criteria that pay be determined by productivity, that no major obstacles to job mobility exist, and that employers be given full flex-ibility in determining the optimal size and composition of their workforces makes reaching an overall conclusion more difficult since different condi-tions exist in the differing sectors of the economy. However, it is clear that movement toward productivity-determined remuneration, elimination of mobility restrictions, and increases in managerial autonomy over the size and makeup of the workforce is occurring in each of the state, collective and private sectors.

In 1978, the state-owned sector employed 78.4% of urban workers and the collective sector 21.6%. By 1994, the figures were 73.3% in the state sector, 21.6% in the collective sector, and 5% in other forms of ownership. The change in hiring practices stands out more clearly when we consider the fraction of new urban labor force entrants going to the state sector: in 1978, it was 72%; but from 1990 to 1993, this fraction fell to 47% with the remaining 53% being absorbed by the non-state sector.[6] In 1978, labor mar-kets did not exist in either rural or urban areas. There has been a dramatic change in the entrepreneurial sector, consisting mainly of the farm sector, which employs 52.8% of the labor force of 614.7 million, from collective serfdom toward unrestricted market arrangements. In the foreign-funded firms, urban and rural collectives and private firms, which, together, employ 29.5% of the workforce, restrictions on hiring, dismissals, transfers and pay, while certainly not absent, are much less frequent and less severe than in the state sector. The state sector, which employs 17.7% of the workforce, has moved from a situation of having absolutely no characteristics of a labor market to a situation where market forces are penetrating the workplace at an accelerating rate.

How much of a sector must be marketized for the benefits of a market system to be present? The major benefits of a smoothly functioning labor market over the pre-reform allocation system include, but are not limited to, the efficiency gains from matching the skills of employees to the needs of firms, the increases in motivation and initiative which spring from giving individuals choice over their employment, and the increases in productivity which arise due to workplace discipline and performance-related rewards.

A parallel must be drawn here between the effects of implementing the dual-track pricing system on resource allocation and the effects of the labor reforms on labor market behaviors on the margin. The benefits of the dual-track pricing system were, first, that it assured continuity of supply while creating an environment where market skills could be learned, and, second, that it created a situation where resources were allocated on the margin on the basis of market prices (Harrold 1992). The restriction on managers'

---

[6] China 1992. Zhongguo Tongji Nianjian. *China Statistical Yearbook,* Tables 4-1, 4-2, and 4-20, and BBC Summary of World Broadcasts, 22 May 1995 and 27 June 1995.

rights to dismiss workers is akin to the continued production of commodities under the plan. Just as the Chinese economy is growing out of the plan, so, too, are state enterprises slowly divesting themselves of redundant and incompetent workers. Even though outright dismissals are still rare, workers' attitudes have changed markedly as the specter of bankruptcies, takeovers of failed firms, and leasing of enterprise assets arise, and the policies of forcing unwanted workers into service companies and into low-pay[7] or unpaid leaves continue. Workplace discipline improves markedly. This discipline is reinforced both by the existence of the huge floating population whose members are willing to work long, hard days and by observation of the extended periods of unemployment and the straightened circumstances of the unemployed.[8] Workers no longer take having a job for granted.

The reforms have introduced a great deal of uncertainty into the work environment. The welfare improvements arising from workers' new-found freedom to choose careers and employers have to be weighed against the increases in uncertainty about job security. The state no longer guarantees the provision of employment and workers are well aware that jobs are no longer "permanent." Even though per capita income is increasing, the benefits of the Chinese reforms are not being spread evenly. Income inequality is increasing, and with it comes the potential for an increase in the dissatisfaction of those whose relative well-being has declined. Additionally, the partial nature of the transition with differences in employee compensation by sector can lead, at least in the short-run to sub-optimal labor allocations. Highly trained individuals may be moving away from state-sector employment, where their pay is low but productivity high, to employment, where their pay is high but productivity low.

Concerns about open unemployment and social instability caused the Chinese leadership to embark on a slow, evolutionary transition to a market economy, a process of outgrowing rather than jettisoning the plan. Profit-motivated managerial demands for the introduction of labor market features into the work environment were initially resisted, experimented with, and only gradually introduced. Under the pre-reform labor system, urban workers were assigned to jobs, left there for a lifetime, and given nearly equal pay regardless of performance. Today, many redundant workers remain in state-owned enterprises; housing and welfare reforms have proceeded slowly, leaving obstacles in the path of job mobility; and the state, still fearful of excessive open urban unemployment, has slowed the implementation on

---

[7] Rawski (1995) reports that 17–28% of the workers in the state-owned sectors of the cities of Shanghai, Chongqing and Shenyang have been forced into *xiagang*, the practice of sending workers home with minimal pay, no bonuses and reduced benefits.
[8] See BBC Summary of World Broadcasts, 5 April 1995, for exerpts of a report entitled, "Investigation and Analysis of Unemployment Situation Among the Urban Workforce," published in the Chinese journal, *Zhongguo Gaige*, 13 February 1995.

management's right to dismiss workers. Despite the incomplete nature of the labor-market reforms, change is profound.

A labor market has emerged and, nascent as it may be, it is affecting attitudes and behavior in significant ways. There is no doubt that large sections of the economy are realizing the benefits of a labor market in terms of the efficiency gains from matching the skills of employees to the needs of firms, the increases in motivation and initiative which spring from giving individuals choice over their employment and the increases in productivity which arise in response to the imposition of workplace discipline and the granting of performance-related rewards. Gradual and partial reform can be very effective.

References

BBC Summary of World Broadcasts. 1995. "Journal Looks at Unemployment: Situation 'More Grim than Ever Before'," Asia-Pacific; China; Internal Affairs. FE/2270/G. April 5, "Solutions Proposed to 'Surplus Labor Problem' in State Enterprises," Asia-Pacific; China; Employment and Society. FE/2309/G. May 22, and "Labor Ministry Issues Data on Employment in 1994," Asia-Pacific; China; Internal Affairs. FE/2340/G. June 27.

Bian, Yanjie. 1994. *Work and Inequality in Urban China*. Albany: State University of New York Press.

Byron, Raymond, and Evelyn Manaloto. 1990. "Returns to Education in China," *Economic Development and Cultural Change*, vol. 38, no. 4, pp. 783–96.

Chan, Wai-Fong. 1995. "Almost 900,000 University Graduates to be Given Priority for Job Vacancies," *South China Morning Post*, April 13, p. 7.

China. 1992. *Zhongguo Tongji Nianjian* (Chinese Statistical Yearbook). Beijing: Chinese Statistical Press.

Christiansen, Flemming. 1992. "'Market Transition' in China: The Case of the Jiangsu Labor Market, 1978–1990," *Modern China*, vol. 18, no. 1, pp. 72–93, January.

Cao, Min. 1995. "China: Workforce Responds to Demands of New System," *China Daily*, December 16.

Davis, Deborah. 1992. "Job Mobility in Post-Mao Cities: Increases on the Margins," *China Quarterly*, no. 132, pp. 1062–87.

FBIS. 1992. "Better Jobs in Guangdong Attract Workers," pp. 56–7, 24 September. 1993. "Officials Comment on Brain-Drain Problem," pp. 40–42, 24 March; "Guangdong Delegation Returns with Job Applications," p. 4, 12 April; "Shanxi Capitol Taiyuan Promotes Job Market," p. 50, 20 August; 1994. "Jiangsu Province Labor Markets Flourist," pp. 56–7, 22 February; and "Shanghai Expands Employment Service Market," p. 55, 4 March.

Fleisher, Belton, Keyong Dong, and Yunhua Liu. 1995. "Education, Enterprise Organization, and Productivity in the Chinese Paper Industry," *Economic Development and Cultural Change*, forthcoming.

Gelb, Alan. 1990. "Worker Incomes, Incentives and Attitudes," in William A. Byrd and Qingsong Lin, eds., *China's Rural Industries: Structure, Development and Reform*. Oxford: Oxford University Press for the World Bank.

Harrold, Peter. 1992. "China's Reform Experience to Date," *World Bank Discussion Papers: China and Mongolia Department*, no. 180.

86 *Maurer-Fazio*

Huang, Wei. 1993. "Market Activates China's Talent Pool," *Beijing Review*, February 1–7, pp. 12–15.
Hussain, Athar, and Juzhong Zhuang. 1994. "Impact of Reforms on Wage and Employment Determination in Chinese State Enterprises, 1986–1991," mimeo.
International Intelligence Report. 1994. "Booming Economy Creates Jobs for Graduates," July 26.
Jamison, Dean T., and Jacques Van Der Gaag. 1987. "Education and Earnings in the People's Republic of China," *Economics of Education Review*, vol. 6, no. 2, pp. 161–6.
Jefferson, Gary, and Thomas G. Rawski. 1992. "Unemployment, Underemployment, and Employment Policy in China's Cities," *Modern China*, vol. 18, no. 1, pp. 47–71.
———, and Yuxin Zheng. 1992. "Growth, Efficiency, and Convergence in China's State and Collective Industry," *Economic Development and Cultural Change*, vol. 40, no. 2, pp. 239–66.
Juan, Kate Yu. 1994. "China Takes Steps to Curb Brain Drain from the Civil Service," *The Straight Times* (Singapore), East Asia Section, p. 17.
Khan, Azizur Rahman, Keith Griffin, Carl Riskin, and Renwei Zhao. 1992. "Household Income and Its Distribution in China," *China Quarterly*, no. 132, pp. 1029–61.
Lu, Hongyong. 1994. "Booming Economy Reshapes Labor," China Busness Daily, October 23–29.
Maurer-Fazio, Margaret. 1994. *An Analysis of the Emerging Labor Market in the People's Republic of China and Its Effect on Rates of Return to Investments in Education.* Ph.D. dissertation: University of Pittsburgh.
———. 1995. "Building a Labor Market in China," *Current History*, September.
Mu, Zi. 1993. "Scramble for Talent Spreads Across Nation," *China Daily*, p. 4, October 26.
Naughton, Barry. 1994. "Reforming a Planned Economy: Is China Unique?" in Chung H. Lee and Helmut Reisen, eds., *From Reform to Growth: China and Other Countries in Transition in Asia and Central and Eastern Europe.* Paris: Organization for Economic Co-operation and Development.
Rawski, Thomas G. 1993. "Progress Without Privatization: The Reform of China's State Industries," in Vedat Milor, ed., *Changing Political Economy of Privatization in Post-Communist and Reforming Communist States.*
———. 1995. "Institutional Aspects of China's Emergence as a Market Economy." Paper prepared for the ASSA meetings held in San Francisco, 7 January 1996.
Shaghai Star. 1994. "1,635 Find Good Jobs at Fair," April 5.
Solinger, Dorothy. 1994. "The Danwei Confronts the Floating Population (Or: The Socialist Work Unit Confronts Migrant Labor)." Paper presented at the Annual Meetings of the Association for Asian Studies. Boston, March.
The Economist. 1992. "China: New Rich," October 10.
Wilson, Jeanne L. 1990. "Labor Policy in China: Reform and Retrogression," *Problems of Communism*, pp. 44–65, September-October.
Yang, Ji. 1993. "Officials Comment on Brain-Drain Problem," *Beijing Review*, pp. 30–1, March 29–April 4.

6

The Role of the State in China's Industrial Development: A Reassessment

Alberto Gabriele
UNCTAD, Switzerland

This paper focuses on China's industrial sector, utilizing both qualitative and quantitative evidence. We show the role of the state in China, far from withering out, is massive, dominant, and crucial to China's industrial development. State-owned and state-holding enterprises are now less numerous, but much larger, more capital-and knowledge-intensive, more productive and more profitable than in the late 1990s. The dominant role of the state in China's industrial development is not necessarily a transitional feature. In the long run, it might consolidate itself as a form of strategic planning, and as a key structural characteristic of market socialism.

Introduction

The unprecedented boom of China's economy has been interpreted by many orthodox analysts more or less as follows. Domestic markets have been almost fully liberalized, first in agriculture and then in industry and services. Previously collectivized land has been given back to peasant households. Most industrial and services enterprises are privately owned, and now produce the bulk of GDP, due mainly to their superior efficiency with respect to state-owned enterprises (SOEs) (see Dougherty et al., 2007).

The country also opened to international trade by joining the WTO, thereby boosting labor intensive exports and acceding foreign, advanced knowledge, thanks to FDI spillovers. In sum, there is nothing so special about China, apart from its size that ensures a virtually unlimited supply

Reprinted with permission from Association of Comparative Economic Studies. All rights reserved. *Comparative Economic Studies* (2010) 52, 325–350.

of cheap unskilled labor to fuel export-oriented industrialization. Yes, relatively egalitarian land distribution, widespread literacy, and an innate, culture-based attitude towards thrift also contribute. However, the bottom line is that China is just one more developing country that is prospering since it traded its obsolete socialist model to embrace capitalism.

Other, more acute, observers do acknowledge the depth of the structural differences between China and 'normal' capitalist countries, but dismiss the applicability of the term 'socialism' as a useful tool to analyze such a strange animal. Lindbeck (2008, p.116), for instance, argues that 'the bulk of production today takes place in private firms' and 'most prices in China are formed on market, the main exceptions being natural resources and public utilities. Moreover, the label "socialism" is not usually associated with a strong reliance on economic incentives, competition, internationalization and (as in China) an apparent neglect of the distribution ... of income, education and welfare'. Therefore, both terms 'state capitalism' and 'market socialism' are inappropriate, and the neutral term 'mixed economy' should rather be utilized to characterize China's economic system. Lindbeck is right when referring to the contradictions between China's present social reality and the traditional goals of socialism, which are particularly stark in the domain of income and social inequalities (see, for instance, Kanbur *et al.*, 2008). Yet, in the present paper we are focusing on some positive (ie, objective) features of China's economic system, rather than on the country's social problems seen in a normative[1] dimension. In this context, we show that Lindbeck's view amounts to a severe underestimation of the role of the state in China's economy, and to an overestimation of the relative autonomy and supposed commanding position of unplanned, market-based regulatory mechanisms. Thus, we consider it as appropriate to retain the term 'market socialism', even if it has to be taken with a grain of salt and to some extent as an *ad hoc* definition.

There are two crucial differences between a 'market socialist' and a capitalist system. The first one is that in a market socialist system the role of the state is both quantitatively larger and qualitatively superior, thereby allowing the public sector as a whole to exert an overall strategic control over the country's development path, especially in crucial areas such as setting the economy-wide rate of the accumulation and determining the speed and direction of technical progress. The second difference is that in a market socialist system, although capitalists endowed with private ownership rights on some means of production do exist, they are not strong enough to constitute a hegemonic and dominant social class, as it happens in 'normal' capitalist countries (see Gabriele and Schettino, 2008). Our approach on the

---

[1] A normative statement is one that states how things ought to be, while a positive statement is one that states factually how things are.

structural differences between capitalism and market socialism is consistent with (although not identical to) that of the late Giovanni Arrighi (2007), who argued that the presently existing Chinese economy is a 'non-capitalist market economy' rooted both in China's ancient economic history and in its more recent revolutionary tradition.

This paper focuses on the role of the state in China's industrial sector. As available statistical data are of a very aggregate nature, the analysis is of preliminary nature, and it can only provide a broad and tentative interpretation of such a vast and unique phenomenon as China's contemporary industrial development. Moreover, too little time has elapsed since the inception of economic reforms to allow for a proper historical evaluation of their ultimate significance.[2] Without underestimating the relevance of such important caveats, the paper concludes that China's state is able to engage in a novel form of strategic planning, employing as a crucial tool its ownership and control rights over the largest and most advanced industrial enterprises. It also carries out huge and ever-increasing investments in infrastructure, institution- and human-capital building, and R&D, on a scale unequaled anywhere else in the world. This public investment drive generates a network of systemic external economies,[3] which in turn decisively enhance the competitiveness, productivity, and profitability of both public and privately owned/controlled industrial enterprises. In the long run, the dominant role of the state in China's industry might consolidate itself as a sustainable structural characteristic of market socialism.

The paper is organized as follows. The next section briefly exposes a few basic facts about China's industrial reforms. The section after that reviews part of a sprawling literature on SOEs' reforms and their relative efficiency and profitability, focusing mainly on studies that covered the 1990s and the early 2000s. The subsequent section presents some statistical evidence on China's industrial enterprises and R&D activities. We show that the role

---

[2] According to a famous statement attributed to Zhou Enlai, even after more than one and a half century it was still too early to evaluate the impact of the French Revolution.

[3] Systemic external economies stem from the ability of individual firms to externalize a number of costs – such as infrastructure building and maintenance, human capital formation, access to free and quasi-free (less than fully protected) knowledge, environmental protection – which otherwise they should have borne directly. Some of these external economies are far from virtuous from a social welfare perspective, such as those resulting in environmental damages. However, on balance, in most countries they favor industrial development, or at least industrial growth. We call them systemic because they are predicated on a number of systemic factors that lie outside the scope of the firm's behavior. These factors, in turn, ultimately depend on the state's willingness and capability to macro-manage strategically the development path of the national economy. Systemic external economies are particularly relevant and crucial in China, consistently with the unique role played by the public sector.

of public industry has been changing but is far from marginal. The performance of public industry in China has improved dramatically in recent years, and is likely to do so even more in relative terms in the near future, due to the collapse of large sections of small-scale, export-oriented manufacturing private firms. Moreover, it has to be taken into account the impact of China's extraordinary R&D effort (the bulk of which is conducted either in large state-owned and state-holding industrial enterprises (SOSHEs) or in public universities and research centers) has important implications for evaluating the overall contribution of the state to industrial development. Finally, the last section concludes.

The Reform of Public Industry in China: Basic Facts

China's industrial scenario, previously dominated by traditional SOEs, has been profoundly modified, first by the surge of township and village enterprises (TVEs) in the 1970s and 1980s, and subsequently by the boom of private- and foreign-funded enterprises (FFEs). Besides the SOEs' restructuring process at firm level, during the present decade, two other major and only apparently contradictory policy trends have become increasingly apparent during the 2000s. One is the adoption of leverage and of a rationalized hierarchical chain as an effective means to maintain state control under a diversified ownership structure. The other is a tendency towards re-centralization (pursued also in domains different from that of industrial policies, as shown by the key 1994 tax reform), which continues unabated and cannot but be further strengthened by the drastic interventions needed to control the exogenous impact of the world financial and economic crisis.

Rounds of SOE reforms have been going on in China since the 1980s. However, the governments' political willingness to accept the social and political costs of radically reforming state enterprises strengthened progressively during the 1990s and the early 2000s. A major turnaround in the performance of state-owned and state-holding firms has become apparent in the second half of the present decade. The reform in China's industrial sector has but accelerated dramatically during the 2000s. Since the late 1990s, private firms have boomed, rapidly overcoming public industry in terms of number, employment, and – to a lesser extent – share of total industrial output. The number of SOEs, conversely, was reduced drastically, as was their workforce, consistent with the thrust of the *zhuada fangxiao* (keep the big, dump the small) policy (see Morel, 2006; Ministry of Commerce, 2008; Wildau, 2008). Private- and FFEs presently constitute the vast majority of firms and generate the bulk of industrial employment (see below, section 'Public and Private Actors in China's Industrial Sector').

Yet, taking into account this trend should not unwarrantedly lead to underestimate the evolving but still crucial role of the state in China's industrial development. The crucial component of China's public industry reform process has been the transformation of many SOEs into state-holding enterprises. These corporations have partial non-public ownership and share trading, and are characterized by harder budget constraints and more indirect forms of control with respect to traditional state enterprises (see Li and Putterman, 2008). Changes aimed at hardening the budget constraint and improve performance have been implemented also in the SOEs that have retained their traditional, fully state-owned status, and many of the worst loss-making enterprises have been closed or (more rarely) privatized.

A key result of SOEs' reforms has been a major turnaround in profitability. By the mid-1990s, SOEs' losses were so high that net profits were less than 0.6% of GDP. By 2007, the picture had changed drastically, with profits reaching 4.2% of GDP in industrial SOSHEs and 2% of GDP in non-industrial SOEs (Naughton, 2008a, b, c).

A major role in the public industry reform process has been played by the state-owned Assets Supervision and Administration Commission (SASAC). The Commission was created in 2002 to represent central-government shareholder interests in large enterprise groups of which there are now 149[4] after having been reduced through mergers. After reorganizations, SASAC-managed firms become joint stock corporations or wholly owned state corporations.[5] SASAC acts mainly as the facilitator and promoter of the effective implementation of reforms, which had been officially launched already in the 1990s, but had not been carried out thoroughly until the political will to get rid of loss-making SOEs became evident, and state support was drastically focused on a limited number of large and ever-growing firms. Public enterprises are now concentrated in few strategic sectors: energy and power, industrial raw materials, military industry and large-scale machinery-building, transport and telecommunications. Some of these sectors are explicitly reserved to state firms; while, in others, spontaneous market forces and regulatory discrimination combine to erect very high barriers to entry for private operators. In both cases, however, the government has strived to avoid the creation of monopolies, engineering the emergence of oligopolistic market structures in which typically two or three large public firms compete with each other.

It should also be taken into account that the true scope of state intervention in China's industry goes well beyond the boundaries of SOSHEs. Even

---

[4] This figure refers to August 2008 (source: Ministry of Commerce, 2008), and might be further reduced by the time this paper is published.

[5] SASAC also strengthened managerial incentives. In 2004, all central SASAC firms signed three-year performance contracts, outlining annual and three-year targets. On the basis of these contracts, SASAC evaluates each CEO's performance. The three-year evaluation criteria are based on growth of capital value and revenues as well as annual profit results.

the most advanced among nominally private enterprises are often connected to the public sector through a number of ownership, finance, and other linkages, to a much larger extent than their counterparts in capitalist countries.[6] A case in point is that of Huawei, a very successful and dynamic producer of telecoms network equipment with sales of about $15 billion in 2008. Huawei is formally private, yet it has been formally supported by the state, and its development strategy seems to be broadly consistent with that of China's industry as a whole. There are similar cases of leading private companies, which are in fact largely connected to public institutions. For example, the white goods company, Hai'er, which is now controlled by Qingdao city SASAC, and that of the computer firm Legend whose biggest shareholder is the China Academy of Sciences (see Naughton, 2008a).

In sum, it would be easy to be caught wrong-footed by the speed and depth of the changes taking place in China's industrial landscape, to the point of interpreting it as an extravagant private-led entrepreneurial unfolding, and concluded that SOEs' assets were being privatized at an accelerated pace and the state's presence in China's industry was withering away. Actually, there has been no mass privatization of major public industrial assets. Notwithstanding the contribution of private firms to production and employment, state-controlled enterprises play a dominant role in most industrial sectors, and the strategic control of key economic levers is still in the hands of public planners (see Kroeber, 2008; Kroeber and Yao, 2008; Wildau, 2008).

A Review of the Literature

Numerous studies analyzed different aspects of SOE reforms. Until the early 2000s, most acknowledged that important changes were ahead and steps to move forward were underway, but concluded that no decisive breakthrough in SOEs' performance had been achieved yet. However, a more favorable trend is evidenced by the most recent works. Zheng *et al.* (2000) analyzed SOEs' productivity performance over the period 1980–1994. They found that productivity did grow, thanks mainly to technical progress, but technical efficiency remained low. Dong and Putterman (2003) argued that hardening budget constraints without relieving SOEs from their social burdens caused a scarcity of non-labor inputs and thus rising redundant labor in the early 1990s. Cull and Xu (2003) found that bank finance – as an alternative to other sources of funding, such as retained profits or direct state transfers – had a positive impact on firms' profitability and on managerial

---

[6] It would be extremely difficult to quantify this phenomenon. Even well-informed case studies on individual firms, like those on Huawei and Hai'er referred to in the text, cannot go beyond a heuristic appreciation of the true measure of control exerted by the state in these enterprises.

flexibility in the 1980s, but this association had been weakening in the early 1990s. Zhang (2004) reviewed the effects of corporatization and stock market listing on SOEs' performance, identifying a rapid trend towards firms' concentration and consolidation, but concluded that results in terms of performance were still modest on balance.

Other studies compared the performances of public and private enterprises. Most of them found that private firms performed better (see Chen, 2001; Gul and Zhao, 2001; Wei and Varela, 2003; Hovey, 2005), while others were inconclusive or did not find a systemic relationship between ownership and firms' behavior (Wang, 2005). Zhang and Parker (2004) analyzed total factor productivity (TFP) trends in China's electronics industry in the 1990s, and found that corporatized SOEs did not perform significantly better than traditional ones, with TFP growing but at a slower pace than in both collective and private electronic firms. Most researchers, however, found that legal person holdings have a positive impact (see Sun and Tong, 2003; Wong *et al*, 2004). In a more recent study, Naughton and Hovey (2007, p. 139) reached similar conclusions: 'state ownership *per* se(is) negatively correlated with performance' while 'legal persons ... have a positive influence on firm performance or value'. On this basis, they put forward policy recommendations favoring various forms of divesture of state ownership in existing SOEs, some of which amount to a transformation of traditional SOEs into state-holding legal persons.

Other recent studies have also identified serious weaknesses in reformed SOEs. Girma and Gong (2008), on the basis of a large micro data set, investigate whether SOEs in China have benefited from the managerial, technical, and organizational skills possessed by multinational firms operating in their country, and conclude that evidence in favor of positive spillovers is weak, due mainly to scarce regional linkages and low level of absorptive capacity. The latter, in turn, was partly caused by a still-undeveloped structure of managers' incentives. Yu and Nikamp (2008) assess the comparative productivity performance of SOEs in high-tech industries from 1996 to 2006. They find that SOEs as a whole experienced an unsatisfactory trajectory of catch-up from 1996 to 2006, with SOEs gaining ground in 1997–2003, but falling further behind FFEs[7] in 2003–2006, due to their inadequate capability to develop indigenous technologies. These results (to be taken as indicative, due to some debatable features of the authors' methodology) might be due in part to the disruptive short-term effects of the major acceleration in SOEs' reform that started in 2003, as shown by Dong and Xu (2008). The

---

[7] There are two main groups of FDI-owned/controlled industrial enterprises (jointly referred to as FDI-funded enterprises, FDIEs) in China. One is that of enterprises owned/controlled by capitalists from Hong Kong, Macao, and Taiwan (HKMTEs). The remaining FDIEs, mainly controlled by large TNCs from the most advanced capitalist countries, constitute the group of FFEs.

authors analyze econometrically the short-term impact of China's major labor restructuring program, which was much more widespread among public-owned rather than private enterprises, and especially in older and SOEs with higher excess capacity. Their most interesting finding is that, far from automatically improving performance and profitability, 'downsizing has serious short-term costs in terms of total factor productivity (TFP)', due largely to its 'psychological' costs in terms of workers' demoralization.[8] They also found that 'private firms tend to have worse allocation efficiency after downsizing but tend to cut wages to a greater extent such that profitability is unaffected, and SOEs tend to have slightly milder deterioration in allocating efficiency, and tend to cut wages to a lesser extent as well ... SOEs have a more positive "catch-up" effect from downsizing, and ... tend to be more protective of labour' (p. 238). Dong and Xu's results illustrate why improvements in the performance of SOSHEs did not become apparent until the mid-2000s, while the bulk of labor shedding took place in late 1990s and early 2000s. Another recent contribution reaching drastic conclusions on the superiority of private enterprises is that of Dougherty *et al.* (2007). The authors provide a quantitative analysis based on a large sample made up by quarter of a million industrial firms, and conclude that '... the private sector ... operates much more efficiently than the public sector' (p. 309).[9]

Since the early to mid-2000s, a discordant strand of literature has been on the ascendance, which tends to be more optimistic regarding the results of past SOEs reforms and to deny the intrinsic superiority of private ownership of industrial enterprises. Some of these studies focus on the interaction between SOEs reforms and China's mushrooming R&D activities, analyzing various aspects of China's national system of innovation (NSI), which has been booming at a historically unprecedented pace and is now the second largest in the world in terms of R&D expenditure (see Mandel, 2004; McGregor, 2007; OECD, 2008a, b; Gabriele and Khan, 2008).

China's NSI is characterized by specific forms of interaction involving public universities and research centers, public enterprises, privately owned and foreign funded industrial firms (see, among others, Gabriele and Khan, 2008; Mazzoleni, 2008; Niosi, 2008). However, even in this flexible, rapidly evolving, and ever-changing context, the role of public organizations remains paramount, especially taking into account that most university-affiliated enterprises are ultimately state owned. In-house R&D activities on the part of public enterprises are a crucial component of any NSI, as

---

[8] An additional factor is probably constituted by the transitional costs of adapting to new forms of labor allocation and organization on the part of both workers and managers.

[9] In our view, the conclusions of this paper are severely weakened by various methodological and interpretative problems. The author can make available a brief unpublished methodological critique to interested readers.

they constitute a key linkage between the creation of knowledge and its productive application. Hu and Jefferson (2004) found high returns to R&D among Beijing's SOEs in the 1990s. However, they also found a suboptimal propensity to invest in R&D on the part of SOEs. Hu *et al.* (2005) showed that in-firm R&D was crucial to 'complement technology transfer—whether of domestic or foreign origin' (p. 780). Hu and Jefferson (2005) argued that, without underestimating the positive impact of the surge in indigenous R&D, China's patent explosion in the early 2000s was mainly due to legal and institutional changes in the competition conditions prevailing in the domestic market, which had been favoring patent holders and strength-ened intellectual property rights protection. It was primarily the competi-tive challenge of FFEs, along with that stemming from the industry's shift towards a high degree of export orientation, which was 'prompting domes-tic Chinese firms to file for more patent applications for their strategic com-petitive value'. The case of patents is an example of a wider trend towards deepening linkages between international trade opening and technological change. FFEs enhance in-bound technological flows, and increased competi-tion forces Chinese exporters to follow close world technological trends (see Kroeber and Yao, 2008).

Another form of interaction between economic and scientific human and non-human assets, in a framework characterized jointly by China's indig-enous drive towards technological development and by the profit-oriented strategies of foreign investors, is the increasing propensity to establish R&D centers in Beijing on the part of many leading Transnational Corporations (TNCs) (Chen, 2008). Fisher-Vanden *et al.* (2006) found that both domestic (such as increasing R&D activities and enterprise reforms) and externally originated factors (technology imports) contribute to an energy-saving bias in China's technological development. In-house R&D activities are crucial to enable firms to develop the absorptive capacity needed for the diffusion of imported technologies. Their findings 'underscore the importance of diverse channels of technical change in driving the economic growth and development of China with likely implications for other developing coun-tries.' (pp. 659–660). Fisher-Vanden and Jefferson (2008) found that in-house R&D is labor- and material-using and capital- and energy-saving, thereby capitalizing on China's comparative advantage, and is mainly aimed at slashing production costs of already-existing products. Conversely, imported technologies, which are comparatively capital-intensive, focus on new prod-uct development: 'These diversified channels of technical change reveal a pattern of technical change in a developing country context that is far more diversified than that suggested by the conventional growth literature' (Fisher-Vanden and Jefferson, 2008, p. 658).

Other authors analyzed comparatively the performance of public and privately owned/controlled industrial enterprises. Holz (2002) showed that the gap between SOEs and non-SOEs was not due to the formers' intrinsic inefficiency, and could be explained simply by SOEs' higher circulation tax rates and capital intensity. Qiu *et al.* (2005a, b) found that restructuring according to corporate law improved firms' governance in the late 1990s, and argued that full privatization was not needed to effectively improve SOEs' performance. Chang (2008) analyzed the diversification of large SOEs in Lanzhou, and concluded that the process was subject to market conditions and firm-specific factors, yet the government played a key enabling role in the reorganization and diversification process.

Jefferson *et al.* (2008) examine differences in levels and rates of productivity growth by ownership type among large and medium industrial enterprises (LMEs). Their firm-level data include both surviving firms that report in both 1998 and 2005 and firms that exit or enter the data set over this period. The authors observe substantial increases in labor and capital productivity across both SOSHEs, and find that the strongest driver of productivity growth was the Schumpeterian process of the exit and entering of firms,[10] due mainly to the thorough firm restructuring and reorganization process, which 'often included changes in ownership (including full or partial privatization)' (p. 3). As the enterprise reform process among LMEs rarely implied full privatization or a shift to private owners of a controlling share, it can be safely assumed that most of the new entrants were reformed mixed state-controlled firms. Jefferson *et al.*, (2008) find that the 'level of productivity of an entering firm in 2005 represents an annual rate of growth of TFP of 18.37% in relation with the productivity of the exiting firm in 1998. This contrasts with a rate of growth of but 8.33% for a surviving SOE' (p. 17).

Many other studies show that 'ownership by legal person entities, which in the large majority of cases means indirect ownership by the state ... tends to positively affect productivity, profitability, and firm performance in general' (Li and Putterman, 2008, p. 374; see also Sun *et al.*, 2002; Delios *et al.*, 2006; Xu and Wang, 1999; Qi *et al.*, 2000; Jia *et al.*, 2005; Holz, 2002). Finally, a particularly interesting study is by Chen *et al.* (2009). The authors analyze a sample of listed companies with different types of ownership to evaluate their relative efficiency, focusing particularly on the group of 149 large enterprises controlled by SASAC, which they call SOEs affiliated to the central government (SOECGs). These elite firms 'excel in almost every way when compared to other ownership types', while mixed enterprises controlled by private investors do not perform particularly well, contrasting 'the claims that firms perform best when the state is completely absent from

---

[10] A likely explanation for the relatively high productivity of entrants is that, exiting firms may be low-productivity firms in need for restructuring. 'Restructuring typically entails a change in formal ownership classification, industrial classification ... often resulting in the assignment of a new ID' (Jefferson *et al.*, 2008, p. 17).

ownership ... at least in the case of China' (p. 172).[11] The authors attribute the relatively favorable performance of SOECGs to the transitional nature of China's economy, and to its weak legal and institutional environment in particular. However, to assume that private ownership would be superior in a fully developed legal and institutional context would be unwarranted. On the contrary, our view is that China's SASAC-controlled elite enterprises are pioneering a form of ownership and management structure, which has a good chance to prove itself quite suitable to deal with the challenges of industrial development in the 21st century.

Public and Private Actors in China's Industrial Sector

Public industry in China, as in other countries, is constituted by industrial enterprises that are controlled by non-private legal entities (be them the state, local governments, or groups of workers). The state-controlled sector of industry is constituted by two components: SOEs and state-holding enterprises (mixed enterprises in which the state holds a majority share). These two groups of enterprises represent the bulk of public industry, and will be referred to jointly as SOSHEs in the remainder of the paper. In addition, there is a smaller category of non-state public enterprises, most of which are local cooperatives and collectives, many of which are small-scale and are located in rural areas.

Adding up all public-owned and public-controlled categories of enterprises, it is possible to gauge the relative weight of the public sector in China's industry.[12] The public sector share has been shrinking fast over the present decade, especially due to the relative decline of TVEs, collectives, and cooperatives, and to the parallel correspondent emergence of a growing number of domestic private enterprises (DPrivEs) (see Table 6.1). In 1998, SOSHEs were still almost 40% of all industrial enterprises, owned 70% of the assets, produced half of the national industrial output and employed 60% of the workforce. SOSHEs' relative weight declined over all these three dimensions, but in an uneven fashion. As a result, by 2007, SOSHEs were only 6% of all industrial enterprises, while (domestic) private enterprises were more than half of the total. Yet, SOSHEs employed over 20% of the

---

[11] In this respect, China's case might not be totally unique. Hanousek, Kocenda, and Svejnar obtain results similar to those of Chen *et al.* (2009) in a quantitative study using firm level data to examine the effects of divesture and privatization on corporate performance in the Czech Republic.

[12] The task of disentangling the relative weight and characteristics of public and private industry, respectively, along various significant dimensions (ie, number, production, investment, productivity, profitability, etc.) has been greatly simplified by the 1998 statistical reform (see Holz and Lin, 2001), but still requires a certain amount of interpretation of available data.

Table 6.1 State-owned and state-holding enterprises (SOSHEs) and (domestic) private enterprises: number, output, employment (% share of industry total, 1998–2007)

Year region	Number of enterprises	SOSHEs		Private enterprises		
		Gross industrial output value	Annual average employed persons	Number of enterprises	Gross industrial output values	Annual average employed persons
1998	39.2	49.6	60.5	6.5	3.1	2.6
1999	37.8	48.9	58.5	9.0	4.5	3.9
2000	32.8	47.3	53.9	13.6	6.1	6.2
2001	27.3	44.4	49.2	21.1	9.2	10.0
2002	22.7	40.8	43.9	27.1	11.7	13.3
2003	17.5	37.5	37.6	34.5	14.7	17.9
2004	12.9	34.8	29.8	43.2	17.4	22.9
2005	10.1	33.3	27.2	45.5	19.0	24.5
2006	8.3	31.2	24.5	49.6	21.2	26.8
2007	6.1	29.5	22.1	52.6	23.2	28.6

Source: CSY (2008).

industrial workforce, produced almost 30% of the output, detained over 40% of industrial assets, and generated 40% of the sector's profits. SOEs proper were less than 3% of all industrial enterprises, producing about 9% of total gross industrial output value (GVIO) and employing 8% of the sector's workforce (see Table 6.1).

However, such a reduced but still sizeable relative weight tells only a rather small part of the story. To evaluate thoroughly the role of the public sector in China's industry it is necessary to examine a number of economic and financial indicators for the three sectors: SOEs, non-state public enterprises, and state-holding enterprises. In turn, these figures will be compared to the corresponding data for privately controlled industrial enterprises. To this purpose, data on various groupings of industrial enterprises from *China's Statistical Yearbook 2008* (CSY, 2008) have been aggregated and decomposed in order to present a clear picture of the public/ private relationships in Chinese industry (see Table 6.2). Indicators of productivity, capitalization, profit-generating capability, capital profitability and efficiency are shown for each group of enterprises (see Table 6.3). The indicators are as follows:

- Labor productivity is measured by the O/L ratio (where O is GVIO and L is the average number of workers).
- Capitalization is the K/L ratio (where K represents the assets endowment).
- The indicator of profit-generating capability is profit generated by each worker; P/L where P represents profits.
- The P/K ratio is the indicator of capital profitability.

Table 6.2 Basic statistics on industrial enterprises, 2007

		Figures and percentages (100 million yuan)									
		Number of enterprises (unit)	Gross industrial output value (current prices)	Total assets	Total profits	Annual average number of employed persons (10,000 persons)					
		N	O	K	P	L	N%	O%	K%	P%	L%
Public enterprises											
State-owned enterprises	SOEs	10,074	36,387	54,723	2,630	646	2.99	8.98	15.50	9.68	8.21
State enterprises (total)	SEs	11,572	55,642	86,040	4,067	1,015	3.44	13.73	24.37	14.98	12.89
Fully public non-state enterprises	FPubNSEs	19,742	14,393	8,666	880	349	5.86	3.55	2.45	3.24	4.44
Fully public enterprises (total)	FPEs	31,314	70,036	94,706	4,947	1,365	9.30	17.29	26.83	18.22	17.33
Private enterprises											
Private enterprises (total)	PrivEsT	244,536	221,653	149,672	12,581	4,606	72.61	54.71	42.40	46.33	58.49
Domestic private enterprises	DPrivEs	177,080	94,023	53,305	5,054	2,253	52.58	23.21	15.10	18.61	28.61
Foreign direct investment enterprises	FDIEs	67,456	127,629	96,367	7,527	2,353	20.03	31.50	27.30	27.72	29.88
State controlled enterprises											
State-owned and state-holding enterprises	SOSHEs	20,680	119,686	158,188	10,795	1,743	6.14	29.54	44.81	39.75	22.13
Mixed enterprises											
Mixed enterprises	MEs	59,779	112,161	107,870	9,541	1,883	17.75	27.68	30.55	35.14	23.91
State-holding mixed enterprises	SHMEs	9,108	64,043	72,148	6,728	728	2.70	15.81	20.44	24.78	9.24
Private-controlled mixed enterprises	PrivMEs	50,671	48,118	35,723	2,813	1,156	15.05	11.88	10.12	10.36	14.68
SHMEs/SOSHEs%		44.04									
SHMEs/MEs%		15.24									

(continued)

Table 6.2 Continued

		Number of enterprises (unit)	Figures and percentages (100 million yuan)								
			Gross industrial output value (current prices)	Total assets	Total profits	Annual average number of employed persons (10,000 persons)					
		N	O	K	P	L	N%	O%	K%	P%	L%
Public industry (total)											
Public-owned and public-holding enterprises	PubOHEs	40,422	134,079	166,854	11,675	2,092	12.00	33.09	47.26	42.99	26.57
Privately owned and controlled enterprises	PrivOCEs	295,207	269,770	185,395	15,394	5,762	87.66	66.58	52.51	56.69	73.16
Total		336,768	405,177	353,037	27,155	7,875					

Note: Sub-groups are composed as follows:
Public enterprises
SEs: SOEs+SJOEs+SSCs
FPubNSEs: COEs+COOP+CJOEs+JSCEs+OJOEs
FPEs: SETs+FPubNSEs
Private enterprises
PrivEsT: DPrivEs+HKMTEs+FFE
FDIEs: HKMTEs+FFEs
Mixed enterprises
MEs: OLLCs+SHCLs
SHMEs: SOSHEs-State total
PrivMEs: MEs-SHMEs
Public industry (total)
PubOHEs: SOSHEs+FPubNSEs
Private industry (total)
PrivOCEs: PrivET+PrivCMEs.
Source: CSY (2008).

Table 6.3 Productivity and profitability indicators

	10,000 yuan			Yuan	
	O/L Labor productivity	K/L Assets per worker	P/L Profit per worker	P/K Capital profitability	K/O Ratio
Public enterprises					
State-owned enterprises	56.3	84.7	4.1	0.05	1.50
State enterprises (total)	54.8	84.7	4.0	0.05	1.55
Fully public non-state enterprises (coops, collectives)	41.2	24.8	2.5	0.10	0.60
Fully public enterprises (total)	51.3	69.4	3.6	0.05	1.35
Private enterprises					
Private enterprises (total)	48.1	32.5	2.7	0.08	0.68
Domestic private enterprises	41.7	23.7	2.2	0.09	0.57
Foreign direct investment enterprises	54.2	41.0	3.2	0.08	0.76
State controlled enterprises					
State-Owned and state-holding enterprises	68.7	90.8	6.2	0.07	1.32
Mixed enterprises					
Mixed enterprises	59.6	57.3	5.1	0.09	0.96
State-holding mixed enterprises	88.0	99.2	9.2	0.09	1.13
Private-controlled mixed enterprises	41.6	30.9	2.4	0.08	0.74
Public industry (total)					
Public-owned and public-holding enterprises	64.1	79.7	5.6	0.07	1.24
Privately owned and controlled enterprises	46.8	32.2	2.7	0.08	0.69
Total (Average for the whole industrial sector)	51.4	44.8	3.4	0.08	0.87

Source: CSY (2008).

- K/O, the capital/output ratio, is a rough indicator of efficiency in terms of capital productivity.[13]

SOEs are on average much larger and capital intensive than most other Chinese industrial enterprises.[14] With respect to the national averages for the entire industrial sector, SOEs' per employee asset endowment is about double, while labor productivity is only slightly higher (Table 6.3, first and last rows).[15] Thus, SOEs' workers utilize on average twice as much capital than the industry's average, but do not translate this advantage into a correspondent productivity gain. SOEs' profitability is also lower than the national industrial average, both in per employee and in per unit of capital terms. Therefore, SOEs do not appear to be among China's most efficient and profitable industrial enterprises.

Conversely, the picture of another category of fully public industrial enterprises, that of Fully Public Non-State Enterprises (FPubNSEs, essentially constituted by cooperatives and collectives), is very different from that of SOEs. They are the smallest group of firms in terms of average labor force size, the most undercapitalized, and those that generate the smaller amount of profits per employee. Yet, they have the lowest capital/output ratio and the highest profits/assets ratio. These small and very light public enterprises occupy a segment of the industry that is virtually at the opposite side from that of SOEs, and utilize their scarce assets in a quite efficient and profitable way. However, their overall weight in China's industrial scenario is limited, both in terms of output and of employment.

The most advanced component of public industry is constituted by state-holding mixed enterprises (SHMEs). In SHMEs, the state owns a larger share than any other shareholder, thereby effectively being able to exercise strategic control. These enterprises are not formally very different from those state-controlled mixed enterprises that are still common (even if much less than a few decades ago) in many capitalist countries. Yet, in the Chinese context, their role is far more crucial, both in quantitative and in qualitative terms. SHMEs are few, large, capital-intensive, and very productive. They

---

[13] Of course, the indicators including the capital term shall be seen as indicative, as they compare a stock variable (the total asset endowment owned by enterprises in a certain moment of time, as a result of an accumulation process that usually lasted for several years and was not homogeneous across different firms) with flow variables such as labor force, output, and profits, each of which refers to a specific year.

[14] Comparing figures in the L and N columns of Table 6.3, it is easy to see that on average each SOE employs about five times more workers than a domestic private enterprise and almost twice as many as a foreign-funded private enterprise.

[15] In Table 6.4, the K/L indicator (assets per worker) is 84.7 for SOEs (first row) against 44.8 for the national average (last row referring to all industrial firms). O/L (labor productivity) is 56.3 for SOEs (first row) and 51.4 for the national average (last row). All the other statements on the relative performance of each group of industrial enterprises in the remainder of this section are based on the same reading of the indicators reported in Table 6.3.

are only 2.7% of all industrial enterprises, a share even smaller than that of SOEs. Yet, they employ over 9% of the labor force, own over 20% of total assets, produce almost 16% of the output, and generate almost a quarter of all industrial profits. Their capital endowment per worker is the highest among all groups of enterprises. SHMEs are industry leaders in terms of labor productivity, with 880300 yuan on average in 2007. This figure is almost 60% higher than that of SOEs and extra-regional FDI-funded enterprises (FDIEs), and also more than double that of DPrivEs and that of privately controlled mixed enterprises (see Tables 6.2 and 6.3).

SHMEs' capital/output ratio (1.13), while lower than that of SOEs, is higher than those of all private and privately controlled enterprises (see Table 6.3).[16] However, we have already found that the enterprise grouping exhibiting the lowest K/O ratio is that of non-state public industry. It is not surprising, after all, that poorly capitalized, small-scale enterprises exhibit a very favorable K/O ratio: it is still theoretically possible for a firm to produce some output, and to realize a profit, utilizing only labor. Such a hypothetical enterprise would exhibit a zero K/O ratio, but would hardly represent a model for industrialization and technical progress. SHMEs are also very profitable, as confirmed by the very high levels of their profits/worker and profits/assets ratios. Both profitability indicators are superior to those of any other large grouping of either public or private industrial enterprises (see Table 6.3). Their interpretation, however, requires a good amount of caution. Across both developed and developing countries, under *ceteris paribus* conditions, profitability among large firms is positively correlated with their market power, which in turn is largely[17] dependent on each country's institutional settings. Thus, in many cases, high profitability could simply be the result of lack of competition, high degrees of monopoly, and corruption, and it cannot be taken as a significant performance indicator. However, an institutional framework allowing some large firms to maintain high, but limited, degrees of monopoly power can also be seen as a second best policy tool to foster the 'profit-investment nexus' (see Akyuz and Gore, 1996),[18] thereby enhancing growth and technical progress.[19]

---

[16] A relatively high K/O ratio is not incompatible with the existence of economies of scale and is not necessarily a symptom of inefficiency in a static context.

[17] Even in the most free-market oriented institutional frameworks, a tendency towards monopoly usually emerges among large firms due to well-known phenomena such as economies of scale, first-move advantages, and the like.

[18] Akyuz and Gore argue that in the most successful East Asian economies 'Government policies played a major role in promoting capital accumulation by creating rents and animating the dynamic interactions between profits and investment. This was achieved through a broader set of measures than those usually identified as selective industrial policies' (p. 461).

[19] As is well known, although he emphasized the role of innovations rather than that of accumulation *per se,* Schumpeter also maintained that some degree of monopoly is preferable to perfect competition.

We are inclined to believe[20] that in the case of China's SHMEs the improvement of profitability indicators should indeed be seen as a positive performance signal, for a variety of reasons. First, the profit-investment nexus approach is more likely to be plausible in a high-growth context (as in nowadays China and in the East Asian NICs in the 1960s and 1970s) than in a slow-growth one, and SHMEs are indeed growing fast (in terms of output and productivity). Second, the biggest headache with public industry in China until recently was precisely that many SOEs were suffering heavy losses. As a result, the overall profitability of the sector was dangerously low, thereby jeopardizing the very financial sustainability of public industry. Third, SHMEs – differently from many SOEs – usually operate in highly oligopolistic but not monopolistic market settings.

These findings on productivity and profitability of reformed public industrial enterprises show that the drastically implemented *zhuada fangxiao* strategy has been rather successful so far. To properly understand their respective roles, weight, and strength, however, it is useful to compare the public sector[21] of China's industry with its private counterpart.

China's private industrial sector is quite heterogeneous, being composed by four uneven categories of enterprises: DPrivEs; private-controlled mixed enterprises (PrivMEs); enterprises with funds from Hong Kong, Macao, and Taiwan (HKMTEs); FFEs, owned by investors from countries different from HKMTEs (FFEs). The latter two categories of enterprises jointly constitute the group of FDIEs. DPrivEs are now over half of the total, employ over one-quarter of the industrial labor force, and produce almost one-quarter of total output. They own only about 15% of industrial assets and generate a slightly higher fraction of total profits (see Table 6.2). DPrivEs' labor productivity is almost identical to that of their similarly small and undercapitalized public counterpart constituted by cooperatives and collectives, and much lower than that of all other categories of industrial enterprises. With respect to profitability, DPrivEs fare poorly in terms of profit/worker, but lead in terms of profit/asset ratio.[22] DPrivEs' K/O ratio is also the lowest of all groupings of industrial enterprises. Yet, it is very similar to that of cooperatives and collectives (see Table 6.3). The latter finding shows that DPrivEs' apparent efficiency in utilizing physical capital to produce industrial goods is not stemming from a supposed intrinsic superiority of private property, but simply by the very low K/L ratios that are a common characteristic of

---

[20] Disaggregated empirical studies carried out in specific sectors would be necessary to gauge rigorously which of these two interpretative approaches is more appropriate in different historical and geographical contexts.

[21] With the term 'public sector' we refer to all SOSHEs, that is both SOEs and SHMEs.

[22] As previously noticed, SHMEs are also very profitable. It is interesting to note that the difference in the respective profit/assets ratios between two very different groupings of enterprises such as SHMEs and PrivDEs is less than 2%.

both DPrivEs and FPubNSEs. In sum, DPrivEs are comparatively small and undercapitalized, and their most valuable contribution to China's overall economic and social development so far is that of creating and maintaining a sizeable share of total employment, utilizing relatively few physical and financial resources (see Table 6.3).

PrivMEs share a number of characteristics with the state-controlled section of mixed enterprises. As such, they are larger and more capital intensive than PrivDEs. They are about 15% of all enterprises, and contribute to about 10% of total industrial capitalization, output, and profits, and to almost 15% of the employment. However, on average, privately controlled mixed enterprises lag behind their state-owned counterparts, as shown by size, labor productivity, capitalization, and profitability indicators. As they are less capital-intensive, however, PrivMEs perform better than SHMEs in terms of K/O ratios (see Table 6.3).[23]

Finally, it has to be taken into account that enterprises are a central but not an exclusive component of each country's overall economic system. The availability of a complex set of what could broadly be seen as 'public goods' has the potential to generate major systemic external economies,[24] thereby decisively affecting enterprises' ability to invest, increase their productivity, promote technical progress, and compete in domestic and world markets. Such economically relevant public goods are well known: infrastructure, education, health, and the like. Here we focus on the NSI in particular, showing that the role of the Chinese state in this crucial area is paramount, and that it is performed both directly (through public institutions such as universities and research centers) and indirectly, through the S&T and R&D activities carried out by public industrial enterprises.

Until the mid-1990s, China's research effort was still very modest, even in purely quantitative terms. In the second part of the decade, however, all S&T and R&D indicators started to skyrocket. In 1996–2000 period, S&T expenditure more than doubled[25] and the share of GDP devoted to R&D activities increased sharply, from 0.6 to 1% (see CSY, 2008, Table 20.44). Research output indicators also exhibited a sustained increase: certified patent applications, for instance, more than doubled (see CSY, 2008, Table 20.38 and 20.44, and Table 6.4). The upward trend continued in the

---

[23] The two groups of FDIEs are quite different from each other. HKMEs are mostly constituted by small- and medium-sized firms exhibiting a behavior very similar to privately controlled domestic mixed enterprises. Conversely, as most FFEs are controlled by large TNCs originating from advanced capitalist countries, they are more capital-intensive than HKMEs, and their labor productivity is higher, as well as their contribution to total industrial capitalization, output, and profits.

[24] Such economies are external essentially because the 'true' price of public goods is not and cannot be fully reflected in real-world markets.

[25] In nominal terms.

2000s, at a pace unequalled anywhere else in the world (see Gabriele and Khan, 2008; Hu and Mathews, 2008). During a period of exceptionally fast economic growth, the R&D to GDP ratio kept climbing, reaching 1.13% in 2003 and almost 1.5% (a figure much higher than that of many OECD countries) in 2007 (see Table 6.4). In sum, over little more than one decade, China leapfrogged from an almost insignificant role in the global research scenario to that of one of its main protagonists.

With respect to the respective role of government and industry – contrary to past experience, when research was almost completely confined to universities and government research institutes – most R&D activities in China are presently financed and performed by industry, similarly to the situation prevailing in the advanced capitalist countries. Actually, the share of total R&D performed by industrial enterprises in China (71%) is about the same as in the US, and higher than that of EU27. In China, however, the role of specialized government research institutions (which perform almost one-fifth of total R&D, and actually carry out the most advanced and ambitious research programs) is more relevant than in the advanced capitalist countries. Conversely, the role of universities is correspondingly minor (see Table 6.4).

The role of the public sector at large in propelling China's unprecedented research effort is overwhelming. It has been pointed out that over 70% of China's R&D takes place in the industrial sector (the rest being performed by fully public research centers and universities). An absolute majority of this R&D activity is carried out by enterprises owned or controlled by the state or other public bodies. Most industrial S&T and R&D activities in China are carried out by large and medium-sized industrial enterprises, who contribute over 80% of the total funding for both S&T and R&D activities.[26] In the LME subsector, SOSHEs contribute almost half of the industry's total R&D personnel and over 47% of the funds. Adding the (small) R&D contribution of non-state public enterprises, both figures increase to well over 50%. The bulk of the remaining R&D activities in the LMEs subsector is performed by foreign-owned enterprises, especially by those owned mostly by large TNCs and classified by CSY as FFEs.

FFEs fund over 20% of LMEs's industrial research and employ 15% of the R&D personnel. The correspondent figures for the other group of FDIEs, those owned by entrepreneurs from Macao, Hong Kong, and Taiwan, are both less than 9%. Fully owned private domestic enterprises fund only 7% of the LMEs' R&D effort and employ 8% of the R&D personnel. Among SOSHEs, the most critical role is that of SHMEs, who are at the core of the R&D effort in China's industry, contributing about 27% of LMEs' total R&D

---

[26] LMEs employ 80% of all the S&T personnel and fund over 80% of both S&T and R&D activities of the entire industrial sector (CSY, 2008, Tables 20.39, 20.40).

Table 6.4 US, China, and EU 27: R&D indicators

I R&D personnel (total)

Million						Compound annual growth rate				
	2002	2003	2004	2005	2006	2002	2003	2004	2005	2006
US	NA	NA	NA	NA	NA	NA	NA	NA	NA	NA
China	1.06	1.09	1.15	1.36	1.5	8.2	5.8	5.3	18.4	10.1
EU 27	2.08	2.09	2.12	2.19	2.28	1.7	0.7	1.6	2.9	4.4
Japan	0.86	0.88	0.9	0.92	0.94	NA	2.9	1.6	2.8	1.5

II. GERD: % of GDP and growth rate

	% of GDP					Compound annual growth rate					Av. 2002–2006
	2002	2003	2004	2005	2006	2002	2003	2004	2005	2006	
US	2.66	2.66	2.59	2.62	2.66	-2.1	2.4	0.9	4.2	4.3	1.94
China	1.07	1.13	1.23	1.33	1.42	22	16.1	19.7	16.6	15.8	18.04
EU27	1.77	1.76	1.73	1.74	1.77	1.8	0.8	1.1	2.7	5.1	1.02
Japan	3.17	3.2	3.17	3.32	3.39	1.6	2.5	1.7	7	4.6	3.48

III. GERD Financing by sector (% of total, 2006)

	IE	GOV
US	65	29
China	69	25
EU 27	55	34
Japan	77	23

(continued)

Table 6.4 Continued

Million	Government	Business enterprise sector	Compound annual growth rate

IV. GERD: Performing by sector (% of total, 2006)

	GOV	HE	IE	PNP
US	11.3	13.5	71	4.2
China	19.7	9.2	71.1	0
EU 27	13.4	22.3	63.1	1.2
Japan	8	13	77	2

GOV	Government
IE	Industrial enterprises
HE	Higher education
PNP	Private non profit

Source: Authors' elaboration based on OECD (2008b), Main science and technology indicators.
NA = Not available.

funds and personnel. Thus, SHMEs constitute the most research-oriented sub-component of mixed enterprises, on one hand, and of public industry, on the other hand (see Table 6.5).

These statistical findings allow us to draw a few stylized conclusions. We saw that (public) research centers and universities carry out about 30% of China's total R&D activities, while the rest is carried out in the industrial sector, mostly among LMEs. SOSHEs fund and execute over half of LMEs' R&D effort. Thus, broadly speaking, the public sector as a whole funds and performs about 2/3 of China's R&D activities. Statistical and descriptive evidence shows that two sub-components of public R&D system play a paramount role. One is constituted by government-funded research centers, which perform most of the basic research and truly scientific activities aimed at approaching or surpassing top world knowledge standards in a number of key areas (see Gabriele and Khan, 2008). The other sub-component is that of SHMEs, which carry out the bulk of China's R&D activities in the industrial sector. Most of the remaining R&D activities are carried out by FFEs, while the role of the domestic private sector is minor.

Table 6.5 R&D activities of large- and medium-sized enterprises, 2007

Status of registration	% of total full-time equivalent of R&D personnel (man-year)	Expenditure on R&D (10,000 yuan)
Total		
State-owned and state-holding	49.73	47.60
enterprises (SOSHEs)	76.65	70.88
Domestic-funded enterprises	11.87	8.62
State-owned enterprises	36.43	33.59
Limited liability corporations	11.26	11.84
State sole funded corporations		
Other limited liability corporations	25.17	21.75
Share-holding corporations Ltd.	18.21	17.88
Private enterprises	7.97	6.99
Enterprises with funds from Hong Kong,	8.35	8.68
Macao, Taiwan	15.00	20.44
Foreign funded enterprises		
Mixed enterprises (MEs)	43.38	39.63
State-holding MEs (SHMEs)	26.61	27.14
Private MEs (PrivMEs)	16.78	12.49
SHMEs/MEs	0.61	0.68
SHMEs/SOSHEs (%)	0.54	0.57

Source: CSY (2008).

Conclusions

In this paper, we argue that the role of the state (to be understood as a holistic term referring to the public sector as whole), far from being withering out, is in fact massive, dominant, and crucial to China's industrial development. Actually, it has been strengthened by the successful implementation of the 'keep the big dump the small' policy, which in turn is consistent with a more general strategy shift towards re-centralization in many areas of economic and social policies. This trend is ongoing and is bound to be further intensified by the massive package of fiscal and other interventions made necessary as a response to the world financial and economic crisis.

State-owned and state-holding enterprises are now less numerous, but much larger, more capital- and knowledge-intensive, more productive and more profitable than in the late 1990s. Contrary to popular belief, especially since the mid-2000s, their performance in terms of efficiency and profitability compares favorably with that of private enterprises. The state-controlled sub-sector constituted by state-holding enterprises, in particular, with at its core the 149 large conglomerates managed by SASAC, is in many aspects the most advanced component of China's industry, and the one in which the bulk of in-house R&D activities take place. The role of the public sector, moreover, goes beyond that of those enterprises that are owned or controlled by the state. In the specific Chinese context, many of the most advanced formally private industrial enterprises are in fact related to the public domain by a web of ownership, financial, and other linkages, to an extent that is qualitatively different and deeper than that of their counterparts in capitalist countries. The public sector is paramount in engineering an extraordinary boom in S&T and R&D activities (both inside the industrial sector and outside, in universities and research centers), and in fueling a massive investment drive aimed at enhancing China's infrastructural and human capital environment. These processes are also likely to generate systemic external economies, which are reaped by public and private enterprises alike, contributing to abating their operative costs and to sustain their competitiveness and profitability. Contrary to other analysts, we believe that the dominant role of the state in China's industry (and, more generally, in China's economy) is not merely a possibly necessary – albeit wasteful – evil, which will be superseded once the transition from a centrally planned to a fully capitalist modern economy will be completed. We rather see it as an ever-evolving but structural characteristic of China's peculiar form of market socialism.

References

Akyuz, Y and Gore, C. (1996): The investment-profits nexus in East Asian industrialization. *World Development* 24(3).

Arrighi, G. (2007): Adam Smith in Beijing: Lineages of the twenty-first century, http://www.amazon.com/Adam-Smith-Beijing-Lineages-Twenty-First/dp/1844671046-#.

Chang, G. (2008): Restructuring of large industrial SOEs in transitional China: A case study in Lanzhou. *Tijdschrift voor Economische en Sociale Geografie* 99(1): 84–93.

Chen, G, Firth, M and Xu, L. (2009): Does the type of ownership control matter? Evidence from China's listed companies. *Journal of Banking & Finance* 33(1): 171–181.

Chen, J. (2001): Ownership structure as corporate governance mechanism: Evidence from Chinese listed companies. *Economics of Plannning* 34(2001): 53–72.

Chen, Y-C. (2008): Why do multinational corporations locate their advanced R&D centres in Beijing? *The Journal of Development Studies* 44(5): 622.

Cull, R and Xu, LC. (2003): Who gets credit? The behavior of bureaucrats and state banks in allocating credit to Chinese state-owned enterprises. *Journal of Development Economics* 71: 533–559.

Delios, A, Wu, ZJ and Zhou, N. (2006): A new perspective on ownership identities in China's listed companies. *Management and Organization Review* 2(3): 319–343.

Dong, X-Y and Putterman, L. (2003): Soft budget constraints, social burdens, and labor redundancy in China's state industry. *Journal of Comparative Economics* 3(1): 110–133.

Dong, X-Y and Xu, LC. (2008): The impact of China's millennium labour restructuring program on firm performance and employee earnings. *The Economics of Transition*. 16(2): 223–245.

Dougherty, S, Herd, R and He, P. (2007): Has a private sector emerged in China's industry? Evidence from a quarter of a million Chinese firms. *China Economic Review* 18(3): 309–334, Elsevier.

Fisher-Vanden, K, Jefferson, G, Ma, J and Xu, J. (2006): Technology development and energy productivity in China. *Energy Economics* 28(5/6): 690–705.

Fisher-Vanden, K and Jefferson, GH. (2008): Technology diversity and development: Evidence from China's industrial enterprises. *Journal of Comparative Economics* 36(4): 658–672.

Gabriele, A and Khan, AH. (2008): *Enhancing technological progress in a market-socialist context: China's national innovation system at the crossroads* Unpublished, MPRA paper No.10695, in http://mpra.ub.uni-muenchen.de/10695/1/MPRA_paper_10695.pdf.

Gabriele, A and Schettino, F. (2008): *Market socialism as a distinct socioeconomic formation internal to the modern mode of production* MPRA paper No.7942, available in http://mpra.ub.uni-muenchen.de/7942/.

Girma, S and Gong, Y. (2008): FDI, linkages and the efficiency of state-owned enterprises in China. *The Journal of Development Studies* 44(5): 728.

Gul, FA and Zhao, R. (2001): *Corporate governance and performance in Chinese listed companies* Paper presented at the AAA International Accounting Section, Phoenix, AZ, January.

Holz, CA. (2002): Long live China's state-owned enterprises: Deflating the myth of poor financial performance. *Journal of Asian Economics* 13(4): 493–529.

Holz, CA and Lin, YM. (2001): The 1997–1998 break in industrial statistics: Facts and appraisal. *China Economic Review* 12(4): 303–316.

Hovey, M. (2005): Do ownership structures stimulate the performance of listed firms in China? Proceedings of the 10th AIBF Banking and Finance Conference, 30 September.

Hu, AG, Jefferson, GH and Jinchang, Q. (2005): R&D and technology transfer: Firm-level evidence from Chinese industry review of economics and statistics. 87(4): 689–700.

Hu, MC and Mathews, JA. (2008): China's national innovative capacity. *Research Policy* 37(3): 1465–1479.

Hu, G and Jefferson, GH. (2004): Returns to research and development in Chinese industry: Evidence from state-owned enterprises in Beijing. *China Economic Review* 15(1): 86–107.

Hu, G and Jefferson, GH. (2005): A great wall of patents: What is behind China's recent patent explosion? *New Economist*, http://people.brandeis.edu.

Jefferson, G, Rawski, T and Zhang, Y (2008): Productivity growth and convergence across China's industrial economy. *Journal of Chinese Economic and Business Studies* 6(2): 121–140, Taylor and Francis Journals.

Jia, J, Sun, Q and Tong, W. (2005): Privatization via an oversea listing: Evidence from China's H-share firms. *Financial Management* (Autumn): 5–30.

Kanbur, R, Quian, Y and Zhang, X. (2008): Symposium on market development and inequality in China. *The Economics of Transition* 16(1): 1–5.

Kroeber, A. (2008): Time for a new story. *China Economic Quarterly* 12(2008): 9–33.

Kroeber, A and Yao, R. (2008): Large and in charge. *Financial Times*, 14 July.

Li, W and Putterman, L. (2008): Reforming China's SOEs: An overview. *Comparative Economic Studies* 50: 353–380.

Lindbeck, A. (2008): Economic-social interaction in China. *The Economics of Transition* 16(1): 113–139.

Mandel, M. (2004): China moves into second place for R&D, http://www.business week.com/the_thread/economicsunbound/archives/2006/12/china_moves_int.html.

Mazzoleni, R. (2008): Catching up and academic institutions: A comparative study of past national experiences. *The Journal of Development studies* 44(5): 678.

McGregor, R. (2007): China develops research sector. *Financial Times* 3 September.

Ministry of Commerce. (2008): Two thirds of China's SOE giants become shareholding companies, http://english.mofcom.gov.cn/aarticle/counselorsreport/western asiaandafricareport/200808/20080805745646.html.

Morel, E. (2006): The changing role of state-owned enterprises in Chinese industrial research: New goals, ownership, and management. University of Kansas, Motorola Foundation Young Scholar, October 2006.

National Bureau of Statistics of P.R.C. (2008): *China Statistical Yearbook (CSY)*.

Naughton, B. (2008a): SOE policy, Profiting the SASAC way. *China Economic Quarterly* (June): 19–26.

Naughton, B. (2008b): Strengthening the center, and premier Wen Jiabao. *China Leadership Monitor* (21): 1–10.

Naughton, T and Hovey, M. (2007): A survey of enterprise reforms in China: The way forward. *Economic Systems* 31(2): 138–156.

Niosi, J. (2008): Technology, development and innovation systems: An introduction. *The Journal of Development Studies* 44(5): 613–621.

OECD. (2008a): *Reviews of Innovation Policy: China*, pp. 648, ISBN 978-92-64-03981-0.

OECD. (2008b): *Main Science and Technology Indicators*, Vol. 2008, No. 1, June, pp. 88–221.

Qi, DQ, Wu, W, and Zhang, H. (2000): Shareholding structure and corporate performance of partially privatized firms: Evidence from listed Chinese companies. *Pacific-Basin Finance Journal* 8(5): 587–610.

Qiu, J, Aivazian, V and Ge, Y. (2005a): Corporate governance and manager turnover: An unusual social experiment. *Journal of Banking and Finance* 26(6): 1459–1481.

Qiu, J, Aivazian, V and Ge, Y. (2005b): Can corporatization improve the performance of SOEs even without privatization? *Journal of Corporate Finance* 11(5): 791–808.

Sun, Q and Tong, WH. (2003): China share issue privatization: The extent of its success. *Journal of Financial Economics* 70(2003): 183–222.

Sun, Q, Tong, WHS and Tong, J. (2002): How does government ownership affect firm performance? Evidence from China's privatization experience. *Journal of Business Finance & Accounting* 29(2002): 1–27.

Wang, C. (2005): Ownership and operating performance of Chinese IPOs. *Journal of Banking & Finance* 29(2005): 1835–1856.

Wei, Z and Varela, O. (2003): State equity ownership and firm market performance: Evidence from China's newly privatized firms. *Global Finance Journal* 14(2003): 65–82.

Wildau, G. (2008): Albatross turns phoenix. *China Economic Quarterly* 12(2): 27–33.

Wong, SML, Opper, S and Hu, R. (2004): Shareholding structure, depoliticization and firm performance: Lessons from China's listed firms. *Economics of Transition* 12(2004): 29–66.

Xu, XN and Wang, Y (1999): Ownership, structure and corporate governance in Chinese stock companies. *China Economic Review* 10: 75–98.

Yu, J and Nijkamp, P. (2008): Ownership, R&D and Productivity change: Assessing the Catch-up in China's High-Tech Industries, Department of Spatial Economics, University of Amsterdam, Research Memorandum no. 10, 2008, http://dare.ubvu.vu.nl//handle/1871/15473.

Zhang, LY (2004): The roles of corporatization and stock market listing in reforming China's state industry. *World Development* 32(12): 2031–2047.

Zhang, Y and Parker, D. (2004): Labour and total factor productivity in the Chinese electronics industry in the 1990s. *International Review of Applied Economics* 18(1): 1-22 1465-3486.

Zheng, JJ, Liu, X and Bigsten, A. (2000): *Efficiency, technical progress, and best practice in Chinese state enterprises (1980–1994)*. Working Papers in Economics no 30, September 2000, Department of Economics Göteborg University.

7
Reforming China's SOEs:
An Overview

Weiye Li[1] and Louis Putterman[2]
[1]*Charles River Associates, USA; and* [2]*Brown University, USA*

After three decades of reform, state ownership still plays a significant if diminishing role in China's industrial sector. We survey studies that focus on the impact of reform on China's SOEs both during the early reform years from 1979 to 1992 and during the years of privatisation and corporatisation since 1993. Most studies find evidence that reforms led to productivity growth in both periods, with both the performance gap and the formal distinction between SOEs and non-SOEs appearing to narrow since the late 1990s.

Introduction

Since China began its long march from the ultra-left socialism of the Mao years toward more market-embracing policies in 1979, its economy has logged the longest sustained period of rapid economic growth in history, by World Bank estimates raising its GDP by a factor of 12 and its GDP per capita by a factor of nine during the 27 years to 2006. The same period has seen China's industrial output grow at least 12-fold, with dramatic changes in industrial structure. Valued at the more market-based prices of 2004, agriculture's share of GDP fell from 42% in 1978 to 13% in 2004, industry's share rose from 29% of GDP to 46% of GDP, and the service sector increased its share from 30% to 40% of GDP (Naughton, 2007, pp. 154–155).[1] The

---

[1] The estimated 12-fold increase in GDP plus Naughton's constant price estimates of industry's output shares at the beginning and end of the period implies that industrial output grew 19-fold. Note that the data indicate far less structural change if current prices, which were artificially high for industry and low for agriculture in 1978, are used.

Reprinted with permission from Association of Comparative Economic Studies. All rights reserved. *Comparative Economic Studies* (2008) 50, 353–380.

total number of secondary industry (including mining, manufacturing, construction, and utilities) workers increased from 69 million to 169 million, and their share of the labour force rose from 17% in 1978 to 22% in 2004, while the urban share of the country's population rose from under 20% to well over 40%.[2]

As late as 1985, petroleum was China's largest single export, accounting for 20% of export earnings. Between 1985 and 1995, China's exports saw a dramatic shift to labour-intensive commodities and a correspondingly large decline in natural resource-based products. According to the International Economic Databank (IEDB), the share of labour intensive products in China's exports increased from 37% in 1984 to 54% in 1994, while the share of agricultural and minerals-intensive products together declined from 49% to 15%.

During the more than quarter century of system change in China, the role and nature of state-owned industrial enterprises has been continuously evolving. In 1980, SOEs were at the heart of China's industrial sector, accounting for 76% of gross industrial output (Jefferson and Singh, 1998, p. 27) and 57% of industrial employment (China Statistical Yearbook 1999, Chapter 5). The SOE share of total industrial output declined steadily, from 77% in 1978 to only 49.6% in 1998. Industrial SOE profits were 15% of GDP in 1978, but fell below 2% of GDP in 1996 and 1997. By 2004, few SOEs remained in their original form, yet some 38% of industrial output was being produced by firms classified as state-owned and by corporations the majority of whose shares were owned by government entities.[3] More privatisation is in the offing, yet a large role for state ownership seems assured at least into the next decade.

SOEs also changed qualitatively, from being units in a command economy tasked with meeting quantitative targets and providing comprehensive services to their employees, to being (in the 1980s and early 1990s) enterprises responding to the price signals of a market economy but retaining the basic SOE organisational form and enjoying easy access to bank credit, to their most recent incarnation as corporations, often with some private shareholders, facing at least a somewhat more disciplined banking system and, for many of the largest among them, an active stock market.

---

[2] China Statistical Yearbook 2006, Chapter 5. An incomplete and subsequently discontinued series shows that manufacturing workforce increased from 53 million in 1978 to 83 million in 2002.

[3] A *caveat* is that, as pointed out by Jefferson and Su (2006), just as many enterprises no longer called state-owned have the state as their largest or majority shareholder, so too some enterprises officially classified as state-owned have only a minority of assets owned by the state. To quote Jefferson and Su (p. 148): 'The association between formal ownership classification and the ownership structure of the assets has become increasingly fluid.'

This paper surveys the literature on the impacts of the reforms of the 1980s and 1990s on state-owned industrial enterprises in China, asking whether and to what degree the introduction of market forces and incentives in the 1980s, and of corporatisation in the 1990s, improved productive efficiency. There is much that the paper does not do, for instance it does not deal extensively with industrial firms of other ownership types, nor does it adequately discuss enterprise finance, the employment effects of SOE reform, or papers focusing on the selection of enterprises for privatisation. Beginning our research with broad ambitions, we were humbled by the size and complexity of the literature on state industry in the world's largest transition economy, and have accomplished only what we could do in limited time.

The paper is organised as follows: The first section gives a brief overview of the process of reform in China's industrial sector and especially its SOEs, with three sub-sections that explain our reform periodisation, then describe the first and second reforms periods in somewhat more detail. The middle two sections survey studies of reform's impacts on SOE performance, with the second section focusing on studies of the reforms up to 1992 and the third section dealing with studies of the reforms from the mid-1990s to the present. In those sections, we devote particular attention to econometric studies of enterprise-level data. The fourth section provides concluding remarks.

Background and Overview

Two phases and two dimensions of industrial reform

In the early 1990s, it was common to contrast China's reform process with the transitions from socialism in East and Central Europe and the former Soviet Union, describing the former as 'gradual' or 'evolutionary' and the latter as 'Big Bang (style)' or 'revolutionary' in nature. Indeed, China's reform process to that time has been called a 'reform without losers' (Lau *et al.*, 2000). Agricultural incomes rose rapidly in the early 1980s, helping to lift at least 200 million people in poorer parts of the country above national and international poverty lines and making a large contribution to the reduction of the *global* poverty headcount (Sala-i-Martin, 2006). By 2000, 76% of the *rural* population aged 16–20 had some kind of off-farm work, and three quarters of these were not working in agriculture even part time (Naughton, 2007, p. 191). Millions exiting agriculture due to increasing farm labour efficiency found employment in township and village enterprises (TVEs), a substantial number of them in industrial jobs. TVE employment grew from 28 million in 1978 to a peak of 135 million in 1996, a 9% annual growth rate. TVE value added, which accounted for less than 6% of GDP in 1978, increased to 26% of GDP in 1996. TVEs' share of industrial output increased from 9% in 1979 to 30% in 1990 and 47% in 2000 (Yano and Shiraishi, 2004; Fu and Balasubramanyam, 2003).

In urban China, initial changes were less dramatic and incomes increased more slowly during the first few reform years. Nonetheless, there was income growth for most urban residents, and its rate of increase accelerated from the mid-1980s so as to achieve the same overall growth as had rural incomes and to restore the old rural-to-urban income gap by 1992. Until that year, at least, state enterprise employment continued to be viewed as attractive from the standpoints of wages, benefits, and job security, and employment in state-owned industrial enterprises grew from 58 million in 1978 to 75 million in 1996.

The sharp difference between China's and the ex-Communist countries' reforms began to blur when, after years of deepening SOE losses, declining state revenues, and a massive accumulation of non-performing loans by the banking system, China's leaders decided to push reform to a new stage. As part of the re-invigoration of the reform process that followed an inter-vention by Deng Xiao-ping in 1992, a new Company Law was adopted in 1994, providing a framework for a process of ownership restructuring that was to include the conversion of SOEs into corporations. A new 'reform with losers' (Naughton, 2007, p. 91) phase began as millions of employ-ees lost their jobs in SOEs, urban collective enterprises, and government and public service units. Layoffs began to surge in 1995, and in the 4-year period from 1996 to 1999 an average of seven million workers were laid off annually, with layoffs exceeding 50 million employees between 1993 and 2004 (Dong and Xu, 2008). According to a retrospective panel survey of 683 firms in 11 cities reported by Garnaut *et al.* (2005, p. 5), 86% of all SOEs had been through the new restructuring process called *gaizhi* (change of system) by the end of 2001. It took various forms, including internal restructuring, corporatisation and public listing of shares, sale, lease, joint ventures, and bankruptcy. Among the surveyed mid- and large-scale SOEs that were restructured, 13% had gone through bankruptcy or debt-equity swaps, 28% were sold or leased out to private owners, 27% introduced employee shareholding, 20% went through internal restructuring, 8% went through ownership diversification including public offerings and pri-vate placement to outside investors, and the remaining 4% became joint ventures. In more than 70% of these cases, *gaizhi* involved the transfer of at least a portion of ownership from the state to private hands (Garnaut *et al.*, 2005, pp. 50–51). Yet despite the disappearance of the smaller SOEs and the appearance of significant pain for SOE employees, in 2004 state-owned enterprises continued to account for 11% of China's industrial output, and the state continued to be the largest shareholder in enterprises accounting for another 21%.

On the Shenzhen and Shanghai stock markets, started in 1991 and trading shares valued at roughly 5% of China's GDP as of 2005,[4] private owners obtained holdings averaging about a third of the shares of corporatised SOEs, but direct and indirect state ownership remained dominant. In one careful study that included 95% of the 1,160 companies with shares listed on the exchange as of 2000 (Liu and Sun, 2003), 8.5% were directly controlled by government departments or agencies. Indirect control was another matter, however. Many of the non-tradable shares of these listed enterprises were in the hands of state wholly owned holding companies or state-controlled non-listed holding companies. When all of these indirect ways that the state ultimately controlled listed companies are combined, the dominant shareholder in 2001 turned out to be the state in 84% of the companies. The 'state' in these cases, of course, includes many different governmental bodies, ranging from central government bureaus to provincial bureaus and many other types of state units.[5]

It is always important to keep in mind that industrial reform in China has progressed simultaneously in two distinct dimensions. Along one dimension, the SOE share of industrial employment and output declined as other kinds of enterprise, initially semi-socialist (TVEs and collectively owned enterprises (COEs)), eventually private (including foreign), came to account for larger and larger shares. Outright privatisation of hundreds of smaller SOEs took place in the 1990s, but the contribution of this privatisation wave to the decline in the SOE share of output was modest compared to that of the entry of non-state enterprises. The second dimension of industrial reform is the one on which we focus in this paper: the gradual transformation of the SOEs themselves, first into the semi-reformed entities that officials hoped could survive in an emerging market economy, and then into corporations facing harder budget constraints with more arms-length control by public asset managers and with some non-public share ownership and share-trading.

Pre-reform, early reform

The many lives of the Chinese state enterprise can be broadly divided into three principal periods. During the 1950s to 1970s, Chinese SOEs fulfilled the traditional role of enterprises in a command economy, being assigned responsibility for meeting specific output targets with an agreed number of employees and payroll, and with assigned allocations of both capital goods and intermediate inputs. Individual enterprises were not judged by profitability, but by fulfilling their assigned roles. To be sure, direction of small and medium enterprises was lodged more at provincial and municipal than

---

[4] If non-circulating shares are included and assumed to be of equal value, the companies traded would have been valued at closer to 18% of GDP in that year.
[5] Yusuf *et al.*, p. 89.

at central government levels, and the economy was governed as much by bureaucratic bargaining and inertia as by fully elaborated plans. And as in all planned economies, profits were by no means irrelevant at the aggregate level, as prices were rigged to generate government revenue that could be plowed back into capital formation. But prices were not meant to serve as guides for production decisions, and enterprise performance was judged by output, not profit.

From 1979 to 1992 – and especially during the half decade from 1984 to 1989 – China's SOEs were the objects of an experiment in 'market socialism'.[6] During this period, they gradually adjusted their orientations away from plans and targets and towards markets and profitability. The strategy of this reform phase borrowed heavily from that used in China's agricultural sector during 1979–1983, especially its 'two tier' (within plan, above plan) feature. Quantity targets were retained but were kept low, and enterprises were encouraged to sell above-plan output and to obtain out-of-plan inputs in market-type transactions at unregulated prices, so that, on the margin, the enterprises' production decisions would be responding to market forces even if many of the transactions were initially with other state units (Byrd, 1989). In a process aptly termed 'growing out of the plan' (Naughton, 1995), the share of an enterprise's activity based on plan targets and input provision would decline, and the share based on autonomous decision-making and market prices would steadily increase. Enterprise financing was shifted from the old system of government grants to a new system of reliance on bank loans repayable with interest, with the hope of signalling a real cost of capital. New hiring began to be done on the basis of shorter-term contracts, to last only 5 years instead of the implicit lifetime contract. To stimulate managers' interest in profit-making, profits were given an important place among the criteria for judging managerial success, enterprises were permitted to retain a portion of profits, some of it for managerial bonuses, and a succession of arrangements to raise the proportion of marginal profits retained were tried out. These included the 'manager contract responsibility system', embraced by the 13th National Party Congress in October 1987, under which the terms of the contracts were extended for at least 3 years (to avoid annual bargaining) and more control rights were delegated to managers (Yusuf *et al.*, 2006, p. 59).

With planned output procurement and input supply phased out, the SOEs, local government owned TVEs, and urban COEs would comprise a predominantly public and collectively owned sector within a market economy in which production would be coordinated by market forces, rather than plans,

---

[6] On the application of the 'market socialist' concept to China, see Kornai and Qian, eds. (2008). Ironically, the Chinese government itself did not adopt the term 'socialist market economy' until after this period had ended and policies were shifting in the direction of still more private ownership.

and where profitability would be at least the most important if not the only determinant of enterprise survival and growth.[7] The high growth sustained by China's economy during most of this period, and the high proportions of output for which the public and collective enterprises were responsible,[8] led some commentators to see in the Chinese case evidence that competition and markets were more important to economic efficiency than private property rights. Even in agriculture, where households had become independent cultivators, farmland was public property contracted out to them by village government.[9]

Reform heats up

Numerous factors combined to bring the early market-socialist phase of reform to a close. On the level of the political elite, those for whom the economic and technological gaps with once-faster-growing Asian tigers had been the main spur to reform probably had little interest in ideological 'halfway houses' like market socialism. They had moved slowly in earlier years mainly to assuage aging revolutionaries. With the latter shuffling off the stage as China moved into the 1990s, this was no longer a consideration. A decade and a half of rapid growth, plus the recent success at staying in power despite popular unrest, may also have emboldened leaders to undertake more radical reforms at the risk of harming some urban workers. Finally, the slowing of the reform process during the 1989–1991 post-Tiananmen-crackdown period had brought with it a deceleration of economic growth, convincing many that the only way forward lay in further reform (Lardy, 2001; Sprayregen *et al.,* 2004).

There were immediate economic drivers as well. As discussed further in the next section, SOE profits had fallen steadily, the ratio of debt to assets had risen sharply, and the stock of non-performing loans on the books of the state banks had grown to alarming proportions.

The adoption of the Company Law in 1994 and the Party's adoption of the policy of 'grasping the large and letting go of the small' (adopted formally at the 15th CPC National Congress) in 1997 marked a turning point for the state sector. 'Letting go of the small' meant letting provincial and lower-level governments dispose of their loss-making enterprises as they

---

[7] As an example of the phasing out of planned allocation, Naughton (2007, p. 93) reports that in the steel industry, the proportion of output allocated by the central government fell to 50% in 1984 and to 7% in 1995.

[8] A total of 70.6% in 1995, of which 34.0% was due to state enterprises, and 36.6% to collective ones (including TVEs).

[9] Commentaries along the lines mentioned include Weitzman and Xu (1994), and Ellerman and Stiglitz (2001). For an interpretive essay on why China experimented with 'market socialist' forms before moving further toward private property rights, see Putterman (2008).

would, and between 1995 and 2000 some 82% of a total of 59,410 small- and medium-sized SOEs, which together accounted for about 33% of overall SOE sector output, underwent restructuring. By the end of 1998, more than 80% of state and collective firms at the level of the county or below had gone through fundamental restructuring, involving direct privatisation in most cases (Zhao, 2006).

'Grasping the large' meant that a small number of large enterprises in industries viewed as strategically important for the government to control, including petroleum, metallurgy, electricity, military industry, and telecommunications, were restructured and placed under the supervision of a newly created State Asset Supervision and Administration Commission (SASAC). Other relatively large SOEs, although not clearly slated for lasting government control, were also not liquidated or privatised outright. These companies were converted to joint stock corporations some shares of which were sold to workers and managers, others of which were made available for purchase and trading by individuals on the Shenzhen, Shanghai, and Hong Kong stock exchanges. Of the remaining shares, the majority was typically held by governmental entities such as provincial SASACs, and by so-called 'legal persons', most of these also public or semi-public entities. During most of 1990s, the limit on the private ownership stake in China's listed firms stood at one-third. Since 2000, however, further change has occurred, with increasing quantities of state-owned shares being sold to non-state entities, including, since 2002, qualified foreign-based institutional investors such as Goldman Sachs, Deutsche Bank, and Merrill Lynch International. According to China Securities Regulatory Commission research, by the end of 2002 some 338 listed companies had experienced a change in control, that is, in the identity of the largest single shareholder (Green, 2003). The so-called 'two-thirds privatization', meaning the rendering tradable of that roughly two-thirds of corporate shares still typically held by the state and state-linked 'legal persons' in the early 2000s, was supported by promulgation of procedures for 'share right splits' in 2005, although tradability of all shares still appears to be unlikely before the early 2010s.[10]

SOEs Entering the Market, 1979–1992

What do detailed studies of Chinese industrial data tell us about the impact of early reforms on enterprise performance? We consider two kinds of studies

---

[10] Share Right Split refers to a process of negotiation between tradable shareholders and the holders of non-tradable shares to set rates of parity between newly released and already traded shares, or to provide alternative forms of compensation, so as to protect incumbent shareholders from suffering declines in wealth as new shares come on the market. On the predicted time-line of transition to full tradability, see Ahn and Cogman (2007).

of the effectiveness of enterprise reform in China in this period. The first type looks at how the productivity of SOEs as a group increased over time, seeking evidence of gains that might be attributed to reform by comparing outcomes and trends of the 1980s and early 1990s to those of the pre-reform era or to the contemporaneous performance of non-state enterprises, which in this period were mainly collectively owned. The second takes advantage of variation in the introduction of specific reform measures at the enterprise level and asks whether enterprises that adopted those measures (or adopted them sooner) did better than others.

Pre- *versus* post-reform and state *versus* non-state comparisons

In the category of studies contrasting performance over time and across enterprise types, we discuss papers by Chen *et al.* (1988) and Jefferson *et al.* (1992, 1996), along with some criticisms of their papers by Woo *et al.* (1993, 1994). Chen *et al.* use annual data for 1953–1985 for aggregate employment, capital stock, and output of independent accounting units within state industry to study trends in multifactor productivity. They conduct growth accounting exercises that make use of both Cobb-Douglas and translog production function estimates of capital and labour output elasticities, using both conventional input series and series adjusted by use of an improved capital price deflator and by removing inputs used to provide services to the enterprises' workforces (such as construction of employee housing). On the basis of the unadjusted data, they find that multifactor productivity rose during 1953–1957 but then fluctuated and stood roughly back at the 1953 level in 1977, followed by a period of fairly strong growth to 1985. The adjusted data yield estimates of stronger growth in the mid-1950s and 1978–1985, with a mild upward trend even during the years of fluctuating productivity, 1957–1978. Because the estimates show long-term productivity growing at only about 1% between 1957 and 1978 *versus* between 4.8% and 5.9% (depending on the precise estimate) from 1978 to 1985, they support the proposition that productivity growth improved noticeably in the early reform period.[11]

Jefferson *et al.* (1992, 1996) carry out similar analyses, using annual observations aggregated to the national level, for the early reform years 1978–1988 and 1980–1992, respectively. These investigations differ from that of Chen *et al.* in using gross rather than net output and considering intermediate inputs as well as capital and labour. Also, they study the

---

[11] Interestingly, they also show productivity to be growing rapidly (at between 3.3% and 5.1%) during 1953–1957, the years of China's Soviet-style and Soviet-aided First Five-Year Plan. Much the same paradox exists for China's agricultural performance data, where the fastest growth rates are registered during 1953–1957, years of gradual collectivisation and imposition of state agricultural procurement, and 1978–1984, years of market liberalisation and decollectivisation of farm production.

productivity trend of government-sponsored collective enterprises above the village level, which includes rural township enterprises and urban COEs, making possible inter-sectoral comparisons. Both papers find positive but modest total factor productivity growth in the state sector, averaging about 2.5% a year and accounting for somewhat under half of total output growth, with the later paper also noting a slow-down in productivity growth during 1988–1992 (the period marked by inflation-fighting efforts and including the post-Tiananmen political crack-down). They find substantially higher rates of TFP growth in the collective sector, around 4.6% according to Jefferson *et al.* (1992), suggesting that the sector's harder budget constraints and more labour-using technology choices led to greater dynamic efficiency.

The favourable assessment of productivity growth in Jefferson *et al.* (1992) is challenged by Woo *et al.* (1993, 1994), who analyse data on a sample of state-owned enterprises and another of TVEs. They find zero TFP growth in SOEs and 8% annual TFP growth in the TVEs. The two sets of studies differ in that Jefferson *et al.* but not Woo *et al.* use a different price deflator for inputs than for outputs, the former but not the latter use a frontier production function approach, and the former but not the latter use aggregate rather than enterprise-level data. Woo *et al.* argue that the price deflators employed by Jefferson *et al.* upwardly bias their estimates of TFP growth in the SOE sector. In a response, Jefferson *et al.* (1994), while not ruling out the possibility of error in constructing their deflator for intermediate goods, defend the need to control for input and output price trends separately. They raise several concerns about Woo *et al.*'s sample data, including that the sample firms appear more closely tied to the plan than state industry as a whole, that the ratio of direct wage payments to value added for the sample firms is surprising high, and that labour's income share in the sample firms grows surprisingly fast.

Inter-enterprise comparisons

We next turn to our second category of studies, those that make possible more direct inferences regarding the impact of reforms by considering variation among individual SOEs in the timing or type of reform measures implemented. We consider, within this class, papers by Lee (1990), Groves *et al.* (1994, 1995), Li (1997), and Shirley and Xu (2001).

Lee (1990) uses 1986 data for 75 large- and medium-sized state enterprises in the Chinese steel industry to test for individual and combined effects of three reform elements, the Contract Management System, Managerial Responsibility System, and the Internal Contract System, each controlled for by a dummy variable. He finds that adoption of any one reform measure has no significant effect on enterprise output, while some combinations of reform measures have a significant positive output effect. The size of the overall reform effect is small, however, less than 3% when the effects of original firm superiority are taken into account. To deal with the possibility that better performing enterprises were chosen for the reform experiments and that the results may therefore not reflect causality running from reform to performance, Lee first runs regression of the reform measure of 1986 on the input and output data of 1980. The results indicate that reverse causality is not significant. He then identifies enterprises that were better performing in 1980 and adds a dummy variable controlling for this to his regressions for 1986. The results imply that both reform measures and original superiority contribute to higher productive efficiency in 1986.

Groves *et al.* (1994) use data from a survey of more than 700 enterprises observed annually during 1980–1989, the C.A.S.S. survey,[12] to study the impact of grants of managerial autonomy on output, and that of increases in the proportion of profit retained by the enterprises on managerial performance. They find that output autonomy and a higher profit retention rate were associated with increases in bonuses as a share of compensation, in bonus per employee, and in reliance on shorter-term contract workers. Further, higher values of the bonus and short-term contract variables, instrumented by their lagged values, had significant positive effects on output, controlling for labour, capital, and materials, and firm and year fixed effects. And enterprise autonomy and a higher profit retention rate improved profit per employee. However, the government budget did not seem to have benefited from the reforms, there being no evidence that the amount of profit remitted to the state increased with these measures. Remitted profit per employee was positively associated with output autonomy in one industry (building materials), but it was significantly negatively associated with marginal profit-retention rates in two industries (building materials and electronics). In their second paper, Groves *et al.* (1995) use the same data set to study incentives and competition in the managerial labour market. They find that poorly performing firms were more likely to have a new manager selected by auction, to be required to post a higher security deposit, and to be subject to more frequent contract review. They find that managerial pay was linked to the firm's sales and profits, and that use of managerial contracts and allocation of managerial positions by auction strengthened the profit link and weakened the sales link. They treat this as evidence that China had achieved some success in creating managerial incentives to increase profitability in SOEs of the early reform era.

Wei Li (1997) also studies the impact of reform and institutional environment measures on productivity using a panel of enterprise survey data

---

[12] This survey was conducted by the Economic Research Institute of the Chinese Academy of Social Science. It covers 769 state-owned enterprises over the years 1980–1989. The central government directly managed 9% of the sample enterprises, provincial governments 10%, municipal governments 72%, and county governments the remaining 9%. Firms were surveyed in four provinces – Jiangsu, Jilin, Shanxi, and Sichuan – that together contributed over 20% of China's industrial output at the time.

covering 272 of the enterprises in the same C.A.S.S. survey, enterprises belonging to four broad industrial sectors in the years 1980–1989. After controlling for enterprise-specific effects by transforming the data to within-firm deviations, and using instruments to predict the profit share, change in factor use and change in the ratio of output to input prices, Li estimates a production function augmented by institutional parameters, jointly estimating a regression for each year as a set of seemingly unrelated regressions. His results show that growth of bonuses had a significant positive impact on the growth of total factor productivity, that competition spurred growth of productivity, and that most productivity growth was attributable to improved incentives.

Finally, Shirley and Xu (2001) use data on 560 SOEs, also in the C.A.S.S. survey, to study the impact on enterprise productivity of performance contracts between SOE managers and the government. Variation in contract terms, time of adoption, and the fact that 10% of the sample enterprises had not adopted such a contract at the end of the study period (1980–1989) permit identification of the effect of the performance contracts. The authors conclude that the contracts did *not* improve performance on average, but that they *did* do so in a little over half of the participating enterprises, which were more likely to be smaller, to face more competition, and to be under the oversight of governments at more local levels. Stronger incentives, longer terms, and managerial bonds were other features associated with better outcomes.

Thus, the available studies find that productivity was increasing in China's SOEs during the 1980s at rates almost certainly higher than had been seen in the 1960s and 1970s but almost certainly lower than those in the collective enterprise sector during the same decade. Studies using enterprise-level data and variation on the timing and details of reforms generally show some positive impact on SOE productivity of the measures considered. A comprehensive picture is difficult to obtain, however, due to the limited number of high-quality studies, the different measures focused on, the different strategies for controlling for the endogeneity of reform measure adoption, and the relatively small data sets used in some studies.

The profitability dilemma

Ultimately, the biggest challenge facing the SOEs during the first decade and a half of China's reforms came from the fact that increasingly competitive market conditions were eroding profits and undermining the ability of SOEs to generate revenues for their government owners and to repay the loans with which they met their financing requirements. As detailed by Naughton (1992), even as output per unit of inputs was rising, the average rate of profit earned by China's SOEs was falling, from 25.2% in 1980 to 16.8% in 1989. Holz (2003) puts profit per unit of equity for the SOE sector at 7.7% in 1993, 6.7% in 1994, 4.1% in 1995, and 2.2% in 1996.[13] Industrial SOE profits had fallen from 14% of GDP in 1978 to 2% of GDP in 1992, with only about half of that decline expected due to the declining SOE share of industrial output.[14] Government revenues, which had overwhelmingly come from SOE profits, had fallen correspondingly. Meanwhile, SOEs had gone from obtaining 62% of their investment in fixed capital from government grants in 1978 to obtaining less than 3% this way by 1997, with bank credit making up most of the difference. As SOEs' ratio of debt to equity climbed from 12% in 1978 to 211% in 1994 (Naughton 2007, p. 307), estimates were suggesting that upwards of half of the loans outstanding of the Chinese banking system – the bulk of it loaned to SOEs – could be considered non-performing.[15]

Not all of these trends were in principle bad ones. Naughton (1992) argued persuasively that the falling rate of profit in the SOE sector – and by the mid-1990s in the TVE sector as well – was largely a sign of the erosion of the monopoly profit rates that had been built into the pre-reform system as a way of financing the state's capital-intensive investment programme. Letting local governments start new SOEs, COEs, and TVEs, and letting enterprises compete with each other and determine their own prices, was bound to reduce profit rates if real competition emerged. The trend had not hurt saving rates, which remained high as China's people put as much into the banking system in the form of household savings as the state was losing in enterprise profits. Enterprise reliance on bank loans, and the debt-asset ratio along with it, was bound to rise due to the intentional reform policy of phasing out direct government financing of investment so that enterprises would have to rely on retained earnings and interest-carrying loans. And much of the profitability differential between SOEs and other enterprises could be attributed to SOEs' historical capital intensity, social welfare obligations, and high tax burdens.[16]

Yet some of the trends were clearly unsustainable. The mounting stock of non-performing loans indicated that neither the state banks nor the SOEs

---

[13] Although the years in question fall in the second stage of our reform periodisation, the reported profits are nevertheless indicative of the trends that motivated changes that began to be adopted in 1994 but the effects of which would not be felt until the late 1990s.

[14] The SOE share of total industrial output had declined from 77% in 1978 to 33% in 1996; see Naughton (2007, p. 300).

[15] While reliable estimates for the mid-1990s are hard to come by, a careful estimate of the total non-performing loans of China's main banks, including loans already taken off the books of the banks and given over to asset management companies tasked with cleaning up the problem, equaled about 42% of outstanding bank loans or 35% of GDP in 2001. See Ma and Fung (2002).

[16] Holz (2003, p. 194) argues that once one controls for higher capital intensity and taxes, SOE profitability actually exceeded that of non-SOEs.

had yet grasped the concept of commercial debt, or, to put it differently, been given sufficient incentives to do so. Failure of new entry to be balanced by exit of less successful firms, another symptom of soft budget constraints, also contributed to the decline in profits. And real labour costs were rising in part due to the SOEs' burden of unfunded pension payouts to a growing number of retirees.

These were the considerations that lay behind the central government's decision, as the mid-1990s approached, to allow local governments to privatise their small enterprises, should they find that expedient, and to seek ways to harden the budget constraints of the medium and large state enterprises by means of a more radical new set of reforms.

Restructuring and Corporatisation, 1993–2007

Obtaining a good picture of how China's public or once-public industrial enterprises performed in the second reform period is in some ways even more difficult than for the first, partly because some dramatic changes are more recent and not yet fully understood, but more importantly because the picture becomes more complicated as more SOEs transition into private and mixed-ownership categories. To organise our investigation of the set of Chinese SOEs that existed around 1992, we find it helpful to distinguish between the smaller enterprises controlled by more local levels of government, the majority of which were either fully privatised, leased to private operators, merged, or shut down in this period, and the medium and large enterprises more likely to be controlled by provincial or central governments, most of which have undergone various forms of ownership restructuring since the mid-1990s. These larger enterprises can then be divided into approximately 1,400 corporatised former SOEs that have issued shares on the Shanghai and Shenzhen stock exchanges, and the remaining roughly 20,000 enterprises that lack publicly traded shares but that nevertheless also often include private domestic or foreign entities among their owners following restructuring (*gaizhi*).

'Letting go of the small'

Information about the disposal of China's small SOEs remains remarkably sparse. According to official data summarised by Zhao (2006), small enterprises accounted for 20% of SOE industrial product in 1993 and this share had fallen moderately to 16% in 1997. By 2004, however, there were less than 32,000 SOEs *versus* roughly 120,000 in the mid-1990s, and most of the SOEs that had disappeared were undoubtedly small enterprises previously controlled by county, municipality, and provincial governments. Some local snapshots of what became of the small SOEs are available. Naughton (2007) refers to Huang and Huang's (1998) report that the city of Zhucheng, in Shandong Province, privatised 85% of its small SOEs and township enterprises by converting them to joint-stock corporations owned by their workers and (especially) managers. Zhao (2006) reports that most enterprises in Zhou district of Zhucheng also became shareholding cooperatives, while in Xing county most SOEs were leased out or auctioned off. He also reports on a programme in Bing county of Heilongjiang province that saw 36% of 158 states or collectively owned small and medium enterprises being turned into shareholding cooperatives, 54% being leased, and the remainder being disposed of by auction, merger, closure, or other methods.

Medium and large SOEs: broad sample studies

In the remainder of this section, we focus on medium- and large-sized state-owned enterprises, the majority of which underwent *gaizhi* between the mid-1990s and early 2000s. Most larger enterprises became limited liability corporations (LLC), or for the largest, limited liability shareholding corporations (LLSC), while on the smaller end of the spectrum, many became joint stock corporations, joint ventures, or domestic private firms. We consider studies that investigate the impact of these reforms on enterprise performance, with an emphasis on the general effects of the reform process as such and also on the more specific effects of the distribution of shareholding between state, mainly state-related 'legal persons', manager and worker insiders, domestic private owners, and foreign investors.

While a disproportionate number of published studies focus on the minority of enterprises that have publicly traded shares, this sub-section looks at studies that include mainly enterprises without listed shares. One of these, Jefferson and Su (2006), uses National Bureau of Statistics data from virtually the entire universe of medium and large SOEs, and a second, Bai *et al.* (2008), looks at an almost equally large set of enterprises. The other four studies that we discuss – Garnaut *et al.* (2005), Yusuf *et al.* (2006), Dong *et al.* (2006), and Li (2008a) – use data from smaller enterprise surveys.

Jefferson and Su (2006) study the impact of conversion to shareholding enterprise form and of changes in the proportion of shares owned by non-state actors using observations for the years 1995–2001 from a sample of roughly 7,000 SOEs of which about 5,300 retained the SOE classification while some 1,500 had been converted to and retained the shareholding enterprise classification as of 2001. Using a two-stage least squares estimation process that treats the change in the proportion of shares owned by non-state agents as an endogenous variable determined by enterprise size, region, and year, they find that growth of value added per unit of capital and growth of value added per worker are significantly positively related to the initial share of non-state assets, to the enterprise conversion event, and to the change in the share of non-state assets, but that the share and conversion variables fail to significantly affect profit per unit of sales.

One of the themes of Jefferson and Su's paper is that conversion to the shareholding form generally does not entail a decline in the value of assets held by the state, but rather an increase in total assets through bringing in the new capital of private investors. Despite this growth of enterprises' capital bases, however, they observe enterprise operations becoming more labour-intensive rather than more capital-intensive. The first clue to this is that in the estimates just discussed, conversion appears to impact capital productivity to a larger degree than it does value added per worker. Conjecturing from this that capital/labour ratios may have fallen, they estimate further regressions that confirm that both conversion and the increase in the non-state asset share have significant negative effects on the capital/labour ratio. This can be interpreted as a shift from the overly capital-intensive input mix for which old-line SOEs were notorious to more efficient, more labour-intensive technologies. Furthermore, while the changes in ownership failed to increase profitability as measured by the profit-to-sales ratio, they *are* found to increase profit per RMB of fixed capital, a measure of return on investment.

Bai *et al.* (2008) study the set of 15,496 enterprises annually surveyed by the National Bureau of Statistics that were still 100% state owned in 1998 and that either remained so (12,630 enterprises) or were privatised to some degree (2,866 enterprises) by 2003.[17] Controlling for firm specific factors including the debt-equity ratio and the percentage of new products in output, and controlling for competition in the relevant market by using a Herfindahl index at the two-digit industry level, they examine the impact of the non-state ownership percentage on a variety of outcomes. They find that non-state ownership is significantly negatively associated with the number of employees, positively associated with wage and with non-wage benefits (welfare) per worker, negatively associated with product price and total assets, and positively associated with profit per RMB of sales. They also estimate a parallel set of regressions in which dummy variables for undergoing an initial sale of shares to non-state owners in the year in question, and likewise for second, third, and fourth waves of partial privatisation, are used as privatisation indicators instead of the private ownership share. For most dependent variables, the first and sometimes the second privatisation event show significant effects which parallel those in the corresponding regressions with private share, while the third and fourth waves are generally insignificant. The implication drawn is that it is the introduction of private ownership, but not its exact amount, that is most important to the outcomes in question. Having private shareholders seem to have positive effects on wages and profits and negative effects on employment, although the effect on product price is insignificant in this multiple waves specification. The authors conclude that partial privatisation in China helped consumers and improved firm performance. They also find that the negative effects of

---

[17] The starting point of the sample used differs from that of Jefferson and Su in that it includes all SOEs and all non-SOEs with over five million RMB in annual sales, a somewhat larger category than the set of medium and large enterprises.

privatisation on employment were small in comparison to those associated with privatisations of other countries.

Econometric analyses of enterprise survey data appear in the book-length study of Chinese enterprise reform by Yusuf *et al.* (2006), and in a companion paper to another book-length study, that of Garnaut *et al.* (2005), by contributors Song Ligang and Yao Yang (2004). The Garnaut *et al.* survey studied by Song and Yao has data on 683 SOEs or reformed SOEs located in 11 mid-sized cities – Harbin, Fushun, Tangshan, Xining, Lanzhou, Chengdu, Guiyang, Weifang, Zhenjiang, Huangshi, and Hengyang – that broadly represent China as a whole, with annual observations for 1995–2001. The Yusuf *et al.* survey includes a similar number of enterprises, 736, located in five larger cities – Beijing, Chongqing, Guangzhou, Shanghai, and Wuhan – with annual observations covering 1996–2001. Unlike the all-SOE sample of Garnaut *et al.*, only 266 of the enterprises in the Yusuf *et al.* survey are SOEs, and of these 140 had not yet undergone ownership restructuring, with the remaining enterprises being former or current COEs or TVEs, *de novo* private enterprises, and foreign-owned enterprises. All sample enterprises operate in one of seven sectors chosen to represent high-, medium-, and low-technology industries. In addition to Song and Yao, the Garnaut *et al.* data are also studied by Li (2008a), while Dong *et al.* study data on 165 urban and rural enterprises located in a single metropolitan area, Nanjing.

Yusuf *et al.* carry out panel fixed effects regression estimates in which the main dependent variable is value added and the explanatory variables include capital and labour inputs, firm type, state and foreign ownership shares, and indicators of amount of competition faced, of the education, appointment process, turnover, and autonomy of the manager, of shareholder meeting voting structure, board composition, and softness of budget constraint. They find that reform improves the performance of SOEs, with the LLSC enterprises performing best, joint ventures second, and LLCs third. Among non-SOEs, they find no significant performance difference relative to non-reformed SOEs for the domestic private, collective, and wholly foreign owned enterprises in their sample, whereas they find that other non-SOEs and joint venture enterprises perform significantly better than non-reformed SOEs and slightly better than reformed SOEs. Firms with managers appointed by the state perform worse than others, and managers with more domestic education perform better than those with less education and those educated abroad (who, they conjecture, may lack comparable ties to local networks). Following a one-share-one-vote rule has a significant positive effect on performance.[18]

[18] Hu *et al.* (2004) also study the 736 enterprise data set, examining the determinants of total factor productivity, value-added, sales, profits, and employment. They find that SOE classification and a low proportion of privately owned shares negatively affect performance, and that operating in a more competitive industry positively affects performance among SOEs but has a weaker or no effect for non-SOEs.

Song and Yao (2004) estimate regressions to investigate the effect on three dependent variables – return on assets (ROA), unit cost, and labour productivity – of the non-state ownership share and of status as fully state-owned, partially privatised but state controlled,[19] and privatised with a dominant private shareholder. Control variables include industry, city, and year dummies, indicators of whether the firm had its debts reduced at privatisation, the debt-asset ratio, and measures of overdue interest and loan payments, overdue taxes, and overdue social security payments. Estimating the regressions both by OLS on three-year moving averages and by a firm fixed effects model, they find that privatisation has a significant effect on ROA; in particular, a fully privatised firm has a profit rate 1.4 percentage points higher than does a fully government-owned one. However, the effect is significant only in the first year of privatisation, and is significant with both estimating methods only for the categorical ownership variables, not the continuous private share measure. The authors argue that labour productivity fails to rise significantly in their sample because of continuing pressures on partially privatised enterprises to maintain employment. They attribute the increase in profitability to an association between private ownership and increased R&D.

Li's (2008a) study uses the same data, but whereas Song and Yao focus on the *share* of private ownership, she studies the impact on firm profitability, leverage, and productivity of the *form* of restructuring (internal restructuring, employee shareholding, sale, lease, bankruptcy, initial public offering (IPO), and joint venture) treated as categorical dummy variables.[20] To address the selection bias problem, she not only applies the standard panel data estimation methods adopted by Song and Yao, but also uses various robustness checks to test particular selection hypotheses. For example, she compares the 1995–1998 performance of the current treatment group (firms undergoing restructuring in the 1995–1998 period) with that of the future treatment group (firms that would undergo restructuring in 1999) to address the concern that the unobserved characteristics correlated with firm performance may not be fixed. Also, she compares the post-restructuring performance of management-controlled firms with that of non-management-controlled firms to test the hypothesis that the management may have run down the firm before restructuring in order to buy it more cheaply. She finds that some forms of restructuring, particularly IPO and joint venture, not only effectively raise firm profitability, but also significantly raise productivity. IPO and joint ventures show the most pronounced impact on firm profitability and productivity, in her study, while sale, lease, and bankruptcy have significant impacts under a group fixed effects model but not under a firm fixed effects model. She estimates that conversion by IPO and joint venture raises ROA

---

[19] That is having the state as largest shareholder.
[20] Owing to this focus, she discards firms that undertook more than one change of ownership form during the sample period, some 20% of the sample.

by 2.3 percentage points compared to unreformed SOEs, significant at the 1% level. This appears roughly consistent with Song and Yao's estimate that a one percentage point increase in private ownership share increases ROA by 0.014 percentage points, significant at the same level. Both estimates are economically significant because the average ROA of the sample in the year 1996–2001 was between –1.17% and –0.93%, so that *gaizhi* could mean a substantial improvement in profitability relative to the average performance.

The survey conducted for Dong *et al.* (2006) by the National Bureau of Statistics studies 60 SOEs, 10 COEs, and 95 TVEs in a single city and its suburban areas. During the covered years of 1994–2001, 63% of the SOEs underwent ownership restructuring, with 11 becoming LLSCs, 20 LLCs, 5 shareholding cooperatives, and 2 fully private firms. A somewhat smaller fraction of the COEs and a larger fraction of the TVEs went through restructuring, with two-thirds becoming private firms and a quarter shareholding cooperatives. Investigating selection, they find that weaker-performing SOEs were restructured first in Nanjing, but that there is no correlation between prior performance and restructuring for firms in the city's rural environs. Then, using both end-of-period group fixed effects and firm fixed effects models to control for selection, they find that restructuring has significant positive effects on the growth rates of value-added per worker, revenue per worker, and TFP, and on the level of the profit-to-assets ratio, for SOEs switching to minority private ownership, but not for SOEs becoming majority privately owned or for restructured COEs and TVEs. They also estimate firm fixed effects models in which the proportion of ownership in private hands, a continuous variable, rather than categorical ownership variables, is used to predict performance. These models show performance to be improving for both SOEs and TVEs as private ownership rises from zero, but they suggest an inverted U-shaped relationship in which performance is maximised in the restructured SOEs when private ownership stands at about 42%, using productivity criteria, or 56% using profitability.

Listed companies

Firms with shares traded on the Shanghai and Shenzhen stock exchanges have received particular attention. Most of the largest of China's SOEs and former SOEs now have traded shares, and in 2004 the revenue generated by traded companies accounted for 22% of national gross industrial output, 68% of all state-owned and state-controlled enterprises' revenues, and 26% of gross industrial output generated by state-owned enterprises and non-state-owned enterprises above 'designated size'.[21] Share

---

[21] Estimated by the authors from Wind Info China Financial Database and China Statistical Yearbook 2005, Chapter 14. Here, state-controlled means having the state as largest shareholder, and designated size means having annual sales above five million RMB.

issuance was hoped to play a central role in the transformation of these enterprises, partly through bringing in private shareholders and creating pressures to improve corporate governance. Ninety-one percent of companies listed on the two exchanges at the end of 2002 began as SOEs, and 83% of total listed assets belonged to enterprises in which a state body, institution, or company was the largest shareholder. Overall, state-owned shares accounted for 31.5%, legal person shares for 28.1%, employee owned shares for 0.4%, and private, tradable shares (of which 93% were held domestically, 7% by foreigners) accounted for 37.4% of the total in 2002.[22] Since 92.6% of legal persons could be traced to state-controlled entities as of 2001 (Delios and Wu, 2005), a clear majority of shares were still publicly owned.

Listed companies present interesting possibilities for analysis due to the potential barometer of performance or at least of expectations of performance that public share prices offer and because of the availability of information about shareholding. Yet assessment of findings is complicated by uncertainty as to the efficiency of pricing in China's young stock markets,[23] the fact that the majority of the companies' shares – those owned by the state, legal persons, and employees – are non-traded, difficulty comparing results obtained for share value *versus* financial performance data, and difficulty identifying the real nature of legal person owners. There is a large literature to draw on, of which we refer to 16 studies, focusing on the effect of share issuance, the impact of owner identity, and aspects of CEO shareholding, political connections, and turnover.

Chen *et al.* (2006) study data from all 1,078 enterprises that issued tradable shares in the period from 1991 to 2000, studying changes in various performance indicators between the 3 years before and the 3 (alternatively, five) years after share issuance. They find that investment and sales significantly increased and that the debt to assets and long-term debt to equity ratios significantly declined after this event, but that three profitability indicators (profit-to-sales, profit-to-assets, profit-to-equity) declined, in two cases significantly. However, firms with a dominant private owner saw less, and less significant, declines in profitability. Moreover, Wei *et al.* (2003) compare share issuers to ordinary SOEs in the 1990–1997 period and find that firms that became listed recorded significant improvements in profitability and other performance indicators relative to those that did not. Jia *et al.* (2005)

---

[22] Foreign-owned tradable shares as of 2002 consisted of those traded in China's B share market and those traded in Hong Kong, known as H shares.
[23] Although observers have often suggested that the vast majority of participants are uninformed 'retail' investors and have compared the markets to casinos, Li (2008b) finds stock prices to be highly responsive to information, in particular promptly upgrading performance expectations upon publication of news that shares of a company's stock had been purchased by a foreign-owned qualified institutional investor.

study 53 firms issuing shares on the Hong Kong stock exchange during 1993–2002 and find 'that listing has led to a median increase of 70% in real net profits, 80% in real sales, 50% in capital spending ... but no improvement in return on sales'.

Turning to shareholder identity, most of the relevant studies point toward either no relationship or a negative relationship between the proportion of shares owned by the state and enterprise performance or share value measures, while finding a positive relationship between the proportion of legal person shares and those measures. Qi *et al.* (2000), looking at the data of all enterprises listed in Shanghai during 1991–1996, found return on equity, ROA, and the market-to-book ratio to be positively correlated with the fraction of shares owned by legal persons and negatively correlated with the fraction owned by the state. Xu and Wang (1999), studying all companies listed on the Shanghai and Shenzhen exchanges during 1993–1995, found either a negative correlation or no correlation between profitability and the proportion of state shares, and a negative relationship between labour productivity and that fraction. Wei *et al.* (2003) find a positive effect of majority private shareholding on profitability, while Bai *et al.* (2004) find a negative impact of the state being the largest shareholder on share valuation among all listed firms in 1999–2001.

Tian and Estrin (2008), studying data for 1994–1998, find a negative relationship between the state ownership share and financial performance measures that include a simplified Tobin's Q. However, a specification that allows for non-linearity generates a U-shaped relationship of superior fit, indicating that once the state's proportion of ownership exceeds 30% or 40% increases in state ownership are *positively* associated with financial performance. Sun and Tong (2003) find no significant relationship between the state's share and profitability, while Sun *et al.* (2002), using data for the 1994–1997 period, obtain the only definitely contrary result, finding an inverted U-shaped relationship between the state share and performance, with a positive sign on state share in a linear specification.

An interesting, if difficult-to-interpret, finding is that ownership by legal person entities, which in the large majority of cases means indirect ownership by the state (Sun *et al.*, 2002; Delios and Wu, 2005; Liu and Sun, 2005; Delios *et al.*, 2006), tends to positively affect performance. Sun and Tong (2003), Xu and Wang (1999), Qi *et al.* (2000), and Sun *et al.* (2002) all find that the higher the proportion of shares owned by legal persons, the higher the profitability. Jia *et al.* (2005), studying 53 companies that issued shares on the Hong Kong stock exchange between 1993 and 2002, also find a positive effect of the legal person share for those companies.

Tian and Estrin (2008) consider the benefits of share concentration as one possible reason why a large set of shares in state hands may sometimes be beneficial. Xu and Wang (1999) considered ownership concentration as a possible determinant of traded enterprises' performance and found a significant positive relationship. A special case of ownership concentration is that of the proportion of shares held by the CEO. Li *et al.* (2007) find that the CEO ownership share is a significant positive predictor of enterprise performance over the period from 1992 to 2000.

While shareholding by the CEO may provide stronger performance incentives, some analysts consider CEO entrenchment to be a possible problem and ask whether the nature of the owners affects the likelihood that CEOs will be dismissed in the event of poor company performance. Kato and Long (2006) study this issue and find that CEO tenure is more closely related to firm performance – as measured by stock market return – among listed Chinese firms with a controlling private shareholder.

A final set of issues that have been studied are ones revolving around the CEO's relationships to the government and Party. Fan *et al.* (2007) investigate whether enterprises managed by CEOs with strong ties to Chinese government officials behave differently from those whose CEOs lack such ties. They find that having a CEO with political connections is a significant predictor that performance will worsen after the issuing of shares. Chang and Wong (2004) use the same Shanghai Stock Exchange survey as Wang *et al.* (2004) to investigate the effects of the assessed decision-making power of the local party committee. They find that greater power of that committee, as reported by management, is associated with significantly worse performance in terms of ROA, return on equity, and return on sales.

We conclude the third section by suggesting that while studies of SOEs in the second phase of China's industrial reforms yield varied results on details, they are generally in agreement that restructuring as partially or wholly private firms has led to improvements in factor productivity, profitability, or both. The studies leave open, however, the question of whether the relationship between state ownership and performance was necessarily monotonic. Among others, the results of Dong *et al.*, for a sample of urban SOEs, and of Tian and Estrin, for companies listed on China's stock markets, suggest that some state ownership was sometimes still helpful to performance, at least during the latter half of the 1990s. Several studies agree that legal person ownership improved corporate outcomes, despite the linkage of the large majority of legal person entities to state actors. And there are other surprising findings, such as Yusuf *et al.*'s failure to find significant performance differences between non-reformed SOEs and the domestic private and wholly foreign owned enterprises in their sample, despite their finding that joint venture enterprises performed significantly better than non-reformed SOEs. Taken together, the results confirm that the influence of state and Party in China's economy remained strong enough, more than two decades after adoption of the 'reform and opening' strategy, that state connections could still be an asset. It remains to be seen whether studies using still more recent data will lead to different conclusions.

What Does It All Mean?

Overviews of China's economic performance since 1979 cannot help but note the country's remarkable pace of economic growth and structural change. Yet, throughout the 1980s, the 1990s, and even into the present decade, an oft-repeated refrain has been that the heart of Chinese industry remains state-owned and controlled, and that – excepting, perhaps, the 'letting go' of the smaller SOEs – change has been relatively superficial. Some studies of the more radical reforms begun in the mid-1990s fail even to mention the preceding decade of change, as if the starting point of the second period's reforms might just as well have been the 'old dinosaurs' of the pre-reform economy. And the fact that many of China's largest companies today, including the large majority of those listed on its stock exchanges, are still state controlled leads to a similar 'waiting for reform to begin in earnest' view on the parts of some observers.

It is implausible that China's economic growth could have progressed so rapidly if the country has been dragging along its state sector like an albatross around its neck for all of these years, as such views imply. To be sure, export-oriented non-state industry, foreign investment, and the private sector together may account for most of China's economic dynamism. Yet it strikes us as reasonable to conclude that the state sector has also been a contributor to China's economic growth, churning out most of the steel, oil, chemicals, equipment, and industrial staples that have permitted the mushrooming of new urban and industrial sites throughout the country, providing the skeleton over which more dynamic sectors could add muscle and flesh, and all the time continuing its own transformation toward more efficient management and greater responsiveness to market signals.

The case can be made that gradual reform in the 1980s, preserving urban living standards while permitting steady growth of industrial output (in contrast to the deep early transition recessions in many ex-Communist countries), was a sensible and successful part of the recipe for China's unprecedented three decades of high growth. Mass privatisation of smaller SOEs, COEs, and TVEs is a fact of the 1990s that remains underappreciated outside of China itself and foreign scholarly circles. The corporatisation strategy for dealing with larger SOEs can also be judged reasonably successful and on track, since a third or more of the shares in these enterprises were successfully sold over a 10-year period, and the next decade or so may well see the majority of the firms in question transition into majority private control. A rush to sell off shares too quickly might well have threatened the whole programme, as the sharp dip in share prices that occurred in the early 2000s (when the government tried to begin off-loading more non-traded shares) suggests.

Estimates of the overall performance of the state and state-dominated sector of Chinese industry tell a story of continuing progress in recent years. Jefferson *et al.* (2008) estimate the combined productivity of labour and capital (multifactor productivity) in various Chinese industrial sectors during 1998–2005 using factor weights derived from production function estimates. While their multifactor productivity measure for the SOEs is only 86% as large as that of foreign-owned and 76% as large as that for domestic private firms in 2005, SOEs recorded a considerably higher annual growth rate of this productivity measure, 16.8% a year, than did that for domestic private (6.3%), foreign (5.1%), COE (7.7%), and 'other' firms (8.5%).[24] Comparing the 16.8% estimate to Chen *et al.*'s (1988) estimate of 4.8%–5.9% multifactor productivity growth during 1978–1985 and Jefferson *et al.'s* (1996) estimate of total factor productivity growth of only 2.5% in state industry during 1980–1992 suggest that the second phase of industrial enterprise reform has after all succeeded in improving upon the achievements of the first. Jefferson *et al.* attribute the strong productivity growth of the 1998–2005 period at least as much to the exiting of poor performers as to improvement in the performance of surviving enterprises.

Also important for judging the success of the second stage of reforms is what happened to profitability. After falling to less than 1% of GDP in 1996–1998, the aggregate profits of the SOE sector recovered to over 1% in 1999, to more than 2% in 2000–2003, and to over 3% of GDP in 2004–2005, despite the rapid growth of GDP itself and the smaller size of the SOE sector. In relation to the SOEs' fixed assets, profits rose almost continuously from 1.6% in 1998 to 9.1% in 2003 and 13.3% in 2005.[25]

The last chapter remains to be written on China's reform and opening, and in particular on the role played in it by the country's state-owned enterprises. But it is clear from the large body of studies to date that the SOEs, while hardly the cutting edge of the reforms, have also not been static entities blocking the way to economic change and growth. Although underperforming relative to other sectors, they have played their part in China's massive growth surge, have been through an ongoing process of institutional transformation, have at least gradually improved their efficiency, and have weathered and (for their surviving remnant, at least) partly recovered from a severe crisis of plummeting profitability.

Acknowledgements

We are extremely grateful to Barry Naughton, Carsten Holz, Gary Jefferson, Xiao-Yuan Dong and Yao Yang for reading a draft full of what for them is

---

[24] Calculations based on the estimates of the log of MFP by sector shown in their Table 5.

[25] Most of these profits were attributable to the 176 large SOEs run by the Central SASAC. (Calculations from China Statistical Yearbook 2006, Chapter 14 with additional information on large SOEs from Xinhua News Agency (2005).) 'Grasping the large' has turned out, thus far, to mean holding on to the goose that lays the golden eggs.

old news, and for pointing out errors and providing wise counsel. The usual disclaimer applies.

References

Ahn, J and Cogman, D. 2007: A quiet revolution in China's capital markets. *McKinsey quarterly perspectives on corporate finance and strategy* 24(Summer): 18–24 http://www.mckinseyquarterly.com/PDFDownload.aspx?L2=5&L3=0&ar=2016.

Bai, C-En, Liu, Q, Lu, J, Song, F and Zhang, JX. 2004: Corporate governance and market valuation in China. *Journal of Comparative Economics* 32: 599–616.

Bai, C-en, Lu, JY and Tao, ZG. 2008: *How does privatization work in China?* MPRA paper no. 6599, posted 06 January 2008.

Byrd, WA. 1989: Plan and market in the Chinese economy: A simple general equilibrium model. *Journal of Comparative Economics* 13(2): 177–204.

Chang, E and Wong, S. 2004: Political control and performance in China's listed firms. *Journal of Comparative Economics* 32: 617–636.

Chen, G-M, Firth, M and Rui, O. 2006: Have China's enterprise reforms led to improved efficiency and profitability? *Emerging Markets Review* 7(1): 82–109.

Chen, K, Wang, HC, Zheng, YX, Jefferson, GJ and Rawski, TG. 1988: Productivity change in Chinese industry: 1953–1985. *Journal of Comparative Economics* 12(4): 570–591.

China Financial Database. Shanghai Wind Information Technological Service Corp. Ltd, http:// www.wind.com.cn/en/home.html.

Delios, A and Wu, ZJ. 2005: Legal person ownership, diversification strategy and firm profitability in China. *Journal of Management and Governance* 9: 151–169.

Delios, A, Wu, ZJ and Zhou, N. 2006: A new perspective on ownership identities in China's listed companies. *Management and Organization Review* 2(3): 319–343.

Dong, XY, Putterman, L and Unel, B. 2006: Enterprise restructuring an firm performance: A comparison of rural and urban enterprises in Jiangsu province. *Journal of Comparative Economics* 34(3): 608–633.

Dong, XY and Xu, LC. 2008: The impact of China's millennium labor restructuring program on firm performance and employee earnings. *Economics of Transition* 16(2): 223–245.

Ellerman, D and Stiglitz, J. 2001: Not poles apart: "Whither Reform?" and "Whence Reform?". *Journal of Policy Reform* 4(4): 325–338.

Fan, JPH, Wong, TJ and Zhang, TY 2007: Politically connected CEOs, corporate governance and post-IPO performance of China's partially privatized firms. *Journal of Financial Economics* 84(2): 330–357.

Fu, XL and Balasubramanyam, VN. 2003: Township and village enterprises in China. *Journal of Development Studies* 39(4): 27–46.

Garnaut, R, Song, LG, Tenev, S and Yao, Y 2005: *China's ownership transformation: Process, outcomes, prospects.* The World Bank: Washington, DC.

Green, S. 2003: *Two-thirds privatization': How China's listed companies are finally privatizing.* The Royal Institute of International Affairs Asia Programme Working paper.

Groves, T, Hong, YM, McMillan, J and Naughton, B. 1994: Autonomy and incentives in Chinese state enterprises. *The Quarterly Journal of Economics* 109(1): 183–209.

Groves, T, Hong, YM, McMillan, J and Naughton, B. 1995: China's evolving managerial labor market. *Journal of Political Economy* 103(4): 873–892.

Holz, CA. 2003: *China's industrial state-owned enterprises between profitability and bankruptcy.* World Scientific: Riveredge, NJ.

Hu, YF, Song, F and Zhang, JX. 2004: *Competition, ownership, corporate governance and enterprise performance: evidence from China.* Hong Kong Institute of Economics and Business Strategy Working paper 1111.

Huang, SA and Huang, LJ. 1998: A further analysis of the "Zhucheng phenomenon." (Zhucheng Xianxiang Zaixi). *Gaige* 2: 38–47, (In Chinese).

Jefferson, GH, Rawski, TG and Zheng, YX. 1992: Growth, efficiency, and convergence in China's state and collective industry. *Economic Development and Cultural Change* 40: 239–266.

Jefferson, GH, Rawski, TG and Zheng, YX. 1994: Productivity change in Chinese industry: a comment. *China Economic Review* 5(2): 235–241.

Jefferson, GH, Rawski, TG and Zheng, YX. 1996: Chinese industrial productivity: trends, measurement issues, and recent developments. *Journal of Comparative Economics* 23(2): 146–180.

Jefferson, GH, Rawski, TG and Zhang, Y. 2008: Productivity growth and convergence across China's industrial economy. *Journal of Chinese Economics and Business Studies* 6: 121–140.

Jefferson, GH and Singh, I (eds) 1998: *Enterprise reform in China: Ownership, transition, and performance.* Oxford University Press: New York.

Jefferson, GH and Su, J. 2006: Privatization and restructuring in China: Evidence from shareholding ownership, 1995–2001. *Journal of Comparative Economics* 34(1): 146–166.

Jia, J, Sun, Q and Tong, W. 2005: Privatization via an oversea listing: Evidence from China's H-Share firms. *Financial Management Autumn* 2005: 5–30.

Kato, T and Long, C. 2006: CEO turnover, firm performance, and enterprise reform in China: Evidence from micro data. *Journal of Comparative Economics* 34(4): 796–817.

Kornai, J and Qian, Y. (eds) 2008: *Market and socialism in light of the experiences of China and Vietnam.* Macmillan: Basingstoke, UK.

Lardy, NR. 2001: *China's worsening debts.* Brookings Working paper, 22 June 2001, http://www.brookings.edu/opinions/2001/0622china_lardy.aspx.

Lau, L, Qian, Y and Roland, G. 2000: Reform without losers: An interpretation of China's dual track approach to transition. *Journal of Political Economy* 108(1): 120–143.

Lee, K. 1990: The Chinese model of the socialist enterprise: An assessment of its organization and performance. *Journal of Comparative Economics* 14(3): 384–400.

Li, DH, Moshirian, F, Nguyen, P and Tan, L-w. 2007: Managerial ownership and firm performance: Evidence from China's privatization. *Research in International Business and Finance* 21(3): 396–413.

Li, W. 1997: The impact of economic reform on the performance of Chinese state enterprises, 1980–1989. *Journal of Political Economy* 105(5): 1080–1106.

Li, WY. 2008a: *The second wave of reform: On the effects of enterprise restructuring in China, 1995–2001.* Brown University PhD Dissertation Chapter.

Li, WY. 2008b: *Does money chase money: Estimating the signaling effects of qualified foreign institutional investors in China's Domestic stock markets.* Brown University PhD Dissertation Chapter.

Liu, GS and Sun, P. 2003: *Identifying ultimate controlling shareholders in Chinese public corporations: An empirical study.* Asia Programme Working paper no. 2.

Liu, GS and Sun, P. 2005: The class of shareholdings and its impacts on corporate performance: A case of state shareholding composition in Chinese public corporations. *Corporate Governance: An International Review* 13(1): 46–59.

Ma, G and Fung, BSC. 2002: *China's asset management corporations.* Bank for International Settlements Working papers no. 115.

National Bureau of Statistics. various years: *China Statistical Yearbook.* China Statistics Press, Beijing.

Naughton, B. 1992: Implications of the state monopoly over industry and its relaxation. *Modern China* 18(1): 14–41.

Naughton, B. 1995: *Growing out of the plan: Chinese economic reform, 1978–1993.* Cambridge University Press: New York.

Naughton, B. 2007: *The Chinese economy: Transitions and growth.* Massachusetts Institute of Technology Press: Massachusetts.

Putterman, L. 2008: China's encounter with market socialism: Approaching managed capitalism by indirect means. In: Kornai, J and Qian, Y (eds). *Market and Socialism In Light of the Experiences of China and Vietnam.* Macmillan: Basingstoke, UK.

Qi, DQ, Wu, W and Zhang, H. 2000: Shareholding structure and corporate performance of partially privatized firms: Evidence from Listed Chinese companies. *Pacific-Basin Finance Journal* 8(5): 587–610.

Sala-i-Martin, X. 2006: The world distribution of income: Falling poverty and convergence, period. *Quarterly Journal of Economics* 121: 351–397.

Shirley, MM and Xu, LXC. 2001: Empirical effects of performance-contracts: Evidence from China. *Journal of Law, Economics, and Organization* 17(1): 168–200.

Song, LG and Yao, Y. 2004: *Impacts of privatization on firm performance in China.* CCER Working paper E2004005.

Sprayregen, JHMPC, Friedland, JP, Miller, NS and Li, C. 2004: Non-performing loans in China: A potential win-win opportunity for foreign investors and China's economy. *Financial World Global Restructuring and Insolvency Review* 2004: 38–39.

Sun, Q and Tong, WHS. 2003: China share issue privatization: The extent of its success. *Journal of Financial Economics* 70(2): 183–222.

Sun, Q, Tong, WHS and Tong, J. 2002: How does government ownership affect firm performance? Evidence from China's privatization experience. *Journal of Business Finance & Accounting* 29(2002): 1–27.

Tian, LH and Estrin, S. 2008: Retained shareholding in Chinese PLCs: Does government ownership always reduce corporate value? *Journal of Comparative Economics* 36(2008): 74–89.

Wang, XZ, Xu, LXC and Zhu, T. 2004: State-owned enterprises going public: The case of China. *Economics of Transition* 12(3): 467–487.

Wei, ZB, Varela, O, D'Souza, J and Hassan, K. 2003: The financial and operating performance of China's newly privatized firms. *Financial Management* 32: 107–126.

Weitzman, M and Xu, CG. 1994: Chinese township-village enterprises as vaguely defined cooperatives. *Journal of Comparative Economics* 18(2): 121–145.

Woo, WT, Fan, G, Hai, W and Jin, Y 1993: The efficiency and macroeconomic consequences of Chinese enterprise reform. *China Economic Review* 4(2): 153–168.

Woo, WT, Hai, W, Jin, Y and Fan, G. 1994: How successful has Chinese enterprise reform been. *Journal of Comparative Economics* 18: 410–437.

Xinhua News Agency. 2005: SOEs See 31.2% Profit Growth in 1st Quarter. 19 April 2005.

Xu, XN and Wang, Y. 1999: Ownership structure and corporate governance in Chinese stock companies. *China Economic Review* 10: 75–98.

Yano, G and Shiraishi, M. 2004: Efficiency of Chinese township and village enterprises and property rights n the 1990s: Case of Wuxi. *Comparative Economic Studies* 46(2004): 311–340.

Yusuf, S, Nabeshima, K and Perkins, DH. 2006: *Under new ownership: privatizing China's state-owned enterprises.* Stanford University Press and the World Bank: Palo Alto, CA.

Zhao, X. 2006: Competition, public choice, and institutional change: Searching for reasons for improved policy efficiency in institutional reform from "Managing large enterprises and cutting small ones loose". *Chinese Economy* 39(1): 5–73.

8

The Changing Role of Money in China and Its Implications

Carsten A. Holz
Hong Kong University of Science & Technology, Hong Kong

Economic development is highly correlated with financial sector development. But the emergence, development, and economic implications of different financial structures are not well understood. This paper analyzes the emergence and development of China's financial structure since the beginning of the economic reforms. By focusing on the functions of money, monetary policy, and financial intermediation, it argues that although agricultural and industrial reforms in the early 1980s have led to significant changes in the financial system, financial liberalization has progressed little since. The creation of new financial institutions and markets throughout the 1990s and the recent abandonment of some of the traditional administrative control instruments do not signify a systemic change as the underlying functions remain constrained.

Introduction

Empirical studies invariably find an intricate link between indicators of financial sector development and economic growth. The faster the deepening of the financial sector, the higher the growth rate of the economy. Financial markets and financial intermediaries are viewed as performing certain functions affecting real variables. Financial markets and financial intermediaries themselves are the response to market friction such as information and transaction costs.[1]

---

[1] Chant (1992) clarifies the conditions under which market friction leads to the emergence of financial intermediation. On the link between financial intermediation and economic growth see, for example, the review articles by Levine (1997), Berthelemy and Varoudakis (1996), and Gertler (1988). Empirical studies include, among others, Levine and Zervos (1998), Thornton (1996), King and Levine (1993a and 1993b).

Reprinted with permission from Association of Comparative Economic Studies. All rights reserved. *Comparative Economic Studies* (Fall 2000) 42(3), 77–100.

But how the financial structure of an economy comes about in practice is not well understood and has not been explored in great depth. "We do not have a sufficiently rigorous understanding of the emergence, development, and economic implications of different financial structures" (Levine 1997, 702), where the term "financial structure" covers "the mix of financial contracts, markets, and institutions" (Levine 1997, 703). In the People's Republic of China (PRC), financial institutions and markets have proliferated rapidly and financial practices have undergone numerous changes since the beginning of the economic reforms in 1978. But we in fact lack a rigorous understanding of why financial reform occurred, how it proceeded, and what its limitations and implications are.

The literature concentrates either on describing actual financial transition experiences or on offering policy recommendations on how to switch to a market-based financial system.[2] While we have some understanding of how the socialist financial system operated,[3] financial system reform during economic transition is often viewed as a step into an abyss from which best to move to a market economy as quickly as possible. McKinnon (1993, p. 223), for example, finds that "in their rush to decentralize decision-making, privatize, and dismantle the apparatus of central planning, reformers inadvertently upset the pre-existing system for sustaining macroeconomic equilibrium. The ability of the reform government to collect taxes and control the supply of money and credit is unwittingly undermined by the liberalization itself." This paper suggests, quite to the contrary, that in the case of the PRC the financial system has been actively used by the government to supplant the dismantled apparatus of central planning in the real economy, and that the status of reform in the financial system may be the deliberate outcome of an attempt to sustain macroeconomic balance and economic growth.

In order to make sense of an otherwise profusion of financial reform events, this paper evaluates financial sector development in terms of changes in the functions of money, financial intermediation, and monetary

---

[2] For example, Caprio, Atiyas, and Hanson (1994), describe financial reform in a number of developed and developing (albeit not transitional) economies with a concluding chapter on lessons and strategies. Cole and Slade (1991) derive generalizations about financial system reform from the experiences of Indonesia, Turkey, and Korea. Miurin (1995) describes Russia's banking reform and its effects.

Caprio and Levine (1994) and McKinnon (1993) offer policy recommendations for transitional economies, Sametz (1991) for the PRC, Claessens (1996) for the choice between radical and gradual banking reform in transitional economies, Sundararajan (1992) for central banking reforms in formerly planned economies, and De Melo and Denizer (1997) for the transition in monetary policy instruments.

[3] Sigg (1981) and Bank of China International Finance Research Institute (1991) cover the socialist banking system of the former Soviet Union in great detail. For the case of the PRC see De Wulf (1986) and Cheng (1981).

policy. (See Figure 8.1, explained in more detail below.) Particular functions of money determine the functions of financial intermediation and monetary policy, which in turn yield a particular financial structure. Financial reform in the PRC has proceeded by lifting one set of restrictions on the functions of money. This led to changes in the functions of financial intermediation and monetary policy with subsequent changes in the financial structure. However, some restrictions on the functions of money are still in place today; these restrictions prevent the development of more market-oriented financial intermediation and monetary policy.

The next section examines how the PRC's pre-reform financial system operated. The third section explains the emergence of China's financial structure in the 1980s and 1990s by focusing on the changing functions of money in the early 1980s. The fourth section investigates whether the most recent financial reform measures represent systemic changes rather than cosmetic alterations without consequences for the functioning of the financial system. The last section concludes.

The Pre-Reform Period Financial Sector: Extension of the Physically Planned Economy

The PRC's modern financial system has its origins in the socialist, planned economy. This section explains the producer vs. consumer goods dichotomy in socialist economic theory and policy, and derives the implications for the financial sector.[4] It focuses on the restricted functions of money with the consequences for financial intermediation and monetary policy. How the PRC's modern financial system emerged through a change in these functions is the subject of the next section.

The centrally planned economy is characterized by two distinct circuits, the household circuit on the one hand and the inter-enterprise circuit on the other hand. (See Figure 8.2.) In the household circuit enterprises make all wage and salary payments to households in cash according to plan; all enterprises are state-owned and follow nationwide wage and salary scales. Households use their cash receipts to save and to consume (as well as to purchase agricultural producer goods). In the absence of household checking accounts, all withdrawal of household savings deposits and all households purchases are in cash.

In the inter-enterprise circuit, enterprises buy producer goods from other enterprises. They are not allowed to purchase consumer goods except for well justified and specially approved purposes. All payment is made through the transfer of deposits between bank accounts, using "transfer," or "book"

---

[4] Kornai (1979) uses this dichotomy to explain the phenomenon of shortage, but devotes only a few lines to the implications for the financial sector.

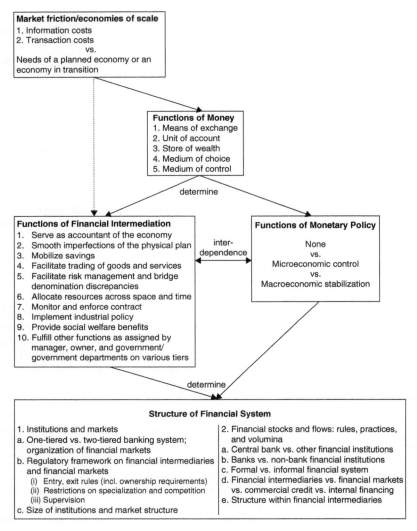

Figure 8.1 Dynamics of financial intermediation

money; enterprises are subject to rigid cash administration through ear-marked accounts in the few instances of cash use, such as for wage payments.

The set of functions of money in this economy differs from the set of functions of money in a market economy in two major respects. (See Table 8.1.) Money in this economy is a medium of control. Money fulfills a control function in that each individual monetary transaction is either planned or subject

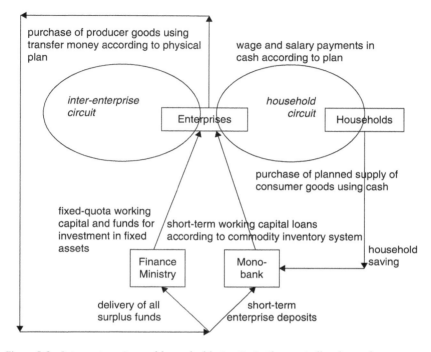

Figure 8.2 Inter-enterprise and household circuits in the centrally planned economy

to government supervision. In the household circuit all wage and salary pay-ments are planned. In the inter-enterprise circuit all monetary transactions follow the physical plan. The two circuits are controlled separately. Consumer goods (in the household circuit) can only be bought with cash, producer goods (in the inter-enterprise circuit) only with transfer money.

For enterprises, money carries neither the medium of choice function nor the store of wealth function. Enterprises have access to their transfer money in bank accounts only if the underlying physical transaction has been approved by the relevant state organ. Enterprises cannot decide themselves when to use their money, and what to use it for.[5] Similarly, government departments may claim the enterprises' transfer money at will.

---

[5] On the medium of choice function see also Dembinski (1988). Dembinski (p. 284) defines the medium of choice function as follows: "This function means that anyone who possesses money is entitled by this fact alone to choose the way in which he will spend it. For the sake of analysis, the permitted range of choice can be splitted into two dimensions: the diachronic one, which specifies the period of time during which this choice has to take place, and the synchronic one which specifies the class of transactions that can be chosen from."

Table 8.1 Functions of money

	Market economy	People's Republic of China			
		pre-reform period (before 1978)		reform period	
		household	enterprise	household	enterprise
Medium of exchange	Y	Y	Y	Y	Y
Standard of value	Y	Y	Y	Y	Y
Store of wealth	Y	Y	N; government may claim funds	Y	Y
Medium of choice when to use	Y	Y; except for rationed goods	N; determined by plan	Y	Y; but government may interfere directly in case of state-owned enterprises
for what to use	Y	Y; but limited to consumer goods and agricultural producer goods *cash plan applies	N; determined by plan and limited to producer goods	Y	Y; for state-owned enterprises limited to producer goods, with investment subject to government approval
Medium of control	N	*limited to use of cash, not suitable for purchase of producer goods *cash plan applies	*limited to use of transfer money, not suitable for purchase of consumer goods; all cash receipts must be promptly submitted to the bank *credit plan/commodity inventory system applies	*still largely limited to use of cash, now suitable for purchase of both consumer and producer goods; use of debit cards *cash plan applies	*state-owned enterprises are limited to the use of transfer money, not suitable for purchase of consumer goods; all cash receipts must be promptly submitted to bank *credit plan applies

Y: Yes; N: No.
The 'medium of exchange' function is also known as 'means of payment' function. The 'standard of value' function comprises the functions of unit of account and measure of relative value.

The control function of money and the lack of medium of choice function for enterprises have implications for monetary policy. Wage and salary payments in the household circuit are subject to strict controls. However, since the planning authorities cannot perfectly account for future household consumption decisions, imbalances between the supply of and the demand for consumer goods may arise. Nevertheless, with household income barely above subsistence level, the supply of consumer goods has to meet little more than the—easily predictable—demand for food and everyday household goods. Excess purchasing power is channeled off through the sale of relatively expensive, rationed luxury goods as well as through savings campaigns.[6] To be on the safe side, prices are state-determined and fixed. In the household circuit there is thus no need for active monetary policy.[7]

In the inter-enterprise circuit imbalances between the demand and supply of producer goods cannot arise as long as all transactions scrupulously follow the physical plan. Disturbances in the implementation of the physical plan, however, may lead to imbalances in the physical sphere. They are of no consequence to the monetary sphere as long as the use of transfer money requires approval by the relevant state organ. In addition, prices are state-determined and fixed. Transfer money in the inter-enterprise circuit serves only as "lubricant" of which a sufficiently large amount has to be kept at hand. In the inter-enterprise circuit thus there is likewise no need for active monetary policy.

Since the existence of financial markets would contradict the concept of a planned economy, financial intermediation in this economy is exercised solely by financial intermediaries. Financial intermediaries implement the control function of money in that they serve as accountants of the economy; a glance at the accounts allows an immediate update over fulfillment of the physical plan. The absence of the medium of choice function of money for enterprises is reflected in the financial intermediary's close scrutiny of each

---

[6] Savings in the PRC in the pre-reform period were on a rather small scale, suggesting no major imbalance on the consumer goods market. In 1978, total per capita savings deposits (not distinguishing between rural and urban population) were equal to 16.4% of average rural per capita annual disposable income and equal to 6.9% of average urban per capita annual income. For comparison, the percentages in 1998 were 197.9% and 78.9%. (ZGTJNJ 1999, 317) Per capita currency in circulation in 1978 was equal to 16.5% of average rural per capita annual income and equal to 7.0% of average urban per capita annual income; the percentages in 1998 were 41.5% and 16.5%. (ZGTJNJ 1999, 111, 317, 624; China Financial Statistics 1952–1987, 5).

[7] The monetary or planning authorities could have used interest rates on household deposits to influence household consumption decisions, but perhaps there was no need—between 1959 and 1979 interest rates in the PRC were adjusted twice, and then only marginally (ZGJRNJ 1990, 167).

individual disbursement of cash (except savings withdrawal by households) and of each transaction using transfer money.

Financial intermediaries smooth imperfections of the planning system by extending short-term working capital loans in accordance with the commodity inventory system.[8] (The finance ministry supplies all funds for investment in fixed assets as well as fixed-quota working capital directly to the enterprise.) However, the financial intermediaries have little decision-making authority since the allocation of loans simply follows the instructions of the planning, fiscal, and production hierarchy. The volume of loans is not constrained by the volume of deposits as the financial intermediaries are free to create money as needed.[9]

Financial intermediaries finally strive to maintain a high savings rate in order for the government to be able to minimize the production of consumer goods,[10] and they facilitate trade by providing cash to the household circuit and sufficient amounts of transfer money to the inter-enterprise circuit. (In Figure 8.1 the first four functions of financial intermediation are characteristic for the centrally planned economy, while functions three through seven are for a market economy.)

Without the need for monetary policy or the fulfillment of any significant allocative function by financial intermediaries, the banking system is reduced to a monobank, in the PRC the People's Bank of China (PBC). Between 1969 and 1977 the PBC was furthermore integrated into the Finance Ministry.

---

[8] The commodity inventory system specifies that (working capital) credit be extended directly to the user in accordance with specific plans and for specific purposes on the basis of material inventories held by the economic unit. Enterprises are required to promptly pay back their loans to the banks when the commodities that were used to back the loan are transferred outside the enterprise. (See De Wulf 1986.) The commodity inventory system represents the socialist economy's application of the "real bills principle."

[9] The centrally planned economy thus upholds a very peculiar version of the banking school. Bank branches can autonomously issue transfer money and cash. But rather than being separate banks each issuing its own, competing money—ultimately checked by the limitations set through a gold standard or other reserve specie in an open economy—all branches of a bank issue the same type of money without reserve or exchange requirement. The absence of the constraints maintained by the banking school does not matter due to the restricted functions money plays in the planned economy and due to fixed prices which perform as an additional safety mechanism.

The origins of the banking school version adopted in the PRC can be traced back to Karl Marx (Marx 1971; Chapter 34) and to the Soviet banking system (see, for example, Sigg 1981; Chapter 4).

[10] Walter (1985, 290) argues for the case of the PRC that after an unsuccessful credit reform in 1956 "the People's Bank [the only financial intermediary] came to focus primarily on developing its savings operations, which, in contrast to the credit reforms, enjoyed strong local Party support."

Emergence of China's Modern Financial Structure: Reforms in the Real Economy Lead to Changes in the Role of Money

The PRC's pre-reform period financial system was inherently stable. But once economic reforms in the real sphere began, the monetary system came under pressure to change.[11] The reform period brought about a fundamental change in the functions of money: as enterprises were given the right to make their own production and investment decisions, transfer money had to acquire the medium of choice function. (See Table 8.1.) This had a number of consequences for the functions of monetary policy and financial intermediation, and finally the financial structure.

In the early 1980s enterprises began to supplement planned wage and salary payments with bonus payments. (See Figure 8.3.) The total wage bill increased and became a priori indeterminate.[12] Rising household income meant that the share of easily planned food and everyday household good purchases in total household expenditures declined. The planning bureaucracy subsequently lost partial control over the extent of cash disbursement and withdrawal by the banking system.[13] The loss of control was exacerbated through the illegal use of cash by enterprises. Imbalances in the household circuit became more likely and could now, with prices successively freed, lead to inflation in the consumer goods market.

The need for active monetary policy in the household circuit arose, while monitoring and enforcement of the cash plan continued. Monetary policy in the household circuit focused on withdrawing excess cash by

---

[11] The secondary literature on economic reform discussions suggests that throughout the 1980s reform of the monetary system was not a topic of interest in itself. For example, Wu (1994) in her book on economic transformation, covering the various economic schools in the PRC throughout the reform period, not once refers to the monetary system. Hsu (1991) in his account of the discussions on economic reform among academics in the PRC during the 1980s likewise does not mention monetary reform.

[12] The central government tried to maintain an upper limit on bonus payments by levying a steep bonus tax. Bonus payments equaling up to four months of wage and salary payments were free of tax, marginal bonus payments equivalent to a fifth month of wage and salary payments carried a 30% tax, those equivalent to a sixth month of wage and salary payments a 100% tax, and those exceeding the equivalent of six months' wage and salary payments a 300% tax. (SC 84/6/28)

[13] For example, while in 1978 easily planned wages, salary payments and agricultural procurement accounted for 55.1% of all cash disbursement by state banks, this percentage dropped to 13.3% by 1998; the share of easily planned sales of goods and services in all cash receipts (receipts of cash by state banks) at the same time dropped from 79.2 to 12.7%. The share of the relatively unpredictable withdrawal and depositing of savings (both in cash) as share of total cash disbursement and receipts by banks rose from 9.6% and 10.7% in 1978 to 64.2% and 63.1% in 1998. (See *China Financial Statistics 1952–1987*; ZGTJNJ 1999, 625.)

150   *Holz*

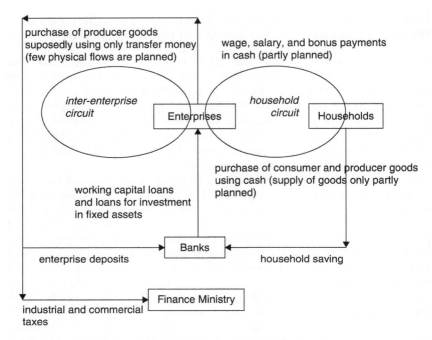

Figure 8.3 Inter-enterprise and household circuits after 1983/84

setting appropriate, centrally determined, nationwide uniform interest rates on household deposits. Between 1978 and 1999 these interest rates were adjusted eighteen times.[14]

In the inter-enterprise circuit the planning and production bureaucracy gradually lost control over physical transactions. The volume and distribution of transfer money, now a medium of choice, began to matter in that excess transfer money could lead to imbalances in the real sphere. Beginning in 1985, prices for producer goods were partially freed in the dual-track price system; by 1993, market-determined prices governed 81.1% of the value of all producer goods sales.[15] Imbalances in the producer goods sector could furthermore through the price of materials and the volume of wages and salaries spill over into the consumer goods sector. Inflation became a threat.

---

[14] See *Jinrong shibao* 97/10/28 and 99/12/6 as well as ZGJRNJ 1997, 493, and ZGTJNJ 1998, 533. During two periods of high inflation, savings deposits of three or more years maturity were inflation-indexed; the first period lasted from 88/9/10 to 91/12/1, while the second began on 93/7/11 with the inflation subsidy dropping to zero in May 1997.

[15] See ZGWJNJ 1997, 482.

The need for active monetary policy in the inter-enterprise circuit arose. As the use of transfer money by enterprises had to be deregulated, it was the extension of *additional* transfer money (credit) to individual enterprises which became central to monetary policy. Economic reform led to a reduction of microeconomic control in the real sphere (partial abandonment of the physical plan and price controls); monetary policy in 1984 took over this transaction-specific, microeconomic control task through an elaborate credit plan system with earmarked loans for individual projects and enterprises.

With transfer money turning into a medium of choice, the financial link between enterprises and superordinate ministry as well as finance ministry had to be severed. Enterprises making their own production decisions could no longer submit all surplus to the finance ministry; a finance ministry receiving less funds could no longer provide enterprises with fixed-quota working capital and investment funds. This led to two reforms in the fiscal system. Enterprises were first allowed to retain funds through partial profit retention in 1979. A 'tax instead of profit delivery' (*ligaishui*) reform followed in 1983 through 1985. At the same time, the task of providing working capital and investment funds fell to the banking system in an effort to 'switch from budget appropriations to credit' (*bogaidai*).

The reforms in the fiscal system implied a much larger volume—and in part a different type—of business for financial intermediaries. Financial intermediaries came to satisfy more than 80% of all working capital needs of enterprises but had no experience with lending criteria except with the 'commodity inventory system' at a time when all monetary flows simply followed implementation of the physical plan. No decision-making mechanisms were in place to determine the allocation of loans to investment projects except the traditional, physical planning system.

Given this lack of experience in allocating resources and given the perceived need for microeconomic control, now exercised through the monetary system, all lending authority became subsumed in the credit plan. Lending decisions incorporated industrial policy measures through an elaborate system of preferential access to credit for priority projects and backbone enterprises; working capital loans at times were barely disguised social welfare payments to enterprises starved of funds since the discontinuation of budget appropriations.

Drawing up the credit plan involved not only the financial intermediaries but also the line ministries superordinate to the borrowing enterprise, the finance ministry of the corresponding tier government, and, in the case of investment projects, the planning commission and the economic (and trade) commission hierarchy. The State Planning Commission (SPC) and ultimately the State Council reserved the right of final approval for the nationwide credit plan. While loans thus were extended in name by financial institutions, in practice lending decisions were made outside the financial system by the traditional planning and production hierarchy.[16] The PBC continued to set all interest rates, subject to State Council approval, at nationwide uniform levels. Financial intermediaries extending loans in accordance with the credit plan drawn up together with or under instructions from other government departments could not be assigned the lending risk. They thus had little incentive to monitor the use of the loans and to enforce repayment.

At the same time as the banking system became inundated with new lending tasks, the PBC exerted strong pressure on financial intermediaries to attract savings deposits from households in order to prevent the build-up of inflationary pressures in the consumer goods sector. On the one hand financial intermediaries faced a limit on overall credit plan lending as well as quotas on different types of loans within this overall limit, while on the other hand the PBC provided the financial intermediaries with insufficient refinancing to fulfill these loan quotas and the overall limit.[17] This led financial intermediaries to exert strong efforts to attract savings deposits. (Financial intermediation thus entered a stage where the first two functions in Figure 8.1 were cast aside and the eighth through tenth function rose to prominence, while the fifth through seventh function are not yet developed.)

The changes in the functions of financial intermediation with an increase in the volume and a diversification in the type of banking business led to a change in the institutional structure. As early as 1979 the Agricultural Bank

---

[16] According to Montes-Negret (1995, 31), the Industrial and Commercial Bank of China in the early 1990s could autonomously decide on less than 20% of its lending. According to Xiao (1997, 371), approximately 40% of all state bank loans in 1991 were "policy loans" (defined in the source as particular lending categories). These loans range from the loans extended to 240 enterprises under the "double-guarantee system" (the state guarantees all inputs, the enterprise guarantees all outputs) with no decision-making authority for the bank, to agricultural procurement loans for which the government only determines volume and purpose.

Not all policy loans are explicitly labeled "policy loans." Local governments and lower-level tier ministries are participating in, if not making some loan decisions; financial intermediaries may not want to lend to enterprises which do not have borrowing approval from their superordinate ministry.

[17] The transition in the credit plan system occurred in two stages. At the first stage (1984–86) banks faced both a credit and a deposit plan with refinancing of the difference guaranteed by higher-level branches of the same bank and ultimately the central bank. Deposits attracted in excess of the deposit plan could be turned into working capital loans by the bank branch itself (*duocun duodai*). In 1987 the deposit plan was abandoned, refinancing through the central bank no longer guaranteed, and the credit plan limit became fully binding.

of China (ABC) and the Bank of China (BoC) re-emerged from departments within the PBC as separate institutions directly under the State Council.[18]

Since the PBC fulfilled both commercial and central bank functions, it increasingly faced difficulties in objectively determining the appropriate volume of transfer money—which now mattered. Furthermore, ABC and BoC complained about the preferential treatment of the PBC's own commercial departments when it came to refinancing decisions. Finally, the PBC had little administrative authority over ABC and BoC which on the provincial and subprovincial tiers enjoyed a status equal to that of the PBC branches. In September 1983 the PBC was therefore turned into a solely central bank; the commercial banking departments of the PBC were renamed Industrial and Commercial Bank of China (ICBC).[19] In 1985 the People's Construction Bank of China (PCBC), formerly a division within the finance ministry in charge of administering the budget appropriations to investment projects, joined the ABC, BoC, and ICBC as the fourth "special" bank.

Development of the PRC's Modern Financial Structure: Changes in Financial Structure But Not in Underlying Functions?

From the mid-1980s to the late 1990s a number of financial reform measures were implemented. However, the concept of two separate moneys was never fully abandoned, and both cash and transfer money continue to be a medium of control.[20] While implementation of the cash plan and

---

[18] The establishment of these "special" banks was in part due to the agricultural reforms in 1978/79 and the opening up to foreign trade in the early 1980s, requiring specialized banking services, but also to the fact that these banks had already existed as separate entities in the years before the cultural revolution. A further reason may have been the desire to avoid concentration of power in an increasingly large and complex financial sector. On the institutional changes and some of the potential reasons for these changes also see Sheng (1989, 37–40) or Qin (1993, 47–57).

[19] The State Council justified this move by the need to change the "present situation of dispersed administration and use of funds." A further aspect was the avowed separation of government and enterprises (*zhengqi fenkai*). The PBC acting as solely a central bank was viewed as an extension of the government controlling – through its conduct of (microeconomic) monetary policy – special banks operating like enterprises (*qiyehua*).

[20] The ABC in mid-1997 prided itself on having strictly adhered to the cash disbursement plan in the first half of the year (*Zhongguo chengxiang jinrongbao* 97/1/ 21). The most recent regulation on the use of cash by enterprises is still in effect (PBC 88/9/23), although it is frequently not enforceable, especially with rural collective-owned enterprises and individual-owned enterprises.

supervision over cash flows are deteriorating, the centrally approved credit plan on the volume and distribution of transfer money is still in effect, albeit since 1998 only in 'indicative' rather than 'imperative' form. The PBC supposedly abandoned credit limits and quotas in favor of money supply targeting with as sole objective currency stabilization (in order to promote economic growth; NPC 95/3/18, Art. 3). Since the passing of the Commercial Bank Law in 1995 (NPC 95/5/10) the special banks are supposed to have turned into 'commercial banks,' making lending decisions based on economic criteria.

But governments concerned about their state-owned enterprises and local economic development continue to interfere in bank lending decisions.[21] After the financial conference of Mid-November 1997 it was announced that starting 1998 the provincial heads and municipal mayors would no longer have any authority to issue instructions to bank directors.[22] Explicit policy loans are now supposedly only extended by the state development banks. Yet the state commercial banks continue to extend loans which are policy loans in all but name. For example, the ICBC since 1994 extends loans to loss-making state-owned enterprises so that these can pay a basic living allowance to their employees.[23] In June 1996 the PBC assigned 300 key large and medium-sized state-owned enterprises as well as large and medium-sized state-owned enterprises in seven cities to individual state commercial banks; the banks are expected to supply sufficient funding.[24] With the

---

[21] *Jinrong shibao* 97/3/29 carried an example of how a county government tried to pressure a rural joint credit cooperative (*lianshe*) to extend loans to county enterprises which would then pay taxes to the county government. It threatened (and in part proceeded) to cut off electricity and water supply to the joint credit cooperative, to stage an investigation of the credit cooperative's lending behavior, and to expel the children of the head of the joint credit cooperative from the local school.

[22] See *Ming Pao* 98/1/11. Banks are traditionally viewed as secondary in rank to productive enterprises and their superordinate ministries, and thus as service institutions for state-owned enterprises. The question of rank reaches back to the early years of the PRC. See, for example, Walter (1985) on the failure of the 1956 credit reforms and the subsequent low status of the monobank PBC. After the failed reforms, "the PBC continued to supply working capital to enterprises virtually on demand" (p. 289).

The establishment of bank branches follows the government administrative structure, and branches may only collect deposits and make loans within their locality. Activities across the borders of the locality must be reported to the PBC. On local financial protectionism see, for example, Ding and Liu (1993).

[23] The ICBC headquarters issues maximum quotas on such loans to each province; if these quotas are not sufficient, the locality may exceed them but should (in urgent cases a posteriori) obtain approval from headquarters. These policy/ special loans are only extended if the local finance or labor department subsidizes the interest payment. Final repayment of the loan is left unclear. (ICBC 13 June 1994)

[24] See *Jinrong shibao* 97/1/9.

proliferation in financial institutions reflecting little more than the creation of financial institutions attached to lower-level tier governments, the pattern of assigning enterprises to individual financial institutions continues on provincial, municipal, county, and township tier.[25]

A tradition of banks as accountants and facilitators of plan fulfillment does not strengthen their authority. Thus banks need continued government support when collecting interest payments and principal from their main borrowers, the state-owned enterprises. In recent years this led to explicit lending contracts between banks and governments, with the bank promising loans to government-selected state-owned enterprises and projects in exchange for government quasi-guarantees of loan repayment.[26]

Banks' limited experience in selecting borrowers and in monitoring and enforcing loan contracts is aggravated by limited access to enterprise information. To amend the information deficit the PBC – true to its traditional practice of exercising microeconomic control – in April 1996 began to issue "credit licenses" to all borrowing enterprises; the license must be renewed at the PBC every year. The credit license contains enterprise information relevant for lending decisions and is to be made available to banks when applying for a loan.[27] But the credit license system has met with strong opposition by enterprises as well as banks which do not want to reveal their past and present lending practices to the PBC. The PBC itself does not have the staff to sufficiently supervise credit licenses and in practice implementation of the regulation has therefore lapsed.

The transition from an 'imperative' to an 'indicative' credit plan for the four state commercial banks reflects little more than an acknowledgment

---

[25] The central government can primarily rely on the four state commercial banks, the provincial government on trust and investment companies as well as regional commercial banks, the municipal government on urban cooperative banks, the county government on rural credit cooperatives, and the township government on rural cooperative funds.

[26] For example, in late 1999 the ICBC Sichuan provincial branch entered a contract with the Yibin municipal government in which it guaranteed Yibin municipality a certain share of the annual increase in its province-wide lending. The municipality promised support in attracting deposits, collecting interest payments and principal, and safeguarding bank assets. (*Jinrong shibao* 99/11/15)

[27] See PBC 95/11/30 and various reports in *Jinrong shibao* such as on 96/3/31, 96/7/ 21, and 96/12/2.

The regulation was first applied in two hundred large and medium-sized cities and then extended by some provinces further down the administrative hierarchy. For the license to be valid, enterprises must submit their balance sheet and profit and loss account for inspection to the PBC annually. When applying for a loan or extending a loan, the bank enters the relevant information in the credit license.

that credit limits in the past few years could not be fully enforced.[28] Within each bank, the credit plan remains imperative as it suits the centralized credit approval structure within each bank in place since 1994.[29] Explicit government industrial policy regulations restrict lending to desirable industrial sectors and projects. The lending limit of the 'indicative' credit plan has not yet met its test, in part because banks have been trying to meet the in 1994 newly implemented ratio requirements, such as a loan-deposit ratio of below 0.75, but also because they are reluctant to assume responsibility for lending in a still rapidly changing economic environment.

Commercial banking remains hampered by continued central control over interest rates. The central government actively adjusts interest rates to regulate the demand for consumer goods and thereby influence the inflation rate. Controlled interest rates together with strict limitations on interbank money market transactions and bank participation in the stock market also help stem inter-regional flows of funds to the most productive regions of China, mainly the coastal regions, that would endanger investment and production in the interior provinces. In this heavily regulated financial environment, private banking has been outright prohibited.[30] Private banks might not only evade the plethora of restrictions but also endanger the stability of the state-owned financial sector burdened with policy tasks.

The limitations to financial intermediation have resulted in an astounding bad loan problem in the state commercial banks. A member of the

---

[28] Already in 1986–88, credit limits were once merely indicative targets, with overshooting not being penalized. Later on, credit limits were again more strictly enforced. (Mehran 1996, 41) For the discrepancy between credit plan limits and actual credit outstanding see Fan et al. (1993, 25) and Xie (1997). In the years 1985 to 1996 actual year-end credit outstanding exceeded the plan by between 21 and 109% (in 1995 and 1985, respectively).

[29] See, for example, *Jinrong shibao* 97/12/20 which states explicitly: "The abandonment of the imperative plan only holds for the commercial bank as a legal person, and does not mean that all tiers of the commercial bank follow deposit-loan ratios and other asset-liability ratios, as if the big bank could be split up into many small banks."

As recently as late 1997 ICBC branches in a particular county were penalized by the Party cell in the municipal PBC branch for exceeding their credit plan limits; some branch directors were suspended for three years. (*Jinrong shibao* 97/11/30)

[30] As recently as 1992 the SC agreed to a PBC instruction explicitly stating that "individuals cannot establish banks or non-bank financial institutions and cannot undertake financial business." (PBC 92/12/10). Likewise, *Renmin ribao* on 6 July 1995 stated that China does not allow the establishment of private banks (according to ZGJRNJ 1996, 17). Newly established nationwide commercial banks such as Huaxia and Minsheng Bank have slightly more complex ownership structures with as owners state-owned enterprises and non-state enterprises under the (state-run) All-China Federation of Industry and Commerce, respectively, but remain if not directly state-owned then state-controlled.

central Party school in 1995 suggested that "according to today's most conservative estimate," the share of non-performing loans in all bank loans is about 25%; "some scholars even think this figure to be around 47%." At end-1995 a 47% share of all loans was equal to 80% of all household savings deposits and 41% ofGDP.[31]

Since mid-1998 the government has countered with a number of measures. In fall 1998 the four state commercial banks received a 270b yuan capital injection, raising their equity from 2.45% of their combined assets at the end of the second quarter of 1998 to 6.15% at the end of the third quarter.[32] After 50 years of almost exclusive lending to state-owned enterprises, banks were finally encouraged to lend to private households for car or house purchases, and to small- and medium-sized enterprises independent of ownership form.[33] Chinese Communist Party (CCP) financial work committees were set up in all four state commercial banks in order to strengthen independence as well as supervision; these report to the CCP Central Committee financial work committee as well as the CCP Central Committee discipline work committee.

But banks have become increasingly cautious now that they are held responsible for at least some of their lending. The annual growth rate of state bank loans fell from its level above 20% between 1993 and 1997 to 15% in 1998.[34] As economic growth in 1998 threatened to slip below the 8% target, the central government in August issued – outside the regular budget – new bonds worth 100b yuan to finance infrastructure investment, equivalent to 6.51% of all investment by state-owned units in China in 1998. These quasi-government, quasi-guaranteed projects then attracted several hundred billion yuan of bank loans.[35] In 1999 the government finally tackled the past bad loan problem head-on by turning bad enterprise loans into equity held by four resolution trust companies. By end-1999 these were poised to take

---

[31] See Zhou (1995), If; ZGJRNJ 1996, 429; and ZGTJNJ 1996, 42.

[32] See ZGRMYHTJJB vol. 15 (1999–3), 21.

[33] Despite the publicity, the volume of such loans has remained small. In mid-1999, 82.15% of total lending by all state banks was to state-owned enterprises (including urban collective-owned enterprises); individual-owned enterprises accounted for only 0.36%, rural collective-owned enterprises, the typical small or medium-sized enterprises, for 2.56%, and a category 'others,' presumably including consumer loans, for 1.01%. (*Zhongguo jinrong* 8/99, 37)

[34] See ZGJRNJ 1998, 509; and *Zhongguo jinrong* 2/99, 38f.

[35] The same pattern repeated itself in 1999, with the government in late 1999 issuing 60b yuan of government bonds to finance infrastructure projects beyond the planned budget expenditures; this is reported to have induced additional bank lending of more than 200b yuan. (*Jinrong shibao* 99/11 /20) On the investment data see ZGTJNJ 1999, 184.

over approximately 5% of the four state commercial banks' loan portfolio.[36] Banks are supposed to make a clean new start.

But their main clientele remain the state-owned enterprises; thus, for example, the state commercial banks on behalf of the government continue to keep close track of cash disbursements to state-owned enterprises. Industrial policy tasks as outlined above continue to restrict bank operations. Discretionary government instructions abound; thus, for example, the state commercial banks following central government orders buy treasury bills, state development bank and resolution trust company bonds. The central bank continues its microeconomic policies from extending poverty alleviation loans to twisting commercial banks' arms for particular lending purposes. The fundamental change in the functions of money and therefore financial intermediation and monetary policy brought about in the early reform period by the need to give enterprises decision-making autonomy remains by far the most significant financial reform measure. All other developments since, implemented gradually throughout the past approximately 15 years, have so far not added up to a final push towards market-oriented functions of money, financial intermediation, and monetary policy.

Conclusions

A focus on the functions of money, financial intermediation and monetary policy yields a number of conclusions on how the development of the PRC's financial sector came about. At a first stage of economic reform, decentralization of decision-making authority in the real sphere required money to acquire the medium of choice function for enterprises. This change in the functions of money in turn led to changes in the functions of financial intermediation and monetary policy, and ultimately to changes in the financial structure.

While the real economy faces a physical constraint (no more products can be distributed than have been produced or stored), no such hard constraint exists in the monetary sphere. This allowed the delay of painful reforms in the real economy, such as the reform of inefficient state-owned enterprises, through the accumulation of non-performing loans. Economic reform appeared successful and gained momentum and support. The government maintained its administrative, microeconomic allocation and control mechanisms over the economy, only now through the monetary sphere.

The pressure to liberalize the financial system further is high. By the late 1990s, in the aftermath of the Asian financial crisis; the extent of non-performing loans was too formidable to be ignored any longer. Non-performing loans

---

[36] The State Economic and Trade Commission by late 1999 has approved and recommended 394 enterprises for a debt-equity swap total of 358.7b yuan, which compares to total loans by all state banks at mid-1999 of 7158.9b yuan. (*Jinrong shibao* 99/11/21 and *Zhongguo jinrong* 8/99, 37)

attribute a clear price to the continuation of administrative, microeconomic allocation and control mechanisms. At the same time, tight central control over the financial sector hampers the development of an increasingly complex economy. Lower-level tier governments responded by extending the formal financial sector through the establishment of local financial institutions. In the second half of the 1990s, an informal financial sector sprang up in the countryside which the central government has since tried to bring under its control.

Yet recent reform measures, while improving the health of the financial sector and redressing the worst mis-allocation of funds, are still based on the principle that the financial sector is a tool of the state to implement various policy and control objectives. Formal financial sector development is still not so much directly driven by market friction (information and transaction costs) as by the needs of a transition economy in the eyes of the government.

The underlying mechanisms of financial sector development discussed in this paper urge caution in the interpretation of indicators of financial structure, such as the ratio of savings to GDP. A high ratio of savings to GDP – and China's ratio of 120.53% in 1998 exceeds that of the US at 38.11% by far-need not imply a high degree of sophistication in financial intermediation, which then supposedly implies strong economic growth.[37] Given the extent of bad loans in China's state-owned banking system and the implicit government guarantee for the banking system, much of the deposits in the PRC's banks simply reflect government debt. China's fast rate of economic growth thus may be highly correlated with measures of financial depth, but the underlying mechanisms are simply expansionary government policies.

Acknowledgments

The author is grateful for criticism and suggestions from Thomas P. Lyons, Judith Banister, Zhu Xiaodong, and the participants of the Asian Pacific Rim Experience Session of the Chinese Economic Association of North America at the 1998 Allied Social Science Association meetings.

References

Bank of China International Finance Research Institute. 1996. *Sulian jinrong qishi nian—jianlun meiguo de jinrong* (Seventy years of finance in the Soviet Union—with a discussion of finance in the USA). Beijing: Zhongguo shuji chubanshe.

---

[37] For example, Levine and Zervos (1998) find a "strong, positive link between financial development and economic growth and [that] the results suggest that financial factors are an integral part of the growth process." On the data see ZGTJNJ 1999, 55 and 624; Federal Reserve internet database (www.bog.frb.fed.us) and *Economic Indicators* (November 1999).

Berthelemy, Jean Claude, and Aristomene Varoudakis. 1996. "Models of Financial Development and Growth: A Survey of Recent Literature," Chapter 1 in Niels Hermes and Robert Lensink, eds., *Financial Development and Economic Growth: Theory and Experiences from Developing Countries*. London: Routledge, pp. 7–34.

Caprio, Gerard, Jr., and Ross Levine. 1994. "Reforming Finance in Transitional Socialist Economies," *The World Bank Research Observer 9*, no. 1, January, pp. 1–24.

Caprio, Gerard, Jr., Izak Atiyas, and James A. Hanson, eds. 1994. *Financial Reform: Theory and Experience*. Cambridge: Cambridge University Press.

Chant, John. 1992. "The New Theory of Financial Intermediation," Chapter 3 in Kevin Dowd and Mervyn K. Lewis, eds., *Current Issues in Financial and Monetary Economics*. New York: St. Martin's Press, pp. 42–65.

Cheng, Hang-Sheng. 1981. "Money and Credit in China," *Federal Reserve Bank of San Francisco Economic Review*, Fall, pp. 19–36.

China Financial Statistics 1952–1987. Beijing: China Financial Publishing House, 1989.

Claessens, Stijn. 1996. "Banking Reform in Transition Countries," World Bank, Manuscript.

Cole, David C, and Betty F. Slade. 1991. "Reform of Financial Systems," in Dwight Perkins and Michael Roemer, eds., *Reforming Economic Systems in Developing Countries*. Cambridge, MA: Harvard University Press, pp. 314–40.

De Melo, Martha, and Cevdet Denizer. 1997. "Monetary Policy During Transition: An Overview," The World Bank, Policy Research Working Paper No. 1706, January.

De Wulf, Luc, and David Goldsbrough. 1986. "The Evolving Role of Monetary Policy in China," *International Monetary Fund Staff Papers 33*, no. 2, June, pp. 209–42.

Dembinski, Pawel H. 1988. "Quantity versus Allocation of Money: Monetary Problems of the Centrally Planned Economies Reconsidered," *Kyklos 41*, no. 2, pp. 281–300.

Ding Hengjiang and Liu Xiaoqi. 1993. "Guanyu defang zhengfu ganyu yinhang jingying huodong de shenceng sikao" (Some profound thoughts on the interference of local governments in bank management), *Jingji yanjiu* #12, December, pp. 29, 45–48.

Economic Indicators. 1999. Prepared for the Joint Economic Committee by the Council of Economic Advisors. Washington, D.C.: Government Printing Office, November.

Fan Gang, Zhang Shuguang, and Wang Limin. 1993. "Shuanggui guodu yu 'shuanggui tiaokong' (shang): gaige yilai wo guo hongguan jingji bodong tedian yanjiu" (Double-track transition and double-track adjustment (Part I): a study of the characteristics of the macroeconomic fluctuations since the beginning of the reforms), *Jingji yanjiu* #10, October, pp. 15–26.

Gertler, Mark. 1988. "Financial Structure and Aggregate Economic Activity: An Overview," *Journal of Money, Credit and Banking 20*, no. 3, Part 2, August, pp. 559–88.

Gertler, Mark, and Andrew Rose. 1994. "Finance, Public Policy, and Growth," Chapter 2 in Gerard Caprio, Jr., Izak Atiyas, and James A. Hanson, eds., *Financial Reform: Theory and Experience*. Cambridge: Cambridge University Press, pp. 13–48.

Hsu, Robert C. 1991. *Economic Theories in China, 1979–1988*. Cambridge: Cambridge University Press.

ICBC (Industrial and Commercial Bank of China). 13 June 1994. *Zhongguo gongshang yinhang yinfa <guanyu dangqian de guoyou gongye kuisun qiye fafang jiben zhuanxiang daikuan de guanli banfa> de tongzhi* (Administrative measures for special loans to presently loss-making industrial state-owned enterprises). Gongyinfa #81/1994. In JRGZZDXB 1994/1, pp. 297–9).

Jinrong shibao (Financial Times). Beijing, daily newspaper.

JRGZZDXB. *Jinrong guizhang zhidu xuanbian* (Selected financial rules and regulations). Beijing: Zhongguo jinrong chubanshe, two volumes per year.

King, Robert G., and Ross Levine. 1993a. "Financial Intermediation and Economic Development," Chapter 6 in Colin Mayer and Xavier Vives, eds., *Capital Markets and Financial Intermediation*. Cambridge: Cambridge University Press, pp. 156–89.

King, Robert G., and Ross Levine. 1993b. "Finance and Growth: Schumpeter Might Be Right," *Quarterly Journal of Economics 108*, no. 3, August, pp. 717–38.

Kornai, Janos. 1979. "Resource-Constrained versus Demand-Constrained Systems," *Econometrica 47*, no. 4, July, pp. 801–19.

Levine, Ross, and Sara Zervos. 1998. "Stock Markets, Banks, and Economic Growth," *American Economic Review 88*, no. 3, June, pp. 537–58.

Levine, Ross. 1997. "Financial Development and Economic Growth: Views and Agenda," *The Journal of Economic Literature 35*, no. 2, June, pp. 688–726.

Marx, Karl. 1971. Das Kapital III: Der Gesamtprozess der kapitalistischen Produktion (Kapital III: The process of capitalist production). Berlin: Ullstein Materialien.

McKinnon, Ronald I. 1993. "Macroeconomic Control in Liberalizing Socialist Economies: Asian and European Parallels," Chapter 8 in Albert Giovannini, ed., *Finance and Development: Issues and Experiences*. Cambridge: Cambridge University Press, pp. 223–56.

Mehran, Hassanali, Marc Quintyn, Tom Nordman, and Bernard Laurens. 1996. "Monetary and Exchange System Reforms in China: An Experiment in Gradualism," Occasional Paper No. 141, Washington, D.C.: International Monetary Fund.

Ming Pao. Hong Kong, daily newspaper.

Miurin, Paolo. 1995. "The Banking System, Monetary Policy and Economic Transformation in Russia: 1992–1994," *MOCT-MOST 5*, no. 1, Winter, pp. 53–70.

Montes-Negret, Fernando. 1995. "China's Credit Plan: An Overview," *Oxford Review of Economic Policy 11*, no. 4, pp. 25–42.

Naughton, Barry. 1985. "False Starts and Second Wind: Financial Reforms in China's Industrial System," Chapter 9 in Elizabeth J. Perry and Christine Wong, eds., *The Political Economy of Reform in Post-Mao China*. Cambridge, Mass.: Harvard University Press, pp. 223–52.

NPC (National People's Congress)

95/3/18 *Zhonghua renmin gongheguo zhongguo renmin yinhang fa* (PRC People's Bank of China law). In ZXZYYHSWQS pp. 309–13.

95/5/10 *Zhonghua renmin gongheguo shangye yinhang fa* (PRC commercial banking law). In ZXSYYHSWQS, pp. 1075–82.

PBC (People's Bank of China).

88/9/23 *Zhongguo renmin yinhang guanyu yinfa <<Xianjin guanli zanxing tiaoli shishi xize>>* (Temporary implementing instructions on the administration of cash). Yinfa #288/1988. In JRGZZDXB 1988/1, pp. 16–23.

92/12/10 *Zhongguo renmin yinhang guanyu qiye, geren bu de banli jinrong yewu de tongzhi* (Circular on enterprises and individuals not being allowed to undertake financial business). Yinfa #284/1992. In JRGZZDXB 1992/1, p. 78.

94/2/15 *Zhongguo renmin yinhang dui shangye yinhang shixing zichan fuzhai bili guanli de tongzhi* (Circular on the asset-liability ratio management of commercial banks). Yinfa #38/1994. In JRGZZDXB 1994/1, pp. 25–31.

95/11/30 Daikuanzheng guanli banfa (Credit License Administration Measures). Yinfa #322/1995. In JRGZZDXB 1995/1, pp. 141–6.

Qin, Chijiang et al. 1993. *Jinrong tizhi bianqian yu songjin zhuanhuan* (Changes in the financial system and the switch from "lose" to "tight" monetary policy). Beijing: Zhongguo caizheng jingji chubanshe.

Renmin ribao (People's Daily). Beijing, daily newspaper.

Sametz, Arnold W. 1991. "The Role of Financial Reform and Development in China's Economic Reform and Development," *Journal of Asian Economics 2*, no. 2, Fall, pp. 337–51.

SC (State Council).

84/6/28 (revised 85/7/3) *Guoying qiye jiangjinshui zanxing guiding* (Temporary regulation on bonus taxes in state-owned enterprises). In ZHRMGHGFLQS vol. 1, pp. 665f.

Sheng Mujie. 1989. *Zhongyang yinhang xue* (Central banking). Beijing: Zhongguo jinrong chubanshe.

Sigg, Hans. 1981. *Grundzuege des sowjetischen Bankwesens: historische Entiwcklung, Struklur und Aufgaben* (Fundamentals of Soviet banking: historical development, structure and tasks). Stuttgart: Haupt.

Sundararajan, V. 1992. "Central Banking Reforms in Formerly Planned Economies," *Finance & Development 29*, no. 1, March, pp. 10–13.

Thornton, John. 1996. "Financial Deepening and Economic Growth in Developing Economics," *Applied Economics Letters 3*, April, pp. 243–6.

Walter, Carl E. 1985. "Dual Leadership and the 1956 Credit Reforms of the People's Bank of China," *The China Quarterly 102*, June, pp. 277–290.

Wu Yu-Shan. 1994. *Comparative Economic Transformations: Mainland China, Hungary, the Soviet Union, and Taiwan*. Stanford, California: Stanford University Press.

Xiao Geng. 1997. *Chanquan yu zhongguo de jingji gaige* (Property rights and China's economic reform). Beijing: Zhonguo shehui kexue chubanshe.

Xie Kangsheng. 1997. "Guanyu quxiao xindai guimo guanli de xianshi tiaojian yu shishi buzhou" (On the actual requirements for and implementary steps of abolishing the administration of the credit volume). *Jinrong yanjiu baogao*, no. 10, 4 May.

ZGJRNJ. *Zhongguo jinrong nianjian* (Almanac of China's finance and banking). Beijing: Zhongguo jinrong nianjian bianjibu. Various years.

ZGRMYHTJJB. *Zhongguo renmin yinhang tongji jibao* (Quarterly People's Bank of China statistics). Beijing: People's Bank of China. Various issues.

ZGTJNJ. *Zhongguo tongji nianjian* (China Statistical Yearbook). Beijing: Zhongguo tongji chubanshe. Various years.

ZGWJNJ. *Zhongguo wujia nianjian* (China price yearbook). Beijing: Zhongguo wujia nianjian bianjibu. Various years.

Zhongguo jinrong (China Finance). Beijing, monthly journal.

Zhongguo chengxiang jinrong bao (China Urban and Rural Finance). Beijing, daily newspaper.

Zhou Tianyong. 1995. "Yinhang daizhang he huaizhang shi daozhi shehui dongdang de yinhuan" (Non-performing loans are hidden dangers bringing about social unrest), *Jinrong cankao*, January, pp. 1–3.

ZHRMGHGFLQS. *Zhonghua renmin gongheguo falu quanshu* (Collected laws of the PRC). Jilin: Jilin renmin chubanshe. Volumes 1–7.

ZHRMGHGGWYGB. *Zhonghua renmin gongheguo guowuyuan gongbao* (State Council Bulletin. Beijing: State Council. Various Issues).

ZXSYYHSWQS. 1995. *Zui xin shangye yinhang shiwu quanshu* (Latest commercial banking manual). Beijing: Zhongguo jinrong chubanshe.

ZXZYYHSWQS. 1995. *Zui xin zhongyang yinhang shiwu quanshu* (Latest central banking manual). Beijing: Zhongguo jinrong chubanshe.

9
China's Monetary Policy and the Exchange Rate

Aaron Mehrotra[1] and José R Sánchez-Fung[2]
[1]*Bank for International Settlements, Switzerland; and* [2]*University of Nottingham, Ningbo, China*

The paper models monetary policy in China using a hybrid McCallum-Taylor empirical reaction function. The feedback rule allows for reactions to inflation and output gaps, and to developments in a trade-weighted exchange rate gap measure. The investigation finds that monetary policy in China has, on average, accommodated inflationary developments. But exchange rate shocks do not significantly affect monetary policy behaviour, and there is no evidence of a structural break in the estimated reaction function at the end of the strict dollar peg in July 2005. The paper also runs an exercise incorporating survey-based inflation expectations into the policy reaction function and meets with some success.

Introduction

China's emergence as a global power raises concerns about its economic policies. Monetary policy commands attention, as maintaining low inflation is crucial for social and economic stability. High inflation could erode the value of Chinese households' large savings in domestic banks – broad money M2 amounted to over 150% of GDP in 2008. And China's policymakers are also concerned about sustaining rapid economic growth. Hence, considering a central bank loss function including inflation and output gaps, as in Svensson (1999), is likely to further our understanding of the conduct of monetary policy in China. But China's institutional features, in particular the limited role of interest rates in the monetary transmission mechanism, precludes estimating benchmark monetary policy reaction functions that are popular for analysing more advanced economies.

Reprinted with permission from Association of Comparative Economic Studies. All rights reserved. *Comparative Economic Studies* (2010) 52(4), 497–514.

The paper models monetary policy in China using a hybrid McCallum–Taylor reaction function (McCallum, 2000; Sánchez-Fung, 2005). The main question we seek to answer is: how does the People's Bank of China react to developments in the economy, in particular to output, inflation and exchange rate gaps? In tackling that question, the investigation estimates reaction functions to capture the monetary authorities' adjustments of the monetary base in reaction to the variables of policy interest. The econometric modelling also estimates a reaction function incorporating a survey-based measure of inflation expectations.

Discussions about China's monetary policy have largely focused on the exchange rate, especially in the context of the 2007–2009 crises, where the country's dollar peg was thought to be important in feeding the global imbalances (Corden, 2009). That is why China's decision of returning to a *de facto* dollar peg in the summer of 2008 generated criticism. In principle, the problem is that fixing the exchange rate renders domestic interest rate policy ineffective in the presence of full capital mobility. But China's capital controls have been largely binding, so that determining the link between movements in the exchange rate and domestic monetary policy is an empirical matter.

Previous studies use quantity-based rules in modelling China's monetary policy, but the ultimate aim was different from the present study. Burdekin and Siklos (2008) examine whether Chinese monetary policy could be modelled using a McCallum-type rule. They first compare the outcomes for money growth in China to those suggested by the McCallum rule, and use the data for estimating the coefficients for the policy rule. Koivu *et al.* (2009) use a McCallum-type rule to forecast inflation in China. Liu and Zhang (2007) used a quantity-based rule as part of a New-Keynesian model to analyse monetary policy in China.

Zhang (2009) compares price and quantity rules in a dynamic stochastic general equilibrium framework for China, and finds evidence that the impact of a price rule in the economy has become more important. He further argues that, when hit by shocks, following a price rule reduces volatility in the economy. But the policy rules examined in the study do not include the exchange rate as a target variable. Zhang (2009) also includes forward-looking inflation terms in the policy rules, but these are based on actual (instrumented) inflation outcomes rather than on surveys.

We find that monetary policy in China has been procyclical in terms of reactions to inflation. The finding matches the fact that accelerated reform policies have generally coincided with increase in bank lending and inflation pressures (Naughton, 2007). But there is evidence of stabilising policy *via* reactions to the output gap, and that may reflect the importance to the authorities of supporting economic growth and employment. Importantly, exchange rate shocks do not seem to significantly impact domestic monetary policy. The outcome probably reflects effective capital controls that have allowed for conducting a largely independent monetary policy in China. There is no evidence of a structural break, in terms of the estimated monetary policy reaction function, following the end of the strict dollar peg in July 2005.

The paper also includes survey-based inflation expectations in the Chinese monetary policy reaction function. Using business surveys to evaluate the relevance of including forward-looking elements in the estimated equations produces evidence of stabilising policy in terms of inflation. But the finding is dependent on the measure of inflation expectations.

The paper proceeds as follows. The next section specifies the empirical monetary policy reaction function, relating it to the specific features of China's monetary policy and institutions. The subsequent section contains the econometric modelling of the benchmark reaction functions. The penultimate section estimates an empirical monetary policy reaction function, including a survey-based measure of inflation expectations. The final section concludes.

Specifying a Mccallum–Taylor Reaction Function

The paper models monetary policy in China using the type of hybrid McCallum–Taylor reaction function studied in Sánchez-Fung (2005) (see also McCallum, 2000). The central bank controls the growth of the monetary base Δb according to the following feedback mechanism

$$\Delta b = a + \beta_1(y - y^*) + \beta_2(\pi - \pi^*) + \beta_3 (e - e^*) + u \tag{1}$$

In equation 1 $(y - y^*)$ is the output gap measured as the difference between actual and potential output; $(\pi - \pi^*)$ is the inflation gap, that is, the difference between actual inflation and the pre-announced annual inflation target. The gap $(e - e^*)$ gives the nominal trade-weighted exchange rate's deviations from a long-run trend path.

The monetary base is the relevant instrument under the control of the policymaker (McCallum, 1988). Interest rates – only infrequently adjusted – have traditionally played a small role in China's monetary transmission mechanism. The authorities announce a variety of interest rates, such as a bank lending rate, rediscount rate, and benchmark rates for loans and deposits of different maturities. But overall the liberalisation of interest rates has proceeded slowly.

In contrast to the limited role of interest rates, intermediate annual money supply targets for M2 have been announced from the mid-1990s. The People's Bank targets a level of the money supply so as to prevent inflation and deflation (PBoC, 2005). Reserve requirement ratios have been adjusted in order to control the money supply, together with open market operations in treasury bonds and central bank bills. The choice of instrument for analysis here corresponds with previous work on China's monetary policy, for example, Burdekin and Siklos (2008), Koivu *et al.* (2009), and Koźluk and Mehrotra (2009). Operating a fixed exchange rate along with strict capital controls has enabled implementation of a fairly independent monetary policy (eg, Ma and McCauley, 2008). Majority state ownership of the banking sector arguably facilitates sterilisation of capital inflows.[1] Formal credit plans formed the basis of commercial bank lending until 1998. Window guidance policy continues to play an important role in Chinese monetary policy, which includes direct guidelines from central bank to commercial banks on lending to the money-holding sector.[2]

The target variables on the right hand side of equation 1 are rationalised by the formal objectives of the People's Bank of China. The announced objective of Chinese monetary policy is to 'maintain the stability of the value of the currency and thereby promote economic growth'.[3] Although the specification of a final target suggests that the value of the currency is important, promoting economic growth is in line with the Chinese government's concern for providing sufficient employment and maintaining social stability. This supports inclusion of the output gap in equation 1. As an expanding output gap may result in inflationary pressures, its inclusion is justified also on the basis of maintaining price stability.

In estimating the output gap in China the analysis applies a Hodrick-Prescott filter to year-on-year growth rates of industrial production, with a conventional smoothing parameter of 1,600.[4] Holz (2004) notes that China's data collection is most advanced for the industrial sector. Industry covered 47% of China's GDP both at the start (1994) and end (2008) of our estimation sample. There is also a strand of research related to the limitations and reliability of Chinese GDP statistics (Rawski, 2001; Holz, 2008). Recent important revisions to GDP data – in particular the 17% upward adjustment to its level in late 2005 – have been due to corrections regarding the size of the service sector.

---

[1] Liu and Zhang (2007) note that there have been persistent deviations from uncovered interest rate parity.

[2] For a thorough description of China's monetary policy, see Geiger (2008); Evenett (2010) discusses China's exchange rate policy.

[3] http://www.pbc.gov.cn/english/huobizhengce/objective.asp.

[4] Although an industrial production series in levels is available in current prices, no deflator is published; hence our choice of year-on-year growth rates (in constant prices) for construction of the output gap. Moreover, during the reform period, Chinese economic cycles have been 'growth cycles', with slowdowns and upturns in growth rates but no fall in the levels series.

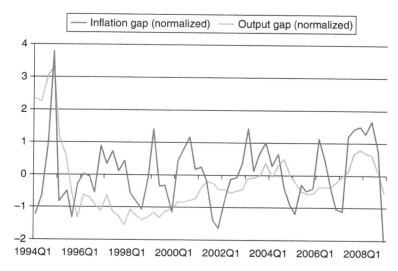

Figure 9.1 Output gap and inflation gap
Note: Both series are normalised by their respective standard deviations.

China does not operate a formal inflation-targeting regime, but annual targets for CPI growth are set by the Central Economic Working Conference. We employ that measure in constructing the inflation gap.[5] For the 1994–1997 period, targets were only defined for retail price inflation (RPI), a variable that is closely correlated with CPI inflation. For those years, CPI inflation targets are constructed using the announced RPI inflation target, and adding the gap between actual CPI and RPI inflation for the previous year.[6] The inflation gap has been negative during most of the sample, as actual inflation has fallen short of the target. Positive inflation gaps have been largely a temporary phenomenon, arising with demand pressures and high lending growth in 1994/1995, and in tandem with food price pressures in 2004 and 2007/2008. Figure 9.1 displays the inflation gap together with the output gap, both series divided by their respective standard deviations. Some co-movement between the two series can be seen for 1994, 2004 and 2008.

The final gap in equation 1 is the exchange rate gap. China has tightly controlled the value of the yuan against the dollar, even after the strict dollar peg was disbanded in July 2005. The fixed exchange rate arrangement

[5] The data are from the China Monetary Policy Report, from 2001 onwards (various issues). The targets prior to 2001 were obtained from the website of the National People's Congress of China (only in Chinese, link available from the authors upon request).
[6] For 1998, when both RPI and CPI targets were announced by the government, this procedure produces a CPI target equal to the officially announced target.

makes China different from some other transition economies (see eg, Granville and Mallick, 2010, for evidence on the role of the exchange rate in Russian monetary policy). The existence of the strict peg during most of the sample ruled out use of the bilateral rate in the econometric modelling. The model produces the impacts of the trade-weighted nominal exchange rate, which is not an operating target, on China's monetary policy. The rate is important from a policy perspective, as it captures imported inflation pressures and changes in competitiveness more extensively than a bilateral exchange rate. The exchange rate gap is defined as the deviation of a trade-weighted exchange rate from its trend. This measure abstracts from the trend appreciation affecting an emerging economy with rapid productivity growth and the ensuing Balassa-Samuelson effect.

Estimating the Monetary Policy Reaction Function

The research plan involves estimating a hybrid McCallum-Taylor policy rule using vector autoregressions (VARs). The strategy allows starting from a single equation specification by focusing on part of the estimated system and subsequently examining richer dynamics *via* an impulse response analysis. The starting point is a benchmark reduced-form vector autoregression:

$$x_t = A_1 x_{t-1} + \cdots + A_p x_{t-p} + u_t \tag{2}$$

In equation 2, the x_t is a $(K \times 1)$ vector of endogenous variables, the A_p are fixed $(K \times K)$ coefficient matrices, and u_t is assumed to follow a K-dimensional white noise process with $E(u_t) = 0$. A four-variable VAR is estimated, including output gap $(y - y^*)$, inflation gap $(\pi - \pi^*)$, annualised quarter-on-quarter change in monetary base Δb, and nominal exchange rate gap $(e - e^*)$. Applying an augmented Dickey-Fuller test reveals that all the series are stationary: a unit root can be rejected for all series at the 10% level when the Akaike information criterion is used to determine lag length, and for the exchange and output gap a unit root can be rejected at the 1% level.[7] Summary statistics for the variables are shown in Appendix A.

The time series data are for 1994Q1–2008Q4, but estimations begin at 1994Q2, due to the use of first-differenced data for monetary base. The year 1994 is an important year in terms of reforms, as the former dual exchange rate system gave way to a single exchange rate framework, the fiscal system underwent a revamping, and policy banks were created to differentiate policy-related financing from commercially oriented activities.

---

[7] When the Schwarz information criterion is used, a unit root can be rejected at 1% level for monetary base as well. Detailed results are available from the authors upon request.

The VARs include three lags, to allow for one full year of dynamics in the level of the monetary base, and estimate the system using ordinary least squares. The system includes a constant and a linear trend. The modelling process reduces the estimated VARs to a parsimonious system by sequentially eliminating all coefficients with t-values below the threshold of 1.00, at each step re-estimating the system and deleting the coefficient with the lowest t-value. The resulting system, estimated with feasible generalised least squares, passes the major misspecification tests for autocorrelation and Autoregressive conditional heteroskedasticity (ARCH) effects.[8]

The equation for the monetary base is the following (with standard errors in parentheses)

$$\Delta b_t = -2.207(y - y^*)_{t-1} + 3.055(\pi - \pi^*)_{t-1} - 0.146\Delta b_{t-1} - 2.073(\pi - \pi^*)_{t-2}$$
$$\quad (0.996) \qquad\qquad (1.017) \qquad\qquad (0.115) \qquad\qquad (0.839)$$

$$+ 0.183\Delta b_{t-2} - 3.004(e - e^*)_{t-2} + 1.277(y - y^*)_{t-3} + 0.276\Delta b_{t-3}$$
$$\quad (0.121) \qquad\qquad (0.888) \qquad\qquad (0.859) \qquad\qquad (0.121)$$

$$+ 2.383(e - e^*)_{t-3} + 11.849$$
$$\quad (0.902) \qquad\quad (3.876) \qquad\qquad\qquad\qquad\qquad\qquad\qquad (3)$$

The estimated equation for the monetary base suggests that the People's Bank conducts a countercyclical policy, leaning against the wind, in terms of the output gap: an increase in the output gap leads to slower growth of the monetary base.[9] But the result for the inflation gap is the opposite: inflation above the government's target leads to an increase in the rate of change in monetary base, suggesting that policy is accommodating increases in inflation.[10] The latter finding is parallel to the argument by Naughton (2007) that the demand for real resources has been accommodated by credit policy, which has then led to inflation. But as the inflation gap has been mostly negative during most of our sample period, inflation has not posed a problem for policy makers in China.[11] The reaction of monetary base growth to

---

[8] The adjusted Portmanteau test for autocorrelation yields a test statistic of 253.24 (p-value of 0.14), and the LM test for autocorrelation with 4 and 1 lags amounts to 76.11 (0.60) and 9.24 (0.90), respectively. The multivariate ARCH-LM test yields a test statistic of 510.00, with a p-value of 0.37.

[9] The result is obtained by calculating the long-run impact, that is, adding up the lagged coefficients of the output gap.

[10] Burdekin and Siklos (2008) find a procyclical response of monetary policy to movements in nominal GDP. However, they do not estimate policy reactions to movements in real output and inflation separately.

[11] According to the International Monetary Fund (2003), both transitory and long-term supply shocks contributed to deflation in China in the late 1990s and early 2000s.

the exchange rate gap is accommodative: exchange rate appreciation leads to a fall in base money growth.

How do the results look if we assume the existence of an interest rate rule and replace the growth in base money in the VAR by the People's Bank of China's benchmark 1-year lending rate?[12] The resulting equation for the interest rate in the VAR is as follows:

$$i_t = 1.137i_{t-1} - 0.023(e-e^*)_{t-1} - 0.244i_{t-2} - 0.043(y-y^*)_{t-3}$$
$$\quad (0.141) \qquad\qquad (0.023) \qquad\quad (0.137) \qquad\qquad (0.028)$$

$$+ 0.034(\pi - \pi^*)_{t-3} + 0.940 - 0.007t$$
$$\quad (0.012) \qquad\qquad (0.361) \quad\; (0.004) \qquad\qquad\qquad (4)$$

In addition to the statistically significant coefficients on lagged interest rates – suggesting important instrument smoothing – and the deterministic terms, only the coefficient on the inflation gap is statistically significant at the 10% level. Further, although its sign would actually suggest a countercyclical policy response, the magnitude of the coefficient is small. The evidence shows that an interest rate rule does not provide an adequate description of monetary policy behaviour in China, at least during the sample considered in the study. The finding is in line with the observation by Liu and Zhang (2007) that a standard Taylor rule does not capture China's interest rate movements well during the 1992–2006 period. We therefore, continue with the benchmark system with monetary base as the central bank's instrument.

The analysis examines the system's dynamics by shocking the VARs and computing impulse responses. If we do not want to take a strong stand on the contemporaneous restrictions to identify the system, we could in principle compute forecast error impulse responses (eg, Breitung *et al.*, 2004). This option creates similar dynamics, as suggested by equation 3, that is, policy is leaning against the wind in terms of the output gap, and accommodative in terms of the inflation and exchange rate gaps.[13]

However, the correlation matrix provides evidence against choosing forecast error impulse responses: the residuals appear contemporaneously correlated, and the correlations in many cases exceed $\pm 2/T^{1/2}$, where T is the sample length. Under such conditions, shocks to the system would not

---

[12] Dai (2006) reports that the PBoC would have adopted interest rates as the intermediate goal in 2004. Nevertheless, in 2009, intermediate targets for monetary aggregates and credit growth were announced by the PBoC. Furthermore, base money can be used as an instrument even with a change in the intermediate target by the monetary authority.

[13] The results can be obtained from the authors upon request.

happen in isolation. So the analysis opts for structural impulse responses with contemporaneous restrictions, in particular the AB Model by Amisano and Giannini (1997). Denoting the structural form errors as ε_t and the reduced form disturbances as u_t as before, the model $Au_t = B\varepsilon_t$ is written as

$$
\begin{bmatrix} 1 & * & 0 & 0 \\ 0 & 1 & 0 & * \\ 0 & 0 & 1 & * \\ * & * & * & 1 \end{bmatrix} \begin{bmatrix} u_t^\pi \\ u_t^m \\ u_t^y \\ u_t^e \end{bmatrix} = \begin{bmatrix} * & 0 & 0 & 0 \\ 0 & * & 0 & 0 \\ 0 & 0 & * & 0 \\ 0 & 0 & 0 & * \end{bmatrix} \begin{bmatrix} \varepsilon_t^\pi \\ \varepsilon_t^m \\ \varepsilon_t^y \\ \varepsilon_t^e \end{bmatrix} \tag{5}
$$

where * denotes an unrestricted element.

The structural shocks are an output shock ε_t^y, a price shock, ε_t^π, a monetary policy shock ε_t^m – defined as a shock to monetary base – and an exchange rate shock ε_t^e. The structure of system 5 implies that the effective exchange rate gap, being determined largely outside of China, is allowed to react immediately to any shock hitting the system. The assumption is reasonable, as we are not using the bilateral USD-yuan rate that was stable during a major part of the estimation sample. The monetary policy reaction function – corresponding to the second row in (5) – is constructed taking account of the policymaker's information set. Although information about the exchange rate is available immediately, data on output and inflation gaps are only available with a lag.

The output gap appears in the third row and is specified to react slowly to shocks hitting the system, possibly due to pre-determined consumption and investment expenditure, as in Rotemberg and Woodford (1999). But the output gap reacts rapidly to exchange rate shocks, to avoid over-identifying the system.[14] The inflation gap reacts slowly to shocks in output or the exchange rate. A slow response is in line with a standard Calvo-pricing scheme, where prices are changed at exogenously determined random intervals (Calvo, 1983), or due to menu costs. There is a policy dimension to the inflation gap variable as it incorporates the government's inflation target. So the inflation gap is allowed to react contemporaneously to a monetary policy shock. As there are $K = 4$ endogenous variables, and $K(K − 1)/2$ restrictions are necessary for exact identification, the system (5) is just identified.

The structural model is estimated using the variance-covariance matrix of the reduced form VAR, with a maximum likelihood estimator and scoring algorithm. Figure 9.2 shows the structural impulse responses 12 quarters ahead. The impulse response graphs show the path of monetary base growth following the various shocks. Appendix B shows the impulse responses computed using the system. In order to illustrate the uncertainty

---

[14] Restricting the coefficient on the exchange rate shock to zero is not supported by the data, judging by the test on over-identifying restrictions.

related to the parameter estimates, the graphs display Hall's 95% percentile intervals, obtained by bootstrapping methods with 1,000 replications (Breitung *et al.*, 2004).

The structural impulse responses partly confirm the results from the monetary base equation of the reduced form VARs: policy is accommodative in terms of an inflation shock and countercyclical in terms of an output shock. The latter finding supports the common perception about the importance of growth and employment for China's policymakers. However, domestic monetary policy does not appear to be very responsive to movements in the exchange rate.[15] This may be the result of relatively binding capital controls, which provide leeway for domestic policy despite the fixed exchange rate, or the possibility to sterilise capital inflows without major implications for domestic interest rates.

It is of interest to consider the robustness of the responses in Figure 9.2 to changes in the structure of the estimated SVAR model. In particular, we investigate the responses to shocks in a system with a Cholesky decomposition of the variance-covariance matrix and the following two orderings of the variables: $\{(y - y^*), (\pi - \pi^*), \Delta b, (e - e^*)\}$ and $\{(e - e^*), \Delta b, (\pi - \pi^*), (y - y^*)\}$. The procyclical response to the inflation gap detected in the benchmark system remains when adopting the alternative models. With the first ordering, the response of policy to an output shock appears to be procyclical and with both orderings there is evidence of a procyclical policy response to the exchange rate. However, there is little theoretical support for the second ordering of variables.[16]

The exercise also considers a five-variable VAR including the benchmark 1-year lending rate: in this system movements in the monetary aggregate should be negatively correlated with interest rates. In the reduced form equations, base money never enters the equation for interest rates with a statistically significant coefficient. The interest rate enters the equation for base money with a counterintuitive positive coefficient. It is difficult to identify shocks in the SVAR methodology including both base money and interest rates, as it is not clear how to simultaneously identify the (assumed) policy shocks. However, simple forecast error impulse responses indicate that there

---

[15] This finding is confirmed by examining the accumulated impact of exchange rate shocks on monetary base in levels instead of growth rates – there is no statistically significant impact on the level of base money. In contrast, structural shocks to output and prices have a statistically significant impact on base money in levels for several quarters.

[16] The dynamics of the structural shocks do not need to seem identical to the coefficient estimates of the reduced form equations, as the structural shocks are identified by theoretical assumptions about the contemporaneous relationships between the reduced form errors. This explains why the policy reaction to the exchange rate gap is countercyclical in equation 2 but the response of base money to a structural shock in the exchange rate is largely insignificant in Figure 9.2.

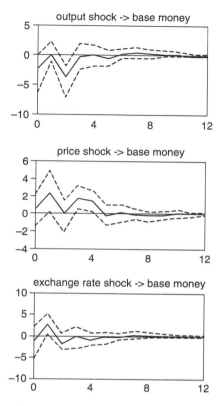

Figure 9.2 Responses of base money growth to various shocks

is no statistically significant impact of a base money shock on the interest rate. This result is expected given the limited role of interest rates in the monetary transmission mechanism, especially in the earlier part of our sample.

We have also estimated the VAR with a different measure of the output gap. Instead of using data on industrial production, we have computed an output gap based on the growth rates of real GDP, with an identical methodology to the one described in the section 'Specifying a McCallum-Taylor reaction function'. The SVAR impulse responses are similar to those obtained with the benchmark model: a price shock is met with a procyclical policy response and the response to an output shock is countercyclical although statistically insignificant. An exchange rate shock is also met with a procyclical policy response when real GDP is used. We emphasise that the findings should be treated with caution, taking into account the arguments in favour of the industrial production data in the section 'Specifying a McCallum-Taylor reaction function'. The robustness tests provide evidence of the procyclical tendencies of China's monetary policy. Detailed results from all robustness tests are available from the authors upon request.

During the sample period there was a major change in China's exchange rate policy: on 21 July 2005 China announced that it was ending the fixed dollar peg, with a subsequent switch to a peg to a basket of currencies. Shortly afterwards the People's Bank provided more information about the composition of the currency basket: the biggest weights were assigned to the US dollar, the euro, the Japanese yen, and the Korean won. Other minor currencies were also included. But actual policy strongly resembled a crawling peg from July 2005 until the summer of 2008, after which China has kept the value of the yuan stable against the US dollar.

Frankel and Wei (2007) estimate that almost all weight on the currency basket was on the US dollar in 2005 and that the dollar's weight was still 'fairly heavy' in 2006.[17] The investigation tests whether monetary policy setting in China experienced a structural break following the change in the exchange rate regime, by computing a Chow forecast test. Because Candelon and Lütkepohl (2001) show that the standard F-test leads to excessive rejections in samples of realistic size, the p-values for the test are obtained by bootstrapping methods with 1,000 replications.

There is no evidence of a structural break in the exchange rate in the third quarter of 2005 – the test statistic's p-value is 0.51. Did the change in the exchange rate regime induce a slow change in domestic policy? The analysis tests for a possible structural break on every observation during the 2005Q4-2006Q4 period. All resulting p-values are far above those normally considered standard for rejecting model stability. The lowest p-value obtained is for 2006Q1 (0.37). The analysis also runs the model until 2005Q2 and performs out-of-sample forecasts 10 quarters ahead. The approach provides an additional test for system stability.

Formally, an h-step-ahead forecast is obtained as

$$\hat{X}_{T+h|T} = \hat{A}_1 \hat{x}_{T+h-1|T} + \cdots + \hat{A}_p \hat{x}_{T+h-p|T} \tag{6}$$

where $\hat{x}_{T+j|T} = x_{T+j}$ for $j \leq 0$ and the $\hat{A}_i$'s $(i = 1,\ldots,p)$ are estimated parameters.

Figure 9.3 shows that the actual observation for 2005Q4 (solid black line) is just on the borderline of the 95% confidence intervals (grey dashed lines), while all other actual observations for base money fall inside the confidence

---

[17] Recent estimates support an increasing weight on the euro in the basket, but since September 2008 almost all weight appears to again go to the US dollar (see Frankel, 2009, and http://content.ksg.harvard.edu/blog/jeff_frankels_weblog/2009/03/11/the-rmb-has-now-moved-back-to-the-dollar/).

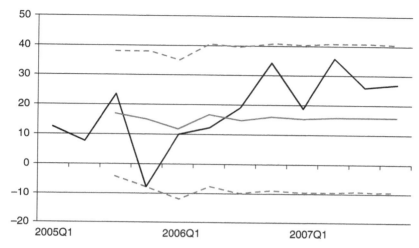

Figure 9.3   Out-of-sample forecast for base money growth (grey solid line)

bands. This provides further evidence that the exchange rate reform has not entailed a structural change in domestic policy. That also supports the findings in the literature about the relative independence of Chinese monetary policy (eg, Ma and McCauley, 2008; Liu and Zhang, 2007).

Monetary Policy Reactions and Survey-Based Inflation Expectations

The previous analysis considers monetary policy reactions to current and past developments in the relevant variables, but does not explicitly include forward-looking terms. Given the empirically well-established lag between a change in the monetary policy stance – or a policy shock – and output and inflation, including a forward-looking variable in a policy reaction function can be easily justified.[18] However, the omission of explicit forward-looking terms does not imply that the hybrid rule would not allow for any forward-looking behaviour in policy making. Indeed, if an increase in output gap is expected to lead to inflation pressures with a lag, then by leaning against the wind with respect to output gap the central bank may be reacting to future inflation pressures. This may arise despite the fact that the coefficient on current and past inflation gap signal accommodative policy behaviour.

China's surveys on inflation expectations are deficient in terms of sample length. The People's Bank of China publishes a survey on inflation

---

[18] Woodford (2000) discusses problems related to excessive forward-looking reactions in monetary policy.

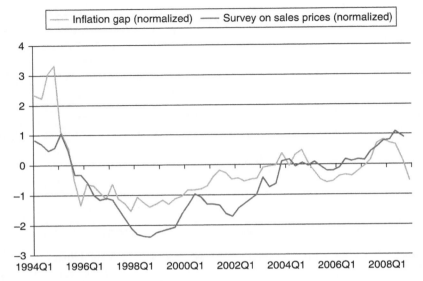

Figure 9.4   Inflation gap and diffusion index on firms' price level of sales
Note: Both series are normalised by their respective standard deviations.

expectations, but the data are available only for the current decade. For that reason the paper employs a business survey on the price level of sales in 5,000 principal industrial enterprises in China, compiled by the People's Bank.[19] The series reflects the firms' judgments on price developments, including the prospects for the next few months. Most firms in the survey are state-owned large- and medium-sized enterprises, covering a total of 27 industries. The data are available for the entire sample.[20] The survey is based on diffusion indices that are quantitative indicators constructed from qualitative answers by firms. The indices are obtained as the difference between qualitative answers indicating either an improving or a deteriorating outlook (an increase or a decrease in sales prices). As the index values range from –100 to +100, the survey does not produce an actual point forecast for the price level or inflation, but it does capture the perceived and expected dynamics of sales prices. Figure 9.4 shows the inflation gap and the survey for price level of sales, with both series normalised by their standard deviations.

Given the difficulty of simultaneously identifying shocks both in terms of actual inflation and the survey-based measure in a SVAR framework, the

---

[19] The People's Bank's survey on inflation expectations is highly correlated with the business survey used in our study for the 2001–2008 period, where both series are available (contemporaneous correlation coefficient of 0.83).

[20] A possible alternative would be to use actual future outcomes for inflation and estimate a forward-looking reaction by GMM, as reported in Zhang (2009). However, our approach relies on surveys on inflation rather than a perfect foresight assumption.

modelling focuses on examining a reduced form equation similar to equation 3, but incorporating the first differences of the price level survey (π^e). The model is estimated using ordinary least squares, eliminating coefficients with t-values below 1.00, and estimating the reduced model *via* feasible generalised least squares. The parsimonious equation for the monetary base is

$$\Delta b_t = -1.569(y - y^*)_{t-1} + 2.541(\pi - \pi^*)_{t-1} - 0.200\Delta b_{t-1} - 1.740(\pi - \pi^*)_{t-2}$$
$$\quad\,\,(0.965) \qquad\qquad\quad (1.078) \qquad\qquad (0.114) \qquad\quad (0.861)$$

$$+ 0.201\Delta b_{t-2} - 3.651(e - e^*)_{t-2} + 0.658\Delta\pi^e_{t-2} + 1.982(y - y^*)_{t-3}$$
$$\quad (0.123) \qquad\qquad (0.974) \qquad\qquad (0.433) \qquad\qquad (0.912)$$

$$+ 0.336\Delta b_{t-3} + 2.798(e - e^*)_{t-3} + 0.645\Delta\pi^e_{t-3} + 6.268$$
$$\quad (0.117) \qquad\qquad (0.920) \qquad\qquad (0.488) \qquad (5.070) \qquad\qquad (7)$$

In equation 7, although the long-run coefficient on the inflation gap is still positive, the one based on survey data carries a negative sign, suggesting that the People's Bank reacts to increases in inflation expectations *via* restrictive monetary policy. But in equation 7 the output gap carries a positive long-run coefficient, which provides some evidence that the countercyclical output gap response identified earlier in the paper actually captures a reaction to inflation expectations.

The analysis considers an alternative measure of inflation expectations computed using an autoregressive univariate model of inflation. An AR(1) model, including a constant term, is estimated as a rolling regression from 1994Q1–1998Q1 to 1994Q1–2008Q4, and at every observation a 4-quarter-ahead out-of-sample forecast is produced. This AR-based measure of inflation expectations does not appear to be statistically significant for the resulting sample of 1998Q1–2008Q4.

Conclusion

The paper models monetary policy in China using a hybrid McCallum-Taylor reaction function. The estimated reaction function allows feedback from developments in the output and inflation gaps, together with the effective trade-weighted exchange rate, using base money as the instrument. The analysis finds that Chinese monetary policy has been procyclical, reflecting an accommodative reaction to developments in the inflation gap. This is in line with the empirical observation that liberalisation policies in terms of reforms and regulation have coincided with increases in lending and inflation. But the reaction to the output gap has been countercyclical, whereas the money supply has not reacted significantly to developments in the exchange rate.

The paper finds stabilising policy behaviour when using business surveys of price developments, suggesting that the People's Bank of China reacts significantly to inflation expectations. The finding is consistent with the estimation of policy reaction functions in a general equilibrium framework, such as Zhang (2009), or in a three-equation New-Keynesian model, as in Liu and Zhang (2007). Similarly, the countercyclical response for the output gap probably reflects reactions to future price developments.

Acknowledgements

We thank Tuuli Koivu, Iikka Korhonen, participants in the 2010 American Economic Association-ASSA Annual Meetings in Atlanta, ACES session on China's exchange rate, and in the 2010 Finnish Economic Association Annual Meeting in Tampere, in particular our discussants Sushanta Mallick and Petri Maki-Franti, for helpful comments and suggestions. All opinions are those of the authors and do not necessarily reflect those of the Bank for International Settlements. Any errors are our own.

References

Amisano, G and Giannini, C. 1997: *Topics in structural VAR econometrics*. Springer-Verlag: Berlin.

Breitung, J, Brüggemann, R and Lütkepohl, H. 2004: Structural vector autoregressive modeling and impulse responses. In: Lütkepohl, H and Krätzig, M (eds). *Applied Time Series Econometrics*. Cambridge University Press: Cambridge.

Burdekin, RCK and Siklos, PL. 2008: What has driven Chinese monetary policy since 1990? Investigating the People's bank's policy rule. *Journal of International Money and Finance* 27: 847–859.

Calvo, G. 1983: Staggered prices and in a utility-maximizing framework. *Journal of Monetary Economics* 12(3): 383–398.

Candelon, B and Lütkepohl, H. 2001: On the reliability of chow-type tests for parameter constancy in multivariate dynamic models. *Economics Letters* 73: 155–160.

Corden, WM. 2009: China's exchange rate policy, its current account surplus and the global imbalances. *Economic Journal* 119: F430–F441.

Dai, M. 2006: Inflation-targeting under a managed exchange rate: The case of the Chinese central bank. *Journal of Chinese Economic and Business Studies* 4(3): 199–219.

Evenett, SJ (ed). 2010: *The US-Sino currency dispute: New insights from economics, politics and law*. Centre for Economic Policy Research: London.

Frankel, J. 2009: New estimation of China's exchange rate regime. *Pacific Economic Review* 14(3): 346–360.

Frankel, J and Wei, S-J. 2007: Assessing China's exchange rate regime. *Economic Policy* 51: 575–614.

Geiger, M. 2008: *Instruments of monetary policy in China and their effectiveness: 1994–2006*. United Nations Conference on Trade and Development, Discussion Paper No. 187.

Granville, B and Mallick, S. 2010: Monetary policy in Russia: Identifying exchange rate shocks. *Economic Modelling* 27(1): 432–444.

Holz, CA. 2004: China's statistical system in transition: Challenges, data problems, and institutional innovations. *Review of Income and Wealth* 50(3): 381–409.

Holz, CA. 2008: China's 2004 economic census and 2006 benchmark revision of GDP statistics: More questions than answers? *The China Quarterly* 193(March 2008): 150–163.

International Monetary Fund. 2003: *Deflation: Determinants, risks and policy options – Findings of an interdepartmental task force.* International Monetary Fund: Washington, DC.

Koivu, T, Mehrotra, A and Nuutilainen, R. 2009: An analysis of Chinese money and prices using a McCallum-type rule. *Journal of Chinese Economic and Business Studies* 7(2): 219–235.

Koźluk, T and Mehrotra, A. 2009: The impact of Chinese monetary policy shocks on East and South-East Asia. *Economics of Transition* 17(1): 121–145.

Liu, L-g and Zhang, W 2007: *A new Keynesian model for analyzing monetary policy in mainland China.* Hong Kong Monetary Authority Working Paper 18/2007.

Ma, G and McCauley, RN. 2008: Efficacy of China's Capital controls: Evidence from price and flow data. *Pacific Economic Review* 13: 104–123.

McCallum, BT 1988: Robustness properties of a rule for monetary policy. *Carnegie-Rochester Conference Series on Public Policy* 29(Autumn): 173–203.

McCallum, BT. 2000: Alternative monetary policy rules: A comparison with historical settings for the United States, the United Kingdom, and Japan. *Federal Reserve Bank of Richmond Economic Quarterly* 86: 49–79.

Naughton, B. 2007: *Chinese economy: Transitions and growth.* MIT Press: Cambridge, MA.

PBoC. 2005: *China monetary policy report, quarter one, 2005. Monetary Policy Analysis Group of the People's Bank of China.* China Financial Publishing House: Beijing.

Rawski, TG. 2001: What is happening to China's GDP statistics? *China Economic Review* 12(4): 347–354.

Rotemberg, JJ and Woodford, M. 1999: Interest-rate rules in an estimated sticky-price model. In: Taylor, JB (ed). *Monetary Policy Rules.* University of Chicago Press: Chicago.

Sánchez-Fung, JR. 2005: Estimating a monetary policy reaction function for the Dominican Republic. *International Economic Journal* 19(4): 563–577.

Svensson, LEO. 1999: Inflation targeting as a monetary policy rule. *Journal of Monetary Economics* 43: 607–654.

Woodford, M. 2000: Pitfalls of forward-looking monetary policy. *American Economic Review* 90(2): 100–104.

Zhang, W 2009: China's monetary policy: Quantity versus price rules. *Journal of Macroeconomics* 31: 473–484.

Appendix A

See Table 9.A1.

Table 9.A1 Summary statistics

Variable	Mean	Min	Max	Standard deviation
Inflation gap	−1.233	−7.202	15.399	4.430
Output gap	0.143	−3.775	7.165	1.908
Base money growth	14.989	−33.416	46.728	13.819
Exchange rate gap	−0.167	−4.116	5.726	2.324

Appendix B

See Figure 9.B1.

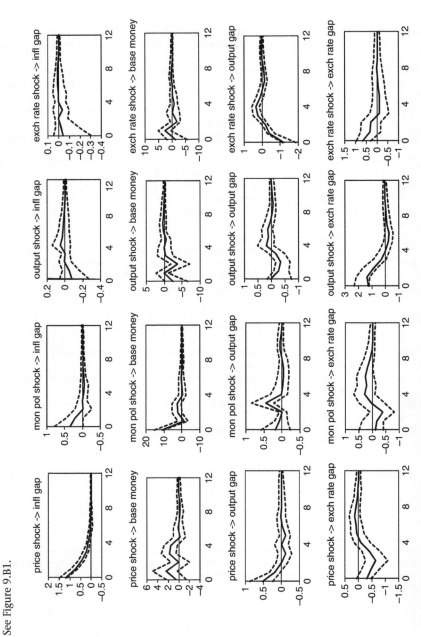

Figure 9.B1 Impulse responses computed using the benchmark VAR

10

The Structure of Chinese Industry and the Impact from China's WTO Entry

Aimin Chen
Sichuan University, China

This paper examines the impact of WTO entry on the change of China's industrial structure. It first investigates the pre-entry structure from both perspectives of changing role of the state and the scale economic characteristics. Post-entry systemic and resource re-allocation effects are then analyzed. Emphasis of the analyses is placed on major industries that are currently highly concentrated with nearly exclusive ownership by the state and on the sectors in which rapid entry by the non-state owned enterprises have taken place. Case studies are provided where more detailed data are available.

I Introduction

China's WTO entry comes at a critical stage of its transition to a market economy.[1] The entry will not only forcefully change the market structure in terms of its concentration and resource allocation among products of different comparative advantages, but also profoundly weaken the dominance of state enterprises in the economy. We call the first effect the scale effect and the second, systemic effect. This article analyzes, from the both perspectives, the current structure of Chinese industry and the impact from China's WTO entry on the structure.

The paper is organized as follows. In the second section, I will first examine the current systemic structure of the Chinese industry using most recent

---

[1] China is hopeful to officially enter the WTO in November 2001. The major issues on the entry have all been resolved. China has finished its negotiations with the U.S. and countries in the European Union, and the remaining negotiation with Mexico will not impact negatively on the anticipated date of entry [*People s Daily* (electronic version), May 25, June 7, June 9, June 21, July 04, and July 27, 2001].

Reprinted with permission from Association of Comparative Economic Studies. All rights reserved. *Comparative Economic Studies* (Spring 2002) 44(1), 72–98.

available data from Chinese official sources, highlighting the declining state dominance in general and the rapid development of certain sectors in particular. In section III, the market structure from scale perspective is examined to evaluate and explain the state of concentration and competitiveness of Chinese firms and the dynamic consolidation that has been taking place. Then in section IV, the scale and the systemic effects of WTO entry are discussed. The author argues that while WTO entry will accelerate the consolidation of Chinese firms, which leaves China's major sectors and industries more concentrated, the severity of the effect on state dominance varies among sectors depending on the systemic structure of the sectors prior to the entry. Since WTO entry will lead to the unprecedented breaking of administrative and ideological barriers in the service and agriculture sectors, we expect a significant weakening of the state dominance in these two sectors. Such effect is much less obvious for the industrial sector, however. The fifth section concludes the paper.

II   The Current Structure: A Systemic Approach

It has been a stylized fact that the state economy is on the decline in all former centrally planned transition economies. In China such decline has accelerated especially in late 1990s. We will analyze the dynamics in three aspects. To guide the analysis, the classification of China's economic sectors is provided in Table 10.1. Many of the tables to follow cover the structure and dynamics of industrial and tertiary sectors. The primary (or the agriculture) sector is analyzed only in the assessment of the impact of WTO entry.

1   The Significantly Weakened State Sector Measured by Urban Employment

China's economy consists of enterprises of various ownership types. Statistically, four types of enterprises are officially listed as the state-owned enterprises (SOEs), the collectively-owned enterprises (COEs), privately owned enterprises and self-employment (we will address the two together as private enterprises hereafter), and other types of enterprises. The last category of "other types" consists of share-holding corporations, foreign founded enterprises, and enterprises founded by entrepreneurs from Hong Kong, Macao, and Taiwan.

The decline in the dominance of the state sector in the urban economy can be seen from the negative growth in the 1990s of the urban employment in the sector (Table 10.2) despite the persisting disguised unemployment in state enterprises. The collectively-owned enterprises have experienced a similar decline of employment. Moreover, the share of total urban employment in the state sector has shrunk from 70.24% in 1990 to 55.58% in 1998 and in the collective sector from 24.10% in 1990 to 12.20 in 1998.

Table 10.1 Classification of Chinese economic sectors

Name	Description

First Sector (Primary Sector)	Agriculture, including
	  Farming
	  Forestry
	  Animal husbandry
	  Fishery

Second Sector	1. Industry
	  Mining and quarrying
	  Manufacturing
	  Production and supply of electricity, water, and gas
	2. Construction

Tertiary Sector	1. **Circulation sector (or first level).** transportation, storage, postal and telecommunications whole sale and retail trade 2. **Service sector (or second level):** banking, insurance, geological survey, water conservancy management, real estate; services for residents, agriculture; and forestry, animal husbandry, fishery, subsidiary services for transportation and communications, comprehensive technical services. etc. 3. **Third level,** education, culture and arts, broadcasting, movies, television, public health, sports, social welfare and scientific research, etc. 4. **The fourth level:** government agencies, political parties, social organizations, military and police service

Source: *China Statistical Yearbook 1999*, pp 104–105.

In the meantime, the private sector urban employment has increased from 4.55% to 20.76% and "other types" increased from 1.11% to 11.45% during the same period (Table 10.3). The non-publicly owned enterprises, which include the last two types of enterprises, together now account for 32.96% of total urban employment. But if we define dominance as possessing more than 50% of the total share, China's state sector, not to mention together with the collective sector as the public sector, is still in dominance.

The data in Table 10.2 also show that, between 1980 and 1990, there was an expansion of employment in all sectors. But, between 1990 and 1998, the state and collective sectors declined, suggesting a more rapid reform and labor resource reallocation in the 1990s.

2 The Lost Dominance in the Industrial Sector Measured by Gross Value of Industrial Output (GVIO)

First, a conceptual delineation must be made to eliminate confusion on the scope of the term "industry." In China, an industry involves non-agricultural activities that turn physical inputs into physical outputs, thus excluding service activities of any kind. China's industrial sector includes

184

Table 10.2 Changing role of enterprises of different ownership types: employment (in 10,000) and its growth (% change in parentheses)

	State-owned Enterprises			Collectively-owned Enterprises			Privately-owned Enterprises & Self employment			Other Types Of Enterprises	
	1980	1990	1998	1980	1990	1998	1980	1990	1998	1990	1998
Total of All Sectors	8019	10346 (29)	8809 (−16)	2425	3549 (46)	1900 (−46)	81.4	670.5 (723)	3231.9 (382)	163.8	1627.6 (894)
Faming, forestry, Animal Husbandry & Fishery	740	737 (−0.4)	525 (−29)	48	42 (−13)	16 (−62)	0.2	0.6 (200)	43.4 (7133)	1.1	5.06 (360)
Mining & Quarrying	621	786 (27)	596 (−24)	76	95 (25)	49 (−48)	NA	NA	13.9 (∞)	0.67	56.96 (8400)
Manufacturing	2601	3395 (31)	1883 (−45)	1346	1773 (32)	742 (−58)	9.5	91.3 (861)	563.9 (518)	135.5	1143.6 (744)
Production & Supply of Electricity, Gas & Water	112	183 (63)	242 (32)	6	9 (50)	11 (22)	NA	NA	NA	1.09	2868 (2348)
Construction	475	538 (13)	444 (−17)	235	357 (52)	311 (−13)	0.4	4.6 (1050)	55.2 (1100)	1.59	91.49 (5654)
Geological Prospecting & Water Conservancy	187	194 (3.7)	113 (−42)	1.0	3.3 (230)	2.0 (−39)	NA	NA	NA	0.04	0.10 (150)
Transport, Storage, Post, & Telecommunications	496	660 (33)	584 (−12)	216	232 (7.4)	79 (−66)	0.8	36.4 (4450)	190.3 (423)	1.63	37.73 (2215)
Wholesale and Retail Trade & Catering Services	1005	947 (−5.7)	694 (−27)	234	762 (226)	414 (−46)	57.1	431.2 (655)	1896.2 (340)	6.00	148.88 (2383)
Banking and Insurance	63	145 (130)	208 (43)	26	51 (96)	71 (39)	NA	NA	NA	0.05	21.90 (43700)
Real Estate Trade*	33	40 (21)	63 (58)	4	4	7 (75)	NA	NA	NA	0.51	19.26 (3676)
Social Services*	130	236 (82)	322 (36)	88	93 (5.7)	68 (−27)	13.0	94.3 (625)	397.2 (321)	15.03	61.02 (306)
Health Care, Sports, & Social Welfare	217	323 (49)	402 (24)	70	69 (1.4)	58 (−16)	0.4	7.0 (1650)	NA	0.05	0.98 (1860)
Education, Culture & Arts, Radio, Film & TV	757	1112 (47)	1408 (27)	60	32 (−47)	41 (28)	0.7 (1981)	3.9 (457)	NA	0.26	1.52 (485)

185

Scientific Research & Polytechnic Services	104	148 (42)	155 (4.7)	1	3 (200)	7 (133)	NA	1.2	NA	0.20	643 (3115)
Government Agencies, Party Agencies, & Social Organizations	476	903 (90)	1079 (19)	14	26 (86)	5 (−81)	NA	NA	NA	NA	NA
Others	NA	NA	84	NA	NA	20	NA	NA	71.8	NA	4.04

Note: "Other Types of Enterprises" include mostly share-holding enterprises, jointly-owned enterprises, limited liability corporations, enterprises funded entrepreneurs from Hong Kong, Macao, and Taiwan, and foreign-funded enterprises. The data did not exist until 1990.

Source: Complied from *China Statistical Yearbook 1994*, p. 98 for the data on Other Types in 1990, all other data are compiled from *China Statistical Yearbook 1999*, pp. 144–149 & 154. The percentage changes are calculated from the data.

Table 10.3 Changing role of enterprises of difference ownership types: share (%) of total urban employment

	Total Employment by All Enterprises (10,000)		State-owned Enterprises		Collectively-owned Enterprises		Privately-owned Enterprises And Self-employment		Other Types of Enterprises	
	1990	1998	1990	1998	1990	1998	1990	1998	1990	1998
Sum of All Sectors	1472.9	15568.9	70.24	55.58	24.10	12.20	4.55	20.76	1.11	11.45
Farming, Forestry, Animal Husbandry & Fishery	780.7	589.5	94.40	89.06	5.38	2.71	0.08	7.36	0.14	0.86
Mining & Quarrying	881.7	715.86	89.15	83.26	10.77	6.84	NA	1.94	0.08	7.96
Manufacturing	5394.8	4332.5	62.95	43.46	32.86	17.13	1.69	13.02	2.51	26.40
Production & Supply of Electricity, Gas & Water	193.1	281.7	94.77	85.9	4.66	3.90	NA	NA	0.56	9.47
Construction	901.2	901.7	59.70	49.24	39.61	34.49	0.51	6.12	0.18	10.15
Geological Prospecting & Water Conservancy	197.3	115.1	98.33	98.18	1.67	1.74	NA	NA	0.02	0.09
Transport, Storage, Post, & Telecommunications	930.0	891.0	70.97	65.54	24.95	8.87	3.88	21.36	0.18	4.23
Wholesale and Retail Trade & Catering Services	2146.2	3153.1	44.12	22.01	35.50	13.13	20.09	60.14	0.28	4.72
Banking and Insurance	196.1	300.9	73.94	69.13	26.01	23.59	NA	NA	0.03	7.28
Real Estate Trade	44.51	89.26	89.87	70.58	8.99	7.84	NA	NA	1.15	21.58
Social Services	438.3	848.2	53.84	37.96	21.22	8.02	21.51	46.83	3.43	7.19
Health Care, Sports, & Social Welfare	399.1	461.0	80.93	87.20	17.29	12.58	1.75	NA	0.01	0.21
Education, Culture and Arts, Radio. Film, & TV	1148.2	1450.5	96.84	97.09	2.79	2.83	0.34	NA	0.02	0.10
Scientific Research & Polytechnic Services	152.4	168.4	97.11	92.04	1.97	4.16	0.79	NA	0.13	3.82
Government Agencies, Party Agencies. & Social Organizations	929.0	1084.0	97.20	99.54	2.80	0.50	NA	NA	NA	NA
Others	NA	179.8	NA	46.67	NA	11.12	NA	39.89	NA	0.84

Table 10.4   Changing role of the state economy

Year	Number of Industrial Firms		Industrial Employment		Value of Industrial Output	
	National Total (10,000)	Share of SOES (%)	National Total (10,000)	Share of SOES (%)	National Total (Billion Yuan)	Share of SOES (%)
1985	518.53	1.81	5,557	68.65	971.65	64.86
1990	795.78	1.31	6378	68.42	2392.44	54.60
1991	807.96	1.29	6551	68.26	2824.80	52.94
1992	862.21	1.20	6621	68.28	3459.9	51.52
1993	991.16	1.06	6626	67.88	4840.2	46.95
1994	1001.71	1.02	6580	66.40	7017.6	37.34
1995	734.15	1.60	6610	66.52	9189.4	33.97
1996	798.65	1.42	6450	62.33	9959.5	28.48
1997	792.29	1.24	6215	65.00	11373.3	25.52
1998	797.29	0.81	4753	52.25	11904.8	28.24

Sources: Calculated from *China Statistical Yearbook*, 1992, pp. 403–404, 1997, pp. 411–412, 1998, pp. 431–432, and 1999 pp. 422–423.

mining and quarrying, manufacturing, and the production and supply of electricity, water, and gas, and construction. The calculation of the gross value of industrial output includes only these listed industrial activities.

As shown in Table 10.4, the share of the gross value of industrial output produced by the state enterprises has decreased from 54.6% in 1990 to less than 28.24% in 1998. It is safe to say that China's state sector has retired from its dominant position in the manufacturing sector, though such position has been well maintained in the public utilities and several other sectors as indicated by the employment shares in Table 10.3.

It is interesting to note, however, that the state sector in 1998 produced 28.24% of GVIO with 57.25% of the labor force compared to about the same share of GVIO produced by 62.33% of the labor force in 1996 and, worse yet, 25.52% of GVIO with 65% of the labor force in 1997. Most obvious reasons are higher efficiency and the release of the disguised unemployment into the explicitly unemployed. The extra labor being shunted away from the sector had zero, if not negative, marginal productivity, holding other factors constant.

3   The Changing Priority of the State Sector: An Inter-Sectoral Perspective

While the overall state dominance measured by total urban employment and the share of gross value of industrial output has declined significantly, the state enterprises have remained dominant in many sectors of the economy.

As shown in Table 10.3, the state has declined significantly in the manufacturing sector, but has remained its dominance or monopoly position in the sector of education, culture and arts, radio, film, and television (97.07% of urban employment); in scientific research and polytechnic services (92.04% of urban employment); in services for farming, forestry, animal husbandry, and fishery (89.06%); in health care, sports, and social welfare (87.2%); in production and supply of electricity, gas, and water (85.9%); in mining and quarrying (83.26%); in real estate trade (70.58%); in banking[2] and insurance (69.13%); and in transport, storage, post, and telecommunications (65.54%).

The state sector has even expanded in absolute size in the public utilities sector, the banking and insurance sector, the education, culture and arts, radio, film and television sector, the real estate sector, and the scientific research and polytechnic services sector. This development not only reveals the priority of the state, but also that the economy as a whole has become increasingly service oriented.

Within the industrial sector, the state dominance exists in the productions that are considered to be vital to national interests. As shown in Table 10.5, the state has kept its dominance of higher than 70% of GVIO in tobacco manufacturing, logging and transport of timber and bamboo, ferrous metal mining and dressing, production and supply of public utilities, petroleum processing and coking, smelting and pressing of ferrous metals, coal mining and dressing, and smelting and pressing of nonferrous metals (51.97%).

Enterprises that have grown most rapidly are those under the ownership type of "Other Types" including mostly share-holding enterprises, joint-ownership enterprises, limited-liability corporations, enterprises funded by entrepreneurs from Hong Kong, Macao, and Taiwan, and foreign-funded enterprises. The growth of employment in these enterprises has accounted for a large portion of the declined shares of the state enterprises. Enterprises in the collective sector seem to have the least favorable growth. Except for noteworthy expansion of employment in scientific research and polytechnic services, all other sectors have either declined dramatically or barely changed (Table 10.3).

Equally noteworthy in Table 10.3 is the changing role of the non-foreign private sector. Private enterprises have grown in the manufacturing sector to hire four times more employees in 1998 than in 1990 and nearly two and a half times more in wholesale and retail trade and catering services during the same period. Entry barriers to private enterprises have continued to exist in public utilities production and supply and mining and quarrying in the

---

[2] In a separate source from The People's Bank of China (February 6, CCTV), the "big four" commercial banks of the Bank of China, the Industrial and Commercial Bank of China, the China Construction Bank, and the Communications Bank of China have total market share of 82.3%, foreign competition 0.6%, and others 17.1%.

Table 10.5 The shares (%) of state enterprises in the industrial sector (1997)

Industries	Number of State-owned Enterprises	GVIO
Coal Mining arid Dressing	15.70	73.49
Petroleum and Natural Gas Extraction	62.65	91.82
Ferrous Metals Mining and Dressing	11.96	33.61
Nonferrous Metals Mining and Dressing	21.91	46.47
Nonmetal Mineral Mining and Dressing	9.05	21.39
Logging and Transport of Timber and Bamboo	61.74	93.99
Food Processing	28.81	39.20
Food Manufacturing	28.59	26.84
Beverage Manufacturing	21.53	45.29
Tobacco Manufacturing	72.61	96.87
Textile Industry	15.52	31.58
Garments and Other Fiber Products	5.43	5.08
Leather, Furs, Down and Related Products	6.89	6.21
Timber Processing, Bamboo, Cane, Palm Fiber and Straw Products	7.46	12.11
Furniture Manufacturing	6.00	5.58
Papermaking and Paper Products	11.73	26.09
Printing and Record Medium Reproduction	21.97	34.23
Cultural, Educational and Sports Goods	8.43	6.86
Petroleum Processing and Coking	14.98	82.55
Raw Chemical Materials and Chemical Products	18.05	46.51
Medical and Pharmaceutical Products	35.30	41.39
Chemical Fiber	15.79	24.39
Rubber Products	12.12	29.60
Plastic Products	7.90	9.92
Nonmetal Mineral Products	10.67	24.62
Smelting and Pressing of Ferrous Metals	14.96	70.39
Smelting and Pressing of Nonferrous Metals	15.41	51.97
Metal Products	7.87	10.59
Ordinary Machinery	13.60	30.65
Special Purpose Equipment	21.19	42.41
Transport Equipment	19.88	47.44
Electric Equipment and Machinery	12.76	16.78
Electronic and Telecommunications Equipment	18.33	22.80
Instruments, Meters, Cultural and Office Machinery	19.56	23.08
Production & Supply of Electric Power, Steam & Hot Water	36.80	72.64
Production and Supply of Gas	71.47	88.90
Production and Supply of Tap Water	43.31	80.75

Source: *China Statistical Yearbook* 1998, pp. 452–453.

industrial sector excluding construction. The branches of the service sector are virtually all off limits to the private sector except in the wholesale and retail trade and catering services. The continued distrust in private enterprises is apparent also from the fact that many sectors are enterable by joint venture firms (under "Other Type"), but not domestic private firms. The entry barriers to domestic private firms but not Other Types of firms also arise from the requirement of production scale and capital investment that are beyond the reach of private firms.

III   The Current Structure: A Scale-effect Approach

Studies of Chinese industrial structure point to two problems: overcapacities in many manufacturing industries, on the one hand, and shortages of high-tech products and infrastructures, on the other. While both aspects are important, we will in this article focus on the overcapacity issue of Chinese industry.

1   How Concentrated Are Chinese Industries?

Official data on concentration ratios of China's industries hardly exist, though in some industries, market shares of leading firms have started to be reported.[3] It has become a standard realization that Chinese industrial firms have been small and that overcapacities have been severe in many industries.

Table 10.6 provides data on the "crowdedness" of Chinese markets in the industrial sector. It is clear that each industry has numerous firms and that the average firm size measured in sales revenues is very small. The profile of the larger firms is also revealed indirectly in Table 10.6. The 1998 data include only SOEs and scaled non-SOEs (those with sales revenues of more than five million yuan), showing a large number of large-scale firms. Though different price systems prevent us from inferring the nature of "smallness" of the firms based on revenues per firm in comparison with other countries, the sheer number of the large firms indicates that the concentration ratios of the largest firms are very low in China's industrial sector.

What then does the numerousness of firms and the overcapacities imply about the nature of the "state monopoly?" The author argues that "state monopoly" is more of a systemic monopolization of the market than share monopolization of the market. The term monopoly virtually refers to the

---

[3] The industry of transport equipment, for example, had a 10-firm concentration ratio of 22.83%, 50-firm concentration ratio of 43.32%, and the industry is said to have scale economies. The industry of electronic and telecommunications equipment, on the other hand, has a 10-firm concentration ratio of 16.62% and 50-firm concentration ratio of 33.98%, but the industry did not seem to have scale economies (Cui and Zhang, 1998).

Table 10.6 Number and size of industrial firms

Industries	1997		1998	
	Number of Firms	Sales Revenues Per Firm (million yuan)	Number of Firms	Sales Revenues Per Firm (million yuan)
Coal Mining and Dressing	11526	12.21	3202	37.20
Petroleum and Natural Gas Extraction	83	2086.36	76	2178.5
Ferrous Metals Mining and Dressing	1948	7.13	577	23.56
Nonferrous Metals Mining and Dressing	3597	9.57	1416	21.72
Nonmetal Mineral Mining and Dressing	10902	3.78	1849	15.54
Logging and Transport of Timber and Bamboo	1197	13.81	634	22.54
Food Processing	27970	12.15	11909	26.71
Food Manufacturing	14304	8.18	5368	20.86
Beverage Manufacturing	12711	11.66	3817	39.03
Tobacco Manufacturing	398	321.94	352	377.44
Textile Industry	21844	19.04	11276	34.26
Garments and Other Fiber Products	17224	9.29	6768	26.29
Leather, Furs, Down and Related Products	8634	11.77	3312	32.66
Timber Processing, Bamboo, Cane, Palm Fiber and Straw Products	14001	3.75	2487	17.84
Furniture Manufacturing	8034	3.34	1470	18.15
Papermaking and Paper Products	13094	8.23	4763	23.62
Printing and Record Medium Reproduction	14359	3.60	3863	12.94
Cultural, Educational and Sports Goods	4921	8.80	1785	28.26
Petroleum Processing and Coking	2356	107.74	1052	224.70
Raw Chemical Materials and Chemical Products	26896	15.68	11303	37.12
Medical and Pharmaceutical Products	5028	23.42	3280	38.54
Chemical Fiber	1292	62.46	803	97.07
Rubber Products	4396	15.64	1785	38.77
Plastic Products	17831	7.17	6016	22.36
Nonmetal Mineral Products	58662	5.52	14496	19.77
Smelting and Pressing of Ferrous Metals	6109	61.10	3260	118.66
Smelting and Pressing of Nonferrous Metals	4297	31.20	2405	63.83
Metal Products	28283	6.37	8132	23.96
Ordinary Machinery	27837	8.88	9282	25.34
Special Purpose Equipment	17916	10.13	6638	25.83
Transport Equipment	18332	21.51	6779	59.18
Electric Equipment and Machinery	17773	17.05	7544	43.56
Electronic and Telecommunications Equipment	7345	50.12	4166	108.00
Instruments, Meters, Cultural and Office	5193	11.31	1821	36.45
Production & Supply of Electric Power, Steam & Hot Water	12164	37.78	4994	100.02
Production and Supply of Gas	361	33.59	291	51.63
Production and Supply of Tap Water	5223	4.94	2363	10.98

Note: The 1998 figures include state-owned enterprises and scaled non-SOEs which are defined as firms with sales revenue of more than five million yuan, whereas the 1997 figures include all independent accounting industrial firms.

Sources: Compiled from *China Statistical Yearbook* 1998 (pp. 444–455) and 1999 (pp. 432–437).

dominance of the state enterprises as a whole, rather than the monopolization of market by individual firms. The competition with each other among
most state firms suggests a low degree of monopolization by individual firms
in the market at least at the national level. The state monopolies will phase
out as a result of both the expansion of private businesses domestically and
the entry of foreign firms following WTO accession. As the reform deepens,
inefficient firms are to be eliminated and efficient firms are to prevail. The
accelerated reform of enterprises is accompanied, therefore, by expansive
consolidation of firms.

2　Too Many Firms in the Markets?

The R Ratio

Does the low concentration ratio carry any implication on the engineering
scale effect about the industries and firms? While generally conclusions in
this regard require statistical analysis of firms' cost structures in relation to
their sizes, anecdotal evidence and the data in Table 10.7 do suggest properties
of similar nature. Table 10.7 shows the production capacity of key firms in
industries and the total output of these industries. The ratio of the industries'
total output to the total capacity of key firms is indicative of the overcapacity
situation and may lead to sensible inference on whether the industries have
too many firms.

Let the ratio of output to capacity be R. If R >1, the industry's total output is greater than the capacity of key firms, indicating that the small firms
are needed to fill the unsatisfied market demand by the key firms. In these
industries, therefore, the key enterprises are leading firms and the markets
are shared by fringe firms. If, for example, R = 1.23, it means that about
20% of the production is produced by fringe firms or that the key firms
have market concentration ratio of 81.3%. The greater is R, the lower are
the concentration ratios of the key firms, and the more evenly distributed
is the market power.

Coal, natural gas, pig iron, and motorcycle industries are observed to have
R >1 with steel industry being the boarder-line case (or R = 1) (see Table 10.7).
Except the motorcycle industry, the other three are perceived as stylized fact
to have many small-scale producers—in fact so many that the government
will close many "small coalmines" as a way to rescue the industry from
heavy losses resulting from over-supply.[4] Another factor contributing to
R >1 is the high demands for energy and material resources relative to their
supplies, consistent with the shortage of energy supply in China. In the case
of motorcycle industry, high demand, relative to that for cars, as well as the

---

[4] The closure of small coalmines is a part of the cracking down on the "Five Smalls" of
small oil refineries, small hydroelectric power plants, small steel plants, small glasses
plants, and small cement production.

ease at which production technology of large firms can be copied by small firms both explain the greater than unit R.

If R < 1, the industry's total output is smaller than the production capacity of its key firms, indicating clearly the existence of overcapacities. The lower is R, the more severe is the situation, which in turn indicates that "too many" firms exist relative to the market demand. The marginal firms' survival under the circumstance may be explained by the fact that the key firms, though larger, are more burdened with retirees and social welfare expenditures on housing, medical service, day care etc. Local protectionism and exit barriers also contribute to their survival. In the cases of R < 1, dynamic adjustments will take place to eliminate the inefficient firms if market is allowed to work.

Table 10.7 shows that overcapacities prevail in most of the listed industries and are most severe in electronic products, which strongly confirms the investigated market situation. In 1996, the production capacity of color television sets was 60% higher than market demand; the capacity utilization rate in the production of air conditioners was 30%; wash machines, 43.3%. 75% of all electronic products were over-supplied, and only 10% under-supplied (Research Group, 1997).

The Cases

Several well-noted cases of over-competition or overcapacities are worth citing to support the findings from Table 10.7. The auto industry, for example, has long been observed to have too many producers. In early 1990s, there were 125 producers in the auto industry with an average annual production of 6000 automobiles (Xia, 1993). In 1996, 47% of all auto producers (more than 100) produced on average less than 1000 vehicles during the first 9 months of production; 67% of the auto firms experienced reduced production from the same period a year before; and there were 116,000 unsold automobiles held as inventory nationwide (Research Group, 1997). At present, almost every Chinese province has its own auto producers, and each province practices local protectionism to set block to cars of other provinces from entering the local market (*China This Week*, CCTV June 24, 2000).

The textile industry had experienced similar overcapacity of 40% above market demand (Research Group, 1997). The government in 1992 set the target to eliminate the overcapacity (*Xinhua Forum*, Nov. 2, 1998) of 10 million spindles and established an aid project to eliminate the overcapacity. Under the "Aide" project, the government would provide a subsidy of three million yuan to an enterprise that idles 10,000 spindles and additional two million for alternative placement of its employees. By October 15, 1998, state textile enterprises had idled 4.32 million spindles, and, of which, 3.56 million were done by large and medium state enterprises. For the first nine months of 1998, 10.8% of, or 450,000, textile workers had been shunted away from the industry through regular or early retirement,

194   *Chen*

Table 10.7   Production capacity and output (end of 1997)

Products	Total Industry Output	Production Capacity of Key Enterprises	Ratio Output to Capacity (R)
Coal (10,000 tons)	137,300.00	74101.00	1.853
Crude Oil (10,000 tons)	16074.14	16194.17	0.993
Natural Gas (100 mil. Cu. M)	227.03	173.97	1.305
Sugar (10,000 tons)	702.58	1028.32	0.683
Liquor (10,000 tons)	781.79	1196.47	0.653
Beer (10,000 tons)	1888.94	2686.54	0.703
Cigarettes (10,000 cases)	3377.42	3789.88	0.891
Chemical Fiber (10,000 tons)	471.62	587.07	0.803
Machine-made Paper and Paperboard (10,000 tons)	2733.20	3509.48	0.779
Sulfuric Acid (10,000 tons)	2036.87	2370.71	0.859
Caustic Soda (10,000 tons)	574.40	662.08	0.868
Soda Ash (10,000 tons)	725.76	743.67	0.976
Synthetic Ammonia (10,000 tons)	3000.28	3864.66	0.776
Chemical Fertilizer (10,000 tons)	2820.96	3624.20	0.778
Chemical Pesticide (10,000 tons)	52.67	75.73	0.695
Plastics (10,000 tons)	685.76	759.92	0.902
Synthetic Detergents (10,000 tons)	279.91	464.11	0.693
Cement (10,000 tons)	51173.80	66016.53	0.775
Plate Glass (10,000 weight cases)	16630.70	20303.79	0.819
Pig Iron (10,000 tons)	11511.41	9357.49	1.230
Steel (10,000 tons)	10894.17	10892.28	1.000
Steel-rolling Capacity (10,000 tons)	9978.93	11512.38	0.867
Metal-cutting Machine Tools (10,000 tons)	18.65	19.83	0.940
Large and Medium Tractors (10,000)	8.24	10.50	0.785
Motor Vehicles (10,000)	158.25	240.00	0.659
Motorcycles (10,000)	1033.42	701.12	1.474
Bicycles (10,000)	2999.29	6274.73	0.478
Household Wash Machines (10,000)	1254.48	2513.95	0.499
Household Refrigirators (10,000)	1044.43	2579.57	0.405
Electric Fans (10,000)	8171.42	13246.33	0.617
Air Conditioners (10,000)	974.01	3317.29	0.293
Microcomputers (10,000)	206.55	402.00	0.514
Color Television Sets (10,000)	2711.33	5069.00	0.535

Source: Compiled from *the China Statistical Yearbook 1999*, pp. 445–447. The ratios in the last column are calculated from the previous two columns.

reemployment in other occupations, self-employment, and extended leaves (*Xinhua Forum,* Nov. 2, 1998). Finally, by the end of 1999, as reported by the State Economic and Trade Commission, the textile industry had turned its heavy losses since 1992 into profits of 800 million yuan (*China Report,* CCTV, Jan. 25, 2000).

China's tobacco industry consisted of 178 firms in 1995, and the market concentration ratio measured by the output of top 14 firms was 34.17% (Shi, 1999), which indicates that the industry is much less concentrated than their counterparts in the US and the Europe. In the 1990s, the capacities of the industry were one third in excess of the market demand (Zhou, 2000).

3 Why So Many Firms?

N_p vs. N_f

The sheer large numbers of Chinese firms arises in part from the fact that, in China, a firm has usually one plant. Let N_p be the number of plants and N_f the number of firms. The two variables approximately equal each other in China. In the West, on the other hand, market concentration ratios based on top corporations and conglomerates that usually have many plants nationwide are high, but the concentration ratios based on top plants would be much lower. In other words, $N_f < N_p$ in the West and $N_f < N_p$ in China may exaggerate the smallness of production scale in engineering perspective. Be that as it may, the same fact (of $N_f < N_p$) contributes to the division of national market and its operation in an efficient way. To illustrate, if corporation x owns plants A, B, and C in three different locations, the corporation then can coordinate the size of the production according to their engineering economic features and demand and supply conditions of the local markets. Such coordination, however, will fail to take place among three plants that are owned by three different firms, or local governments as in the case of China. Instead, they try to compete with each other by building up their capacities and by protecting their local markets. Now if we expand the case to N firms, with each trying to outrun others and protecting its own market, it's hardly surprising that we have as many firms as shown in the table.

Local Protectionism

Unnecessary replication of production facilities has been a long noted problem in China as a result of deregulation in Chinese industries and firms' effort to snatch a share of the market that had long been a sellers' market. But when the market turned into a buyers' market in the 1990s, production facilities became redundant and overcapacities resulted. Instead of letting the market eliminate the inefficient firms, local protectionism prevailed by subsidizing these firms and by blocking products from other jurisdictions to enter the local market. Either way, it protects the inefficient firms and aggravates the overcapacity situation.

The Coexistence of Free Entry and Exit Barriers

It has been widely acknowledged that China has had a low rate of firm bankruptcies and a low rate of employee turnovers. In other words, Chinese state enterprises face exit barriers, and the overcapacities persist as a result. These firms are not at liberty to cut the labor force to the efficient size because of the concern for labor welfare that allows only gradual reduction of disguised unemployment accumulated in the past decades. In many cases, firms have no freedom to leave an unprofitable business and shut down for the same reason. The central government sets an annual number of medium to large scale SOEs that are allowed to go bankrupt in large municipalities, and local governments have their own quota for local state enterprises.

Meanwhile, the government remains reluctant to allow transfers of property rights to employees at the zero share-price regardless the worth of the firms. Many small firms in Sichuan, for example, suffer from being unable to "die" (*Summary Report,* 1998).

4   The Consolidation of Chinese Firms

Competition as a result of the overcapacities has led to the consolidation of firms. Firms in 1998 experienced unprecedented asset regrouping. Regrouping of assets in China refers to mergers and acquisitions in the conventional sense as well as combined operations of firms following administrative orders. Anecdotal evidence also tends to indicate that multi-plant firms have been on the rise.

The merger, acquisition, as well as combined operation have been most prevalent among publicly traded share companies. Between 1997 and April 1998, 538 of the 810 publicly traded firms, or 66% of the total, had undergone certain form of assets regrouping. Of the 538,15% had undertaken transfers of the controlling share-holding among institutional investors; 13% transfers of non-controlling share-holding; 17% mergers and acquisition; 34% co-ownership through share exchanges and cross-firm investment; 11% transfers of assets and ownership rights; 6% assets exchanges; and the remaining 4% other forms (Yang, Gao, and Li, 1998).

Large producers have emerged in the process of merger, acquisition, and assets regrouping.[5] The consolidation has also led to greater competitiveness and profitability of firms. Many of China's industries have matured from their infancy. In some industries, such as the consumer electronics products, the domestic producers have not only established their dominance in Chinese market, but also started to compete in the international markets. The first eight months of 2000 saw a 40.7% increase in the export value of electronic products and the exports have become higher value added (*The Economic Daily,* October 3, 2000).

---

[5] Most noteworthy is the merger of the three companies: Shanghai Baoshan Steel Mill (formerly one of the largest steel mills owned by the central government), Shanghai Metallurgical Holding Company (formerly owned by the Metallurgical Bureau of Shanghai with four subsidiaries that have shares publicly traded), and Shanghai Meishan Enterprise Group. The merger has created a largest steel producer with assets of 12 billion dollars (or 20% of the steel industry's total assets) and production capacity of 15 million tons of steel, or 14% of total steel production in China (*World Daily,* August 18, 1998).

IV   The Impact of WTO Entry on The Structure of Chinese Industry

1   General Assessment: The Openness and the Extent of Monopolization

The severity of the impact of WTO entry depends, in general, on the openness and the extent of monopolization. The openness refers to the exposure of firms to foreign competition, whereas the monopolization refers to the firms' market shares in the domestic market. A firm can be a monopoly in the domestic market and yet face fierce foreign competition. Meanwhile, a firm can be nearly perfectly competitive in the domestic market but protected from foreign competition. The more closed is a sector to foreign competitions, the greater shock it will bear after the accession; the more monopolized is an industry, the more dramatic will be the decline in the market shares of the monopolistic firms.

2   The Impact on the Three Sectors

Table 10.8 reveals useful information for our analysis of the impact of WTO entry on China's agriculture and industrial sectors. It shows the composition of bilateral trade of major goods between the US and China. While the data in the table do not correct the official US trade statistics for trade via Hong Kong and the absolute size of the trade surplus (or deficits) is subject to debate, they do indicate the comparative advantages of the goods between China and the US and among themselves.

As shown in Table 10.8, the last column numbers of the ratio of Imp/Exp, or the ratio of imports from China to exports to China, indicate the comparative advantages. If the ratio is smaller than one, the US has comparative advantage in the good's production, and if it is greater than one, China does. The greater is the ratio, the more advantageous is China in producing the good. The magnitudes of the ratio suggest that China has the greatest comparative advantage in the productions of apparel, clothing, and textiles, followed by leather, travel goods, sports equipment, feather and down articles, toys, etc. The table indicates, on the other hand, that China is a net importer of aircraft, spacecraft, and parts, oil seeds, grains, and fruits, fertilizers, and aluminum products.

Table 10.8, however, is by no means a comprehensive list of exports and imports between the US and China. Many high-tech and service industries, such as telecommunications and internet development, are unlisted. The summary of the impact is highlighted in Table 10.9.

The Agriculture Sector

Agriculture production in China has been primarily family-based as a result of decollectivization. While there are numerous producers, the state continues to monopolize the wholesale distribution of grains. Moreover, the sector

Table 10.8   Major US exports to and imports from China, 1999 ($ millions)

Product Category	Exports	Imports	Ratio of Imp/Exp
Boilers, machinery, and mechanical appliances	2,572	10,661	4.145
Aircraft, spacecraft, and parts	2,317	29	0.013
Electrical machinery, equipment, and parts	1,985	15,804	7.962
Fertilizers	932	1	0.001
Optical, photographic, and precision instruments	792	2397	3.027
Paper, paperboard, and pulp	541	542	1.002
Plastics and articles	522	2736	5.241
Chemicals	478	1,110	2.322
Oil seeds, grains, and fruits	371	88	0.237
Vehicles	213	1190	5.587
Aluminum and articles	179	157	0.877
Iron and steel articles	140	1563	11.164
Furniture, bedding, cushions, etc.	63	6325	100.397
Footwear and the alike	41	8901	217.098
Toys, games, and sports equipment	38	12074	317.737
Ceramic products	28	920	32.857
Apparel, clothing, and textiles	7	7092	1013.143
Leather, travel goods, handbags, and similar articles	4	3217	804.25
Feather and down articles: artificial flowers, artificial human hair	2	947	473.5
All other products	1488	12057	8.103
Total	13118	87787	6.692

Note: The data in this table do not correct the official US trade statistics for trade via Hong Kong.
Sources: The last column figures are calculated from the previous two, and the rest are from Hufbauer and Rosen (April 2000).

has been protected from foreign competition through tariff, quota, export subsidies, and other means. It is, therefore, characterized by low monopolization and low openness. The massive disguised unemployment in the sector has driven marginal productivity down to nearly zero, if not negative. The low level of mechanization and technology application leaves the sector at disadvantage relative to foreign competition, especially in bulk commodities such as dairy products, meats, soybeans, wheat, corn, rice, cotton, and barley. The statistics on the bilateral trade between the US and China shows that agriculture goods of oil seeds, grains, and fruits are one of the four listed groups of goods in which China has comparative disadvantage.

The WTO accession requires lowering of overall average tariff for agricultural products to 17%, and even lower by 2004 and for some products from the US. China will cease to subsidizing its exports and will adopt a tariff rate quota (TRQ) system (i.e. a system in which imports up to the quota level are charged a minimal tariff-usually 1-3%—and imports above that level a high tariff) that provides strong incentive for state enterprises to purchase bulk commodities at world market rates. The TRQ will apply on bulk

Table 10.9   Sectoral impact of WTO entry

The Sectors	Impact Assessment
Agriculture	**Strong overall impact** Domestic sector at disadvantage in general. Sector-wide reallocation of labor to other sectors.
Industry & Construction	**Unclear overall effect** The impact varies among its sub-sectors. Reallocation of resources among sub-sectors. Firms to consolidate.
Tertiary	**Strong overall impact**
The first level: transportation, storage, postal and telecommunications, whole sale and retail trade **The second level:** banking, insurance, geological survey, water conservancy management, real estate; services for residents, agriculture; and forestry, animal husbandry, fishery, subsidiary services for transportation and communications, comprehensive technical services, etc.	Unprecedented breaking of entry barriers in the **first and second** levels of the sector, e.g. the wholesale and retail trade channels, telecommunications, banking, and insurance services. Ending of state monopoles.
The third level: education, culture and arts, broadcasting, movies, television, public health, sports, social welfare and scientific research, etc.	Many entry barriers to remain or uninterested by foreign competition or in the **third** level of the sector. State monopolies to stay.
The fourth level: government agencies, political parties, social organizations, military and police service	The **fourth level** is naturally intact

commodities such as soybean oil, wheat, corn, rice, cotton, barley, wool, sugar, palm oil and rapeseed oil.[6]

Moreover, China will for the first time provide full trading rights (the right to import and export) and distribution rights (wholesaling, retailing, maintenance and repair, transportation, etc.), which will eliminate an important layer of non-tariff protection to Chinese firms (Government Releases, 1999 and Whitehouse Factsheets, 2000). Table 10.8 shows that agriculture goods of oil seeds, grains, and fruits are one of the four listed groups of goods with the ratio of Imp/Exp smaller than 1 or, in other words, with comparative disadvantage.

---

[6] For details of the WTO agreement between China and the US, see US government releases on Market Access and Protocol Commitments (April 1999) and While House Factsets (February 17, 2000).

As a result, one would expect a strong overall effect from WTO entry on the entire sector and a sector-wide labor resource reallocation to other sectors. Within the heavily impacted sub-sectors, consolidation of land may emerge in the long run to regain economies of scale.

The accession will also end the long-existing state monopoly in China's grain marketing at the wholesale level. As recently as June 1, 1998, China's State Council, in an effort to maintain grain price stability and minimize losses by state grain bureaus, issued a new stipulation (No. 244) to enforce the administrative control of grain pricing and state monopoly in grain marketing. The stipulation explicitly states that only state grain bureaus can purchase grains from farmers and they must do so within their own counties (Chen, February 2000). The Stipulation has reaffirmed government's grain price control and minimized competition from private grain dealers and among state grain enterprises. The impact of foreign competition following WTO entry will, therefore, be most profound.

The Industrial Sector

In this sector, China has agreed to reduce average tariffs from 24.6% in 1997 to 9.44% and to implement two thirds of tariff cuts by 2003 and the rest by 2005 (with a limited number of exceptions), bringing tariff levels to levels comparable with major trading partners and below those of most developing countries. China will also phase out all quantitative restrictions on imports. Moreover, as in the agriculture sector, China will provide full trading rights and distribution to foreign firms in most industries.

The effects of the entry on this sector are by no means uniform. An important feature is the concurrence of foreign entry and domestic consolidation. As analyzed previously, China's industrial sector features low concentration and overcapacities in production. The consolidation among Chinese producers in the reform process and in preparation of the WTO entry, however, has increased their competitiveness, making domestic fringe firms phase out. The number of firms in each industry, therefore, will decrease despite the entry of foreign firms if exit barriers are eliminated.

Sectors producing labor-intensive products such as textile products, toys, umbrellas, shoes and hats will benefit from the accession to the WTO because of their greater access to foreign markets. In the bilateral trading with the US, these goods have enjoyed the highest margin of trade surplus as shown in Table 10.8. But China's comparative advantage in labor-intensive products is shrinking because of the competition of cheaper labor from other developing countries.

Industries that have recently grown out of their infancy and become capable of competing with foreign firms will meet the challenge and experience dynamic changes, such as consumer electronic products of color television, wash machines, refrigerators, fans, and air conditioners. China also has comparative advantage and certain degree of competitiveness in the international market in shipbuilding industry because of its comparative advantage in factor supply (Research Group, 1997).

Sectors producing products such as beverage, beer, and consumer chemical goods will have more difficult time coping with the changes. China has also lagged behind in automobiles, computers, and aircraft, spacecraft and parts. These industries not only have no comparative advantage exporting but also face fierce international competition for domestic market. Table 10.8 shows that aircraft, spacecraft and parts are among the few that China imports more form the US than it exports to the country.

It is recognized that China's auto industry, though unlisted in Table 10.9, will be heavily impacted by its WTO entry. We have already noted that the industry has had many producers with sub-optimal scales. Consolidation in the industry, however, has been taking place. The major Chinese auto companies have also formed joint venture with foreign firms. The question to be answered is whether Chinese auto firms will have enough time to phase out their infancy before July 2006 when tariffs on autos will decrease from the current rates of 100% and 80% to 25%. The rapid development in recent years seems to suggest that even the auto industry will survive WTO entry as long as China no longer insists, as it had done, on having its own complete production as a security strategy and as a national pride. Meanwhile, China does not commit to allowing foreign firms to enter wholesaling of tobacco and wholesaling and retailing of salt (*Whitehouse Factsheets,* 2000), leaving these industries to continue to be protected.

To summarize, the overall effect of WTO entry on China's industrial sector is that increased foreign competition will force domestic firms to cut costs, adopt new technology, and boost exports. The rise or fall of Chinese firms following the entry, however, varies significantly among industries in the sector and among firms in each industry. Resource reallocation will take place among industries within the sector.

The Service Sector
As shown in Table 10.1, the service sector (or the tertiary sector) consists of four levels. WTO entry will have diverse impact on the different levels in this sector.

As we know, the Chinese concessions to gain entry into the WTO have been major reductions of entry barriers in the areas of distribution and telecommunications services, leaving the first level of the tertiary sector greatly impacted as a sub-sector. The foreign competition as a result of WTO entry will also prevail in the banking, insurance, professional and technical services (including accounting services, management consulting and taxation services, legal services, and agricultural, engineering, and urban planning services), thus affecting in a comprehensive manner the second level of the tertiary sector. Foreign involvement in these areas will not only force the Chinese firms to continuously cut cost and keep abreast of technological development, but also bring higher quality services at lower prices, thus benefiting significantly Chinese consumers. The lower prices have already been observed in telecommunications services.

WTO accession, however, will have a limited effect on the third level, consisting of education, culture and arts, broadcasting, movies, television, public health, sports, social welfare and scientific research, etc. Books, magazines, newspapers are one exception.[7] There will also be increased quota of foreign films imported to China and there has been at least one reported case of foreign film company starting business in China. The fourth level, consisting of government agencies, political parties, social organizations, military and police service, will remain intact. While one would not expect any foreign involvement in the fourth level of the sector for most obvious reasons, the remaining entry barriers in the third level result primarily from ideological concerns and the lack of comparative advantage of foreign competition. The state monopolies are, therefore, to continue in the third level of China's service sector.

3   The Systemic Effect of the WTO Entry: The Ratio of SOE/ (SOE+NSOE+FE)

WTO entry, which allows privately owned foreign firms to operate and employ workers in many Chinese industries that have been off-limits to domestic private firms, will further weaken the dominance of the state and change the systemic structure in favor of the non-state sector. Let SOE be state-owned enterprises, NSOE non-state enterprises, and FE foreign enterprises. The state dominance is therefore reflected in the ratio of SOE to SOE plus NSOE and FE.

The dominance of the state in the agriculture sector lies primarily in agricultural services, and the most important of which is the wholesale distribution of grains. WTO entry will break the barriers in the services to agriculture, thus reducing SOE and increasing FE. It is reasonable to expect a smaller ratio of SOE/(SOE + NSOE + FE) after the entry because, while the decline of SOE tends to be offset by the decline of NSOE, the net increase in FE seems unambiguous.

To bear directly the impact of the structural change, however, are primarily private firms in the short run. In the long run, the unemployed farmers as a result of WTO entry, for example, will migrate into towns and cities and become re-employed by urban private sectors. The impact on the private firms, therefore, is short-run and distributional, whereas the impact on reducing the dominance of the state sector is permanent.

---

[7] For books, magazines and newspapers, China will allow foreigners to provide wholesale services within three years from the date of accession and retail services within five years (Whitehouse Factsheets, 2000).

The systemic impact in the industrial sector is unclear. The ratio of SOE/(SOE+NSOE+FE) may change in either direction following the entry. The state dominance will persist in some industries where Chinese state-owned large enterprises possess comparative advantage over foreign competition and have become more competitive in the process of consolidation in preparation for the entry. Since the process eliminates many small firms and the large state enterprises may effectively gain the lost shares of these firms, the entry of foreign enterprises may not necessarily lead to, at least in the short run, the decline of the state.

The most striking systemic impact will be the termination of state monopolies in many of the services where entry barriers have long lasted, thus creating entirely a new growth environment for China's private enterprises. China's public utilities sectors and state propaganda apparatuses such as TV-radio broadcasting, media services, banking and insurance, wholesale trade, air and rail transportation, and education services have been primarily off-limits to domestic private firms, and it takes WTO entry to break the barriers. The significance of the entry is, therefore, far beyond the fact that Chinese consumers have already started to experience lower prices and better quality of the services. Entry barriers in the third level of the service sector are remaining as a result ideological concerns and the lack of comparative advantage of foreign competition. The state will continue to dominate in the fourth level of the service sector, again, for most obvious reasons.

V   Concluding Remarks

China's long sought WTO accession is approaching its final stage at a critical time of China's economic transition. The structure of Chinese industry has changed significantly since the launch of economic reforms two decades ago in both scale and systemic aspects.

The role of the state (represented by state-owned enterprises) has declined measured by the share of the gross value of industrial output and by both the size and the share of urban employment. The state, however, has maintained its dominance in many industries where products and services have been considered vital to national interests and has even experienced expansion in employment size in several service industries.

Meanwhile, many industries in China are characterized by numerousness of firms, sub-optimal scale of production, as well as severe overcapacities. These characteristics arise from the lack of multi-plant firms, the local protectionism, as well as the existence of exit barriers. Facing the challenge of foreign competition ensuing the WTO accession, the Chinese firms, especially in the industrial sector, are consolidating and catching up. The impact of WTO entry is by no means uniform across the sectors of the economy.

The agriculture sector is predicted to have strong overall effect as the sector has had low degree of openness despite the low degree of monopolization.

Resource reallocation, primarily rural labor, is expected to flow toward other sectors. Systemically, the role of the state in the sector is expected to decline, primarily reflected in the sharing of trading rights and distribution that have long been monopolized by the state.

The industrial sector, on the other hand, is predicted to have an unclear overall impact from WTO entry. Some sub-sectors are to benefit from expanded foreign markets and will further extend their comparative advantage; some will contract in the effort to consolidate and become competitive; and yet some will shift resources to other industries. Thus, reallocation of resources in this sector occurs primarily among its own industries. Systemically, the state dominance will persist in some industries where Chinese state-owned large enterprises possess comparative advantage over foreign competition and have become more competitive in the process of consolidation prior to the entry. Since the process eliminates many small firms and the large state enterprises may effectively gain the lost shares of these firms, the entry of foreign enterprises may not necessarily lead to, at least in the short run, the decline of the state.

Finally, China's service sector is predicted to experience strong overall effects from the accession. Retail sales excepted, this sector characterizes most pronounced state dominance prior to the accession, such as in banking, insurance, telecommunications, and wholesale distribution. WTO entry marks the sharing of market for the first time with any non-state enterprises in these industries. While state monopolies are ending in this sector, resources are also expected to flow into the sector as the economy becomes more advanced and privatized. Consumers in China have already started to experience the benefit of increased competition in anticipation of WTO entry.

In sum, the WTO entry may cause considerable redistribution of resources and income between sectors and among individual firms and consumers. The long-run effect is that it will not only enhance the competitiveness in the Chinese economy and force firms to cut cost and adopt more advanced technology, but also accelerate the systemic reform of Chinese firms and the decline of the sate dominance. This research, however, is an early attempt to address these aspects of WTO entry, and it intends to provoke future researches to extend and deepen the issues discussed here.

References

Chen, Aimin, "Has China's State Sector Really Turned the Corner?" presented at a session of the annual meetings of the Allied Social Science Associations, January 2001.

———, "Unemployment and Labor Market Development in China," presented at the International Symposium on 21" Century China and Challenge of Sustainable Development, September 3–5, 1999, Washington DC.

———, "Inertia in Reforming China's State-owned Enterprises: The Case of Chongqing," *World Development*, Vol. 26, No. 3, pp. 479–495. 1998.

Cui, Minxuan, and Zhang, Cunping, "The Comparison of Scale Economies of Chinese Enterprises," *China Industrial Economy*, No. 5, 1998, pp. 53–58.

Frazier, W Mark, "Coming to Terms with the 'WTO Effect' on U.S.-China Trade and China's Economic Growth," *The National Bureau of Asian Research*, September 1999.

Frazier, W. Mark and Hansen, M. Peter, "China's Accession to the WTO: A Candid Appraisal from U.S Industry," The National Bureau of Asian Research, September 1999.

Hufbauer, Gary Clyde and Rosen, Daniel H., "American Access to China's Market: The Congressional Vote on PNTR." *International Economics Policy Briefs*, April 20, 2000, Institute for International Economics.

"Market Access and Protocol Commitments," *Government Releases*, April 1999.

Research Group, the Industrial Economy Research Institute, Social Science Academy of China, "Chinese Industry's Change from Quantity Expansion to Quality Enhancing," *China's Industrial Economy*, June 1997, pp. 5–14.

Shi, Yaodong, "The Problems Facing China's Tobacco Industry and Their Solutions," *China's Industrial Economy*, Feb. 1999, pp. 42–47.

Summary Report on the Status of Ownership Restructuring of SOEs under County Governments in Sichuan, August 1998, System Reforms Commission of Sichuan Provincial Government.

White House Fact Sheets, February 17, 2000.

Zhou, Huizhong, "Interjurisdictional Competition in an Imperfect market: The Case of the Chinese Tobacco Industry," paper presented at an ASSA session, January 2000.

Zhou, Shuhan, and Wang, Yanzhong, "The Development of Chinese Industry in the 21st Century and Strategies," *China Industrial Economy*, February 1999, pp. 5–9.

11
Effect of Migration on Children's Educational Performance in Rural China

Xinxin Chen[1], *Qiuqiong Huang*[2], *Scott Rozelle*[3], *Yaojiang Shi*[4], *and Linxiu Zhang*[5]
[1]*Peking University, China;* [2]*University of Arkansas, USA;* [3]*Stanford University, USA;* [4]*Shaanxi Normal University, China; and* [5]*Chinese Academy of Sciences, China*

Migration is one of the main ways of alleviating poverty in developing countries, including China. However, there are concerns about the potential negative effects of migration on the educational achievement of the children that are left behind in villages when one or both of their parents out-migrate to cities. This paper examines changes in school performance before and after the parents of students out-migrate. Surprisingly, we find that there is no significant negative effect of migration on school performance. In fact, we find that educational performance improves in migrant households in which the father out-migrates.

Introduction

Migration is widely known by researchers and policy makers as one of the main ways of alleviating poverty in developing countries (Todaro, 1989). Many positive effects have been identified. Having a migrant may increase a household's income per capita significantly (eg, Du *et al.*, 2005). Migrant remittances have been shown to help reduce income inequality in countries such as Mexico (eg, Benjamin *et al.*, 2005; McKenzie and Rapoport, 2007). Increases in out-migration can lead to increased investment in assets related to agricultural production and other investments in source communities (de Brauw and Giles, 2007). Giles (2006) shows that access to migration offers a risk-coping mechanism that allows households to reduce the variability of income caused by shocks affecting agricultural production.

Reprinted with permission from Association of Comparative Economic Studies. All rights reserved. *Comparative Economic Studies* (2009) 51, 323–343.

Migration itself, however, is not costless. In recent years, a group of researchers have raised concerns about the potential negative effects of migration on the educational outcome of the school-aged children that are left behind in rural areas when one or both of their parents out-migrate to cities for work. McKenzie and Rapoport (2006) found that children in migrant households are less likely to be attending school and complete fewer total years of schooling than children in non-migrant households. One of the main reasons may be that migration results in significantly less parental supervision of school attendance and the loss of any positive influence through learning at home (Hanson and Woodruff, 2004). There may be other effects. For example, students may have less time to spend on studying because they have to do more housework when parents out-migrate. Similar findings of adverse effects of migration on children's schooling are also observed in Philippines (Battistella and Conaco, 1998).

On the other hand, researchers have also found a positive relationship between migration and education of migrant children. Remittance transfers, by relaxing a household's liquidity constraint, allow investment in education and thereby can increase educational attainment of children in migrant households. For example, Cox Edwards and Ureta (2003) found that receiving remittances reduces the likelihood of quitting school among individuals aged 6–24 years in El Salvador. Similar arguments are also found in Glewwe and Jacoby (2004). In addition, migration, by increasing household income, can contribute positively to child development (Blau, 1999; Duncan *et al.,* 1994). Overall, migrant children could benefit from the positive income effect of migration.

The impact of migration on the educational performance of children that are left behind is also an important and emerging issue in China. The migrant labour force has been growing rapidly since the 1990s in China, surpassing 100 million individuals (de Brauw *et al.,* 2002). Migrants also are moving further away from home and leaving for a longer period of time (Rozelle *et al.,* 1999). Since most of China's migration is by individuals instead of entire households, in most cases the school-aged children are left behind in the village when their parents move to the city for work (Wu, 2004). Researchers have claimed that school performance of migrant children is adversely affected (Li, 2004; Tan and Wang, 2004; Wang and Wu, 2003; Zhou and Wu, 2004).

If migration indeed has a negative impact on education of the next generation, the government may want to respond. In fact, in the long run, Heckman (2005) actually argues that the government probably should start to modify education policies to favour children of migrants.

The overall goal of this paper is to examine the effect of migration activities of parents on the educational performance of their children and provide policy makers with information about whether or not they need to do anything to change the school systems and childcare systems in China's rural and urban areas. To meet the overall goal, we will pursue two specific objectives. First, we compare the distribution of children's scores across different types of households (migrant and non-migrant households) and over time (before and after one or both parents out-migrate). Second, we examine whether migration negatively affects the school performance of migrant children.

Data

The data used in this paper come from a survey conducted by the authors in 2006. The sample was drawn from 36 primary schools in 12 townships in Shaanxi province, one of the nation's poorest provinces. The sample was drawn using a four-stage clustering design with random sampling procedures employed at each stage. In each stage, we randomly chose six counties that were selected from 93 counties in Shaanxi province; two townships from each county; and three primary schools were randomly chosen from a list of all primary schools with six years of schooling (or all *wanxiao*) in each township.

The sample students were selected during the final stage of sampling. The sample included all students that were in the entering year of the sixth grade classes in each of the sample schools. On average, there were 1.4 sixth grade classes per school, ranging from one to three. Since the survey was conducted in September and the school year in China runs between early September and mid-July, all of the sample students had just completed the fifth grade about 2 months ago. In total, the sample included 1,649 children and their families. Approximately 45% of the sample students were girls. The ages of the students ranged between 10 and 16 years.[1] In addition, since we sampled from the population of students that made it to the sixth grade, we did not track down those that either dropped out or accompanied their parents to the city before the sixth grade. Fortunately, according to the information from the principal questionnaire-based interviews, this is not a serious problem. The drop-out rate in our sample is low. More than 98% of the children that started first grade were still in school in the sixth grade.

In addition to interviewing students directly, we also elicited information about the students from their homeroom teachers (or *banzhuren*). In more than 90% of the cases, the homeroom teacher had been with the students for at least 2 years. In China, homeroom teachers are in charge of administering students' school programme in addition to teaching one or two

---

[1] Although the ages of children ranged from 6 to 16, only few children in the sample were older than 14.

subjects. For many reasons, the homeroom teacher was intimately familiar with the school performance and family life of each student.

The measure of one of the key variables, educational achievement, is based on the math and Chinese language scores of the students from the calendar year 2001/2002 (the year in which the students were in the first grade) to 2005/2006 (the year students were in the fifth grade). Fortunately, students in all the sample schools keep in their possession a booklet that records their math and Chinese scores for each semester during their schooling. The scores were copied by our enumerators with the assistance of the homeroom teachers. Therefore, the educational achievement variables are measured with great accuracy since they are record-based.

In our analyses, we use the second term (or the spring semester) math and Chinese language scores to measure educational achievement because they are based on standardised tests (and not any other work during the year). The tests are standardised in two dimensions. First, the questions are the same for all schools within the same township. Second, the final exams were graded according to the same set of criteria by a township-wide panel of teachers.[2]

In order to measure another key variable, the migration status, we collected detailed information on the migration histories of each student's family. The first set of information came from the survey questionnaire that was filled by students and their family with the supervision of enumerators. In the questionnaire, we have a section that asked for the migration status of each parent during the first grade and during the fifth grade. If the parents were both out of the village, we called one of the parents and asked them these questions over the telephone. As a way of cross checking, the homeroom teacher was asked to verify the information on migration status.

On the basis of migration status, there are two types of households in this study: *migrant households* (or those households in which at least one parent out-migrated during the period between 2002 and 2006) and non-migrant households. Recognising that the effect of migration on student performance may be affected by *which family member* out-migrates (ie, father, mother or both), we further subdivided the migrant households into six types of households: *Any Parent Migrated* households (ie, households in which both parents lived at home in 2002 and at least one parent – either the father; mother or both parents – out-migrated by 2006); *Father Migrated*

---

[2] The results of our analyses, however, do not depend on the choice of using the second term scores from the first and fifth grades. As a robustness check, we also used average scores for the whole year instead of just for the second semester. In another check, we compared scores that averaged scores from first and second grade to scores that averaged scores from fourth and fifth grade. Our results remain largely the same in these cases.

Only (*or mother-stayed-at-home*) households where only the father out-migrated by 2006 but was at home in 2002; *Father Migrated* (*Unconditional*) households where the father was at home in 2002 but out-migrated by 2006 (including households in which the mother was either at home or not at home in 2006); *Mother Migrated Only* (*or father-stayed-at-home*) households where only the mother out-migrated by 2006 but was at home in 2002; *Mother Migrated* (*Unconditional*) households where the mother was at home in 2002 but out-migrated by 2006 (including households in which the father was either at home or not at home in 2006); and *Both Parents Migrated* households where both parents were at home in 2002, but out-migrated by 2006. It should be noted that the six types of households are not mutually exclusive. For brevity, when we talk about all of these households as a group, we call them *New Migrant* households to distinguish them from households that were already in the migrant labour force in 2002 (which are not included in our study). In addition, we define *Never Migrant* households as those in which both parents stayed at home in both 2002 and 2006.

In addition to educational achievement and migration status, we also collected information on variables that can help us explore whether the effects of migration on the school performance of children are heterogeneous across households that are different in several aspects. First, as family wealth may improve the learning outcomes of students (Brown and Park, 2002), we asked the parents whether their house was worth more than 5,000 yuan or not as a proxy for family wealth.[3] Admittedly, this is a crude measure of wealth. However, given that our sample size is larger than 1,600, financial and time constraints dictated that we used this measure instead of implementing a long questionnaire to collect detailed information on income and assets from all different sources as well as information on consumption.

---

[3] There are several issues to discuss when considering our measure of income. The value of the house only includes the part of the house used for domicile purposes and the value of assets that were used for farming and non-farm businesses was not included. Yuan is the Chinese currency. One dollar was about 7.6 yuan during the time of our survey. Finally, we admit that we only have a rough proxy for income. Because of this it is possible that we will not be able to identify the impact of income on grades (since the coefficient of the variable could be biased down to zero). The cross sectional variation for income (using our measure), however, does show that there is at least a negative correlation (richer households have children with higher grades). In fact, there are reasons to expect a positive effect of income on grades. The literature (eg, Kandel and Kao, 2001) has shown that the positive relationship between the father's migration and the school performance partly stems from the financial resources provided migration, which lowers the likelihood of children's labor force participation and increases resources for consumption of education-related goods.

Second, since previous studies have also documented the effect of the number of children in a family on the school performance of each child (eg, Hanushek, 1992; Steelman and Mercy, 1980), we collected information on whether a student had any siblings or not and the number of siblings.

Finally, we also collected information on other variables that may affect school performance. We collected information on each student's gender, age, whether they were student cadres and whether they had mentors to help them study. The survey questionnaire also included questions on the characteristics of parents and households: each parent's age, educational attainment, the household's land holdings and the total number of other household members.

Migration and Educational Performance

Similar to the migration status in many other poor rural areas in China (Rozelle *et al.*, 1999), many households were already in the migrant labour force in 2002, the first year of our sample. In 236 households (about 15% of the 1,594 sample households), either one parent or both parents migrated (Table 11.1, column 1, rows 1–3). In most migrant households (149), the father was the parent that out-migrated (while the mother stayed at home).

In addition, similar to the migration trend in the rest of China (as reported in de Brauw *et al.*, 2002), the number of new migrant households rose rapidly during the period between 2002 and 2006. Among the 1,358 non-migrant households in 2002 (column 1, row 4), one or both parents in 220 households entered the migrant labour force between 2002 and 2006 (row 4, columns 2–4). After subtracting the 81 households that migrated in 2002 but returned to the village in 2006 from the 220 New Migrant households (column 5, rows 1–3), the total migrant households rose to 375 households in 2006 (row 5, columns 2–4), a 9% rise from the 2002 migration level.

More than 70% of the households did not participate in migration activities at all during this period (column 5, row 4). The existence of these non-migrant households as well as new migrant households offers a unique opportunity to examine the relationship between the migration activity of parents and the school performance of children. In the rest of the paper, we will focus on comparing the school performance of the children of the 1,138 Never Migrant households and those of the 220 New Migrant households.

If one were naively to have sought out parents of New Migrant households and asked them for the record of their children's scores over the years, one would likely have found that the scores have fallen since the first grade. It is understandable how the findings of such an inquiry could raise concerns about the potential negative impact of migration on school performance. However, the falling scores may not be a problem that can be

Table 11.1 Patterns of migration in sample households in 2002 and 2006, Shaanxi Province, China

	Migration status in 2002	Migration status in 2006			
	(1) Number of households in 2002[a]	(2) Father Migrated Only (mother stayed home)	(3) Mother Migrated Only (father stayed home)	(4) Both Parents Migrated	(5) Return migrants (rows 1–3)[b] Never migrant (row 4)
(1) Only father migrated	149	94[c]			55
(2) Only mother migrated	18		9[c]		9
(3) Both parents migrated	69	7	5	40[c]	17
(4) Neither parent migrated	1,358	131[d]	35[d]	54[d]	1,138
(5) Total number of households	1,594	232	49	94	1,219

Data source: Authors' survey.

[a] Column (1)=Column (2)+Column (3)+Column (4)+Column (5).

[b] The households in column 5, rows 1, 2 and 3 are return migrants (or those households in which households had a migrant in 2002 and by 2006 had returned home. These households are dropped from the multivariate analysis.

[c] The diagonal elements in the first three rows of the 2006 matrix (row 1, column 2; row 2, column 3; row 3, column 4) are *Always Migrant* households. These households are dropped from the multivariate analysis.

[d] Total new migrants (or those households in which the parents did not migrate in 2002 and migrated by 2006) is found in row 4 by summing columns 2, 3 and 4).

solely blamed on migration. As our data show, not only have the scores of the students from the New Migrant households fallen (by about 1 point – from 71.6 to 70.8), but also those from other households including never migrant households have fallen (by about 3 points from 73.7 to 70.6). According to our data, this is true for both math and Chinese scores. When asking teachers about this trend, we were told the pattern of falling scores is easily explained by two factors: The materials covered in the fifth grade are much more advanced and difficult than those in the first grade; and, in general, the fifth grade teachers grade harder than the first grade teachers. Since these two factors affect students from both New Migrant and Never Migrant households, the general trend of falling scores is not surprising and clearly cannot be solely attributed to parents' migration activities.

If the interviewers had sought out Both Parents Migrated households or Mother Migrated households, the results of interviews might raise an additional source of concern about the effect of migration on the grades of the children of new migrants. In our sample, students from Both Parents Migrated households had lower average test scores during their fifth grade year (69.9 points) than those from Never Migrant households (70.9 points). Similar results were found in a number of Chinese studies (eg, Li, 2004; Tan and Wang, 2004; Wang and Wu, 2003; Zhou and Wu, 2004). Although the difference is not statistically significant, the fifth grade scores of the children of Mother Migrated (Unconditional) households (70.6 points) were also lower than those of Never Migrants. While we will explore this result further in the forthcoming analyses, it may be that it is these types of findings, which appear in our cross section of fifth grade households, that have made the effect of migration on school performance a high-profile issue. Interestingly, if the interview team had chosen Father Migrated (Unconditional) households (72.0 points), they would have found that on average scores of children from these households were slightly higher than those from Never Migrant households. The differences in the relationship between students' scores and parents' migration activities among different types of households indicate that the effect of migration on school performance is a complicated issue and those relying exclusively on cross-sectional data should exercise caution in any interpretation.

The need to exercise caution is reinforced when we compare the first grade scores in 2002 in addition to comparing the fifth grade scores in 2006. Although students from Both Parents Migrated households scored lower than those from the Never Migrant households in 2006, Figure 11.1 shows they already scored lower in 2002 when they were in the first grade. In other words, on average the scores of the students from Both Parents Migrate households were already lower *before their parents migrated*. This finding from our panel data indicates we should not jump to the conclusion that migration hurt children's school performance. Moreover, the distribution of the scores of the non-migrant children appears to actually move slightly closer

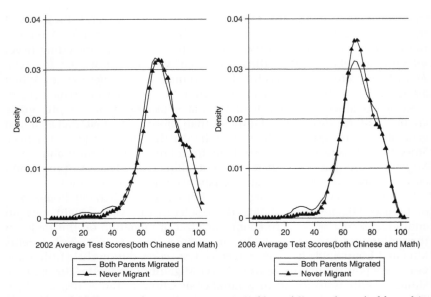

Figure 11.1 Distribution of average test scores in Never Migrant households and in Both Parents Migrated households in 2002 and 2006 using Kemel Density, Shaanxi Province, China
Date source: Authors' survey

to that of the migrant children over years. The distribution of the scores of non-migration students shifts to the left in contrast to its distribution in 2002 (a higher peak in the middle and thinner tail at the upper end). Although the distribution of the scores of migrant children has a thicker tail at the lower end in contrast to its distribution in 2002, its distribution does not shift as much as that of non-migrant children. Overall, it appears that the gap between the scores of migrant children and non-migrant children actually was narrowing slightly between 2002 and 2006. From this seemingly narrowing gap, one might infer that migration helps improve school performance. However, t-tests show that the means of the two distributions are not statistically significantly different either in 2002 or in 2006.

Further analyses of our data reveal that school performance may be explained by many factors other than migration activities. These factors may change over time and differ between migrant and non-migrant households. More importantly, these variations may be masking the relationship between migration and school performance. For example, as mentioned earlier, the difficulty of class materials and teachers' grading attitude change over time, which affect students' scores. In addition, school performance may differ by a household's wealth – or more specifically in our study, the value of the housing assets of the household.[4] According to our data, students from wealthier households score systematically higher than those from poorer households (on average about 2 points higher). This result is consistent with previous findings that the grades of children from better-off families often are higher since these children have access to better nutrition and better studying facilities, including access to extra reading materials and exercise books (Princiotta *et al.*, 2006).[5]

If either a household's wealth or some of other factor differs systematically with a household's migration status, two-way correlations between a family's migration status and the grades of its children could be misleading. For example, de Brauw and Giles (2007) find that migrant households, while poorer, improve their family's income status after migration. Higher income could have a positive effect on the grades of migrant children over time that might offset any other adverse effects. Therefore, further analyses are needed to explore the impact of migration on educational achievement while holding as many other factors constant as possible.

Methodology

The objective of this study is to examine the effects of migration on the student's educational performance. In order to evaluate the effects of migration, conceptually we are making migration the treatment. In other words, our sample students are divided into a treatment group (those that were in households in which the parent(s) out-migrated) and a control group (those in Never Migrated Households). With this set-up, we are interested in understanding the mean impact of 'treatment on the treated,' which is the average impact of grade retention among those treated (Smith and Todd, 2005):

$$
\begin{aligned}
TT &= E((Y_1 - Y_0)|X, D = 1) \\
&= E(Y_1 \mid X, D = 1) - E(Y_0 \mid X, D = 1)
\end{aligned}
\tag{1}
$$

where we denote Y_1 as the outcome (the scores of students – in our case) after the parent of the student out-migrated and Y_0 as the outcome if a student's parent did not out-migrate. In equation 1, our treatment is denoted by $D = 1$, which stands for the students whose parent(s) out-migrated and for whom Y_1 is observed and $D = 0$ stands for the student whose did not

---

[4] The term, wealth, when used in the rest of the paper will refer to the value of housing assets only.

[5] Scores may also differ among households with different household demographic compositions. According to our data, students from households in which there are no siblings (70.3 points) scored slightly lower than those from households with siblings in 2006 (71.5 points). Such a finding is consistent with Brown and Park's study (2002), which found that children with older siblings have significantly higher test scores than their peers.

out-migrate and for whom Y_0 is observed. As in reality we do not observe either the counterfactual mean, $E(Y_0|X,D = 1)$, or the mean outcome for the students had they not been retained in a grade after they were retained, we need to employ a difference-in-difference estimation approach (DD). Using the DD approach allows us to compare the outcomes before and after a student repeated a grade with students not affected by the treatment (those who were not retained).

In addition to the standard DD estimator (Smith and Todd, 2005), we implement three other DD estimators: an 'unrestricted' version that includes $Y_{t'}$ as a right-hand variable, an 'adjusted' version that includes other covariates in addition to the treatment variable (in our case they are a series of control variables from 2002 or the pre-programme period), and an unrestricted/adjusted model that combines the features of both the 'unrestricted' and 'adjusted' model. The unrestricted and adjusted DD estimators relax the implicit restrictions in the standard DD estimator that the coefficient associated with $Y_{t'}$ (pre-programme outcome) and covariates in t' (pre-programme period) equals one. The combination of unrestricted and adjusted DD estimators relaxes both of these assumptions. In summary, the models to be estimated are as follows:

Model (1), Restricted and Unadjusted:

$$\Delta Score_i = a + \delta\, MIGRATE_i + \varepsilon_i$$

Model (2) Restricted and Adjusted:

$$\Delta Score_i = a + \delta\, MIGRATE_i + \beta X_i + \varepsilon_i$$

Model (3) Unrestricted and Unadjusted:

$$\Delta Score_i = a + \delta\, MIGRATE_i \\ + \gamma\, Score\_beforemigrate_i + \varepsilon_i$$

Model (4) Unrestricted and Adjusted:

$$\Delta Score_i = a + \delta\, MIGRATE_i \\ + \gamma\, Score\_beforemigrate_i + \beta X_i + \varepsilon_i$$

In addition to the set of DD estimators, we also use a matching approach to check and see whether our results are robust to our choice of estimators. Matching estimators match a student in the treatment group with an observably similar student from the control group and interpret the difference in their school performance as the effect of the parents' migration activities. The key assumption underlying the matching estimator is the Conditional Independence Assumption (CIA), which states that non-participation outcome, $Score_0$, is independent of parents' migration status after being conditional on a set of observable characteristics (Rosenbaum and Rubin, 1983).

In order to implement our matching estimator, we follow a series of well-established steps (Caliendo and Kopeinig, 2008). First, since matching is only justified over the common support region, we check whether there is a large overlap in the support of the covariates, Z, between the New Migrant and Never Migrated households. In our study, we use propensity scores as a tool to enforce a common support. Fortunately, the common support is fairly wide in our sample.[6] In the second step, we choose the method of matching. In our analysis, we use the nearest neighbour matching method with replacement. Following Smith and Todd (2005), we match students based on the log odds ratio and standard errors are bootstrapped using 1,000 replications. The last step is to assess the matching quality. Since we do not condition on all covariates but on the propensity score alone in PSM, it has to be checked whether the matching procedure is able to balance the distribution of the relevant covariates in both the control and treatment group. To do so, we use balancing tests described in Dehejia and Wahba (1999, 2002). The balancing tests were satisfied for all covariates. In order to guard against the potential source of bias (shown by Abadie and Imbens, 2002), we also implement the *Bias-Corrected Matching* estimator developed by Abadie and Imbens (2006).[7]

Finally, since all matching methods only match observations based upon observable covariates, they do not account for all unobservable covariates. To control for part of the unobservable factors, in particular, those factors that are time-invariant, we extend the cross-sectional matching estimator to a longitudinal setting and implement a difference-in-differences matching (DDM) estimator. With DDM we can exploit the data on the Migrant households in 2002 to construct the required counterfactual, instead of just using the data in 2006 (as is used in matching). When implementing DDM, we use both PSM matching and bias-corrected matching. In our PSM estimators, we match using the log odds ratios. In both PSM and bias-corrected matching, the nearest neighbour matching methods with replacement is used. In addition, we also compute the 'adjusted' version where observations in the control group are weighted by the number of times they are matched to an observation in the treatment group. For more information about the exact specification and the theory of our approaches, see a more complete working paper at www.reap-china.com.

---

[6] Graphs of distributions of propensity scores that show the common support are available upon request.

[7] This is achieved by using the STATA command 'nnmatch.'

Results of Multivariate Analysis

Although we do not report the full version of the regressions from models 1 to 4 for brevity purposes, the DD analyses perform fairly well. The results from the DD regressions (and throughout the rest of the analyses) show that the estimates of the treatment effect (ie, the coefficient on the Any Parent Migrated dummy variable) are largely the same across all four specifications (models 1–4). However, the Unrestricted and Adjusted specification (model 4) generates a much higher goodness-of-fit statistic (or R^2) than other specifications (almost certainly because of the importance of capturing beginning scores, which embodies the unobserved ability of a student, and other covariates). Therefore, in the rest of the analyses, when reporting the results, we will mostly focus on the results from the Unrestricted and Adjusted model. The DD analyses also produce estimates with expected signs and significance. For example, the scores of older students drop relatively more than those of younger students (row 4, column 4). This finding is reasonable since students that enter primary school at an older age may have an initial advantage because they are relatively more mature (Fredriksson and Öckert, 2005), but the initial advantage gradually disappears as younger children catch up over the course of primary school.

The most important finding from the basic regression models is that we reject the hypothesis that migration affects school performance negatively (Table 11.2).[8] In all four models, the coefficient on the Any Parent Migrated household dummy variable is *not* negative. In fact, the coefficients are all positive and significantly different from zero. The magnitudes of the coefficients range from 1.16 to 3.18, meaning that, everything else held constant, after any parent in a household out-migrated between the first and fifth grade, the scores of the children of the migrants actually rose relative to the children of Never Migrant households. In other words, unlike claims made by some researchers, migration did not hurt school performance. At least in the migrant households in our sample area, migration has improved school performance.

The results hold when we examine other types of migrant households: no negative effect of migration on school performance is found. In the rest of Table 11.2, for each of the four specifications, we look at the effect of migration on school performance in all six types of migrant households.[9] In 20 out of the 24 cases the coefficient is positive. The coefficients are

---

[8] In Table 11.2 we only report the coefficients on the treatment variable. The rest of the results are suppressed for brevity but are available from the authors upon request. We report the results for 24 different regressions.

[9] For completeness in Table 11.3, we include the results of the effect of Any Parent Migrated on school performance, but, in fact, this is a duplication of the results from Table 11.2, row 1.

Table 11.2 Evaluating the effects of migration activities of parents on school performance of students in all six types of migrant households using difference-in-difference, Shaanxi Province, China[a]

Treatment variable (MIG$_i$)[b]	Outcome variable ($\Delta Score_i$) = $Score_{i,2006}$—$Score_{i,2002}$			
	(1)	(2)	(3)	(4)
	Restricted and unadjusted	Unrestricted and unadjusted	Restricted and adjusted[c]	Unrestricted and adjusted[c]
(1) Any_Parent_migrated	3.183	2.327	2.169	1.164
	(3.72)***	(3.03)***	(2.58)**	(1.65)*
No. of observations R^2	1,575	1,575	1,549	1,549
	0.01	0.27	0.10	0.43
(2) Father_Migrated_Only (mother stayed home)	4.634	3.812	3.630	2.356
	(4.27)***	(4.09)***	(3.45)***	(2.73)***
No. of observations R^2	1,577	1,577	1,549	1,549
	0.01	0.28	0.10	0.43
(3) Father_Migrated (Unconditional)	3.812	2.879	2.984	1.508
	(4.10)***	(3.52)***	(3.24)***	(1.98)**
No. of observations R^2	1,595	1,595	1,551	1,551
	0.01	0.27	0.10	0.43
(4) Mother_Migrated_Only (father stayed home)	0.839	0.156	–0.861	–0.121
	(0.45)	(0.08)	(0.45)	(0.07)
No. of observations R^2	1,576	1,576	1,549	1,549
	0.00	0.27	0.09	0.43
(5) Mother_Migrated, (Unconditional)	0.903	0.444	–0.147	–0.541
	(0.73)	(0.37)	(0.12)	(0.48)
No. of observations R^2	1,587	1,587	1,551	1,551
	0.00	0.27	0.09	0.43
(6) Both_parents_migrated,	1.367	0.615	1.040	–0.536
	(0.79)	(0.38)	(0.58)	(0.35)
No. of observations R²	1,575	1,575	1,549	1,549
	0.00	0.27	0.09	0.43

Data source: Authors' survey.

[a] Four versions of specifications are used in the difference-in-difference estimation. An unrestricted model includes $Score_{i,2002}$ as a right-hand side variable. This removes the restriction in the standard DD model that the coefficient on $Score_{i,2002}$ equals one. An adjusted model includes other covariates in addition to the treatment variable. Model (1) is the standard DD model and is restricted and unadjusted. Mathematically, model (1) is expressed as $\Delta Score_i = a + \delta MIG_i + \varepsilon$, where i is the index for students $\Delta Score_i$ is the before – after change in the school performance of student I, that is, scores from the fifth grade minus scores from the first grade: MIG_i is the treatment variable and δ is the parameter of interest, which measures the treatment effect. Model (2) is unrestricted and unadjusted, which is expressed as $\Delta Score_i = a + \delta MIG_i + \gamma Score_{i,2002} + \varepsilon_i$. Model (3) is unrestricted adjusted. Model (3) is expressed as $\Delta Score_i = a + \delta MIG_i + X_i \beta + \varepsilon_i$, where X_i is a vector of covariates that include the characteristics of students, parents and households, and a set of township dummy variables. Model (4) is unrestricted and adjusted and is expressed as $\Delta Score_i = a + \delta MIG_i + \gamma Score_{i,2002} + X_i \beta + \varepsilon_i$.

[b] The treatment variable MIG_i takes the following six forms:. *Any Parent_Migrated*, which is a dummy variable that is equal to 1 if both parents lived at home in 2002 and at least one parent (either the father; mother or both parents) out-migrated by 2006. *Father_Migrated_Only (mother stayed at home)* is a dummy variable that is equal to 1 if only the father out-migrated by 2006 but was at home in 2002. *Father_Migrated (Unconditional)* is a dummy variable that is equal to 1 if the father was at home in 2002 but out-migrated by 2006 (including households in which the mother was either at home or not at home in 2006). *Mother_Migrated_Only (Father stayed at home)* is a dummy variable that is equal to 1 if only the mother out-migrated by 2006 but was at home in 2002; *Mother_Migrated (Unconditional)* is a dummy variable that is equal to 1 if the mother was at home in 2002 but out-migrated by 2006 (including households in which the father was either at home or not at home in 2006). *Both_Parents_Migrated* is a dummy variable = 1 if both parents were at home in 2002, but out-migrated by 2006.

[c] The coefficients on the township dummy variables are not reported here for the sake of brevity.

[d] Robust t-statistics in parentheses.

*Significant at 10%; **significant at 5%; ***significant at 1%.

only negative for Mother Migrated Only households (row 4) and Mother Migrated (Unconditional) households (row 5) when the Restricted and Adjusted (column 3) or Unrestricted and Adjusted specification (column 4) is used. In each of these four cases, however, the *t*-statistic is smaller than 0.50, indicating there is no statistically significant effect of migration on school performance. Interestingly, as in the case of Any Parent Migrated households (row 1), when the father out-migrates (rows 2–3), the scores of migrant children improve.

So why is it that migration does not appear to have a negative effect on the scores of migrant children, and in some cases even appears to have a positive effect? Although we cannot answer this question from our analyses, one possible reason is that the income effect is relatively large compared to the adverse effect of less parental supervision. If migration leads to higher income, as found in Du *et al.* (2005), the migrant households that experience rising incomes may be able to provide better nutrition, improved access to educational supplies and burden their children with less housework. This may have a positive effect on school performance. The positive income effect is probably behind our finding that the largest positive effects are found in the Father Migrated Only households (Table 11.2, row 2). This result may arise since not only would children in such households benefit from higher incomes from migration, they would also suffer relatively less from falling parental care since the mother is still at home. Such an interpretation is also consistent with other findings. For example, Kandel and Kao (2001) found a positive relationship between fathers' migration and students' grades.

Matching results

The results of cross-sectional matching analysis, regardless of the method of matching, also reveal that migration has no significant negative effect on the school performance of students. When Propensity Score Matching is used to examine the effect of migration on school performance for all six types of New Migrant households, there are no cases in which the coefficient on the treatment variable is negative and statistically significant (Table 11.3, column 1, rows 1a, 2a, 3a, 4a, 5a and 6a). The same is true when Bias-Corrected Matching is used (column 1, rows 1b, 2b, 3b, 4b, 5b and 6b). In fact, results from matching are quite similar to those from the DD analyses. When we use Bias-Corrected Matching, which perhaps generates better estimates and standard errors, we find that the coefficients on the treatment variables in the Father Migrated Only household model and Father Migrated (unconditional) household model are positive and statistically significant and the magnitudes are similar to those from the DD analyses. In addition, and importantly, the findings remain largely the same when the DDM estimator is used (results not reported for brevity sake – please see our working paper at www.reap-china.com).

Table 11.3 Evaluating the effects of migration activities of parents on school performance of students in all six types of migrant households using matching and difference-in-difference matching, Shaanxi Province, China[a]

Treatment variable[b]	Matching[a]		Difference-in-difference matching	
	Average treatment effect for the treated	*t*-stat/ *z*-value[c]	Average treatment effect for the treated	*t* stat/ *z*-value[c]
Any_parent_migrated				
(1a) Propensity score matching	1.16	(1.02)	0.31	(0.28)
(1b) Bias corrected matching	1.57	(1.60)	2.12	(1.86)*
Father_Migrated_Only (mother stayed home)				
(2a) Propensity score matching	2.04	(1.36)	1.12	(0.77)
(2b) Bias corrected matching	3.59	(2.96)***	3.12	(1.93)**
Father_migrated, (Unconditional)				
(3a) Propensity score matching	1.57	(1.20)	2.35	(1.93)**
(3b) Bias corrected matching	2.19	(2.04)***	2.52	(1.99)***
Mother_Migrated_Only (father stayed home)				
(4a) Propensity score matching	–0.63	(–0.22)	–1.1	(–0.39)
(4b) Bias corrected matching	–0.94	(–0.43)	1.93	(0.58)
Mother_migrated (Unconditional)				
(5a) Propensity score matching	–0.45	(–0.26)	–1.51	(–0.88)
(5b) Bias corrected matching	–0.46	(–0.32)	0.82	(0.48)
Both_parents_migrated				
(6a) Propensity score matching	–0.22	(–0.09)	–0.56	(–0.23)
(6b) Bias corrected matching	–0.28	(–0.13)	0.97	(0.43)

Data source: Authors' survey
[a] Propensity scores are estimated using the same set of covariates as in Table 11.2.
[b] The treatment variables are described in note b in Table 11.2.
[c] t-Statistics are reported for propensity score matching and z-values are reported for bias-corrected matching in parentheses.
*Significant at 10% level; **significant at 5% level; ***significant at 1% level.

Conclusions

In this paper, we have tried to understand whether or not the school performance of children suffers when their father, mother or both parents migrate from the village into the city. Despite the perception that is commonly found in the literature and the press, our results, somewhat surprisingly, show that there is no effect of migration on the school performance of the children from migrant households. Comparing the change in the grades before and after parents out-migrate between children from migrant households and those from non-migrant households, we can reject the hypothesis that migration harms the grades of migrant children. In fact, in the analysis of some migrant households, especially in those in which the father out-migrates, migration is shown to have a statistically significant and positive effect on the performance of migrant children. We also find that the effects of migration on children's school performance are not systematically different for households that are more or less wealthy households. Neither are the effects different across households that have one or more than one child.

Based on these results, it might be tempting to conclude that policy makers do not need to take any action since there is no measurable effect of migration on school performance. If there were, education officials might want to reduce class sizes or hire more qualified teachers to improve the mentoring programme in schools in which there were many children of migrants. Boarding schools might offer some of the services that parents originally carried out before they entered the migrant labour force. Ultimately, measures can be promoted to offer the children of migrants who lived in China's cities better access to urban schools so parents would not have to leave their children behind. However, all of these programmes are costly. Although there might be good reason to implement such policies anyhow, according to our results, they should not be carried out on the ground of the negative effect of migration on school performance.

Although we have tried a number of alternative approaches to identify the effect of migration, and although the findings are largely robust, if the assumptions underlying our methodologies were not valid, our estimates could be bias. Even though we control for many observed and time-invariant unobserved factors, there still may be factors that are known to the parents of migrants and potential migrants but are not be observable to the econometrician. For example, it may be that all parents who were in the village with their children in 2002 worry about whether or not their migration decision would negatively affect the school performance of their children. If it is the case that those parents who – though having an opportunity to migrate – believed that the grades of their children would suffer decided not to migrate, while those that believed their children's grades would not suffer decided to migrate, then our results would be subject to selection bias.

If there was, in fact, such a selection bias and we did not account for it (as we were unable to – due to the absence of any effective instrumental variable), would our results be useless? We believe not. We believe even if there was a selection bias our results are showing that when rural parents out-migrate, the grades of their children do not suffer. It is true that part of the reason for the zero effect may be exactly this selection effect – parents do not go when they believe the grades of the children would suffer. But, from society's point of view, there is less cost in terms of school performance of its children due to migration.[10]

---

[10] There is also another potential source of endogeneity that we are not able to account for in the analysis. It is possible that unaccounted for shocks, either in the local economy or in individual households, affect both parents' migration activities and students' grades. If these shocks systematically affect all the households, then it is possible that our coefficients also are biased due to the fact that we did not account

Acknowledgements

The authors would like to thank Chengfang Liu, Renfu Luo who have spent uncountable days coordinating the survey and cleaning data. A special thanks to all the enumerators, school principals and students. We are also grateful for the useful comments from Belton Fleisher and two anonymous referees. We acknowledge grants to support field research from The Ford Foundation (Beijing), Chinese Academy of Sciences (KSCX2-YW-N-039) and support for follow-up research from the National Natural Science Foundation of China (70803047). The Natural Science Foundation of Zhejiang Province (Y607420) and the Social Sciences Foundation of Zhejiang Province (07CGLJ005YBQ).

References

Abadie, A and Imbens, GW. 2002: *Simple and bias-corrected matching estimators.* Technical report, Department of Economics, UC Berkeley.

Abadie, A and Imbens, GW. 2006: Large sample properties of matching estimators for average treatment effects. *Econometrica* 74: 235–267.

Battistella, G and Conaco, MCG. 1998: The impact of labour migration on the children left behind: A study of elementary school children in the Philippines. *Journal of Social Issues in Southeast Asia* 13: 220–241.

Benjamin, D, Brandt, L and Giles, J. 2005: The evolution of income inequality in rural China. *Economic Development and Cultural Change* 53: 769–824.

Blau, DM. 1999: The effect of income on child development. *Review of Economics and Statistics* 81: 261–276.

Brown, PH and Park, A. 2002: Education and poverty in rural China. *Economics of Education Review* 21: 523–541.

Caliendo, M and Kopeinig, S. 2008: Some practical guidance for the implementation of propensity score matching. *Journal of Economic Surveys* 22: 31–72.

Cox Edwards, A and Ureta, M. 2003: International migration, remittances, and schooling: Evidence from El Salvador. *Journal of Development Economics* 72: 429–461.

de Brauw, A and Giles, J. 2007: *Migrant labor markets and the welfare of rural households in the developing world: Evidence from China.* Working paper, Michigan State University.

de Brauw, A, Huang, J, Rozelle, S, Zhang, L and Zhang, Y. 2002: The evolution of China's rural labor markets during the reforms. *Journal of Comparative Economics* 30: 329–353.

Dehejia, RH and Wahba, S. 1999: Causal effects in nonexperimental studies: Reevaluating the evaluation of training programs. *Journal of the American Statistical Association* 94: 1053–1062.

Dehejia, RH and Wahba, S. 2002: Propensity score-matching methods for nonexperimental causal studies. *Review of Economics and Statistics* 84: 151–161.

---

for this type of unobservable heterogeneity. In this case, it is difficult to determine the direction of the bias. These shocks could be either negative (eg, the family suffers a crop failure or family sickness) or positive (eg, the family receives an inheritance or enjoys a bumper crop) and can lead to negative or positive bias in our estimates.

Du, Y, Park, A and Wang, S. 2005: Migration and rural poverty in China. *Journal of Comparative Economics* 33: 688–709.

Duncan, GJ, Brooks-Gunn, J and Klebanov, PK. 1994: Economic deprivation and early childhood development. *Child Development* 65: 296–318.

Fredriksson, P and Öckert, B. 2005: *Is early learning really more productive? The effect of school starting age on school and labor market performance.* IZA Discussion papers, 1659, Institute for the Study of Labor.

Giles, J. 2006: Is life more risky in the open? Household risk-coping and the opening of China's labor markets. *Journal of Development Economics* 81: 25–60.

Glewwe, P and Jacoby, HG. 2004: Economic growth and the demand for education: Is there a wealth effect? *Journal of Development Economics* 74: 33–51.

Hanson, GH and Woodruff, C. 2004: *Emigration and educational attainment in Mexico.* Working paper, University of California, San Diego.

Hanushek, EA. 1992: The trade-off between child quantity and quality. *The Journal of Political Economy* 100: 84–117.

Heckman, JJ. 2005: China's human capital investment. *China Economic Review* 16: 50–70.

Kandel, W and Kao, G. 2001: The impact of temporary labor migration on Mexican children's educational aspirations and performance. *International Migration Review* 35: 1205–1231.

Li, X. 2004: The investigation on the rural migrant children (in Chinese). *Journal of Women Study in China* 10: 35–37.

McKenzie, D and Rapoport, H. 2006: *Can migration reduce educational attainment? Evidence from Mexico.* The World Bank Policy Research Working paper series no. 3952.

McKenzie, D and Rapoport, H. 2007: Network effects and the dynamics of migration and inequality: Theory and evidence from Mexico. *Journal of Development Economics* 84: 1–24.

Princiotta, D, Flanagan, KD and Hausken, EG. 2006: *Fifth grade: Findings from the Fifth grade follow-up of the early childhood longitudinal study, Kindergarten class of 1998–99.* National Center for Education Statistics No. 2006–2038.

Rosenbaum, PR and Rubin, DB. 1983: The central role of the propensity score in observational studies for causal effects. *Biometrika* 70: 41–55.

Rozelle, S, Guo, L, Shen, M, Hughart, A and Giles, J. 1999: Leaving China's farms: Survey results of new paths and remaining hurdles to rural migration. *The China Quarterly* 158: 367–393.

Smith, J and Todd, P. 2005: Does matching overcome LaLonde's critique of nonexperimental estimators? *Journal of Econometrics* 125: 305–353.

Steelman, LC and Mercy, JA. 1980: Unconfounding the confluence model: A test of sibship size and birth-order effects on intelligence. *American Sociological Review* 45: 571–582.

Tan, S and Wang, X. 2004: The study on the migrant children (in Chinese). *Journal of Education in Hubei* 20: 11–12.

Todaro, MP. 1989: *Economic Development in the Third World.* Longman: New York.

Wang, Y and Wu, X. 2003: A case study of the migrant children (in Chinese). *Investigation of the Youth* 4: 7–10.

Wu, N. 2004: The problems on the rural migrant children (in Chinese). Unpublished Manuscript, China National Institute for Education Research.

Zhou, Q and Wu, H. 2004: A mother of 13 years old. *XinhuaNet,* May 26.

12

How Has China's Economic Emergence Contributed to the Field of Economics?

Gary H. Jefferson
Brandeis University, USA

China's economic transformation demonstrates that the paths of transition and development are broader and more varied than generally predicted by economic research relating to other countries. Research focused on China's experience contributes to the scope and richness of the economics literature in notable ways. The China literature illustrates and makes more vivid established insights and paradigms, including those of Nobel laureates whose work relates to development and institutions. Furthermore, China is inspiring new insights and understanding regarding the central role of institutions. This paper, in particular, focuses its review on the literature that expands our understanding of the process of induced institutional change.

Introduction

Noteworthy innovations in the field of economics over the past three decades, particularly in the field of institutional economics, have coincided with China's transformation from a relatively minor, centrally planned economy to a burgeoning economy with the highest sustained rate of economic growth on record. China is now poised to become the world's third largest economy and is widely expected to regain by mid-century its position last enjoyed circa 1820 as the world's largest economy (Maddison, 2003). Measured in terms of GDP at purchasing power parity (PPP), the overtaking of the US economy may materialise within a single decade.[1] Of

---

[1] In its recent revision of relative purchasing power parity measures of GDP, the World Bank estimates that China's GDP is 40% less than previously reported by the Bank. http://web.worldbank.org/WBSITE/EXTERNAL/NEWS/0,,contentMDK:21589281

Reprinted with permission from Association of Comparative Economic Studies. All rights reserved. *Comparative Economic Studies* (2008) 50(2), 167–209.

course, it is difficult to isolate the impact that China's economic transformation has had on the field of economics. Other important changes have occurred in recent times, including economic transitions in Eastern Europe, the former Soviet Union, and Vietnam and the rapid globalisation of the world economy, involving the establishment and expansion of the World Trade Organization and the deepening and expanded reach of a growing array of financial markets.

Nonetheless, my thesis in this paper is that China's dramatic economic transformation has itself inspired a broad body of research that substantially enriches the field of economics. While I will argue that the China-related economic literature is noteworthy in numerous respects, one feature stands out. Many country economic analyses address the issue of why a particular country has not lived up to its performance expectations. Usually, the answer is deemed to be obvious. That is, the country did not follow the appropriate policy; it deviated in fatal ways from orthodox policy prescriptions associated with the so-called Washington Consensus. Alternatively, if the country indeed did appear to have conformed to the tenets of this neo-liberal doctrine, the literature probes the question as to why a country that dutifully carried out the policy consensus did not reap the expected benefits.

China is different. Much of the China literature addresses a contrary puzzle: with institutions and policies that have deviated greatly from established orthodoxy, how could China be performing so well? China's economic emergence has contributed to the field of economics simply by posing this very different puzzle and forcing members of our discipline to come to terms with the fundamental contradiction between expectations shaped by theory and the observed outcomes. Certainly no body of literature has focused on this puzzle to the extent that the China literature has. Since the nature of the puzzle is so fundamentally different from the usual formulations that spur research, it should not be surprising that the literature addressing this puzzle represents a unique contribution.

This paper argues that research on China's experience deserves attention for its focus on two areas. First, as both a transitioning economy and a developing economy, China provides a large, heterogeneous, fast evolving laboratory for testing and illustrating many important and enduring insights of the economics discipline. The paper focuses on the work of economics Nobel laureates whose insights and conclusions have been made far more vivid and accessible when viewed through the lens of China's economic

---

~pagePK:34370 ~ piPK: 34424~theSitePK:4607,00.html. This revision adjusts China's PPP measure of GDP to somewhat less than one-half that of the US. However, at the time of the writing of this paper, China's exchange rate is widely believed to be substantially undervalued in relation to the US dollar.

experience. These insights include, but are not limited to, the work of Solow in growth, Lewis, Kuznets, and Sen in development and Buchanan, Coase, and North in institutional economics.

Second, research on the Chinese experience expands the scope of economic analysis. The story of China's economic experience is about the evolution of a system involving complex interactions and feedback mechanisms that cut across institutions and time. Much of the answer to the puzzle of China's distinctiveness has to do with viewing economic transition as a *series of interrelated process* rather than a *collection of events,* that is, the process of reassigning property rights, the process of becoming a market economy, the process of technology transfer and innovation, and the process of learning and adapting mental models to new economic realities. As such, China-related research emphasises and expands the scope of the endogenous nature of economic reform and development.

For example, the restructuring of only a small proportion of China's state-owned enterprises (SOEs) was the immediate and direct outcome of state action. Edicts, such as those liberalising new entry and sanctioning enterprise restructuring, had little direct impact on SOE performance. However, the competition that resulted from liberalisation did create pressures and opportunities that altered the relative marginal benefits and costs of institutional change. Such changes in the incentive structure motivated local government officials, managers, workers, and outside investors to search for new governance arrangements and new technologies that led to China's incremental enterprise restructuring. This cursory account of China's corporate governance reform is but one example of China's reform experience that illustrates the dynamic, endogenous character of China's transition and development process.

China's government has played a central and on-going role in the economy's transition. The transitions of Eastern Europe and the former Soviet Union (EEFSU) and that of China reflect a key difference. Whereas the functioning and authority of the EEFSU political systems collapsed, China's ruling party and central government have remained intact with the legitimacy and administrative capacity to steer China's economic transformation. China's government has played a central role in reassigning property rights from the state to individuals, thereby incentivising workers, managers, and investors to serve as agents of economic growth. If there is an unfinished chapter relating to China's experience, it is likely to be how property rights, now extensively in the hands of individuals and non-state organisations, are operating through feedback mechanisms to reshape the structure and functioning of China's government and political system.

China's experience offers a now irrefutable lesson. Economic transition and development is a far more complicated phenomenon than simply putting in place the principal elements of the neoclassical model, whose policy implications have been dubbed the Washington Consensus, or even adhering to an enlarged doctrine that incorporates the basic tenets of the New Institutional Economics (NIE). With respect to the latter, stressing that there are many paths to the fulfillment of different visions of a market economy, Murrell (1991) argues: 'The institutions of capitalism come in many varieties and cannot be put in place instantaneously. There are many alternative reform paths, depending upon the importance attributed to each of these institutions' (p. 59). More than any other country, China's experience gives life to this insight.

The following sections examine these themes as well as the specific literature on China that develops these themes. In writing this essay, I faced a tension between giving an account of China's economic reform and then identifying the literature that maps into this paradigm of transition and development or undertaking a full review of the literature from which a synthesis of various themes would naturally emerge. In principle, the latter approach seemed preferable, but given my somewhat inflexible priors regarding the essential lessons of China's reform experience as well as the difficulty of confronting the now vast literature on China's transition and development, I judged the full immersion approach to be infeasible.[2] Hopefully, there would be substantial agreement in the conclusions arising from the two approaches. How differently these two approaches to carrying out this assignment might have turned out I leave to you, the reader, to assess. While this paper no doubt misses important contributions, it attempts to capture the essential character of the forest if not all the trees that populate it.

The paper is organised as follows. The next section highlights some of the quantitative impacts of the growth of China-related economic research on the field, including the coming on line of extensive data sets and proliferation of journals, books and compilations relating to China's economy. The third section describes the distinctive nature of the puzzle that shapes the China research agenda – why China's economy is performing as well as it is given China's deviation from economic orthodoxy. One theme of this paper is that the research that chronicles and analyses China's economic transformation vividly illustrates and in some cases deepens the insights of important areas of the established economics literature. The fourth section 4 illustrates this theme. The fifth section develops a second theme regarding the distinctive contribution of China-related research; that is the focus on understanding the evolution of economic systems as a process that cuts across institutions and time. This section sets out an analytical framework into which we situate much of the salient research on China's economic experience. The sixth section reviews and synthesises that research and the

---

[2] I believe that the last comprehensive review of the literature relating to China economic reforms was conducted by Perkins (1988).

seventh section investigates the distinctive features of China's economy and assesses the extent to which these may or may not limit the transferability of analyses and lessons drawn from the Chinese experience to other countries and regions. Finally the last section reviews the key conclusions of the paper and speculates on new directions for China-related economic research.

Quantitative Impacts

Before examining the intellectual contributions that China's economic emergence and performance have inspired, it may be useful to acknowledge two quantitative measures of China's contribution to the field of economic research. One is the rich trove of economic data that has been collected, in part by government agencies and in part by research groups outside the Chinese government. The other quantitative measure of research inspired by China's economic emergence is the variety and volume of research outputs, journals, articles, conferences, and workshops that seek to make sense of China's experience.

Some of the data now available on China's economy are unparalleled in their scope and completeness. Among these are firm-level data based on the annual collection by China's National Bureau of Statistics (NBS) of data from China's nearly 300,000 large-, medium-, and small-scale industrial enterprises with annual sales exceeding five million Rmb (approximately $700,000). Within this group, the NBS collects more detailed data on the now approximately 30,000 large- and medium-size enterprises (LMEs). These data sets include nearly 100 variables on the economic and financial condition of China's LMEs and another 100 variables describing various science and technology inputs and outputs including R&D spending, new product development, and patenting. A similar detailed annual survey is conducted by China's Ministry of Science and Technology spanning the nation's approximately 4,000 research institutes. The NBS also administers an annual survey of China's most energy-intensive industrial firms. This survey, which has recently been extended to include all of China's LMEs, includes for each firm a profile of the quantity and value consumed, from which individual prices can be imputed, for 20 different energy types. China's Ministry of Commerce maintains detailed data on trade and foreign direct investment (FDI), including that which is more detailed than normally available, such as the ownership shares of exporting firms and exports originating from the special zones at the six-digit SIC level.[3] In addition, the

---

[3] While these data sets are unusually detailed, significant aspects of these data have yet to be fully reconciled with those of other nations. Also, see the NBER website http://www.nber.org/~confer/2007/cwt07/cwt07prg.html for a workshop on this topic as well as the websites of Robert Feenstra and Chad Bown for information on current data and recent research using these trade data.

NBS and other Chinese organisations, including the Ministry of Agriculture, regularly conduct household surveys that have supported extensive research on migration, fertility, educational and occupational choice, and other forms of household behaviour. Researchers have conducted a host of other special surveys that are too numerous to reference here. That conducted by Li *et al.* (2007, 2008) of village elections and household insurance and consumption patterns allows for an investigation of the impact of village elections on health care services and consumption risk-sharing at the village level. This research is but one illustration of the extreme heterogeneity of China's economy, including that of households, firms, and village administrative and political structures, which allows for a rich array of research agendas focused on China (see Li *et al.*, 2007, 2008).

Some of these data, especially data for the broad income accounts that are passed up through multiple lower jurisdictions to the central NBS, include numbers that are of questionable accuracy (see Holz, 2003, 2004). Other survey data, particularly that collected from individual firms, remain proprietary and difficult to access. Nonetheless, collections of these data, usually combined at various levels of aggregation, are conveniently complied and accessible in the form of specialised statistical yearbooks, often online, that span many topics, including energy, finance, science and technology, foreign trade, various industries, as well as individual sub-jurisdictions, including cities and provinces.

A more widely conspicuous consequence of China's economic emergence has been the proliferation of workshops, conferences, working papers, and published scholarly articles describing, analysing, and comparing China's economic experience. China research continues to be a growth industry. Some of these initiatives have resulted in the establishment of whole new programmes or centres at well-known research organisations, including the Brookings Institution, the Carnegie Endowment, and the National Bureau of Economic Research, as well as at many universities. In recent decades international organisations, notably the World Bank, IMF, and OECD, have dedicated substantial resources for extending advice to, and publishing analyses and policy papers about, China.[4]

At the same time China's research has led to the inauguration of new journals, including the *China Economic Review* and numerous Chinese language journals as well as new and existing economic journals that substantially if not exclusively publish the research on China. Thus, China research now provides a steady source of materials for publication in journals, such as the *Journal of Comparative Economics*, the *Economics of Transition*, the *Journal of*

---

[4] See, for example, Brandt and Rawski (2008), a compilation of research papers resulting from a broad effort to match specialists in functional areas, such as economic transition, agriculture, and industrial organisation with their counterparts who specialise in China.

Development Economics, and many others.[5] At the 2008 ASSA meetings held in New Orleans, the programme included no fewer than 43 papers on the subject of China. In addition, approximately 315 authors, co-authors, or discussants with Chinese surnames appeared on the 480 panels, a strikingly high proportion of Chinese researchers given that it was only about 20 years ago that a substantial flow of young Chinese students began to do PhD work overseas.[6]

One of the benefits of this proliferation of data and research outputs is that it supports a stream of analysis, evaluating the performance of China's evolving institutions and those that vie to replace them. By enabling private and public entrepreneurs to gain a deeper understanding of the deficiencies and possibilities for China's institutions, including enterprises and banks of various ownership forms, the IPR system, and other private and public institutions, this research expands the nation's social science knowledge base, thereby facilitating institutional change.

The Puzzle – What Is It?

Reviewing the landscape of economic reform and transition over the previous two decades, Lin (2005) observes, 'The most prevalent reform policy advice according to the existing neo-classical economics theories is the "Washington Consensus"' (p. 248).[7] Dani Rodrik (2004), Zhang Jun (1997), and others pose the China puzzle, that is, since China inaugurated its reform process in the late 1970s, its economy can be characterised by the following conditions, which taken together depart substantially from the Washington Consensus and the tenets of shock therapy. These deviations include

- a weak system of private property rights;
- a repressed financial system;
- continuation of an authoritarian political system;
- corruption, low ranking of transparency;
- deviation from best practice in corporate governance; and
- a weak legal system and law enforcement.

---

[5] These include journals published in Japan, such as the *Journal of Chinese Economic Studies* and the *Journal of Econometric Study of Northeast Asia.*
[6] The count of economists with Chinese surnames cannot distinguish among the country or region of origin, for example, Mainland China, Taiwan, Hong Kong, the US.
[7] According to Williamson (2002), who is generally viewed as the author of the Washington Consensus (Williamson and Miller, 1987), the doctrine consists of 'ten reforms that I originally presented as a summary of what most people in Washington believe Latin America (not all countries) ought to be undertaking as of 1988 (not all times).' Subsequently, the Washington Consensus became widely viewed as the intellectual foundation for the shock therapy proposed by economist for the transitional economies of Eastern Europe and the former Soviet Union.

In fact, Zhang's list above reveals that China's puzzle involves far more than its deviation from the tenets of the Washington Consensus. Just as fundamental, China's transition and development experience deviates from the policy prescriptions that can be derived from the approach of the NIE. Since its reform began in 1978, China's institutional arrangements have run counter to the basic tenets of the NIE that stress the interactions of institutions, economic incentives, and behaviour of individuals and thereby shape the performance of the overall economic system.

In summarising the transition experience of Eastern Europe, Lipton (2007) notes that 'Most governments concluded that reform was a seamless web, such that liberalisation and structural reforms must be woven together simultaneously'. He and other advocates of the shock therapy approach view economic transition as bundles of reforms that stand in fixed proportions and fixed sequence. Deviations from these complementarities and sequences render piecemeal reforms substantially ineffectual.[8]

Yet, in 1993, 15 years into its reform, nearly the same duration as the EEFSU transition from 1990 to the present, China's economy was anything but a 'seamless web' of simultaneous reform. After a decade and a half of reform, state-owned units still accounted for 61% of total government revenue and captured an even larger share of total investment in fixed assets. Also, in 1993, 43% of total industrial output originated from state industry. Moreover, these figures considerably underestimate the role of public ownership at that time, as *collective ownership* continued to play a substantial role throughout China's economy.[9] Because constitutional protections of private property were not added to the constitution until 1999 and even then required still further clarification in 2004 and 2007, it was understandable that the growth of private ownership was tentative during the first decades of China's reform. Although the proportion of public ownership has declined over the past 15 years, it remains significant, particularly within the financial system. Furthermore, observers would argue that China's political system, which ultimately drives the reform process, remains substantially unreformed. In 2004, John Williamson, the individual most closely associated with the Washington Consensus, characterised China's movement towards the constituent policy prescriptions as 'unambiguous but slow'.[10] In 2005, the Heritage Foundation and the *Wall Street Journal* ranked China 112

---

[8] Also see Fischer and Gelb (1991) and the World Bank (1996) for accounts of blueprints and sequencing across key dimensions of the orthodox reform agenda.

[9] According to the China Statistical Yearbook 2006 (NBS, 2006, Ch. 15, Industry, Explanatory Notes on Main Statistical Indicators), 'Collective enterprises constitute an integral part of the socialist economy with public ownership.' Political sub-jurisdictions, such as municipalities, towns, and villages, generally own a substantial share of such collective-owned enterprises.

[10] John Williamson, 'The Washington Consensus as Policy Prescription for Development' (http://info.worldbank.org/etools/bspan/Presentation   View.asp?PID=520& EID=257).

out of 155 countries in their Index of Economic Freedom, an overall score that barely improved on China's 1995 rank (Miles *et al.*, 2005).

Given China's weak compliance with the core principles of the Washington/NIE Consensus, how has it been possible for China to establish and sustain such impressively high rates of economic growth? Much of the China-related research establishes its distinctiveness by addressing this question. The difference in the reform styles of China and the EEFSU countries has made the debate over the respective advantages and disadvantages of gradual *versus* big bang reforms meaningful. In the absence of China's experience, it is likely that the economics profession would view the rapid, comprehensive reform scenario as the only theoretical and empirically valid approach. Instead, the arguments have become far more nuanced.

Illustrating The Basic Models

While part of the body of literature on China's economy is distinctively innovative, much of the contribution of the recent China research is found in the application, confirmation, and extension of well-established models, including those of a number of Nobel laureates. One effect of this literature has been to make the core insights of these classic works more vivid and broadly applicable. The ability of the China literature to illustrate the power of now-established paradigms is particularly relevant for demonstrating the central role and functioning of technology and institutions, particularly in the context of economic transition and development.

From a broad, macroeconomic perspective one of the most basic and enduring insights that is central to China's experience is the critical role of rising productivity in driving China's economic growth. Above all, China's experience underscores the fundamental lesson of Solow's neoclassical growth model (1956). That is, the prime driver of the sustained growth of living standards is *productivity growth* that arises from combinations of technological change, institutional change, and their interaction, and in turn continuously shifts out the economy's production function. While at any moment in time the most proximate and conspicuous source of China's economic growth has been the sheer volume of savings and investment, the key driver in China's rapid increase in capital-deepening and living standards has been on-going productivity change that offsets the diminishing returns associated with China's torrid rates of investment.

The central importance of productivity growth in China's economic transformation should not be diluted by the myriad of TFP studies that have been applied to China, including those of this author and his colleagues. Most of these studies, including Maddison (1998), Young (2003), and Perkins and Rawski (2008), show the growth of TFP accounting for less than one-half of China's growth in per capita income. The Perkins-Rawski study, for example, estimates that, during 1978–2005, 60% of China's economic growth was attributable to investment in fixed capital and education; they conclude that only 40% resulted from TFP growth.

Nonetheless, as Hulton (1975), Prescott (1998), and Easterly (2001) emphasise, the standard productivity growth equation is seriously misspecified. It is indeed ironic that a year after introducing his neoclassical model of growth, which demonstrates that sustained capital deepening and rising living standards require on-going productivity growth, Solow in 1957 followed with his growth accounting paper in which capital deepening is presented as an independent, exogenous phenomenon – a 'source' of economic growth. While growth accounting accounts for the respective roles of capital, labour, and productivity change as proximate sources of growth, taken by itself growth accounting is an atheoretic description of the growth process. Growth accounting identifies the *accounting* contributions to growth and rising living standards, not the *economic* contributions.[11]

Hence the productivity studies cited above utilise a misspecified economic structure that seriously underestimates the true contribution of productivity growth, since the growth of productivity drives both the demand for investment through technical change and the supply of savings by increasing the savings per capita needed to finance new rounds of investment. While Easterly's (2001) section heading 'It's Technology, Stupid', conveys his basic proposition bluntly, he elegantly illustrates his argument with references to countries in which large forced investments in physical and human capital have yielded little payoff in the absence of underlying technological change. By contrast, China illustrates the Solow model as it was intended to work. It is difficult to image that in the absence of reform, opening, and technology transfer, that China's economy would be raising living standards any more rapidly than the negligible rate at which living standards rose in the last decade of the pre-reform period when investment rates exceeded one-third. While China's high rate of savings and low rate of population growth may have contributed to higher levels of living standards, sustained rates of growth of living standards have relied on sustained productivity growth.[12]

---

[11] Perkins and Rawski acknowledge the fundamental role of productivity growth in driving the measured contribution of capital: 'The rise in the contribution of capital did not occur independently of the rise in productivity... . Thus it was the jump in productivity growth (after 1978) that led to a higher GDP growth rate that made possible the greater contribution of capital' (p. 19).

[12] In the spirit of endogenous growth theory, the emphasis on productivity growth does not preclude the possibility that China's high rates of savings and low population growth have themselves contributed to productivity growth. Specifically, they may have affected productivity by promoting human capital investment, which may increase returns to scale at the firm level or facilitate technology spillovers from the broad economy to individual firms (see Romer, 1986). The point is that to the extent that high savings rates and limited population growth have contributed to

A vivid illustration of the importance of productivity growth in driving the demand for human capital investment is shown by Naughton (2007). Even as Table 8.1 of his text documents a dramatic expansion of educational attainment, at the same time, Figure 8.4 shows, paradoxically, over the same period a two-and-a-half-fold increase in the returns to education, a juxtaposition of surging supply and rising returns that would seem to violate the principle of diminishing returns. Clearly, the rise in labour's productivity associated with the abolition of the labour allocation system, corporate governance reform, and the opening of the economy to inflows of new technology have elevated the returns to human capital thereby motivating the surge in human capital investment in China.[13]

While Solow's, 1956 model underscores the centrality of productivity change, the power of China's technological advance and institutional change also operates through other well-known models. The elevation of several hundred million Chinese out of poverty during the 1980s and 1990s, illustrates the power of the insights of Lewis (1954) and the follow-on work of Fei and Ranis (1964) into the dynamics of the dual economy.[14] The literature on China's rising regional and sectoral cleavages and the resulting migration frames our understanding of the largest reduction in poverty in human history spanning a single generation (Ravallion and Chen, 1999).

However, the dual economy model is fundamentally a story about productivity growth – that is of differential rates of productivity growth between the industrial and agricultural sectors that result in allocative inefficiencies that in turn drive factor reallocations, notably labour migration. Hence the Solow and Lewis and Fei and Ranis models are fundamentally linked by their shared reliance on productivity growth to spur rising efficiency and living standards. Brandt *et al.* (2008) demonstrate this importance by calculating the economic contribution of TFP in agriculture to China's overall growth; agricultural reform contributes to the pool of surplus labour whose productivity multiplies as it migrates to higher wage jobs in the urban industrial sector.[15]

While the conventional two-sector model is generally associated with two distinct regions, rural agriculture and urban industry, and the sources of differential urban-rural productivity gains are assumed, not described, in

---

the sustained growth of living standards, they have done so through their indirect contributions to productivity growth.

[13] See Zhang *et al.* (2005) for an account of the sources of China's rising returns to education.

[14] Naughton (2007, Figure 9.1) shows two substantially different estimates of the decline in poverty – an official Chinese estimate and a World Bank estimate. However, both involve more than 25% of China's rural population escaping poverty status.

[15] For China, Hsieh and Klenow (2007) estimate potential gains from allocative efficiency to be in the vicinity of 40%; for India, the potential gains are close to 60%.

that model, China researchers tell a more complete, nuanced story. That story engages the central role of institutions and the migration of workers from farm to factory *within* China's vast rural economy as well as between China's rural and urban sectors. In China, the rapid implementation of the Household Responsibility System (HRS) fundamentally altered incentives in the farm sector (Lin, 1992a,b; Rozelle and Li, 1998), thus spurring the rise of agricultural productivity and rural incomes. The replacement of China's collectives with family-managed farms offers powerful confirmation of the tenets of the NIE regarding how institutions shape individual incentives, behaviour, and economic performance. Although China's agricultural reforms remains incomplete, since land transfer rights remain with local governments, the powerful impetus to work effort and productivity make the HRS arguably the most single important institutional innovation that has fueled China's economic transformation. It is difficult to locate another example of such a fundamental reassignment of property rights that has exhibited such widespread effects and by underscoring the importance of institutions and incentives so clearly illustrates the logic of North and Coase.

During the first decade of the reform era, rising agricultural productivity, in turn, spurred fresh demands for basic consumer goods and agricultural inputs and implements manufactured by China's rural township and village enterprises (TVEs). During the decade of the 1980s, much of the impetus for China's migration and rising incomes occurred within the rural sector as the TVE workforce rose to more than 120 million in 1994 and its share of China's total gross industrial output expanded to 27.5%, double its level in 1985. Yet, by 2000, well into China's privatisation movement, the share of collective-owned industry, of which the TVEs were but a part, had fallen to just 6.6% of total Chinese industry (NBS, 1994, p. 373; 1995, pp. 401, 364; 2004, p. 513). Although driven by the early surge in agricultural productivity and incomes, the rise and fall of China's TVEs underscores how much of China's advance has proceeded in stages with a variety of sectors leading the transformation at different times.

The widespread impact of China's decollectivisation movement also underscores the central importance of institutional change in driving China's reform process. In fact, Easterly's shock message might have been 'It's *institutional* change, stupid', since the core driver of China's transformation has been institutional change to at least the same degree as technological change. The Chinese experience has shown how inseparable institutional change and technological change are as long-term drivers of productivity growth.

Researchers have documented and reported on the highlights of each of these reform stages, including the work cited above on agricultural productivity growth, Groves *et al.* (1994), Hay *et al.* (1994), Jefferson and Singh (1999) on the managerial reform of SOEs, and Byrd (1992), Weitzman and Xu (1993), and Putterman (1995) on TVEs. One feature that all of these analyses share is their focus on transitional institutions in which control rights became better defined but nonetheless retained notable ambiguous features. In each case, however, the literature documents substantial efficiency gains associated with the strengthened, if still substantially incomplete, control rights. The transformations of collectives, SOEs, and TVEs are all accounts of the reassignment of property rights and the 'becoming' of market institutions in the spirit of Buchanan (1979). The market institutions, in turn, evolved from episodes of North-like learning with successions of mental models and from Schumpeterian creative destruction that arose from liberalisation in the 1980s that enabled a growing role for prices and new entry. In the sixth section, we examine the literature's characterisation of these transitional institutions and their processes of change in greater depth.

While the analysis of transition in Eastern Europe and the FSU is about the impact of economic policy, the China literature is more focused on the economics of inducements to institutional change. In the remainder of this paper, we construct a model of China's transition and development that provides a context for situating the key contributions of both the general and China-specific literature.

Induced Institutional Change

Against the backdrop of China's gradual, evolutionary economic transition, the literature that documents the process of induced institutional change, however fragmented, stands out as a principal contribution of the China-related economic research. As with other applied research, analyses of induced institutional change in China have developed against the background of established theoretical and analytical perspectives. The theoretical antecedents include the work of Buchanan (1979), Coase (1960, 1992), North (1990, 1994), Schumpeter (1942), and Sen (1988). While this classic literature is not built on formal structures or models, Ruttan (2001) reviews the rather sparse literature that formally attempts to construct and estimate models induced institutional change.

Although the NIE has fundamentally recast economics, its focus is largely static. That is, its method of analysis is comparative statics, which assesses the relative merits of two or more distinctive sets of institutional arrangements, involving different configurations or assignments of property rights assignments, as in the Coase Theorem.[16] However, within the NIE literature there is relatively little emphasis on the *process* by which property rights become reassigned or better specified. The central issue in the paradigm of

---

[16] Another example analyses the implications of alternative assignments of property rights, such as the right of the lender to monitor for the purpose of mitigating problems associated with asymmetric information in credit allocation, for example Dewatripont and Maskin (1995).

induced institutional change is what conditions drive or induce institutions and their embodied property rights assignments to evolve over time.

Reviewing the literature on the subject, Ruttan summarises the problem in terms of demand and supply conditions that drive institutional innovation. Within the commercial arena, private entrepreneurs investigate and pursue opportunities for institutional change until the marginal benefit and cost of institutional innovation roughly equate. However, in the public arena, Ruttan (2001) postulates:

> Institutional innovation will be supplied if the expected return from the innovation that can be captured by the political entrepreneur exceeds the marginal cost of mobilizing the resources necessary to introduce the innovation. To the extent that the private return to the political entrepreneurs is different from the social return, the institutional innovation will not be supplied at a socially optimal level. (p. 130)

In his summary of the induced innovation literature, many of the illustrations reviewed by Ruttan involve the emergence of disequilibria between the marginal return and marginal cost of institutional change that result from changes in factor endowments or technical change.[17] When the underlying disequilibria emerge, competition becomes critical as it enables market participants to calibrate the gains to institutional change as measured by the observable differences in the returns to good performers and bad performers. Having calculated these potential gains, agents can then decide whether the expected gains exceed the costs of adopting the new institutional arrangements.

Schumpeter and North explicitly focus on the role of competition. Schumpeter views the role of competition from a systemic, macroeconomic perspective as the well-spring of the capitalist system that drives its continuous reinvention. While Schumpeter's focus (1942) on 'the perennial gale of creative destruction' is generally associated with the phenomenon of technological change, like North he sees competition as the driving force behind all forms of change: '(what counts is) the competition from the new commodity, the new technology, the new source of supply, the new type of organization...' (p. 84). By contrast, North has a more microeconomic, behaviour-centred perspective in which incipient competition, which may even exist in a collective setting such as an array of township and

---

[17] Ruttan particularly focuses on a case study of institutional innovation conducted by Hayami and Kikuchi (1981) in a Philippine village involving changes in technology and resource endowments associated with the introduction of high yielding varieties of rice and a national irrigation system. These changes led during 1966–1976 to a shift from share tenure to lease tenure and to a dramatic increase in sub-tenancy arrangements (p. 362).

village-owned enterprises, spawns meaningful incentives for search and learning and for the ensuing adoption of institutional and technological change. North celebrates this link between competition and learning: 'While idle curiosity will result in learning, the rate of learning will reflect the intensity of competition amongst organizations. Competition, reflecting ubiquitous scarcity, induces organizations to engage in learning to survive...' (p. 362). Thus, while for Schumpeter, capitalism is a precondition for Schumpeterian 'creative destruction', from North's more eclectic perspective, competition may function as a key motive for driving individual organisations or whole economies from one system to another. North's broad interpretation of the role of competition gives it the powers to motivate a once-socialist, centrally planned economy like China's to 'grow out of the plan', to use Naughton's phrase (see Naughton, 1995). North's elaboration on the role of competition inspires us to consider the explicit processes whereby competition destroys institutional arrangements devised under the old planned economy, creating in their stead market-oriented capitalist institutions.

If competition has been the driving force of China's institutional transition, then the literature must face the question of what conditions have opened the door to competition. The process of China's opening or liberalisation clearly differs from the EEFSU model of reform agents rapidly opening the spigots of market activity. China occupies the opposite end of the spectrum, in which its reform agents initially limited market activity to a 'bird cage', to use Chen Yun's metaphor, in service to the command economy only to come under the spell of the gains from sustained incremental increases in the scope of the market. Lau *et al.* (2000) identify the source of these political and economic gains as deriving from 'reform without losers'.

Rather than viewing China's institutional change as a purely endogenous phenomenon, Bromley and Yao (2006) formulate a model of multi-layered institutional arrangements. In their model, constitutional and legislative authorities at the top of the political hierarchy frame the legal architecture that shapes the rules, norms, and behaviour of lower-level institutions that are nested within the institutional hierarchy. Initial, exogenous changes in constitutional and legislative rule-making induce changes in the design and functioning of lower-level institutions. Changes in lower-level institutions, in turn, operate through feedback mechanisms, such as monitoring and learning by higher-level authorities, to induce changes at the top of the institutional hierarchy. Hence, once in motion, the process of institutional change can feed on itself to sustain an ongoing, path-dependent process that is reinforced by feedback driven by competition, search, and learning, which, in the case of China's economy, together serve to alter the mental models of the agents responsible for reform. In this spirit, Jefferson and Rawski (1994) characterise China's reform experience as a 'process rather than an event' that incorporates aspects of Hirschman's 'unbalanced' development model in which imbalances and disequilibria force new reform initiatives through systems of feedback and learning. The following section characterises the three central elements of China's 'process of becoming' and induced institutional change.

Three Elements of China's Reform Process

This section is organised into three subsections that describe the essential elements and literature relating to the three elements of the China-related literature on induced institutional innovation. These are transitional institutions, competition and learning, and a generally stable, pragmatic, political environment.

- *Transitional institutions.* Transitional institutions are viewed as having two distinct defining characteristics. First, they embody a fundamental institutional weakness, typically associated with a state-centred or unclear assignment of property rights (eg a legacy of state ownership). Second, they are susceptible to competitive pressure, that is, able to phase out or evolve into a higher-order, market-oriented institution, while continuing to lag behind best practice. An extensive literature has accumulated that analyses and documents China's institutional deficiencies while also attempting to identify the factors that motivate efforts to improve their functioning.[18]
- *Competition and learning.* A recurring theme of the China literature is the role of competition as the key driver of institutional reform in China's economy. This literature describes and documents the sources of the competition, created both internally and through China's opening. A portion of the literature analyses the nature of the learning resulting from the competition, including the formulation of new 'mental models' that enable the design, adoption, and diffusion of new institutional arrangements.
- *A generally, stable, pragmatic political environment.* A key aspect of China's transition has been a political system that has been responsible for reassigning, clarifying, and mediating property rights, while maintaining a stable macroeconomy and political economy and itself being susceptible to institutional change.

The interaction of these three elements, transitional institutions, competition and learning, and a stable, pragmatic political economy, go a long way towards identifying the ingredients of China's heretofore successful economic reform process. Taken together these three elements shift the prism of the NIE literature from that of an emphasis on the nature of 'good' institutions to that of the process of becoming better institutions. Each of

---

[18] Guo (2005) provides a broad context for understanding the certain advantages associated with the relative 'backwardness' of China's institutions.

these three elements has been necessary; none is sufficient, for shaping China's robust reform path. The omission of any one of the three elements would have disabled the reform process or at least implied a fundamentally different reform trajectory.

No one article in the China literature describes all three elements and their interactions sufficiently. The literature addressing the essential character of each of these conditions is reviewed below. Some, describe the central aspects of individual parts of the process, such as Weitzman and Xu (1993) for transitional TVEs and Qian and Xu (1993) for regional experimentation and competition. Others, such as Qian (2002) and Jefferson and Rawski (1994) attempt to integrate the elements of transitional institutions and competition, Bromley and Yao (2006) introduce the key third element of the role of political economy. As yet, however, none has fully integrated these into a single model of institutional evolution. Highlights of the literature are reviewed below.

Transitional institutions

The transitional institution that first began China's reform process was the rural collective. The fact that it was made up of production teams that were, in turn, collections of households made it capable of being restructured by making the household the irreducible unit of production. The fact that, in some collectives, one or few households took the lead in agricultural production, particularly in those areas that specialised in husbandry, made decollectivisation more feasible. Moreover, by leasing, not selling, land use rights to households, decollectivisation side-stepped the issue of land transfer rights and instead struggled with the more tractable problem of distributing machinery, livestock, and crop revenues across households.

According to Qian (2000), the first recorded practice of household responsibility farming took place in December 1978 in the Xiaogang Production Brigade of Fengyang County in Anhui Province, where 20 farmers representing as many households put their fingerprints on a 'contract' to divide the commune's land among the households. By doing so they also promised to fulfill the procurement quota of grain to the state. Under the HRS, households became residual claimants and obtained almost all control rights over production, except for the right to transfer their ownership rights. With the HRS resulting in dramatic gains in farm productivity and household incomes, by the end of 1983, 98% of the production teams in China had adopted the new household-based farming system. What conditions led to this institutional revolution in China's countryside?

The following conditions first opened the door for and then propelled the decollectivisation of agricultural production and adoption of the HRS.

- Following the trauma of the Great Leap that resulted in man-made famines, the death of tens of millions, and later the disturbances of the

Cultural Revolution, including the suspension of higher education for a decade, China's political leaders were desperate to restore the legitimacy of the Party and political system. One initiative authorised experimentation in China's poorer areas to raise economic productivity and living standards. The tragic errors of the Maoist era thus altered the ideology of China's political leadership, making it easier – indeed imperative – to initiate institutional change.

- The dramatic success of the household responsibility experiment among a small number of production teams in Anhui Province inspired its spontaneous adoption across much of China, which raced ahead of the Party's acceptance of the grass roots decollectivisation movement. Once the substantial payoff to adoption of the HRS had become widely demonstrated, it became relatively easy for the Chinese Communist Party (CCP) to give its full recognition.

Lin (1987, 1995) proposes that the rapid diffusion of the HRS through China's countryside can be explained by the induced institutional innovation hypothesis of Hayami and Ruttan (1985). According to Lin (1987):

For the institution to be adopted, as Hayami and Ruttan postulated, it was necessary that gains to the innovators be large enough to offset the social costs involved in changing the relationships. The costs to attain consensus should be smaller if it is easy to divide the team endowments and to parcel out the team obligations to the households. The costs should also be smaller when the merits of the new system have come to light through the performances of those households that have already adopted the new system (p. 411).

Lin (1987) and Fan (1991) view the decollectivisation movement as resulting from the widespread recognition of a large differential between crop yields under the collective system and those potentially available under an incentivised farming scheme, estimated to be as large as 30% in favour of the latter. Lin (1987) hypothesises that the specific payoff to decollectivisation was a function of the size of production teams, where large teams made efficient monitoring and reward more difficult. He also hypothesised that rates of diffusion of the HRS were determined by the cost of transitioning to the new system. Transition costs rose in relation to the proportion of farm output dedicated to crop production *versus* husbandry, since much of the latter was already managed by individual households within the collective. In addition, the less the use of machinery, which was relatively indivisible, the easier the dissolution of the production team. At the same time, the greater use of draft animals, whose numbers made them relatively divisible, led to higher rates of diffusion of the HRS. Using provincial level data for the period 1981–1983, Lin finds reasonably robust support for this analytical framework for balancing the marginal cost and marginal benefit of decollectivisation.

Following the initial spurt in agricultural productivity during the first half of the 1980s, it became evident that under the land-assignment scheme the lease of use-rights alone created insufficient incentives for farmers to invest, while also encouraging small-scale farming and the excessive scattering of plots.[19] The growing perception of the costs of the leasing of fragmented plots *versus* the benefits of assigning residual ownership rights, including the right of sale, to farmers, has spurred active debate and search for politically acceptable solutions to the land ownership issue that challenges the most basic tenets of the socialist doctrine. Although the central government remains unable to resolve the dispute over the matter of privatising agricultural land, the search for resolution has encouraged local governments to allow permissive institutional experimentation, including hiring in farm labour, sub-leasing, and longer land contracts extending in some cases more than 15 years (Bromley and Yao, 2006).

This marginal cost–marginal benefit model of institutional restructuring also resonates with China's SOE reform experience. One of the Chinese names for the state-ownership, ownership by all of the people (*quanmin suoyouzhi*), readily captures the condition of the SOE as a 'tragedy of the commons'. Like trees in a public forest that can be freely used as firewood, the essential institutional problem is that, with weak monitoring, stakeholders with access to the SOE, notably managers, workers, and officials, enjoy the ability to enter and strip the assets, either directly in the form of theft or indirectly in the form of shirking that yields rewards in excess of their real contributions. The result is a leaching of the assets of the SOE. When these assets are replenished through subsidies or loans that become bad loans, the SOE crosses the line from an exhaustible commons to an inexhaustible public good.[20] As in Jensen and Meckling's classic (1976) characterisation of agency costs, the SOE problem is essentially a monitoring problem – a weak assignment of managerial control rights. SOE managers lack the motivation and authority to monitor the productivity of inputs and calibrate the warranted rewards.

Within this institutional setting in which wages are compressed, so long as the skilled and motivated workers face no opportunity cost for shirking, that is, the right to migrate to a job that rewards in accord with skill and effort, the low-effort and low-pay equilibrium persists. In the absence of a market in labour quality, workers of all ability levels shirk. This low-level

---

[19] Bowlus and Sicular (2003) also show that the absence of land markets that function across villages contribute to both labour shortages and surpluses.

[20] See Jefferson's (1998) characterisation of the state-owned enterprise as a public good.

equilibrium was finally disrupted in the latter half of the 1980s when China's government carried out two reforms.[21]

The first policy reform was liberalisation that allowed for the entry of new enterprise forms, including the expansion of TVEs, joint ventures involving shares of foreign ownership, and individual household enterprises (*getihu*). Unlike their SOE counterparts, managers operating within these enterprises types enjoyed a relatively full range of the managerial control rights that frame both a more profit-oriented motivation and the ability to monitor and reward the workforce to increase the firm's profit.

The second reform that disrupted the low-level shirking equilibrium gave workers the right to search for work. Until the mid-1980s, China's workers and graduating students were typically assigned jobs in SOEs with no right or opportunity to transfer to the non-state sector where reward for extraordinary skill and effort could be found.[22] However, by the end of the 1980s, with the abolition of the labour allocation system and proliferation of non-state enterprises, top-tier workers could exit to work settings in which managers enjoyed the authority to monitor and reward workers in accord with their skill and effort.

These changes essentially created a market for labour quality where such a market had previously been absent in China. Unfortunately, China's SOEs did not have the managerial capacity to compete for labour quality. The transitional characteristics of the SOE system then came into play. The emergence of functioning markets for labour quality outside the SOE system motivated the most productive SOE workers to exit to higher wage jobs in the newly established enterprise sector. The exit of high productivity workers from SOEs led to relative reductions in average productivity levels and revenues in the state sector, thereby limiting wage increases there relative to those available in the emerging non-state sector.

This growing wage disparity, documented in national wage statistics,[23] then motivated the next tier of productive workers to exit, with further

---

[21] See Jefferson's account of the problem of markets in labour quality within China's SOEs, 'Missing Markets in Labor Quality: The Role of Quality Markets in Transition,' http://people. brandeis.edu/~jefferso/res.html.

[22] During the academic year 1986–1987 when the author was teaching in the School of Economics at Wuhan University, he observed that the graduate students were not quite as diligent as he had anticipated. They explained that this was due to the fact they anticipated assignments under the labour allocation system that were not likely to require them to use their advanced economics training.

[23] In 1985, the average wage of staff and workers in SOEs was 0.845 that of the firms operating under other types of ownership. From 1985, the relative SOE wage fell year-on-year until 1993 when it stood at 0.712, a 16% decline over 8 years. Thereafter, as managers acquired greater rights to set compensation and furlough workers (ie *xiagang*), the relative wage of SOE workers began to rise. Jefferson *et al.* (forthcoming) document a rapid rise in the relative productivity levels of SOEs from 1998 to 2005.

declines in productivity, revenue, and relative compensation. The process of adverse selection arising from the inability of SOEs to compete in markets in labour quality disrupted the SOE low-level shirking equilibrium. During the late 1980s and early 1990s, as successive tiers of productive workers exited, SOE performance continued to deteriorate in relation to the non-state sector.

By creating more financial and managerial challenges for SOEs, the emergence of markets in labour quality forced local governments and the SOE supervisory agencies either to increase subsidies continuously, reform managerial control rights to enable SOE managers to compete in labour quality markets, or to liquidate or sell off the enterprises. All of these occurred in some measure.[24] Where governments reassigned control rights to SOE managers, the government in some measure extended the *market in labour quality* to China's SOEs.[25] Creating these markets in labour quality replicated conditions associated with the classic case of the creation of a Coasian market in water quality. With a clear assignment of managerial control rights (to the manager) and low transaction costs, management (the downstream party) could compensate labour (the upstream party) to provide higher quality labour services.

During the decade following the government's 1995 decree to 'retain the large (SOEs) and let the small (SOEs) go', the number of SOEs fell dramatically. Even among the large- and medium-size enterprises, the proportion of SOEs declined from 64% in 1996 (12,216) to just 11% (3,396) in 2006. Among those retained by the state, Premier Zhu Rongji called for the implementation of 'modern management systems' seemingly with some effect. Although during 1985–1995, the relative productivity of enterprises that retained their SOE status declined, during 1995–2005, starting from a relatively low level, the productivity of China's SOEs grew more rapidly than that of the economy's non-state enterprises (see Jefferson *et al.*, forthcoming, Table 5).

Various studies point to the role of competition in motivating SOE restructuring. Li *et al.* (2000), for example, start with the recognition that for most SOEs, local governments, which hold the residual claim on after-tax profits, also have the right to decide whether or not to shift these residual claims

---

[24] See the survey of Jefferson *et al.* (1999) of differential assignments of managerial control rights in samples of SOEs and TVEs.

[25] Bai *et al.* (2000) argue that in the absence of an umbrella safety net, such as unemployment insurance, SOEs continue to play a critical transition. Because independent institutions for social safety are lacking and firms with strong profit incentives have little incentives to promote social stability due to its public good nature, SOEs are needed to continue their role in providing social welfare. Charged with the multitasks of efficient production as well as social welfare provision, SOEs continue to be given low-profit incentives and consequently, their financial performance continues to be poor.

to management, that is, to privatise. According to their hypothesis, when competition becomes sufficiently intense, thus eroding or threatening to erode, profitability and tax revenue, local governments are induced to shift residual claims to the manager. This link between competition and enterprise restructuring is probably the most frequently tested causal hypothesis in the Chinese enterprise reform literature.[26] The model of missing markets in labour quality is useful for understanding at least one set of dynamic processes involving spillovers from liberalisation and competition that has motivated the restructuring or liquidation of China's SOEs.

China's dual-track system, which framed the emergence of the markets in labour quality sketched above, served as the administrative and pricing framework for a range of institutions to phase out of their plan structures. Lau *et al.* (2000) document the Pareto-improving impacts of both the agricultural and industrial market liberalisations under the dual-track system. To best appreciate the central role of the dual-track system, however, one must understand how it encapsulated the whole of China's economic transition in which phase outs in one sector created spillovers in the form of supply and demand linkages and competition that enabled or incentivised other sectors to grow out of their plans. By dramatically raising agricultural productivity, the supply of surplus labour, and rural incomes during 1978–1984, decollectivisation set the stage for the rapid emergence and expansion of the TVE sector during the 1984–1994 period. Responding to the rise in purchasing power in China's vast rural economy, TVEs at once filled empty product niches, expanded supply chains, and generated new sources of competition for SOEs. At the same time, the opening of export markets even as the planned trade system remained in force, paved the way for foreign investment and joint ventures, which also competed with SOEs for domestic and overseas markets and quality labour. By 1994, the robustness of the TVE and foreign sectors had substantially eroded the advantages that SOEs had once enjoyed. The cost-benefit calculus of SOE restructuring shifted in favour of reform and SOE restructuring accelerated rapidly. In this sense the TVEs and JVs served as the bridge between China's successful agricultural reforms and the deepening, if delayed, state sector reform during the latter half of the 1990s.

Other institutions that embody the attributes of ambiguous assignments of property rights and susceptibility to competition remain in critical phases of their transition, none more so than the banking system, which has absorbed hundreds of billions of dollars in public funds to recapitalise its depleted assets.[27] However, it too is exhibiting responsiveness to rising

---

[26] Cao *et al.* (1999), Li *et al.* (2000) and Li (1997) all find empirical evidence to support this view.

[27] Lardy (1998, 2002) documents these losses, chronicles the government's attempts to reform the banking system, and describes the rule changes associated with China's accession to the WTO.

competition with China's financial sector, particularly as the provisions of the WTO agreement governing financial liberalisation have taken effect. Keidel (2007) investigates how over the past decade China's financial sector has turned in a credible performance with a respectable ICOR, rising returns to investment, a high degree of financial stability, and the ability to sustain high growth.[28] Like the SOE reform scenario sketched above, Keidel's model of induced restructuring focuses on institutional complementarities, in this case within the financial system. He argues that the successful strengthening of China's financial system has resulted from the 'two-part' or dual-track structure in which the publicly financed portion of the system provides a stable backdrop to the emerging private institutions and market operations. The two parts perform mutually complementary roles; one providing stability, the other serving as a competitive impetus to restructuring. As the WTO provisions for financial sector liberalisation take hold, foreign competition and inflows of foreign capital ensuing rising ownership shares in the Chinese banking system sustain reform progress, as the element of state ownership and backup the necessary ingredient of stability and confidence. Of course, this somewhat idealised account implies the right mix of liberalisation and competition with suitable control and guarantees as if driven by an enlightened despot. This involves the role of China's generally stable, pragmatic political environment, which is addressed later in this section.

Jefferson and Rawski (2002) explicitly apply the Coase Theorem to formulate their analysis of the development of China's market in corporate assets. They argue that reforms involving the clarification of Chinese corporate asset ownership and the reduction in transaction costs resulting from financial sector reform and the development of company and contract law have led to the emergence of an active market in corporate assets, mergers, and acquisitions. China's emerging stock markets are a key element of this market in corporate assets. The access these markets are giving to foreign firms includes the opportunity for foreign financial institutions to purchase substantial blocks of shares in China's state-owned banks thereby clarifying the property rights assignments within these banks and creating access to foreign banking technology and management practices.

Viewed through the lens of a Coasian missing market, each of the transitional institutions described above can be seen as embodying a missing market of one form or another, whether rights over the use of land and the disposition of crops in farm production, the supply and demand for quality labour services in SOEs, the right to issue, monitor, and collect loans in financial services, or the right to transfer corporate assets. China continues to struggle with other realms of missing markets, including intellectual

---

[28] See recent estimate of returns to investment by Bai *et al.* (2006) and Jefferson *et al.* (2006). Both find increasing return to capital in the China's secondary (industrial) sectors.

property and environmental quality. George Stigler said of the Coase theorem, that its logic cannot be questioned, only its domain (Stigler, 1989). Research on China's transitional institutions has served to considerably expand our appreciation of the expanding domain of the Coase theorem.

The innovative feature of the China literature is its ability to deepen our understanding of the dynamic processes that are leading to the creation of varieties of markets and capitalist institutions where such markets and institutions had not previously existed. The examples of the agricultural decollectivisation movement and state enterprise reform show how initial steps by the government can disrupt existing equilibria and set in motion, whether intentional or not, pressures to extend and deepen the reform of transitional institutions in accord with the logic of Coase.

This section clearly points to competition as the driving force for China's transition. The next section examines the role of competition and its corollary, learning, in motivating and directing the search for institutional innovations. Thereafter, the section looks at the critical role of government and the political system in initiating and orchestrating the reform initiatives that motivate and enable individuals and organisations to search ways of adopting and achieving more efficient institutions.

Competition and learning

In the neoclassical paradigm, competition plays a critical role in setting prices and motivating static economic efficiency. Schumpeter (1942) and North (1994), however, view competition in a dynamic setting; it is the mainspring of economic progress.

It is difficult to appreciate the degree of competition that lay latent in China's economic system at the beginning of its reform process.[29] One of the unintended accomplishments of the socialist era was to create the preconditions that facilitated the burst of competition that followed from the economic liberalisation of the 1980s. The sporadic emphasis on decentralisation during the socialist era was associated with the construction of relatively complete sets of industries across many of China's then 29 provinces. In the wake of the decentralisation movements, by 1980 most provinces had a steel mill, a textile factory, a factory producing heavy transportation equipment, and multiple factories established for the production of beer, bicycles, TVs and other household appliances, as well as a wide variety of other

---

[29] Mao's decentralisation movement accompanied the Great Leap. In 1958, the number of SOEs subordinated to the central government was reduced from 9,300 in 1957 to 1,200 in 1958 (Qian, 2002, p. 25). Recentralisation followed the Great Leap disaster. The second wave of decentralisation (1970) shared many features of the 1958 decentralisation but went even further. Qian (p. 27). The number of SOEs under central government supervision fell from 10,533 in 1965 to just 142 in 1970.

manufactured goods.[30] According to Xu (2006), at the outset of the reforms, almost all of the two thousand counties in China had SOEs producing agricultural machinery; 300 countries had steel plants, more than 20 provinces had SOEs producing automobiles or tractors. Small regional SOEs produced 69% of China's total fertiliser output and 59% of its cement. Moreover, because in 1980 19 of these provinces had populations that exceeded 25 million, of which eight had populations that matched or exceeded the size of Great Britain, with sufficient liberalisation, the proliferation of factories created the prospect of high levels of competition and the ensuing restructuring with the potential for multiple plants competing at minimum efficient scale.

Qian and Xu (1993), Qian and Weingast (1997), and Qian *et al.* (2006) offer a critical insight regarding how China's system of regional government has fostered decentralised, experimental transition and inter-regional competition.[31] Although, under its constitution, China is not a federalist system, in important ways, China's regional governments are more powerful than their counterparts in most federalist countries. Most governmental functions are administered by regional governments. Wong (2006) documents the total expenditure of China's regional governments in the early 2000s to have been about 70% of the national level, a proportion that is far larger than that of the world's largest federalist countries, including the US (46%), Germany (40%) and Russia (38%).

According to Qian and Xu (1993) during the early stages of reform,'... the central government delegated more autonomous power and provided stronger incentives to regional government in trying out reforms and in promoting economic growth'. One consequence of this delegation is that provincial and municipal leaders have aggressively competed by shaping their policies – tax, subsidies, public infrastructure investment, education, and technology policies – to gain advantage in attracting new investment, both domestic and foreign.[32] In accord with the central government's policy for China's provinces of 'compete to become rich quicker', provincial officials anticipated that when their province enjoyed higher growth than others, the head of the province would be afforded greater power and be more likely to be promoted (Xu, 2006, p. 3).

---

[30] These bundles of regional production capabilities are documented in Naughton (2007).

[31] Young (2000) argues that substantial barriers to trade exist between Chinese provinces. Other research (eg Bai (2004) and Long and Zhang (2008)) since 1990 find a clear trend toward greater regional specialisation.

[32] Chinese policy makers refer facetiously to the '10 + 1' policy paradigm, that is, 'If province X will give you those 10 incentives, then our province will give you those 10 plus this one more.'

The second source of the competition that is driving China's transition and development is the economy's remarkable openness to the global economy; from just 9.8% in 1978, China's trade ratio rose to 63.9% in 2005 (NBS, 2006).[33] The speed of China's opening had its roots partially in the 19th century and first half of the 20th century during which commercial links were established between the mainland and the economies of Hong Kong, Macao, Taiwan, and the Chaozhou people of Southeast Asia. The four special economic zones, Shenzhen, Zhuhai, Xiamen, and Shantao, established in the early 1980s to rekindle these historical commercial links became the initial impetus for China's burgeoning trade and FDI.[34] Commercial operations in these areas rapidly extended access to supply chains, experienced managerial know-how, and advanced overseas technologies.

Using a large cross-country sample, Aghion *et al.* (2006) confirm that foreign entry induces productivity growth among the relatively productive domestic firms, particularly in technologically advanced industries. Deng and Jefferson (2008) extend that work using large- and medium-size industrial enterprise data for China to show that, in response to foreign entry, Chinese-owned firms that operate closer to the technology frontier defined by their foreign are able to raise productivity, while those firms that are more distant from the frontier are frequently restructured. As North might anticipate, the China literature finds that competition associated with foreign entry results in overall productivity advance by domestic Chinese firms. However, as Schumpeter predicts, while competition strengthens some firms, it also enfeebles weaker firms, often setting them on the path to restructuring or liquidation.

According to North (1994), the link between competition and institutional change is not automatic. In this model of induced institutional change, the phenomenon of learning is the critical avenue linking competition and institutional change. North memorialises this connection: 'While idle curiosity will result in learning, the rate of learning will reflect the intensity of competition amongst organisations. Competition, reflecting ubiquitous scarcity, induces organisations to engage in learning to survive...' (p. 362).

In addition to their finding that foreign entry results in a bifurcation of productivity response, with strong productivity gains in stronger firms and declines in weaker firms, Deng and Jefferson (2008) find a similar response in R&D spending. As higher productivity firms increase their R&D expenditure, weaker firms cut back on R&D spending. Consistent with the finding of Deng and Jefferson, Girma *et al.* (forthcoming), also using Chinese firm-level data, show that foreign entry accelerates the pace of new product development. In a similar vein, even after controlling for firm-level R&D expenditure, Hu and Jefferson (2008) show that rising concentrations of industry FDI in China contribute substantially to the incidence of new

---

[33] The trade ration is defined conventionally as (imports+exports)/GDP.

[34] See Naughton (2007), Ch. 1, 'Legacies and Settings.'

patent applications. Hence, a substantial body of China-related literature confirms the important role that international competition plays in motivating learning that leads to productivity upgrading, R&D intensification, patent development, and rising product quality.

While the literature cited above focuses on technical learning within industry, Bromley and Yao (2006) argue that system-wide learning, including that arising from early productivity advances in agriculture, emboldened the reformers to further modify their ideology and thus to undertake yet further institutional innovation in other sectors. According to Bromley and Yao, China's early reform process was:

> ...a process of individual leaders gradually revising their beliefs, experimenting on a few modest fronts, observing the results of those new institutions, learning from those pilot projects, revising the analytical and prescriptive models of their economic advisors, crafting yet another set of new institutional arrangements, and continuing to watch, learn, revise, observe, and then revise accordingly (p. 44).

In their seven-stage description of China's reform process, which they entitle 'China's Decision to Create a Market-Based Economic System is an Endogenous Outcome of the Partial Reform Process', Jefferson and Rawski (1994) describe key changes that occurred in the early 1990s:

> The rise of pro-market sentiments among the political and administrative elite represents the biggest feedback of all in China's partial reform process. In the early 1990 s these changes coalesced into a stunning reversal of deep-seated attitudes. Ideas that only ten years earlier stood far beyond the limits of permissible discussion now took center stagey. China's Communist Party announced a national goal of creating a decentralized market economy. (Decision, 1993, p. 150)

This decision of the 14th Party Congress, as well as decisions exhibiting changing attitudes towards the role of private property in Chinese society, including the 1999 constitutional amendment placing private business on an equal footing with the public sector, offer vivid examples of the evolution of a succession of North-like mental models that have framed the gradual, but generally continuous advance of China's reform agenda.[35] The remaining

---

[35] Wu (2000) describes the transformation of a mental model associated with the Fourth Plenum of the 15 CCP National Congress (1989). According to Wu, that Congress 'rejected the Soviet-style view that the quality of the socialist state was proportional to the size of the state sector.. (The Congress called for) an economic system based on the principle of "Three Benefits": ...the domain of the state system shall be narrowed; develop multiple forms of public ownership; encourage the development of the non-public sector such as private enterprises.'

question relating to this model of interactions among transitional institutions, competition and learning, and the political environment is: What has been the role of government and China's political economy in initiating and sustaining China's economic transition and institutional change? The following section examines the role of China's political economy and the literature that describes its functioning in China's reform process.

A generally stable, pragmatic political environment

Governments oversee the transition process. Apart from its focus on individual policy choices, the transition literature affords less attention to the role of government than it should. The role of government has been particularly important for China where the political system has managed a gradual, long-duration transition spanning decades. As the overseer of a long-duration transition process, China's political system has not only defined the speed and scope of reform, it has shaped the mental models that inform the reform process, both for decision makers and the general public, and established the means for generating feedback and learning so as to enable mid-course corrections to China's reform strategy. Furthermore, as the initiator and arbiter of rule changes that create the regulatory architecture for China's transitioning economy, China's political system and its own evolution are themselves critical subjects for research and analysis.

Both China's leaders and researchers have created various mental models of the essential nature of China's reform process. The most inclusive and best-known mental model of China's reform doctrine was set forth by Deng Xiaoping in his famous expression: 'groping for stones to cross the river', which in a single phase captured the dimensions of speed, learning, and the centrality of path dependency in shaping China's economic transformation. Invoking the metaphor of the 'orchestra conductor', Bromley and Yao (2006) offer an alternative image of the methods by which China's 'authoritative agents' oversee legal and regulatory change.

Although groping for stones and orchestrating music offer very different images of China's reform process, these contrasting metaphors can be viewed as representing different segments in the time line of China's reform process. At the outset of the reform process, reform agents first groped as they learned to read music, studied the sounds of the different instruments, accessed the capabilities of members of the orchestra, and gained experience in sequencing and harmonising the range of instrumentation. The contrasting Deng and Bromley-Yao metaphors underscore the extraordinary accumulation of learning and experience by China's reformers while still allowing that China's political system retains its distinctive experimental, regressive, and sometimes dissonant character.[36]

---

[36] Consistent with the Bromley-Yao imagery, Wei (1997) assigns to his reform agents the responsibility of delegating 'different parts of a reform program into groups.

In broad strokes (to mix metaphors), from an *ex post* perspective, the Chinese government and CCP have effectively orchestrated the reassignment of property rights from the state to individuals and organisations. The conductor metaphor captures North's (1994) conception of the political system as the authority responsible for setting rules and for assigning and clarifying property rights so as to 'shape perceptions about the payoffs' to various forms of behaviour. The reshaping of these perceptions about payoffs are moving millions of individual actors within China to restructure their local institutional environments. This reassignment, in turn, motivated by the goal of incentivising China's economy to rapidly enhance living standards has substantially restored and maintained the Party's performance legitimacy, as sought by Deng and his party colleagues. However, as discussed later, the reassignment of property rights has itself set in motion new forces that are challenging that legitimacy.

One element of China's successful transition that has received surprisingly little attention has been the ability of China's political system to at once advance its reform agenda while maintaining a stable political environment. Popov (2007) emphasises the critical role of state institutions: 'The ability of state institutions (can be) understood as the ability of the state to enforce its own rules and regulations...'. According to Popov, '...the data seem to suggest that both authoritarian and democratic regimes can have strong rule of law and can deliver efficient institutions, whereas under the weak rule of law, authoritarian regimes do a better job in maintaining efficient institutions than democracies' (p. 28). Popov concludes that 'It is precisely this strong institutional framework that should be held responsible for both (China's and Vietnam's success), where strong authoritarian regimes were preserved and CPE institutions were not dismantled before new market institutions were created...' (p. 3).

Djankov *et al.* (2003) analyse the tension between disorder and dictatorship, which is the tradeoff between social losses due to private expropriation and social losses due to state expropriation. They represent this tradeoff in the form of the Institutional Possibilities Frontier (IPF), that is, a locus of points, such that disorder (dictatorship) cannot be reduced without increasing dictatorship (disorder). In their formulation, dictatorship compensates for the absence of established, well-functioning rule of law, and is therefore consistent with Popov's view that under a weak rule of law, authoritarian regimes perform better in maintaining efficient institutions than

---

Within each group, there is strong interdependence. Across groups there is no strong interdependence' (p. 1,236). The gradual reform process entails the implementation of rapid, simultaneous reform within interdependent groups, while coordination across groups may proceed more slowly.

democracies.[37] However, the Djankov-Popov model may be increasingly unsuited for China.

Enjoying the economic fruits of a stable political regime, China's leadership and much of its intelligentsia and prospering middle class remain leery of the risks associated with moving too quickly along the IPF so long as dictatorship is able to orchestrate the reassignment of property rights and maintain a stable political environment in which these rights can be broken in, exercised, and mediated. However, the reassignment of property rights, originally motivated by the determination of China's party leadership to incentivise the economy and re-legitimate the Party, has created a growing circle of individuals and organisations that are intent on both securing these newly acquired rights and extracting from them the maximum returns. As the owners of corporate assets, homeowners, landowners, and owners of intellectual property exercise their newly acquired rights, these rights are increasingly likely to come into conflict with established interests as well as the interests of other newly empowered groups.

As a result of the reassignment and democratisation of property rights, China is experiencing an increasingly wide range of social divisions and discontents. These divisions centre on the rights of individuals on opposite sides of divides regarding the nation's growing income disparities, a quality environmental, and access to social services and insurance. In its effort to achieve a 'harmonious society', China's leadership is aware of the growing need of the political system to mediate conflict over contending rights and resource allocation priorities.[38]

However, the ability of the political system to mediate conflicts in the assignment and exercise of rights requires legitimacy that cannot be fulfilled through achieving high-growth performance alone. In order for the political system to mediate China's growing economic and social conflict that has raised from the devolution of property rights the ruling party will most likely require procedural legitimacy that can only be achieved through formal electoral procedures. That is, China may be returning to a condition of 'class struggle', this time not one imposed from the top down as in the Maoist era, but one that operates through popular channels similar to those

---

[37] Josef Brada inquires how China 'evolved from a government that gave us the Great Leap Forward, the Great Famine, and other economic and social disasters...to one that seems almost Socratic in its steering of economic reform.' Brada continues, '...this is not the message of the classical public choice school of thought like Tullock and Olsen.' Brada's question goes to the heart of the question concerning the nature of the Chinese leadership's objective function that underlies the 'generally stable, pragmatic political environment,' which is the focus of this section. I leave it to another to identify the objective function of the Chinese leadership and CCP that answers Brada's question.

[38] Elements of this argument are set forth in Jefferson and Zhang (2007)..

in advanced democratic states. The agent with the authority to mediate these struggles will need to emerge from a formal political contest in which the losers know that they can look forward to a day, stretching but a few years into the future, when they can again contest for power in a fair and transparent manner. According to Naughton (2006):

> ...the growth of independent economic powers, the increasing education and sophistication of the population, and the expanding demands for property rights and personal security will challenge the Party. Powerful interest groups currently grouped within the Communist Party will fragment, struggle over distribution of spoils and protection from losses. At some point, interest groups will stare at each (other) over a chasm of social chaos, and decide that a real rule of law and political democracy are better than a fight to the death. A truce in the struggle for wealth and power is more likely to lead to political democracy than is a carefully constructed harmonious society.... (p. 10)

This particular feedback loop, the blowback from China's broad popular reassignment of an array of property rights, is a phase of China's transition process and its institutional becoming that promises to offer a rich mine for students of political economy for decades to come.[39]

Summarising, the central argument of this section is that the most distinctive body of literature inspired by China's economic transformation is that which gives insight into the phenomenon of induced institutional change. This contribution is important not only because the literature in this field is sparse but also because China's 30-year transition and development process has been shaped by the process of induced institutional change. No one or two of the three elements set forth here, the transitional institutions, competition and learning, and a stable, pragmatic political environment, could have resulted in the reform trajectory that has materialised over the past three decades. Interactions among all three of the three elements have been necessary to induce China's sustained institutional change.

China's Distinctiveness? – The Limits of Transferability

China's intellectuals and policy makers often refer to China's 'special characteristics' (*tese*). These characteristics, which generally relate to China's size,

---

[39] In spite of this assessment that a process of political transition or blowback is underway, the view of Wu (2000) is not atypical: 'The key feature of the old system is the unification of the three entities – the party, the government, and the economy.... The interrelationship that arises from this unification is deep and complicated.... (Soviet) people, particularly the social and political elites, have tremendous interest in maintaining the old system....As such the reforms face enormous resistance.'

geography, history, and institutions, are touted as features of China that make it highly distinctive, thus causing its economic challenges not to be easily understood or addressed through the usual analytical framework or policy remedies.

But the implications of uniqueness operate in both directions. Just as the special characteristics of the Chinese situation may justify unorthodox analytical and policy approaches, these special characteristics may also limit the applicability of China's experience, including the economic literature that it has inspired, to other areas of the world. China's four special economic zones that were facilitated by historic commercial links with Hong Kong (Shenzhen), Macao (Zhuhai), Taiwan (Xiamen), and the Chaozhou people of Southeast Asia (Shantou) may not take such fertile root in India or Africa, or even Vietnam. The substantial administrative decentralisation of China's economy may have enabled a process of regional initiative, experimentation, and gradual transition not available to many other administratively more centralised economic systems. The pronounced aversion to social chaos rooted in the wars and upheavals of the 19th and 20th centuries, reinforced by the collapse of the Soviet Union, and Party control may sustain a greater tolerance for authoritarian control and slow-paced reform than displayed elsewhere. The list can be greatly extended.

Still, China is populated by *homo economicus,* who has responded in generally predictable ways to the incentivisation of China's economy. Reassignments of property rights, including the restoration of the family farm, homeownership, labour mobility and the purchase and sale of corporate stock, have engendered generally predictable behaviour. Moreover, as a member of the IMF–World Bank system and the WTO, China is bound to behave by sets of rules that govern other nations. Furthermore, instructive comparisons may be drawn with India, the US, the European Union, and other multi-country federations of significant size. In addition, China shares certain cultural attributes with other East Asian economies, notably Taiwan, Hong Kong, South Korea, and Japan, including higher than average propensities to save, high literacy rates, active industrial policy, and various cultural attributes that invite comparisons with the experiences of these countries.[40]

---

[40] See, for example, Rawski (forthcoming) regarding China's culture, market, and entrepreneurial legacies. Roland (2004) notes that Sachs and Woo (1994) attribute China's recent high growth rates to the country's 'backwardness' in the immediately preceding period. Seen in a long-run historical perspective, however, Roland argues that China has been anything but backward. For example, Chinese agriculture, which was the initial engine of growth early in the transition, has always been among the most productive in the world. I therefore suggest that one of the clues to the success of China's transition is not its 'backwardness' at the onset of the transition but the inherited high level of knowledge and culture relative to its economic performance.

Comparisons may be in order for yet another reason. Once the list of *ceteris paribus* conditions has been accounted for and notable differences persist, contrasts also can be helpful. Perhaps the most conspicuous condition that sets China aside from virtually every other country is its sheer demographic scale and rapidly rising living standards. As Xu (2006) points out, 'The current size of the Chinese economy, in terms of GDP, is larger than the sum of 83 countries in Eastern Europe, the former USSR and all of Africa' (p. 1). As a result of this scale, MNCs see China as an essential part of their global footprint thereby bestowing on Chinese policy makers prerogatives, such as claims on technology transfer as a condition for market access, that are simply unavailable to smaller countries. A more enduring advantage of scale is that it has enabled China to become the world's largest producer and consumer of many conventional industrial staples and high-tech products, such as steel, TV sets, PCs, and cell phones, with the likelihood that the Chinese economy will one day dominate global production in the areas of specialised machinery and equipment, automobiles, and aerospace vehicles. Yet, the same scale characteristics cause China to project conspicuous impacts on world markets. The important role of government in creating public goods, such as food and product standards, intellectual property rights, and environmental protection, are all magnified in the Chinese case. Such scale causes interest groups and politicians in seemingly threatened countries to be far more vocal in their criticism of China than would be the case if China were but the name of a region spanning 83 separate nation-states. Hence, China's economic experience is likely to offer the most illuminating illustration of the costs and benefits of national scale.

As Sala-i-Martin (2002) has shown, China's sheer size can also be decisive in overturning conclusions regarding our understanding of fundamental economic beliefs, often relating to globalisation. While most literature using the country economy as the unit of analysis concludes that over the past 30 years or more global income distribution has become increasingly unequal, using the household as the unit of observation Sala-i-Martin arrives at a contrary finding; once China's preponderant number of households are taken into account, global income distribution is shown to have become more, not less, uniformly distributed.[41]

In a real sense, one of China's most enduring contributions to the economic literature may be not be a deepened understanding of how China is achieving economic prosperity; rather it may be the fading of a certain perspective on China that has all but vanished. Not long ago, much attention was given to China's institutional uniqueness. In 1992, the CCP adopted the

---

[41] Likewise Sala-i-Martin (2002) shows that as China's middle class grows and graduates into the ranks of the world's relatively high income population, China, by itself, has the capacity to reverse this convergence trend and become a key source of an increasing maldistribution of global income.

phrase 'socialist market economy' to describe its model involving extensive state and social ownership and state interventions that advantage returns to labour in relation to those to capital, land, and other natural resources. Whether China is creating institutional arrangements that are distinctly different from their Western counterpart institutions is a key question. Some, such as Roland (2004) believed at least a decade or so ago this to be the case:

> Based on its existing stock of cultural knowledge (which differs strongly from that in the West), China, like other Asian countries, has developed unique fast-moving institutions in achieving its recent growth trajectory. Thus, China is experimenting with its own institutions for the market economy instead of importing Western institutions. Whether Asian capitalist institutions are more efficient is not the right question to ask here. A more appropriate question relates to the one posed earlier about institutional transplantation: what would have happened if Western-style institutions had been directly imported into a cultural context that exhibits deep differences from those of the West?

The possibility of China's experience creating alternative sustainable, even superior, institutional arrangements drew thoughtful attention, including that of Weitzman and Xu (1994). Investigating the surprisingly robust expansion of China's TVEs during the late 1980s and early 1990s, Weitzman and Xu speculated on the exceptional ability of communities of TVE stakeholders to resolve prisoners' dilemma-type free-riding problems internally without the inclusion of explicitly defined property rights. During the subsequent decade, however, the vast majority of China's TVEs have been privatised either in the form of shareholding firms or private companies.

As the forms of Chinese governance come increasingly to look like those of the OECD economies, the literature is less focused on the unique features of China's institutional arrangements. Lee et al. (2001), for example, speculate that China's corporate sector is evolving towards the Anglo-Saxon model, rather than the Japanese-Korean variant of the Asian model. To support their argument, the authors point to several emerging conditions that imitate the US–UK corporate economy model: among listed companies outside investors are becoming increasingly visible while restrictions are imposed on bank ownership, high labour market flexibility, including the relative ease of layoffs, and competitive and open domestic markets, including large numbers of foreign owned companies.

Other observers of China's transition are downplaying the distinctiveness of China's institutions. In his recent review of China's transition and development experience, emphasising the tendency for China's institutions to converge towards those of the world's more successful developing countries, Naughton (2007) refers to China as 'becoming "a normal country".' Putterman (2004) alludes to 'China's brush with market socialism'. He proposes that China evokes an image from space exploration, that is, the image of a 'fly by' or 'a close encounter on the path to a very different destination' (p. 1). Although China probably represents the 'last best chance' to engage the imagination of economic system theorists in an alternative universe of economic institutions, China's leadership and intelligentsia now seem to be headed towards familiar institutional terrain.[42] Rather than have this question of just how 'special' China's reform characteristics are drift out of sight, the matter is worthy of active assessment, debate, and understanding whatever the outcome may be.

Nonetheless, it increasingly appears that the uniqueness of China's experience is not and will not be the nature of its institutions, rather its uniqueness is the manner in which its earlier institutions have become reconfigured – that is their process of becoming – so as to bear the resemblance they do to capitalist institutions. Thus China's uniqueness is likely to be far less in its destination than in its journey.

Conclusions and Future Contributions

This essay is motivated by the question: 'How has China's economic emergence affected the field of economics?' Although no single model or collection of the China-related literature is likely to warrant a Nobel Prize, the literature that has been inspired by China's experience over the past 25 years has contributed to the field of economics in two important ways. First, the most populous country in the world with its variegated and fast moving institutions has generated a wealth of insights and empirical findings that vividly illustrate the insights of the established economics literature, including that of numerous Nobel laureates.

While some insights receive vivid support from China's experience, the robustness of other hypotheses remains to be established. Key among these is whether as China's living standards rise, patterns of income inequality and environmental quality will evolve in a manner consistent with Kuznets' well-known 'inverted U' curve (see Kuznets, 1966). Economists will surely investigate and document these associations, or ponder their absence, as China continues its advance. One reason to anticipate that income inequality will moderate in China is that, as a condition for China's continued economic advance, productivity cleavages will need to become less acute. In order for China's GDP to catch up with that of the US, China's GDP will

---

[42] Japan provides an interesting case of a country having received accolades for its special economic, institutions, culture, and achievements. While this admiration diminished as a result of the nation's apparent shift to a low-growth trajectory, Japan does retain its distinctiveness with respect to the Toyota system, involving just-in-time inventory, industrial policy, and close ties with suppliers (see Ezra Vogel, *Japan as Number One* ,1979).

need to multiply by a factor of five or more in relation to the US. At this point, even when China's GDP matches that of the US, China's considerably larger population will result in its GDP per capita being only one-quarter that of the US. However, it appears that the productivity of China's coastal industry is already at least one-quarter that of the US. The implication is that if China's GDP catch-up involves an equi-proportional growth of all regions and sectors of five-fold or more in relation to the US, then the productivity of China's coastal industry will grow to exceed that of the US. This is highly unlikely; since the growth of coastal industry productivity already exhibits a slowdown. As a result, GDP catch-up for China is likely to rely much more than it has in the past on productivity growth outside of coastal industry. It is therefore likely, but not certain, that China will conform to Kuznets' prediction that income inequality will follow the 'inverted "U" pattern'.[43]

The path of environmental quality in China, critical to China and the world, also remains to be determined. The extent to which Kuznets' environmental 'inverted U' curve defines the trajectory of China's environment may depend on the power of Amartya Sen's notion of 'value endogeneity'. As living standards in China have risen, China's middle class, the media, and political leadership have taken heed of the present and potential economic costs and health hazards caused by polluted water and dirty air. That environmental quality is weighing more heavily in China's social objective function than it did 30 years ago vividly illustrates the endogenous nature of the social values that may lead to China moderating or reversing its environmental deterioration.[44]

The second area in which China's economic experience has inspired a large body of literature, the process of induced institutional change, is theoretically more distinct and novel than that concerning reversals of income inequality and environmental degradation. Because this literature is fragmented and seldom directly speaks broadly to the nature of induced institutional change, this essay attempts to assemble the pieces into a reasonably coherent analytical framework. By reducing the essence of induced institutional change to interaction among just three elements, transitional institutions, competition, and learning, and a stable, pragmatic political environment, the model devised herein certainly oversimplifies the rich set of conditions that are driving China's economic transformation. Technology

---

[43] See Jefferson *et al.* (2006) who document distances between the technology frontiers of China and the US-Japan and internal patterns of productivity differences.

[44] Of course, as in the US, certain pollutants, such as sulphur dioxide and nitrous oxides, may exhibit a turning point, while others, such as carbon emissions, do (have) not. As Naughton reports (2007, p. 490), ambient air quality has improved in many Chinese cities as gas and electricity use has substituted for coal for cooking and heating in many homes; also, leaded gasoline has been omitted. At the same time, as automobile use surges, concentrations of nitrous oxides have increased.

transfer, trade, FDI, comparative advantage, internal migration, and other factors are each strong candidates for the short list of key factors that are motivating China's economic advance. While these drivers of economic transformation have not been the focus of this essay, in order for these factors to come into play, certain institutional conditions need to be in place. At the same time, as these factors come into play, they serve to hasten the speed and expand the scope of institutional change. The story of induced institutional change is therefore both a precondition and a consequence of these complementary drivers of China's growth.

As a laboratory for induced institutional change, China's experience continues to unfold. That the factors motivating China's institutional change have had surprisingly fortuitous effects over the past 30 years is no guarantee that China will continue to defy the more pessimistic predictions in the future. China's political leadership has orchestrated the reassignment of broad swaths of property rights to its citizenry. The feedback from this reassignment is sure to reshape China's political institutional landscape. North notes (1994): 'It is the polity that defines and enforces property rights, and in consequence it is not surprising that efficient economic markets are so exceptional' (p. 361). North's observation reminds us that wrong turns along the path of political change will deliver bumps, obstacles, and reversals along the road to more efficient markets. The chapter analysing the conditions that induce China's political transformation has yet to be written.

China's unfolding transformation will continue to generate notable contributions to the field of economics. As more Chinese researchers enter the field of economics and the scale and complexity of the Chinese economy grows, and with it its impact on the rest of the world, the contributions of the China-related economics research will only become more important.

Acknowledgements

I appreciate the helpful discussions and insightful comments provided during visits to the Chinese Center for Economic Studies at Fudan University, the Chinese Center for Economic Research at Peking University, and the Center for Economic Development Research at Wuhan University. In addition, I was greatly assisted by comments and suggestions from Josef Brada, Loren Brandt, Albert Hu, Albert Keidel, Ma Ying, Dwight Perkins, Peter Petri, Louis Putterman, Thomas Rawski, Su Jian, Xu Chenggang, Yao Yang, Zhang Jun, and Zhang Yifan. Research support provided by the US National Science Foundation (award # SES-0519902) is also gratefully acknowledged.

References

Aghion, P, Blundell, R, Griffith, R, Howitt, P and Pranti, S. 2006: *The effects of entry on incumbent innovation and productivity.* NBER Working Paper, w12027.

Bai, C-en. 2004: Local protectionism and regional specialization: Evidence from China's industries. *Journal of International Economics* 63(2): 397–417.

Bai, C-en, Hsieh, C-tai and Qian, Y. 2006: The returns to capital in China. *Brookings Papers on Economic Activity* 1: 60–102.

Bai, C-en, Li, DD, Tao, Z and Wang, Y. 2000: The multitask theory of state enterprise reform. *Journal of Comparative Economics* 28(2000): 716–738.

Bowlus, A and Sicular, T. 2003: Moving toward markets? Labor allocation in rural China. *Journal of Development Economics* 71(2): 561–583.

Brandt, L, Hsieh, C-tai and Zhu, X. 2008: Accounting for growth and structural transformation in China, 1978–2004. In: Brandt, L. and Rawski, TG (eds). *China's great economic transformation.* Cambridge University Press: New York.

Brandt, L and Rawski, TG. 2008: *China's great economic transformation.* Cambridge University Press: New York.

Bromley, DW and Yao, Y 2006: Understanding China's economic transformation: Are there lessons for the developing world? *World Economics* 7(2): 73–96.

Buchanan, JM. 1979: *What should economists do?* Liberty Press: Indianapolis.

Byrd, WA. 1992: *Chinese industrial firms under reform* published for the World Bank, Oxford University Press: Washington, DC.

Cao, Y, Qian, Y and Weingast, BR. 1999: From federalism, Chinese style to privatization, Chinese style. *Economics of Transition* 7(1): 103–131.

Coase, R. 1960: The problem of social cost. *Journal of Law and Economics* 3: 1–44.

Coase, R. 1992: The institutional structure of production. *American Economic Review* 82(4): 713–719.

Decision. 1993: China's central government decision on resolving several problems concerning the establishment of a socialist market economic system. *Renmin ribao (People's Daily)*, November 17, p. 1.

Deng, P and Jefferson, GH. 2008: *Foreign entry and the heterogeneous growth of firms: Do we observe "creative destruction" in China?* Working paper, Brandeis University.

Dewatripont, M and Maskin, E. 1995: Credit and efficiency in centralized and decentralized economies. *Review of Economics and Statistics* 62: 541–555.

Djankov, S, Glaeser, E, La Porta, R, Lopez-de-Silanes, F and Shliefer, A. 2003: The new comparative economics. *Journal of Comparative Economics* 31(4): 595–619.

Easterly, W. 2001: *The elusive quest for growth: economists' adventures and misadventures in the tropics.* MIT Press: Cambridge, MA.

Fan, S. 1991: Effects of technological change and institutional reform on production and growth in Chinese agriculture. *American Journal of Agricultural Economics* 73: 266–275.

Fei, JCH and Ranis, G. 1964: *Development of the labor surplus economy: Theory and policy.* Richard D. Irwin, Inc.: Homewood, IL.

Fischer, S and Gelb, A. 1991: The process of socialist economic transformation. *Journal of Economic Perspectives* 5(4): 91–105.

Girma, S, Gong, Y and Görg, H. (forthcoming): What determines innovation activity in Chinese state-owned enterprises? The role of foreign direct investment. *World Development.*

Groves, T, McMillan, J, Hong, Y and Naughton, B. 1994: Autonomy and incentives in Chinese state enterprises. *Quarterly Journal of Economics* 109(1): 183–209.

Guo, X. 2005: Houfa youshi xinlun – jianlun zhongguo jingji fazhan de dongli (A new theory of the advantages of backwardness – a concurrent theory of the strengths of China's economic development). *Development economics research: research topics on the advantages of backwardness,* The Economic Development Research Center, Wuhan University, July 2005.

Hay, D, Morris, D, Liu, G and Yao, S. 1994: *Economic reform and state-owned enterprises in China, 1979–1987*. Clarendon Press: Oxford.

Hayami, Y and Kikuchi, M. 1981: *Asian village economy at the crossroads: An economic approach to institutional change*. University of Tokyo Press: Tokyo (and Johns Hopkins University Press, Baltimore, 1982).

Hayami, Y and Ruttan, V. 1985: *Agricultural development: An international perspective*. Johns Hopkins Univesity Press: Baltimore, MD.

Holz, C. 2003: "Fast, clear and accurate": How reliable are Chinese output and economic growth statistics? *China Quarterly* 117: 122–163.

Holz, C. 2004: Deconstructing China's GDP statistics. *China Economic Review* 15: 164–202.15.

Hsieh, C-tai and Klenow, P. 2007: Misallocation and manufacturing productivity in China and India (unpublished manuscript).

Hu, AGZ and Jefferson, GH. 2008: A great wall of patents: What is behind China's recent patent explosion? unpublished manuscript. http://people.brandeis.edu/~jefferso/Great%20Wall,%20submitted%20manuscript,%20Jan.%202006.pdf.

Hulton, CR. 1975: Technical change and the reproducibility of capital. *American Economic Review* 65(5): 956–965.

Jefferson, GH. 1998: China's state enterprises: Public goods, externalities, and coase. *American Economic Review* (Papers and Proceedings), May 1998.

Jefferson, GH, Hu, AGZ and Su, J. 2006: The sustainability of China's economic growth. *Brookings Papers on Economic Activity* 1: 1–60.

Jefferson, GH and Rawski, TG. 1994: How industrial reform worked in China: The role of innovation, competition, and property rights. In: Bruno, M and Pleskovic, B (eds) *Proceedings of the World Bank Annual Conference on Development Economics 1994*. World Bank: Washington, DC pp. 129–156.

Jefferson, GH and Rawski, TG. 2002: China's emerging market for property rights: Theoretical and empirical perspectives. *Economics of Transition* 10(3): 585–617.

Jefferson, GH, Rawski, TG and Zhang, Y (forthcoming): Productivity growth and convergence across China's industrial economy. *Journal of Chinese Economics and Business Studies*.

Jefferson, GH, Mai, L and Zhao, JZQ. 1999: Reforming property rights in China's industry. In: Jefferson, GH and Singh, IJ (eds) *Enterprise Reform in China: Ownership, Transition, and Performance*. A World Bank Research Publication, Oxford University Press: New York.

Jefferson, GH and Zhang, J. 2007: China's political reform: A property rights interpretation. unpublished manuscript, May 15, 2007.

Jenson, MC and Meckling, WH. 1976: Theory of the firm: Managerial behavior, agency costs, and ownership structure. *Journal of Financial Economics* 3: 305–360.

Keidel, A. 2007: China's financial sector: Contributions to growth and downside risks. Prepared for the Conference, "China's Changing Financial System: Can it Catch Up With or Even Drive Economic Growth," Networks Financial Institute, Indiana State University, January 25, 2007.

Kuznets, S. 1966: *Modern economic growth: Rate, structure, and spread*. Yale University Press: New Haven.

Lardy, N. 1998: *China's unfinished economic revolution*. Brookings Institution Press: Washington, DC.

Lardy, N. 2002: *Integrating China into the global economy*. Brookings Institution Press: Washington, DC.

Lau, L, Qian, Y and Roland, G. 2000: Reform without losers: An interpretation of China's dual-track approach to transition. *Journal of Political Economy* 108(1): 120–143.

Lee, K, Hahn, D and Lin, J. 2001: China and the East Asian model: A "comparative institutional analysis" perspective. Institute of Economic Research, Seoul National University, Working Paper Series, No. 41. January 2001.

Lewis, A. 1954: Economic development with unlimited supplies of labor. *Manchester School of Economics and Social Studies* 22: 139–191.

Li, W. 1997: The impact of economic reforms on the performance of Chinese state-owned enterprises. *Journal of Political Economy* 105(5): 1080–1106.

Li, G, Xu, CL and Yao, Y. 2007: Health shocks, village elections, and long-term income evidence from rural China. November 2007, presented on the panel 'Institutions and Economic Development,' January 5, 2008, Allied Social Science Associations, New Orleans 2008.

Li, G, Xu, CL and Yao, Y. 2008: Governance, finance, and consumption insurance: Evidence from Chinese villages. undated, presented on the panel 'Institutions and Economic Development,' January 5, 2008, Allied Social Science Associations, New Orleans 2008.

Li, S, Li, S and Zhang, W. 2000: The road to capitalism: Competition and institutional change in China. *Journal of Comparative Economics* 28: 269–292.

Lin, JY 1987: The household responsibility system in China: A peasant's institutional choice. *American Journal of Agricultural Economics* 69(2): 410–415.

Lin, JY. 1992a: The household responsibility system in China's agricultural reform: A theoretical and empirical study. *Economic Development and Cultural Change* 36(3): S199–S224.

Lin, JY. 1992b: Rural reforms and agricultural growth in China. *American Economic Review* 82(1): 34–51.

Lin, JY. 1995: Endowments, technology, and factor markets: A natural experiment of induced institutional innovation from China's rural reform. *American Journal of Agricultural Economics* 77: 231–242.

Lin, JY. 2005: Viability, economic transition and reflection on neoclassical economics. *Kyklos* 58(2): 239–264.

Lipton, D. 2007: Eastern Europe. *The concise encyclopedia of economics,* The Library of Economics and Liberty, http://www.econlib.org/library/Enc/Eastern Europe.html (accessed 17 August 2007).

Long, C and Zhang, X. 2008: Organization choice with credit constraint: Industrial clusters in China. Presented on the panel "Institutions and Economic Development," January 5, 2008, Allied Social Science Associations, New Orleans 2008.

Maddison, A. 1998: *Chinese economic performance in the long run.* Organization for Economic Cooperation and Development: Paris.

Maddison, A. 2003: *The world economy historical statistics.* OECD Publishing: Paris.

Miles, MA, Reulner, EJ and O'Grady, MA. 2005: *Index of economic freedom. The link between economic opportunity and prosperity.* The Heritage Foundation: Washington, DC and The Wall Street Journal (New York).

Murrell, P. 1991: Can neoclassical economics underpin the reform of centrally planned economies? *Journal of Economic Perspectives* 5: 59–76.

Naughton, B. 1995: *Growing out of the plan.* Cambridge University Press: Cambridge.

Naughton, B. 2006: Reframing China policy: The carnegie debates, debate 2: China's economy (arguing against the motion) The Carnegie Endowment for International Peace.

Naughton, B. 2007: *The Chinese economy: Transitions and growth.* MIT Press: Cambridge.

NBS (National Bureau of Statistics). 1994: *China Statistical yearbook 1994.* China Statistics Press: Beijing.

NBS (National Bureau of Statistics). 1995: *China statistical yearbook 1995.* China Statistics Press: Beijing.

NBS (National Bureau of Statistics). 2004: *China statistical yearbook 2004.* China Statistics Press: Beijing.

NBS (National Bureau of Statistics). 2006: *China statistical yearbook 2006.* China Statistics Press: Beijing.

North, DC. 1990: *Institutions, institutional change, and economic performance.* Cambridge University Press: Cambridge, New York.

North, DC. 1994: Economic performance through time. *American Economic Review* 84(3): 359–368.

Perkins, DH. 1988: Reforming China's economic system. *Journal of Economic Literature* 26: 601–645.

Perkins, DH and Rawski, TG. 2008: Forecasting China's economic growth to 2025. In: Brandt, L and Rawski, TG (eds) *China's great economic transformation.* Cambridge University Press: New York.

Popov, V. 2007: Shock therapy versus gradualism reconsidered: Lessons from transition economies after 15 years of reforms. *Comparative Economic Studies* 49(1): 1–32.

Prescott, EC. 1998: Lawrence R. Klein Lecture 1997: A theory of total factor productivity. *International Economic Review* 39(3): 525–551.

Putterman, L. 1995: The role of ownership and property rights in China's economic transition. *The China Quarterly* Vol. 144, (Special Issue: China's Transitional Economy) pp. 1047–1067.

Putterman, L. 2008: China's encounter with market socialism: Approaching managed capitalism by indirect means. In: Kornai J and Qian Y (eds). *Market and Socialism in the Light of the Experiences of China and Vietnam.* Palgrave Macmillan: Basingstoke (forthcoming).

Qian, Y. 2000: The process of China's market transition (1978–98): The evolutionary, historical, and comparative perspective. *Journal of Institutional and Theoretical Economics* 156(1): 151–171.

Qian, Y. 2002: *How reform worked in China?* Mimeo, UC Berkeley.

Qian, Y, Roland, G and Xu, C. 2006: Coordination and experimentation in M-form and U-form organizations. *Journal of Political Economy* 114(2): 366–402.

Qian, Y and Weingast, BR. 1997: Federalism as a commitment to preserving market incentives. *Journal of Economic Perspectives* 11(4): 83–92.

Qian, Y and Xu, C. 1993: Why China's economic reforms differ: The M-Form hierarchy and entry expansion of the non-state sector. *The Economics of Transition* 1: 135–170.

Ravallion, M and Chen, S. 1999: When economic reform is faster than statistical reform: Measuring and explaining income inequality in explaining income inequality in rural China. *Oxford Bulletin of Economics and Statistics* 61: 75–102.

Rawski, T forthcoming: Social capabilities and Chinese economic growth. In: Tang Wand Holzner B (eds). *Social Transformation in Contemporary China.* University of Pittsburgh Press: Pittsburgh.

Rodrik, D. August 2004: Growth strategies http://ksghome.harvard.edu/~drodrik/ Growth Strategies.pdf.

Roland, G. 2004: Understanding institutional change: Fast-moving and slow-moving institutions. *Studies in Comparative International Development* 38(4): 109–131.

Romer, P. 1986: Increasing returns and long-run growth. *Journal of Political Economy* 94: 1002–1037.

Rozelle, S and Li, G. 1998: Village leaders and land-rights formation in China. *American Economics Review (Papers and Proceedings)* 88(2): 433–438.

Ruttan, VW. 2001: *Technology, growth, and development: An induced innovation perspective.* Oxford University Press: New York.

Sachs, J and Woo, W. 1994: Structural factors in the economic reforms of China, Eastern Europe, and the former Soviet Union. *Economic Policy* 9(18): 101–145.

Sala-i-Martin, X. 2002: *The disturbing "rise" in global income inequality.* National Bureau of Economic Research Working paper, w8904, April, 2002.

Schumpeter, JA. 1942: *Capitalism, socialism, and democracy.* Harper: New York 1975 [originally published 1942].

Sen, A. 1988: The concept of development. In: Chenery, H and Srinivasan, TN (eds). *Handbook of Development Economics.* Vol. 1, Chapter 1, pp. 9–26. Holland: Amsterdam.

Solow, R. 1956: A contribution to the theory of economic growth. *Quarterly Journal of Economics* 70(1): 65–94.

Solow, R. 1957: Technical change and the aggregate production function. *Review of Economic and Statistics* 39: 312–320.

Stigler, G. 1989: Two notes on the coase theorem. *Yale Law Journal* 99(3): 631–633.

Vogel, E. 1979: *Japan as number one.* Harvard University Press: Cambridge.

Wei, S. 1997: Gradualism versus big bang: Speed and sustainability of reforms. *The Canadian Journal of Economics* 30(4b): 1234–1237.

Weitzman, M and Xu, C. 1994: Chinese township and village enterprises as vaguely defined cooperatives. *Journal of Comparative Economics* 1(3): 276–308.

Williamson, J. 2002: Did the Washington consensus fail? Outline of speech at the Center for Strategic & International Studies, Washington, DC, 6 November 2002.

Williamson, J and Miller, MH. 1987: *Targets and indicators: A blueprint for international coordination of economic policy.* Policy Analyses in International Economics, No. 22, Institute for International Economics: Washington, DC.

Wong, C. 2006: *Can China change development paradigm for the 21st century? Fiscal policy options for Hu Jintao and Wen Jiabao after two decades of muddling through?* Mimeo, University of Washington.

World Bank. 1996: *From plan to market.* The World bank: Washington, DC.

Wu, J. 2000: China's economic reform: Past, present and future. *Perspectives* 1(5), April 30, 2000.

Xu, C. 2006: Chinese reform an Chinese regional decentralization. 29 November 2006, presented at the Macau Conference.

Young, A. 2000: The razor's edge: Distortions and incremental reform in the people's republic of China. *Quarterly Journal of Economics* 115: 1091–1136.

Young, A. 2003: Gold into base metals: Productivity growth in the people's republic of China during the reform period. *Journal of Political Economy* 111(6): 1220–1261.

Zhang, J. 1997: *Economics of dual track system: Chinese economic reform (1978–1992).* Shanghai United Press: Shanghai.

Zhang, J, Zhao, Y, Park, A and Song, X. 2005: Economic returns to schooling in urban China. *Journal of Comparative Economics* 33(4): 730–752.

Index

272 *Index*

Printed and bound by CPI Group (UK) Ltd, Croydon, CR0 4YY